The Gospel of Thomas *and* *Jesus*

FOUNDATIONS & FACETS
REFERENCE
SERIES

PUBLISHED VOLUMES
Robert W. Funk, *New Gospel Parallels. Vol. 2: John and the Other Gospels*
John Dominic Crossan, ed., *Sayings Parallels: A Workbook for the Jesus Tradition*
John S. Kloppenborg, *Q Parallels: Synopsis, Critical Notes, and Concordance*
Vernon K. Robbins, *Ancient Quotes & Anecdotes: From Crib to Crypt*
Robert W. Funk, *New Gospel Parallels, Vol. 1,2: Mark*
Arland D. Jacobson, *The First Gospel: An Introduction to Q*
Stephen J. Patterson, *The Gospel of Thomas and Jesus*

The Gospel of Thomas *and* *Jesus*

Stephen J. Patterson

POLEBRIDGE PRESS
Salem, Oregon

Library of Congress Cataloging-in-Publication Data

Patterson, Stephen J., 1957-
    The Gospel of Thomas and Jesus : Thomas Christianity, social radicalism, and the quest of the historical Jesus / Stephen J. Patterson
     p. cm. — (Foundations & facets. Reference series)
    Includes bibliographical references and index.
    ISBN 0-944344-31-3 (alk. paper) : $26.95. — ISBN 0-944344-32-1 (pbk. : alk. paper) : $17.95
    1. Gospel of Thomas-Criticism, interpretation, etc. 2. Bible. N.T. Gospels-Criticism, interpretation, etc. 3. Jesus Christ-Words. 4. Q hypothesis (Synoptics criticism) 5. Jesus Christ-Historcity. I. Title. II. Series.
BS2860.T52.P385   1993   91-35781
                                                  CIP

For
Deborah

Contents

Acknowledgements

I first undertook the present study as a dissertation topic while a student in the New Testament program at the Claremont Graduate School. The monograph offered presently is a much revised version of the resulting dissertation. As such, it was from start to finish undertaken with much careful guidance on the part of many helpful mentors. These include foremost my dissertation advisor at Claremont, Prof. James M. Robinson, and my advisor during a year of research at Heidelberg, Prof. Gerd Theissen. Their probing questions were instrumental in helping me to formulate the thesis presented in these pages. I would also like to thank Prof. Burton L. Mack and Prof. Vincent L. Wimbush, whose helpful comments and suggestions have proven indispensable, and Prof. Helmut Koester, who has provided much encouragement along the way, and from whom I have learned much about the Gospel of Thomas. Finally, I would thank those who consented to read and comment upon drafts of various chapters, especially Prof. Jon Daniels, Prof. Ron Cameron, Prof. Hans–Martin Schenke, and members of the Claremont New Testament Seminar. Special thanks go to Prof. Julian Hills, whose thorough editing has made this a much better volume. The merits of the book, without the aid of colleagues such as these, would be greatly diminished. Any shortcomings, regarding which I may well have ignored perfectly sound advice, are to be credited solely to my own account.

Stephen J. Patterson
St. Louis
August, 1991

Introduction

For many centuries it has been known that in antiquity there was a certain gospel attributed to the apostle Thomas. Though the tides of Christian late antiquity had washed this Thomas gospel into near silent obscurity, along with a score of other early Christian works held by later guardians of orthodox tradition to be heretical, echoes of its existence could be heard in lists of banned books, descriptions of codices now lost, and occasionally in a passing remark from the volumes of the Church fathers. Hippolytus, the third-century Roman antipope, even purports to quote from it in his heresiological work known as the *Refutatio*. Yet the quotation is but a snippet, like so many fragments of ancient books now lost, tantalizing the modern imagination with the thought of esoteric texts of a time gone by:

> They (the Naasenes) say that not only the mysteries of the Assyrians and Phrygians, but also those of the Egyptians support their account of the blessed nature of the things that were, are, and are yet to be, a nature which is both hidden and revealed at the same time, and which he calls the sought-for kingdom of heaven which is within man. They transmit a tradition concerning this in the Gospel entitled According to Thomas, which states expressly, "The one who seeks me will find me in the children from seven years of age and onwards. For there, hiding in the fourteenth aeon, I am revealed."[1]

Hippolytus' comments only serve to make matters worse. That the book would have been a source of delight to such folk as the heretical Naassenes only lends to it the added allurement of forbidden fruit, contraband. To recover such a

---

1. *Ref.* 5.7.20; the translation is that of H. Attridge, "Appendix: The Greek Fragments," in B. Layton, ed., *Nag Hammadi Codex II*, 1. 103. Attridge gives full account of the Greek and Latin *testimonia* on pp. 103–9; see also H.-Ch. Puech, "The Gospel of Thomas," in E. Hennecke and W. Schneemelcher, eds., *New Testament Apocrypha*, 1. 278–80.

book would be the height of fantasy! Normally such yearnings of the historian of early Christianity go unsatisfied. The lost is seldom found.

In December of 1945 an Egyptian peasant from the small town of al-Qasr in upper Egypt, near Nag Hammadi, was with his brother at the base of a cliff gathering peat to be used as fertilizer in the family fields. In the course of their digging, Muhammed and Kalifah 'Ali came upon an ancient jar, whose lid had evidently been sealed to protect its contents. When Muhammed 'Ali broke the jar, out tumbled a hoard of books, which together constitute what may well be the most important archaeological discovery of the twentieth century for persons interested in the study of the New Testament and early Christianity. The thirteen fourth century codices carted home that day by Muhammed Ali contained roughly fifty different ancient tractates, all of which are Coptic translations of works written originally in Greek. Most of these tractates were either previously unknown, or, like the Gospel of Thomas, thought to have been lost long ago. The Gospel of Thomas occurs on pages 32–51 of Nag Hammadi Codex 2. The lost had been found.

After more than a decade of being bought, sold, traded, smuggled, and finally transcribed for study, material from the collection gradually became available to the scholarly public. A German translation of the Gospel of Thomas was published in 1958 by Johannes Leipoldt,[2] based upon photographs of the conserved original papyrus leaves published by Pahor Labib in 1956.[3] One year later an editio princeps—the first edition of the Coptic text itself—was published by a consortium of scholars, together with translations in Dutch, English, French and German.[4] The publication of this new gospel text generated a flurry of scholarly activity. Studies appeared touting the discovery as nothing less than the key to recovering the lost sayings of Jesus, the antidote to all of the historical-critical skepticism wrought upon the canonical gospels by scholars from the form critical school. Still others sought to put out the fire of enthusiastic fervor by discounting the newly recovered book as the work of heretics, untrustworthy and unreliable.

By the end of the 1960s the smoke began to clear, allowing for a survey of the situation after this initial round of discussion. Much progress had been made. A critical text was accessible.[5] The challenges of the language had spawned a new generation of Coptologists to repopulate the ranks of the New Testament guild of scholars. And much had been done toward the better understanding the gnosticizing theology of the Gospel of Thomas.[6] But many

2. Leipoldt, "Ein neues Evangelium," cols. 481–96.
3. Labib, Coptic Gnostic Papyri.
4. A. Guillaumont, et al., The Gospel According to Thomas.
5. See previous note. This has been replaced more recently by B. Layton's critical edition of Nag Hammadi Codex 2 in the series Nag Hammadi Studies (see note 1). A third critical text, with a fresh translation (both by Marvin Meyer) is available in J. Kloppenborg, et al., Q—Thomas Reader, 129–55.
6. See esp. E. Haenchen, Die Botschaft; B. Gärtner, Theology; and the observations of T. Säve-Söderbergh, "Gnostic and Canonical Gospel Traditions," 552–59.

fundamental questions remained unanswered. For example, one could still not point to any scholarly consensus regarding the basic nature of this document. Was it a gospel harmony, combining elements from the canonical gospels for the purpose of promoting a specific theology? Or was it an entirely new document, dependent upon its own traditional sources, channeling the sayings tradition into a traditional form quite distinct from that developed by the canonical writers? A failure to reach a consensus around a resolution of these questions had also prevented any definitive statement about the date of the Gospel of Thomas. If it could be shown that Thomas made use of the canonical gospels, it seemed that one would at least have to relegate it to the second century, and thus of little relevance for addressing the acute problem of Christian origins. On the other hand, if one could not assume some measure of dependence upon the canonical New Testament texts, then the matter of Thomas' dating was really wide open, and its potential for reshaping some of our assumptions about earliest Christianity very significant. Still other questions remained completely unaddressed. For example, who had created and used this text? What sorts of lives would they have led, if indeed one might suppose them to have taken seriously Thomas' injunctions about life and its living? And how might these 'Thomas Christians' be imagined in relation to other early Christian groups known to us through the documents they produced?

When I began to ask the question of how Thomas Christians and Thomas Christianity might have fit into the overall development of ancient Christianity, I found that after yet another decade of study, though significant progress had been made in many areas of research on the Gospel of Thomas, these preliminary questions still had not been satisfactorily answered. The result was a bottleneck in the study of this important document that was impeding progress on many fronts. The present study is an attempt to move beyond this impasse, in the hope that, at the very least, the discussion of these matters might begin to flow once again.

The resulting work falls into three parts. Part I addresses the question of Thomas' place in the literary development of the Jesus tradition, and focuses specifically on the much debated question of the Thomas tradition's relationship to the synoptic gospels and their sources. After an attempt to place this question in proper perspective (Chapter 1), I offer an argument for viewing Thomas as a witness to an essentially autonomous tradition, that is, as a writing that does not rely upon the synoptic gospels for its material. Chapter 2 makes this case with respect to Thomas' specific content. Chapter 3 does the same with respect to Thomas' form, or genre, as a sayings collection.

If Part I seeks to locate Thomas within the literary development of the Jesus tradition, Part II searches for a place for Thomas within the social-historical development of that tradition. Of first priority, of course, are the issues of Thomas' date and provenance. Once the question of Thomas' relationship to the synoptic gospels has been worked out, certain current theses about these matters fall readily into place; they are summarized briefly in Chapter 4. But in turning then to the more vexing question of how Thomas Christianity as an early Christian movement fits into an overall scheme of how early Christianity developed, I found that surprisingly little had been done to describe the shape and character of Thomas Christianity itself, beyond the application to it of such socially nondescript terms as 'gnostic,' or 'proto-gnostic,' and the rather sweeping assumptions that have been made about the social-historical background of gnosticism as 'urban,' or 'the province of the erudite elite.' With such a wealth of material in Thomas suggesting how one might live life with a certain depth of meaning and understanding, it seemed entirely possible, indeed prerequisite, to strive for a more nuanced description of Thomas Christianity from a social-historical point of view. This description constitutes Chapter 5. There it is argued that the dominant ethos among Thomas Christians was a kind of social radicalism, similar to what Gerd Theissen and others have described as operative among those early Christians who focused upon the tradition of Jesus' sayings, including (though not primarily) homelessness, willful poverty, begging, the rejection of family and local piety, and a critique of the political powers that be.

With a description of Thomas Christianity in hand, it was then possible to attempt to locate this particular group of early Christians within the broader historical development of the various groups that grew out of the Jesus movement. Chapter 6 argues the thesis that if the tradition of social radicalism, which Theissen and other's have argued stands behind the synoptic sayings tradition, tended in synoptic Christianity to be subject to gradual domestication, even as the synoptic sayings themselves were "domesticated" through their incorporation into the synoptic gospels, Thomas Christianity tended rather to perpetuate the tradition of social radicalism, even as it also perpetuated the literary tradition of the sayings of Jesus.

This, of course, had consequences—both social and theological. Chapter 7 examines the social consequences the perpetuation of social radicalism would have had for Thomas Christianity. Specifically, here I look at a variety of evidence from various early Christian sources which suggests that as the Jesus movement moved into the latter part of the first century conflict between wandering radicals and local authorities became ever more common. As Thomas Christianity itself sought to perpetuate this form of life and authority it too would have inevitably fallen into such conflicts. With this hypothesis in the background, Chapter 8 proceeds to the question of Thomas' theology. Is there a relationship between the theological developments one finds in Thomas—especially its esoteric or gnosticizing tendencies—and the social-historical developments tracked in Chapters 5–7? I would argue that there is: the social radicalism of Thomas Christianity finds its theological correlary in the anti-cosmic stance of Gnosticism. Moreover, as the socially radical itinerancy of Thomas Christianity became ever more problematic in the face of growing settled communities with local leadership, those Thomas Christians who continued the tradition of itinerant social radicalism hardened their com-mittment to a gnostic view of the world and the path of salvation that lay in the interpretation of Jesus' secret sayings.

Finally, in Part III one last question about Thomas and the Jesus tradition is posed: how might the Gospel of Thomas contribute to a better understanding of the historical figure of Jesus himself. Much of the early excitement over the newly discovered gospel had to do with the prospects it offered for recovering heretofore unknown material from the preaching of Jesus himself, but on this front Thomas has over the years been largely disappointing. It gives us little in the way of new information about Jesus, and only a few previously unknown sayings that anything like a consensus of scholars might attribute to Jesus. However, while the prospects for finding new information about Jesus in the Gospel of Thomas are dim, Thomas may nevertheless open up new ground in that it provides one with a fresh, critical perspective from which to view old information. The discussion of the historical Jesus has, since the nineteenth century, focused primarily upon the synoptic gospels. Their traditions, how-ever influenced by the early Christian kerygma, are still thought to hold out the greatest hope for recovering a picture of Jesus from written sources. But it has not always been clear the extent to which the synoptic tradition had been influenced by the kerygmatic claims it makes about Jesus. Here, Thomas may be of some help. Since Thomas often makes use of the same traditional material, yet gives an account that is independent from the synoptic version, it stands to give us the needed critical distance from which to view some very old and familiar texts in a new light, and to bring a number of tradition-historical issues to a much sharper resolution than has been possible without Thomas. In this way it can help us to clarify the overall history of the Jesus tradition, to sift out the earlier layers from the later ones, and thus to arrive somewhat closer to the origins of that tradition. Thus, though Thomas does not provide the startling new evidence some may have once hoped for, it does provide us with a resource that enables us to use the tools and methods of critical scholarship more effectively. Chapter 9 is an attempt to begin such critical analysis, and to draw some general conclusions about how Thomas may ultimately come to reshape much critical thinking about Jesus.

The Gospel of Thomas

and the Literary Development of the Jesus Tradition

1

The Gospel of Thomas and the Synoptic Gospels   A Question of Method

Since its publication in 1958 the relationship of the Gospel of Thomas to the synoptic gospels has been one of the important focal points of its critical discussion. For the present study it is a point of no small significance, for if, as many have argued, the Gospel of Thomas is dependent upon the synoptic texts for its traditions, it might be possible to think of Thomas Christianity as a small and relatively insignificant spur, diverging from the main stream of the Jesus movement—a "perversion" of the Jesus tradition,[1] whose more original, and hence more authentic voice is to be heard in the synoptic texts themselves. On the other hand, if the Gospel of Thomas is not dependent upon the synoptic gospels, but rather has its own roots, which reach deeply into the fertile soil of early Christian tradition, tapping these sources no less "authentically" than did the authors responsible for shaping the canonical texts, then Thomas presents those who wish to think critically about the problem of Christian origins with something much more important: another point of view from which to peer down into the murk of earliest Christianity. To the historian of early Christianity, for whom new sources with which to ply the trade are seldom forthcoming, these are relatively high stakes. Consequently, this question has produced a rather extensive discussion and debate.[2]

Unfinished Business

Given the considerable amount of discussion which has already been devoted to this subject, it might be tempting at this juncture simply to point to

1. The pejorative comes from Grant and Freedman, *Secret Sayings*, 110.
2. A full account of the debate is to be found in Patterson, "The Gospel of Thomas and the Synoptic Tradition."

the large number of scholars who have come to voice the opinion that the Gospel of Thomas represents an independent tradition, lay claim to a growing *communis opinio*, and so proceed to Part II of this study without further ado. But this is to be avoided. In the first place, though it seems now that there is a growing acceptance of this position, especially among North American scholars, there is still a good deal of reluctance in other quarters to embrace this trend. Influential Thomas scholars such as J.-E. Ménard in France, and B. Dehandschutter in Belgium, continue to defend the position that Thomas is dependent upon the synoptic gospels.[3] Two recent German contributions to the discussion have presupposed the notion that Thomas depends upon the synoptics, citing Wolfgang Schrage's work[4] as decisive for having established this fact.[5] Thus, that a consensus on the problem of Thomas' relationship to the synoptics has been claimed on both sides of the issue (and on both sides of the Atlantic) shows that there really is no consensus on this issue at all, but rather what one might call a certain "continental drift."[6] Yet another vote for Thomas' independence here would only exacerbate this problem, and not contribute to its solution.

In the second place, while proponents of the view that Thomas derives from an independent tradition have done well in pointing out the problems associated with the dependency thesis, studies which have argued in a more positive way for Thomas' independence have, on the whole, been carried out on only a limited scale.[7] A notable exception to this is the Claremont dissertation of John Sieber, which treats in a comprehensive way all of the Thomas-synoptic parallels.[8] Yet even Sieber does not go far enough in this

---

3. Ménard, L'Évangile selon Thomas; Dehandschutter, "L'Evangile de Thomas;" "The Gospel of Thomas and the Synoptics;" "La parabole de vignerons homicides;" "Les paraboles de l'Evangile selon Thomas."

4. Schrage, Das Verhältnis.

5. Lindemann, "Zur Gleichnisinterpretation;" and Schnider, "Das Gleichnis vom verlorenen Schaf." Of course this view of Thomas is not unanimous on the continent; see esp. Vielhauer, Geschichte der urchristlichen Literatur, 624–29; Schramm, Der Markus-Stoff bei Lukas, 9–21; and Schenke's review of Schrage in TLZ 93 (1968) 36–38.

6. In the case of German scholarship this shows up in the lack of attention given to Thomas (and to non-canonical gospels in general) in recent years. Fieger's very recent book, Das Thomasevangelium (1991), is the first German monograph-length study on Thomas to appear since the mid-1960's, a period of more than twenty years.

7. Montefiore's often cited study ("A Comparison") deals only with the parables tradition. Higgins' early study ("Non-Gnostic Sayings") is similarly valuable for its insights, but limited in scope, dealing with fewer than twenty individual sayings. Cullmann's remarks on Thomas ("Das Thomasevangelium") address the question of Thomas' sources in broad enough terms, but he does not provide the sort of detailed analysis of individual sayings, such as that offered by Montefiore and Higgins, that would be necessary to confirm his insights. The most extensive treatment of the Thomas material from the point of view of its fundamental independence is perhaps that provided by Crossan in his major study of aphorisms in the Jesus tradition (In Fragments), wherein almost all of Thomas' sayings are at least mentioned. But valuable as they are, Crossan's observations are made under the presupposition that Thomas represents an independent tradition, a position for which he offers no new arguments (see his p. x).

8. Sieber, "A Redactional Analysis."

respect, since his study is restricted to redaction-critical matters. In most cases, he does not provide an overall tradition-historical comparison of the parallel texts, but confines himself to combing Thomas for traces of synoptic redaction. The result is an important study, but one which convinces only to the extent that one is convinced by Sieber's judgment about what constitutes synoptic redaction in each individual case. The failure of Sieber's study to make a larger impact on the overall discussion is no doubt owing also, at least in part, to the fact that it was never published, and thus remains, after more than twenty years, largely unknown and ignored, especially in continental New Testament circles.

Robert McL. Wilson's study, too, might be mentioned as an exception, in that it treats almost all of Thomas' sayings at one time or another.[9] But the impact of his work has also been somewhat less than dramatic, and understandably so, for though Wilson seems on the whole to regard Thomas as deriving from an independent tradition,[10] in the course of his analysis of individual sayings he seldom arrives at a conclusion that would confirm this thesis. In fact, only a relatively small number of Thomas' sayings are ascribed by Wilson to an independent gospel tradition. Most he judges to have been either derived from or influenced by the synoptic gospels, or created relatively late by a gnostic redactor.[11] In the end, the difference between Wilson on the one hand, and Robert Grant and David Noel Freedman (who also allow for the possibility that a few of Thomas' sayings—but only a few—might have come from an independent tradition[12]) turns out to be only a matter of degree.

Finally, one must mention the work of James M. Robinson and Helmut Koester, whose studies and scholarly influence have probably done the most to encourage scholarship toward the position of Thomas' independence.[13] But while their efforts have provided an overall conceptual framework within which to understand Thomas as a product of an independent tradition-history, they must be supplemented with a more direct tradition-historical comparison of the parallel texts themselves. Koester seems conscious of this fact when, in his ground-breaking article, "GNOMAI DIAPHOROI: The Origin and Nature of Diversification in the History of Early Christianity,"[14] he relies upon the work of Montefiore to establish, as preliminary to his discussion, the

---

9. Wilson, *Studies.*

10. Wilson, *Studies,* 87–88.

11. These categories are laid out in Wilson, *Studies,* 147–48. In the course of his analysis in Chapter 4 ("Thomas and the Four Gospels") Wilson suggests that Thom 56 is from an independent tradition (p. 56); so too, "possibly," Thom 32 (p. 61) and 39 (p. 75). Normally, however, one must settle for a noncommittal "merits further study," or "open to further question." Thus, while Wilson's study remains extremely valuable, his tendency to equivocate on most issues leaves one without much specific support for one position or another.

12. *Secret Sayings* ,101; note the important concession here.

13. See esp. the studies collected in Robinson and Koester, *Trajectories.*

14. Published originally in *HTR* 58 (1965) 279–318; later reprinted in Robinson and Koester, *Trajectories,* 114–57 (subsequent references will be to the article as it appeared in *Trajectories*).

position that Thomas represents an independent tradition.[15] The strength of Koester's argument is that it renders the Thomas tradition comprehensible in its own terms, and thus ultimately affirms Thomas' independence. Nonetheless, in order to avoid becoming circular, his work requires a foundation in firm tradition-historical evidence and the skeptic might well ask whether Montefiore's study, valuable as it is, is not too limited in scope in that it deals only with the parables tradition.

It is the position of this study that the Gospel of Thomas is indeed the product of a tradition-history that is basically independent of the synoptic tradition. Just as it is possible and legitimate to speak of a synoptic tradition, and synoptic Christianity, or a of Johannine tradition, and Johannine Christianity, so too is it appropriate to speak of the Thomas tradition, and Thomas Christianity as a distinctive theological and social-historical current within early Christianity. But this position is not to be taken for granted; arguments must be summoned which deal in a more comprehensive way with the history of the Thomas tradition. Part I of this study is devoted to this task.

Placing the Problem in Perspective

What constitutes a convincing literary source theory? The literary dependence of one text upon another is not easily proven. Comparatively speaking, New Testament scholars seem rather prone to such theories, as the half a dozen or more examples which come to mind involving New Testament texts might suggest. Yet even among such relatively optimistic ranks few such theories have gained universal acceptance. Nonetheless, the extensive discussion they have generated has left behind a good amount of collective experience with such matters, upon which one might draw as a backdrop against which to consider the problem of Thomas' relationship to the synoptic gospels. Much of this discussion has revolved around the question of the relationships which exist between the synoptic gospels themselves on the one hand, and on the other the question of John's relationship to these three. Thomas' relationship to the synoptic gospels presents essentially the same issues that have been dealt with and resolved to the satisfaction of a great majority of scholars in this prior discussion. Thus, in order to place the Thomas question in perspective, and provide the current debate with a few methodological ground rules, it may prove helpful to review the main points of this discussion and its results.

Beginning with the synoptic problem, it may justly be claimed that the predominant way of explaining the synoptic interrelationships today is the two-source hypothesis. As a literary source theory it is not based solely upon the observation that the synoptic gospels share a significant amount of traditional material in common, a fact which in itself might be explained more

15. Koester, "GNOMAI DIAPHOROI," 131–32.

easily by appealing simply to the circumstance that all three synoptics are the product of early Christian authors with access to the same body of traditional material. Rather, both of its prongs, the theory of Markan priority and the Q hypothesis, are based on a combination of two factors: similar *content*, including a high degree of verbal correspondence between parallel versions of given pericopae, and a corresponding *order* in the arrangement of the pericopae they hold in common. In the case of Markan priority, the strength of the thesis has traditionally been the observation that Mark seems to dictate the order followed by Matthew and Luke. Matthew and Luke agree with each other only when they both agree with Mark; they never diverge simultaneously from the Markan order, and after Mark 6:7 neither deviates from the Marcan order at all (before 6:7 Luke deviates on its own from Mark's order four times, Matthew only twice). Thus, the strongest argument for Markan priority concerns a common synoptic order. But it is supported in a very important way by the relatively close textual correspondence to be found between Mark's version of various pericopae and their parallels in Matthew and Luke, which extends also to material serving a distinct function in the Marcan narrative, which in Matthew or Luke is either ill-understood or plainly rejected.

In the case of Q, it is perhaps the very high degree of verbal correspondence found between Matthew and Luke in such Q passages as Luke 3:7–9//Matt 3:7–10, and Luke 7:7–11//Matt 11:9–13, that carries the weight of the hypothesis. Yet the important studies of Vincent Taylor,[16] together with the more recent contributions of Joseph B. Tyson[17] and Petros Vassiliadis,[18] all of which point to residual cases of Q's original *order* in Matthew and Luke's similar ordering of parallel Q pericopae, are not to be overlooked as a significant second leg supporting the Q hypothesis.

While it is this combination of a shared content and order that links the synoptic gospels so intimately together in a relationship of literary dependence, it is the lack of these linking factors between the synoptics and John that leads most Johannine scholars today to the conclusion that John represents a separate tradition altogether.[19] To be sure, John and the synoptics do share a number of well known pericopae, but when one examines this synoptic-like material in John, a number of factors mitigate against the explanation that it derives from the synoptic gospels themselves:

1) Some of this material is paralleled quite closely in the synoptic tradition, but upon closer examination reveals itself to have come from a tradition-history distinct from that to be traced behind and through the synoptic texts,

16. Taylor, "The Order of Q," and "The Original Order of Q."
17. Tyson, "Sequential Parallelism."
18. Vassiliades, "The Original Order of Q."
19. For discussions of the long developing trend in this direction see Haenchen, "Johanneische Probleme," 19–22; Robinson, "The Johannine Trajectory," in Robinson and Koester, *Trajectories*, 234–35; Neirynck, "John and the Synoptics," 73–79.

thus ruling out literary dependence. An illustrative example is to be found in the the story of the Healing of the Centurion's Servant (John 4:46–54, par. Luke 7:1–10//Matt 8:5–13. The pericope comes to Matthew and Luke in the synoptic tradition via their shared sayings source, Q, where it is included apparently as a story of exemplary faith in Jesus' word.[20] John's version of the miracle, the expansion of a pre-Johannine story in which the miracle as an inducement to belief in Jesus must have found much clearer expression,[21] likely came to the fourth evangelist via the Semeia Source.[22] John's direct dependence upon one of the synoptics or their source at this point is ruled out by 4:51–53. If John were dependent here upon the synoptic tradition, these verses, which have no parallel in the synoptic versions of the story, would have to be attributed to the redactional activity of the fourth evangelist. But given John's tendency to undercut and criticize the miracle-inspired faith encouraged in these verses, this is unlikely. More probable is the view that vss 51–53, together with vs 54, derive from the Semeia Source used by John, giving voice to its own christological perspective. The fourth evangelist uses the tradition critically, inserting his or her own perspective in vs 48.[23] At any rate, one may clearly see here that the tradition-historical lines are not to be drawn in this way: Q ● Matt/Luke ● John. Rather, vss 51–53, 54 demonstrate that John has another, non-synoptic source. Thus, despite the close similarity between the Johannine and synoptic versions of this story, close tradition-historical analysis shows that the literary dependence of one upon the other is highly unlikely. One must reckon instead with a common ancestor somewhere in the depths of early Christian tradition.[24]

2) Some of this synoptic-like material in John finds a parallel in the synoptic gospels, but the amount of verbal correspondence between the respective versions is so limited that a relationship of textual dependence can scarcely be assumed. An illustration is to be found in the Preaching of John the Baptist (John 1:19–34, par. Mark 1:2–11; Luke 3:1–22; Matt 3:1–17). The shared elements are enough to suggest that one has to do here with related traditions: 1) the reference to Isa 40:3 (John 1:23; Matt 3:3//Mark 1:2–3//Luke 3:4–5); 2) a similar tendentious saying on the relationship between John and Jesus (John 1:26–27; Matt 3:11//Mark 1:7–8//Luke 3:16); 3) a similar epiphany tradition (John 1:32–34; Matt 3:16–17//Mark 1:10–11//Luke 3:22). Yet nowhere does the actual verbal correspondence extend beyond a few key words. In a tradition-historical situation such as obtains for early Christianity, wherein a

---

20. So Robinson, "Kerygma and History," 57.

21. Note the conversion inspired by the proofs in vss 51–53 and the numeration of the "sign" in vs 54, which emphasizes the significance of the quantity of miracles as accumulated evidence; so Robinson, "Kerygma and History," 57–58.

22. So Bultmann, *The Gospel of John*, 203; and Fortna, *The Fourth Gospel and Its Predecessor*, 58–65.

23. So Bultmann, *Gospel of John*, 207; Robinson, "Kerygma and History," 58.

24. See Bultmann's discussion of the problem, *Gospel of John*, 204–5.

story might have been told in various quarters in different ways and thence taken up independently into literary works, the common occurrence of a key word, or a similar plot, does not guarantee that one author drew the story from another. A relationship of literary dependence in such cases must therefore be ruled out for lack of evidence.

3) Finally, there is some material in John which, though in terms of its form and content closely resembles the sort of material one finds in the synoptic tradition, has no real parallel there. A good example is the Healing of the Paralytic (John 5:1–9a). There are stories of Jesus healing a paralytic in the synoptic gospels as well (Mark 2:1–12//Luke 5:17–26; cf. Matt 9:1–8), but even though in these scenes Jesus uses a similar treatment to effect the cure (cf. John 5:8; Matt 9:6; Mark 2:11; Luke 5:24) the stories themselves are clearly different episodes. Note, for example, the different settings, the different histories of the one who is healed, the different ways in which pathos is created in John 5:7 and Mark 2:4//Luke 5:19, and the different charges brought against Jesus by the authorities as a result of the episode.

If one adds to this material, which I have been calling "synoptic-like," the great mass of material in John generally considered to be more distinctive of the Johannine tradition, such as the long Johannine discourses and the Prologue, it is scarcely possible to argue for John's dependence upon the synoptics on the basis of content. John clearly has its own sources for traditional material, which are independent of the synoptic tradition.

As for order, the case is similarly to be decided in favor of Johannine independence. Anyone wishing to argue for John's dependence on the synoptics would be obliged to explain in terms of Johannine redaction John's multiple trips to Jerusalem over against Mark's single journey, the Johannine transposition of the clearing of the Temple to a point much earlier in the narrative, and the numerous other major discrepancies in the Johannine narrative as distinct from the synoptic view presented in Matthew, Mark and Luke.

While not all would agree with the view that John is not dependent upon the synoptic gospels, there are few who would disagree that the case for or against a literary relationship between John and the synoptics must be worked out in terms of these basic considerations. Thus, my purpose in reviewing this somewhat elementary discussion is not necessarily to make a new case for an independent Johannine tradition, but rather to provide the Thomas debate with a set of consistent and agreed upon ground rules, absent from many previous Thomas studies. For the Gospel of Thomas does not present any tradition-historical dilemmas that have not been encountered already in this prior discussion. There is no reason to treat the problem of Thomas' sources differently from similar problems arising out of the discussion of the relationships prevailing among the canonical gospels, under the pretext that Thomas is an "apocryphal" gospel, as if the invocation of this term somehow implies at the same time the adjectives "late" or "secondary."[25] In a source-critical discussion the term "apocryphal" means absolutely nothing, and the status of "canonical" cannot lend privilege in the debate. Unless one assumes both that the canonical gospels are all earlier than Thomas and that after their composition the canonical gospels henceforth served as the sole source of traditional Jesus material, replacing all other oral and/or written sources, the question of Thomas' sources must remain open, to be addressed using a standard that is consistent with that used to adjudicate the source-critical problems associated with the canonical gospels themselves. Neither of these assumptions is tenable.[26]

It remains, therefore, to ask: Is Thomas' relationship to the synoptic gospels to be considered analogous to the literary relationships that prevail among the synoptic gospels themselves, or rather to the looser relationship that exists between John and the synoptics, that is, sharing oral, and perhaps also common written sources, but on the whole carrying on as two more or less independent traditional streams? Put otherwise, does the Gospel of Thomas represent an exotic spin-off from the main stream of synoptic Christianity, or is it, like John, the document of yet another early Christian school of thought, what one might call "Thomas Christianity"? In the following two chapters I will argue for the latter of these options in a manner consistent with the ground rules laid down in the source-critical discussion of New Testament texts reviewed above. My assumption is that in order to be convincing, a theory of literary dependence must show not just that two texts share a good deal of material in common, but specifically that 1) between the texts in question there is a consistent pattern of dependence, i.e., that one author can be seen regularly to build upon the text of the other, rather than on yet another, shared source (oral or written); and that 2) the sequence of individual pericopae in each text is substantially the same. In the chapters to follow it will be shown that while Thomas and the synoptic texts do in fact share a large body of common material, there is neither a consistent pattern of dependence of one text upon the other, nor a substantial amount of agreement in the way each text has ordered the material they share.

---

25. Cf. Dehandschutter's remarks in "L' Évangile de Thomas," 510, and Robinson's critique in "On Bridging the Gulf," 166–67.

26. It is no longer possible simply to assume that Thomas belongs to the second century (see Chapter 4, pp. 113–18). As for the second assumption, if it is not self-evidently improbable, Koester's study, *Synoptische Überlieferung*, has shown it to be patently false.

2

The Autonomy
of the Thomas Tradition

A Question
of Content

Thomas and the synoptic gospels share a significant amount of material in common. Roughly half of Thomas' sayings have parallels of one sort or another in the synoptics. But when one examines this material closely, with careful attention to the clues each saying provides as to its oral and written history within the broad traditions of earliest Christianity, one finds little to suggest that the author who compiled the sayings collection known as the Gospel of Thomas was even aware of the synoptic texts. To the contrary, one finds a situation rather similar to that which I sketched out in the previous chapter with respect to John and the synoptic gospels. Specifically, there are three groups of sayings affording comparison with the synoptic tradition, all of which cast the argument decisively in the direction of Thomas' fundamental independence. They are "synoptic twins," "synoptic siblings," and "synoptic cousins" respectively.

Synoptic twins are Thomas sayings which have very close parallels in the synoptic gospels. They are like twins, however, in that though their similarities are such that one may be sure they derive from a common origin, their differences reveal that, proceeding from a common point of departure, each version has developed in ways that are unique. Just as biological twins develop characteristics that are quite their own once they have parted and begun to live independent lives, responding to the circumstances in which they find themselves, so too these synoptic twins exhibit tradition-historical differences which show that each member of the pair has enjoyed a life of its own. Their relationship to the synoptic tradition is analogous to the example encountered in John 4:46-54 and its synoptic parallels (see pp. 13-14).

Synoptic siblings are Thomas sayings which have loose parallels in the

17

synoptic text, sharing with their synoptic counterparts a common structure or outline, a common thought, and sometimes key vocabulary. Yet they may be distinguished from synoptic twins in that they lack the degree of close verbal correspondence that would tempt one to posit the literary dependence of one text upon the other. Their relationship to the synoptic tradition is therefore analogous to that of John 1:19–34 (see pp. 14–15).

Synoptic cousins are yet a another grade removed from the synoptic tradition. These are sayings which have no synoptic parallels, but which, in terms of their traditional form and content, offer no grounds for distinguishing them chronologically or topically from sayings in the synoptic tradition itself. One might compare them with the occasional *agraphon* (or 'unwritten saying') appearing in the Pauline tradition, or among the Apostolic Fathers, which, though unattested in the synoptic tradition, nonetheless may be ascribed to the same early, creative period in ancient Christianity that also produced the material collected into the synoptic tradition. Their relationship to the synoptic tradition might be considered analogous to that of John 5:1–9a (see p. 15).

Each of these three groups, "synoptic twins," "siblings," and "cousins" will be dealt with in turn.

Synoptic Twins

If Thomas were dependent upon the synoptic gospels, it would be possible to detect in the case of every Thomas-synoptic parallel the same tradition-historical development behind both the Thomas version of the saying and one or more of the synoptic versions. That is, Thomas' author/editor, in taking up the synoptic version, would have inherited all of the accumulated tradition-historical baggage owned by the synoptic text, and then added to it his or her own redactional twist. In the following texts this is not the case. Rather than reflecting the same tradition-historical development that stands behind their synoptic counterparts, these Thomas sayings seem to be the product of a tradition-history which, though exhibiting the same tendencies operative within the synoptic tradition, is in its own specific details quite unique. This means, of course, that these sayings are not dependent upon their synoptic counterparts, but rather derive from a parallel and separate tradition.

Thom[1] 2:1/92:1/94:1-2 *Seek and Find* (Luke 11:9//Matt 7:7, Q)

2 [1]Jesus said, *"Let one who seeks not stop seeking until he finds.* [2]When he finds, he will be disturbed. [3]When he is disturbed, he will marvel, [4]and will reign over all."*[2]

---

1. The translation of Thomas used throughout this work is based on Scholars Version Thomas, published in Robert Miller, ed., *The Complete Gospels*. However, I have introduced a number of changes to facilitate the work of comparison to the synoptic tradition. The text used is Meyer's Coptic text in Kloppenborg, et al., *Q—Thomas Reader* and Attridge's Greek text in Layton, *Nag Hammadi Codex II.*

2. The extant Greek version of this saying (POxy 654.5-9) reads:

92 ¹Jesus said, *"Seek and you will find.* ²In the past, however, I did not tell you the things about which you asked me then. Now I am willing to tell them, but you are not seeking them.
94 ¹Jesus [said], *"One who seeks will find,* ²and for [one who knocks] it will be opened.*"

In Thomas and Q one is presented with four different versions of this saying, which may not be viewed as different stages in a single line of tradition-historical development. Each has both primary and secondary elements not shared with the others. Given the tendency within the tradition for like sayings to attract, or to expand with analogous formulations,[3] the single-stich form found in Thom 2:1 and 92:1 is no doubt primary over against the double-stich form of Thom 94 or the triple-stich form in Luke 11:9//Matt 7:7, Q.[4] On the other hand, the gnosticizing expansion in Thom 2 and the revealer language appended to the simple saying in Thom 92 represent secondary developments not to be found in Thom 94 or Q. Thom 94, whose form is secondary in the sense that a second stich has been added to complement the first, no doubt preserves a primitive feature in presenting the couplet as an independent saying, without the interpretive elements so in evidence in Thom 2 and 92. Q's version is probably the most developed of the four. Here an earlier double-stich version has been expanded with a third member, Αἰτεῖτε, καὶ δοθήσεται ὑμῖν (Ask, and it shall be given to you). This adapts the older saying to serve as an introduction to the Q section on answer to prayer (Luke 11:10–13//Matt 7:8–11, Q) and creates for it a new point of reference not typical of the seeking-finding *topos*, whose natural referent is the wisdom quest, not the meeting of needs through prayer.[5] Thus, both its expanded form and the resulting new application are secondary. Given these circumstances it is very unlikely that one or all of the various versions collected by Thomas derive from the synoptic text. (For Thom 92:2, see below under "synoptic cousins.")

Thom 4:2 *First and Last*
(cf. Matt 19:30//Mark 10:31; Luke 13:30// Matt 20:16, Q)

4 ¹Jesus said, "The person old in days will not hesitate to ask a little child seven days old about the place of life, and that person will live. ²*For many of the first will be last,* ³and will become a single one."[6]

---

¹[Jesus says], "Let one who [seeks] not stop [seeking until] he finds.
²When he finds, [he will be astounded].
³And having been] astounded, he will reign,
⁴and [having reigned], he will [rest]."
3. Bultmann, *Geschichte*, 86–87, 88–89.
4. Bultmann, *Ergänzungsheft*, 35.
5. Koester, "Gnostic Writings," 238–44.
6. The extant Greek version of the saying (POxy 654.21–27) reads:
   ¹[Jesus says], "A [person old in] days will not hesitate to ask a [little child seven days] old about the place of [life, and] that person will [live].
   ²For many of the [first] will be [last, and] the last first
   ³and [will become one]."

The attestation of this saying in Q and Mark, in different contexts and with differing applications, justifies Bultmann's designation of it as an independent saying from the oral tradition.[7] Furthermore, there is evidence to suggest that our saying is not even uniquely Christian, but rather belongs to a *topos* with deep Jewish roots.[8] Its mere appearance in Thomas can therefore not be taken as proof of dependence on the synoptic gospels; there are simply too many other possible sources from which Thomas might have received it. The fact that it occurs here in yet another context, and applied in a way that is not attested in the synoptic texts, indicates that it probably did not come to Thomas via the synoptic tradition.

Schrage's argument for Thomas' dependence here is not convincing.[9] It rests on the supposition that the Coptic version of Thom 4:2 depends upon the Coptic versions of Matt 19:30//Mark 10:31, since Thomas here follows the Coptic New Testament in rendering ἔσονται (they will be) with ναρ‾rather than with the more usual cενα (I Future) or εγνα (II Future), or with a form of ϣωπε (to become). But in other ways Thomas' Coptic is different from the Coptic versions of the New Testament (e.g., in introducing the saying with χε [for . . .] rather than ᴧε [but . . .]), so that one may be sure that the Coptic scribe was not simply copying sayings from a Coptic New Testament codex. Rather, the translational oddity could easily be explained if Thomas' Coptic translator had cut his teeth in the more familiar text of the New Testament, and either remembered the parallel New Testament text or even consulted it as a means of negotiating difficult translational problems. At any rate, similarities in the Coptic translations of these two documents may tell us something about early Christian scribal practice, but virtually nothing about the literary relationship between the Greek documents they are translating.[10]

Thom 5:2/6:5–6 *Hidden Made Manifest*
(cf. Mark 4:22//Luke 8:17; Luke 12:2//Matt 10:26, Q)

5 [1]Jesus said, "Know what is in front of your face, and what is hidden from you will be disclosed to you. [2]*For there is nothing hidden that will not be revealed.*"[11]
6 [1]His disciples asked him and said to him, "Do you want us to fast? How should we pray? Should we give alms? What diet should we observe?" [2]Jesus said, "Do not lie, [3]and do not do what you hate, [4]because all things are disclosed before heaven.

---

7. Bultmann, *Geschichte*, 191; cf. pp. 78, 84, and 110.
8. Strack and Billerbeck, *Kommentar*, 1.830 (*Baba Bathra* 10b: "I saw a world turned upside down: the highest had become the lowest, and the lowest the highest.")
9. Schrage, *Das Verhältnis*, 32–33.
10. *Contra* Schrage, *Das Verhältnis*, 11, 15, and n. 46.
11. The extant Greek version of this saying (POxy 654.27–31) reads:
    [1]Jesus says, "[Know what is in front of] your face, and [what is hidden] from you will be disclosed [to you.
    [2]For there is nothing] hidden that [will] not [be] brought to light,
    [3]and (nothing) buried that [will not be raised]."

[5]*For there is nothing hidden that will not be revealed,* [6]*and there is nothing covered that will remain without being disclosed.*"[12]

The independent use of this saying by both Mark and Q, in slightly different versions but in quite different contexts and to different ends, clearly indicates that it circulated at one time as an independent saying.[13] In Thomas one encounters two new slightly divergent forms of it, a single-stich version, which uses only the hidden/manifest schema (Thom 5:2), and another double-stich version similar to that found in Q but reversing the order of its members (Thom 6:5-6).[14] Each introduces a new application of the saying not attested in the synoptic tradition.[15] But perhaps the most telling argument against Thomas' dependence upon the synoptics here is the fact that both Thom 5:2 and 6:5-6 are locked into their respective clusters of sayings through catchword connections: 5:2 is linked to 5:1 by ϩⲏⲡ (hide) and 6:5-6 is connected to 6:4 by ⲟⲟⲗⲡ (disclose).[16] This suggests that these clusters were already formed at an oral stage of transmission, when the catchword connection still retained its mnemonic function.

Harvey K. McArthur has duly noted that the Greek version of Thom 5:2 agrees with Lukan redaction in 8:17a insofar as both have the formulation ὁ οὐ φανερὸν γενήσεται (which will not be brought to light) against Mark 4:22a: ἐὰν μὴ ἵνα φανερωθῇ (except to be brought to light). He takes this as evidence of Thomas' dependence on the synoptic text.[17] But the Q form of the saying

---

12. The extant Greek version of this saying (POxy 654.32-40) reads:
[1][His disciples] ask him [and] say, "How [should we] fast? [How should] we [pray]? How [should we give alms]? What [diet] should [we] observe?"
[2]Jesus says, "[Do not lie,
[3]and] do not do [what] you [hate,
[4]because all things are apparent before] truth.
[5][After all, there is nothing] hidden [that will not be brought to light].
13. Cf. Bultmann, *Geschichte*, 86-87.
14. A question arises here as to which of the versions of Thomas, the Greek from POxy 654 or the Coptic from Nag Hammadi, preserves the more original Thomas text. In both Thom 5 and 6, I would hold that the Coptic text represents the more original version. In the case of Thom 5, the additional clause in POxy 654.31 is found also on a burial schroud from Oxyrhynchus (cf. Hennecke [Schneemelcher, ed.], *New Testament Apocrypha*, 1:300), and therefore may simply have been a popular saying at Oxyrhynchus, in this way finding a place in an Oxyrhynchus version of Thomas. In the case of Thom 6, the similarity of the Coptic version to Q seems to speak for its greater age; however, that Thom 6:6 might represent a harmonization of Thomas toward the synoptic text here is not to be ruled out.
15. Thus in the four different versions of this logion one is presented with four different applications: in Q its use is hortatory (μὴ φοβεῖσθε [do not fear], Luke 12:4//Matt 10:28, Q); in Mark it urges mission activity; in Thom 5:2 it refers to revelation through perception; and in Thom 6:5-6 its application is ethical. This wide variation speaks for a logion that circulated independently.
16. If one follows Grenfell and Hunt's reconstruction (*Oxyrhynchus Papyri*, 8) of the Greek Thom 5:1b (ln. 28) the catchword is evident also in the POxy version of the text: κεκρυμμένον/κρυπτόν (being hidden/hidden) in POxy 654.28, 30 and ἀναφαίνεται/φανερὸν (be revealed/revealed) in POxy 654.38, 39.
17. McArthur, "Dependence," 287.

also uses the relative construction (see Luke 12:2b//Matt 10:26b); therefore, one may assume that a form of the saying using the relative clause circulated quite apart from Luke 8:17a. In fact, Luke 8:17 itself probably stands under the influence of the Q text; it is not a purely Lukan invention. Thus, there is no reason to suppose that Thomas could not have composed the saying in this way without direct knowledge of Luke 8:17a.

Finally, if it is the case that Thomas lies on a "gnosticizing" trajectory,[18] it is difficult to imagine why, if its author knew the saying in either its Lukan (8:17) or Q (Matt 10:26//Luke 12:2) form, he or she would have omitted the second stich of each, which features the theme of knowledge and makes use of the favored terminology of Gnosticism ($\gamma\iota\nu\acute{\omega}\sigma\kappa\epsilon\iota\nu$).[19]

Thom 9 The Sower (cf. Matt 13:3-9//Mark 4:2-9//Luke 8:4-8)

9 [1]Jesus said, "Look, the sower went out, took a handful (of seeds), and scattered (them). [2]Some fell on the road, and the birds came and gathered them. [3]Others fell on rock, and they did not take root in the soil and did not produce heads of grain. [4]Others fell on thorns, and they choked the seeds and worms ate them. [5]And others fell on good soil, and it produced a good crop: it yielded sixty per measure and one hundred twenty per measure."

A number of excellent treatments of the relationship between the synoptic and Thomas versions of the Sower are already available,[20] so that only the most pertinent points need be summarized here. Mark's version of the parable, which is taken up and used by Matthew and Luke, contains the following secondary features not in Thom 9: the Markan introduction (4:2; cf. Matt 13:4; Luke 8:4b), a transitional section (4:10-12; cf. Matt 13:10-13; Luke 8:9-10), and the allegorical interpretation (4:13-20; cf. Matt 13:18-23; Luke 8:11-15).[21] Of course, it is not inconceivable that an excerpter might have left out these features as not essential to his or her own plan. But Thom 9 also shows no trace of Mark 4:9 (see also Matt 13:9; Luke 8:8b); had he or she known and used Mark, or any of the synoptic versions of this parable, it would be difficult similarly to explain the absence of this phrase, which otherwise functions often in the Gospel of Thomas as the conclusion to a parable (see e. g. Thom 8:4; 21:10; 63:4; 65:8; and 96:3). Furthermore, Crossan has detected in Mark's somewhat convoluted explanation of the fate of the seed cast upon rocky soil (4:5-6) a redactional preparation for an element of the (secondary) allegorical expansion (cf. 4:16-17).[22] The Thomas version neither shares this awkward-

---

18. So Robinson, "LOGOI SOPHON," 71-113.
19. Cf. Grobel, "How Gnostic is the Gospel of Thomas," 368.
20. See, e.g., Montefiore, "A Comparison," 225, 229, 235, 242, and 244; Crossan, "The Seed Parables," 244-45; Jeremias, Gleichnisse Jesu, 24, 99, 149-50; Sieber, "Redactional Analysis," 155-62; Sheppard, "A Study of the Parables," 142-68; Schrage, Das Verhältnis, 42-48.
21. Jeremias, Gleichnisse Jesu, 75-77; Bultmann, Geschichte, 202; Dodd, Parables, 180-81, 183-84.
22. Crossan, ""The Seed Parables," 147-48.

ness[23] nor shows any awareness of it,[24] offering rather a statement that makes good agricultural sense: "Others fell on rock, and they did not take root in the soil and did not produce heads of grain" (9:3).

There are, of course, secondary features in the Thomas version of the parable that are not found in any of the synoptic versions: the embellishment of the yield to 120-fold (Thom 9:5),[25] and perhaps the streamlining of the elaboration of the yield to two rather than three amplifications.[26] But such secondary features do not prove that Thomas is dependent upon the synoptic gospels; rather, the fact that these secondary features are not the same as those found in the synoptic tradition suggests that Thomas did not know the Markan version of the parable (in any of its synoptic forms), but rather acquired it via another tradition-history, in which it had retained earlier features in some respects and undergone a certain amount of secondary development of its own in others.

Thom 10 *Fire on Earth* (cf. Luke 12:49)

10 Jesus said, "I have set a fire upon the world, and look, I am tending it until it blazes."

It is neither necessary nor plausible to account for Thom 10 by resorting to a theory of dependence upon Luke 12:49. It is not necessary because Luke did not invent this saying but likely received it through the Q tradition, where it was clustered with the two other ἦλθον-sayings in Luke 12:51–53//Matt 10:34–36.[27] It was therefore no doubt available to Thomas from other sources; Luke was not its soul proprietor. It is not plausible because precisely that which Luke adds to this Q cluster (Luke 12:50) is missing in Thomas.[28] Without imagining Thomas carefully removing everything of redactional significance from the Lukan passage with all the skill of a modern redaction critic, it is scarcely conceivable that Thomas used Luke as a source here. It is also not likely that Thomas took this saying from Luke's source for it, Q. In Q it is combined with the sayings found in Luke 12:51–53//Matt 10:34–36. Thomas does have a version of these sayings, but preserves them elsewhere (see Thom 16). With no obvious redactional reason for separating the saying in

---

23. In contrast to Matthew, who takes up the Markan formulation without significant alteration (cf. Matt 13:5–6).

24. In contrast to Luke, who seems to know the Markan version but corrects it—note that the ultimate fate of the seed is the same in Luke: ἐξηράνθη (it was withered) Luke 8:6//Mark 4:6.

25. Jeremias, *Gleichnisse Jesu*, 23; Montefiore, "A Comparison," 225. Cf. the 100-fold embellishment in Mark 4:8, par.

26. Crossan, "The Seed Parables," 248–49.

27. For the argument that Luke 12:49 comes from Q see Patterson, "Fire and Dissension," 124–25.

28. Most agree that 12:50 is a Lukan creation. März ("Feur auf die Erde," 483–84) summarizes the Lukan stylistic and linguistic features: ἔχειν (to have) with the infinitive in vs 50a; πῶς (how) used as an exclamation, συνέχειν (to be in anguish), τελεῖν (to finish), and ἕως ὅτου (until) in vs 50b.

Thom 10 from those found in Thom 16, we must assume that Thomas simply did not encounter them as a cluster (as in Q), but as separate, independently circulating sayings.

Thom 14:4, 5 *Concerning Diet*
(cf. Luke 10:8-9, Q; Mark 7:15, 18// Matt 15:11, 18)

14 [1]Jesus said to them, "If you fast, you will bring sin upon yourselves, [2]and if you pray, you will be condemned, [3]and if you give alms, you will harm your spirits. [4]*When you go into any country and walk from place to place, when people take you in, eat what they serve you and care for*[29] *the sick among them.* [5]*After all, what goes into your mouth will not defile you; rather, it is what comes out of your mouth that will defile you.*"

Thom 14 is a cluster of three sayings connected thematically around the question of proper dietary practice. Thom 14:1-3 has only remote parallels elsewhere in early Christian literature, and thus will not be dealt with here. Versions of Thom 14:4 and 14:5 occur in the synoptic tradition, but embedded secondarily in more developed traditional units: 14:4 is paralleled by a saying forming part of Q's mission instructions to the seventy (Luke 10:2-12//Matt 9:37; 10:7-16),[30] and a version of 14:5 has been appended in Mark to a controversy dialogue on clean and unclean meal practice (Mark 7:1-23//Matt 15:1-20).

Grant and Freedman view the final clause of 14:4 (ΝΕΤϢϢΝΕ Ν̄ϨΗΤΟΥ ΕΡΙΘΕΡΑΠΕΥΕ Μ̄ΜΟΥ [. . .and care for the sick among them]) as a spur revealing the ultimate origin of this saying in Luke 10:8-9, since it makes sense in the Lukan context but strikes one as out of place here in Thomas among sayings dealing with dietary practice.[31] Indeed, the phrase does seem out of place, but this in no way proves that Thomas has taken the saying from out of its Lukan context. On the contrary, if Thomas' author/editor had drawn the saying from Luke in order to include it here, it would be difficult to imagine why he or she would have whittled Luke's Sending of the Seventy-two down to this single verse, and yet stopped short of completing the editorial task, leaving the offending spur to clash with 14:1-3 and 14:5. Another solution seems much more plausible. Thomas' author likely knew a version of Luke 10:8 from another tradition-history, in which it circulated as an independent saying, as yet not combined with the other elements forming Q's Sending of the Seventy-two. It was included here in Thomas without much editorial concern to to adapt it to the Thomas context.

As for 14:5, its parallel in Mark 7:15 probably circulated at one time as an

---

29. Or "heal"

30. On the inclusion of the mission instructions in Q, and their extent, see Schulz, *Q*, 404-408; Kloppenborg, *Formation*, 77, 192-97; and Vaage, "Q," 72-300.

31. Grant and Freedman, *Secret Sayings*, 136; cf. Grant, "Notes on the Gospel of Thomas," 176. A similar position is taken by Wilson, *Studies*, 70-71; Gärtner, *Theology*, 35-36; and Blomberg, "Tradition and Redaction," 181.

independent saying;[32] therefore, it should not be at all surprising to find it here without its Markan context. Thomas apparently has acquired the saying via a tradition-historical stream in which it was not enclosed in the secondary apophthegmic form found in Mark.[33]

Thom 16 *Not Peace, but Dissension* (cf. Luke 12:51–53//Matt 10:34–36, Q)

16 ¹Jesus said, "Perhaps people think that I have come to cast peace upon the world. ²They do not realize that I have come to cast conflicts upon the earth: fire, sword, war. ³For there will be five in a house: three will line up against two and two against three, father against son and son against father, ⁴and they will stand alone."

Schrage is convinced by a certain amount of verbal agreement between Thomas and both Matthew and Luke that Thomas here presents one with a "mixed text," drawn in part from Matthew, in part from Luke.[34] But the case is not so clear cut as Schrage insists. He is correct that Thomas' ΜΕΕΥΕ (to think) in 16:1 can correspond to δοκεῖν (to think) in Luke 12:51a,[35] but he overlooks the fact that this verb derives from Luke's source (Q) here,[36] and hence may not be used to link specifically Thomas and Luke. Thomas' use of ΠШРΧ (conflict) in 16:2 could perhaps reflect Luke's redactional use of διαμερισμον (division) in 12:51b.[37] But ΠШРΧ may also be used to translate the Greek verb διχάζειν (to turn against), as it does in the Sahidic and Bohairic versions of Matt 10:35; thus, here Thomas may just as well reflect a primitive version of the saying more akin to Q's version, not Lukan redaction. The fact that elsewhere in 16:2 Thomas includes a remnant of Luke's Q source in CΗϤε (sword)[38] suggests this as the more likely alternative. Add to this the

---

32. The analysis of Mark 7:1–15 falls into two basic schools of thought: 1) vss 1–8 formed the original controversy dialogue, to which the subsequent verses (including vs 15) eventually gravitated as originally independent logia (so Bultmann, *Geschichte*, 15); and 2) vs 15 itself was the occasion for the composition of 7:1–14, with various theses as to the original extent and subsequent development of vss 1–14 (see esp. Dibelius, *Formgeschichte*, 222–23: vss 1–5 formed the original introduction to vs 15; vss 6–14 were a later Markan insertion). Under either reconstruction, vs 15 is to be viewed as an originally independent logion.

33. McArthur's point ("Dependence," 286), that both Matt 15:10 and Thom 14:5 specify things entering the "mouth" (Mark speaks simply of that which "goes into" a person), need not be taken as an indication that Thomas' author/editor knew and used Matthew's version of the saying. The subject matter, after all, is "eating"; that both specify what goes into the "mouth" could easily be ascribed to an independent effort by both authors to clarify the saying.

34. Schrage, *Das Verhältnis*, 58–59; see also Snodgrass, "Gospel of Thomas," 31.

35. Schrage, *Das Verhältnis*, 58.

36. So Schulz, *Q*, 258, following Harnack, *Sayings*, 86; Bussmann, *Studien*, 80; Wernle, *Frage*, 73; Schmid, *Matthäus und Lukas*, 276 and n. 2; Trillig, *Das wahre Israel*, 171. See also Sellew, "Reconstruction of Q 12:33–59," 647; and Patterson, "Fire and Dissension," 122.

37. Regarding διαμέρισμον as redactional, see Schulz, *Q*, 258, following Harnack, *Sayings*, 86–87; Wernle, *Frage*, 73; Schmid, *Matthäus und Lukas*, 276; *contra* Bussmann, *Studien*, 80.

38. Cf. Matt 10:34b: μάχαιραν (sword); Matthew here reflects Q: so Harnack, *Sayings*, 86–87; Schmid, *Matthäus und Lukas*, 276, n. 2; Wernle, *Frage*, 73; Schweizer, *Matthew*, 250; Schulz, *Q*, 258; Sellew, "Reconstruction of Q 12:33–59," 649; Patterson, "Fire and Dissension," 123.

observation that in their very different versions of this sentence Thomas and Luke share virtually nothing else in common and the case for reliance upon Luke here becomes rather weak. Luke and Thomas intersect again in that they both include the saying in Luke 12:52 (cf. Thom 16:3a). But this material may derive from Q;[39] thus, again their shared material may not be used to demonstrate Thomas' dependence upon Luke. The same is to be said for Thomas' (16:3) and Luke's (12:53) shared order in the next line: father-son/son-father (cf. Matt 10:35). Luke no doubt preserves the Q order, Matthew having reversed it to conform more closely to Mic 7:6.[40]

As for the relationship between Matthew and Thomas, Schrage argues for Thomas' use of the Matthean text on the basis of their shared vocabulary: cHqe (sword) = μάχαιραν (Thom 16:2; Matt 10:34b) and ноүхе (to cast) = βάλλειν (Thom 16:1, 2; Matt 10:34b).[41] But both of these words were already in Matthew's Q source,[42] and therefore may not be used to link Thomas to Matthew.

In looking for more positive evidence for Thomas' independence here, it is to be noted that Thomas transmits this saying as a single logion, in contrast to Matthew and Luke, both of whom combine it with other traditional material. Matthew combines it with another Q saying, Matt 10:37-38 (cf. Luke 14:26-27), to form a longer ending to his version of the Markan Sending Out of the Twelve (cf. Mark 6:7-13). It is striking that Thomas also preserves this second saying, but separately and in two slightly different forms (see Thom 55 and 101). If there is a reasonable explanation for why Thomas' author/editor might have broken these up—reformulating the second saying in two different ways!—it has not yet been offered. Dependence upon Matthew thus seems very unlikely. As for Luke, there the saying is introduced redactionally by Luke 12:49-50, thus forming the larger unit.[43] Since Thomas preserves a version of the saying in Luke12:49 elsewhere (see Thom 10), dependence upon Luke here poses similar problems. The simplest solution to this tangle of traditions is to judge that Thomas did not draw here upon Matthew or Luke, but rather acquired the saying from circles in which it had not been combined directly with these other traditional sayings.

---

39. Klostermann, *Matthäusevangelium*, 91-92; Bussmann, *Studien*, 80; Patterson, "Fire and Dissension," 123; *contra* Schulz, *Q*, 258-59 and nn. 563 and 570.

40. Bussmann, *Studien*, 80; *contra* Schulz, *Q*, 259. In tradition-historical terms, Bussmann's view seems more plausible. As has been learned from the parables tradition, there is a general tendency to harmonize toward LXX parallels (so Jeremias, *Gleichnisse Jesu*, 26-27.)

41. Schrage, *Das Verhältnis*, 58.

42. For μάχαιραν as deriving from Q, see Schulz, *Q*, 258, who follows Harnack, *Sayings*, 86-87; Wernle, *Frage*, 73; Schmid, *Matthäus und Lukas*, 276; *contra* Bussmann, *Studien*, 80; so also Sellew, "Reconstruction," 249." On βάλλειν in Q, see Schulz, *Q*, 258, again following Harnack, *Sayings*, 86; Schmid, *Matthäus und Lukas*, 276; *contra* Bussmann, *Studien*, 80; so also Sellew, "Reconstruction," 648.

43. On the status of Luke 12:49-50, see p. 23, n. 27 and 28.

Thom 20 *The Mustard Seed*
(cf. Matt 13:31-32//Mark 4:30-32//Luke 13:18-19, Mark/Q overlap)

20 [1]The disciples said to Jesus, "Tell us what heaven's kingdom is like." [2]He said to them, "It is like a mustard seed. [3]⟨It⟩ is the smallest of all seeds, [4]but when it falls on prepared soil, it produces a large plant and becomes a shelter for birds of the sky."

Though Schrage[44] and others[45] have attempted to demonstrate that Thom 20 is a mixed text, relying upon the synoptic versions of the parable and combining elements from each, a close examination of these texts renders this theory very improbable.

First, the parable is attested in both Mark (4:30-32) and Q (Luke 13:18-19//Matt 13:31-32),[46] so that one may be quite certain that the parable is older than any of these sources, and probably circulated widely among early Christians. Therefore, if one is to argue that Thomas depends on one or more of the canonical gospels for this parable, one must show unequivocally that elements in the Thomas version mirror the unique editorial hands of the canonical writers. This is not possible.

In the case of Mark, Schrage admits that though Thomas and Mark share many features, none of these can serve as proof for Thomas' dependence upon Mark, since they all may stem from a pre-Markan tradition, that is, a primitive tradition common to both Mark and Thomas.[47] In fact, all of their common features are also attested independently in the Q version of the story, thus assuring us of their primitive origins. One feature peculiar to Mark is the fact that the Mustard Seed is paired with another parable, the Seed Growing Secretly (Mark 4:26-29). Both parables may have come down to Mark as part of H.-W. Kuhn's proposed pre-Markan parables collection.[48] Whether they were paired first in the pre-Markan collection or were already told together at an earlier oral stage cannot be determined.[49] In any event, the fact that Thomas seems to know neither this collection nor the pairing of the Mustard Seed with the Seed Growing Secretly renders Thomas' dependence upon Mark only a remote possibility at best. Similarities between the Coptic versions of Mark 4:30-32 and Thom 20 are not enough to offset such factors. They may suggest something about later Christian scribal practice, but cannot tell us much about the relationship of the original Greek texts to one another.[50]

44. Schrage, *Das Verhältnis*, 61-66.
45. See, for example, Sheppard, "A Study of the Parables," 175-83.
46. This is an instance of Mark/Q overlap; so Laufen, *Doppelüberlieferung*, 174, and n. 1.
47. Schrage, *Das Verhältnis*, 62. Sheppard misses this point entirely when he writes: "There is nothing in Logion 20 to lead one to suspect that Thomas knew any tradition of the similitude other than that found in Mark" ("A Study of the Parables," 182).
48. H.-W. Kuhn, *Ältere Sammlungen*, 99-146.
49. For pairing as a feature of the tradition see Jeremias, *Gleichnisse Jesu*, 89-91.
50. The most striking detail Schrage observes is the use of сōвк пара (smallest) to translate μικρότερον (smallest) in both Thom 20:3 and the Sahidic version of Mark 4:31. He

Matthew and Luke, on the other hand, have probably taken the parable from Q (Luke 13:18-19//Matt 13:31-32). In Q, or perhaps already in the traditions known to Q's author, the parable was, as in Mark, paired with another, but in this case the Parable of the Leaven (Luke 13:20-21//Matt 13:33). Although Thomas does indeed know this latter parable as well (see Thom 107), its positioning at some remove from the Mustard Seed suggests that he did not encounter the two as a pair. This, of course, indicates that the parables came down to Thomas via another tradition-historical stream altogether. Schrage would dispute this, pointing out that Thomas' use of ⲧⲙⲛ̄ⲧⲧⲉⲣⲟ ⲛ̄ⲙ̄ⲡⲏⲩⲉ (heaven's kingdom) mirrors the redactional βασιλεία τῶν οὐρανῶν (heaven's kingdom) of Matthew, who tends to follow Jewish custom in avoiding the use the divine name (cf. "God's kingdom" throughout Mark). But Thomas avoids reference to "God" no less assiduously than Matthew, and never refers to "God's kingdom." Thus, this convergence should sooner be attributed to common Jewish roots than to literary dependence of Thomas upon Matthew.

It has often been pointed out that Thomas' reference to "prepared soil" (20:4) seems to be a secondary feature, reflecting the gnosticizing tendencies of the Thomas trajectory.[51] Whether this is the case may be disputed;[52] it would at any rate not indicate that Thomas was dependent upon the canonical gospels, but simply that its version had undergone secondary development of its own. It should also be noted that in comparison to Thomas, both Q and Mark use forms of the parable in which the final sentence has been reformulated to conform more closely to the wording of Ezek 17:23. Apparently Thomas acquired the tradition from circles in which it was told or written in less biblicistic fashion, and in this respect preserved in an older, or more pristine form.[53]

Thom 21:5, 9 *The Thief/The Reaper* (cf. Luke 12:39//Matt 24:43, Q; Mark 4:29)

21 ²Mary said to Jesus, "What are your disciples like?" ²He said, "They are like little children living in a field that is not theirs. ³When the owners of the field

---

maintains that the use of ⲡⲁⲣⲁ to formulate the superlative is rare; it is found only twice more in the Sahidic New Testament (2 Cor 11:5 and 12:11). One might question how remote this coincidence really is (Thomas uses the formulation again in 107:3), but even if one were to assume that Thomas' use of ⲡⲁⲣⲁ in this way precisely here is no accident of translation, one could at best say that the translation of Mark 4:31 into Coptic influenced the way in which a Christian scribe chose to translate Thom 20:3 (or vice versa), nothing more.

51. Grant and Freedman, *Secret Sayings*, 140; Gärtner, *Theology*, 232; Cerfaux and Garitte, "Les paraboles du Royaume," 319; Schrage, *Das Verhältnis*, 65-66; Montefiore and Turner, *Thomas*, 34, 52-53, 55; Crossan, "The Seed Parables," 258.

52. Proper "cultivation" of discipleship is certainly not a theme unique to Gnosticism; cf. the Parable of the Sower (Matt 13:3-9, 18-23//Mark 4:2-9, 13-20//Luke 8:4-8, 11-15; Thom 9)!

53. See Jeremias, *Gleichnisse Jesu*, 27, Crossan, "The Seed Parables," 258. Montefiore ("A Comparison," 227) also notices the phenomenon, but in a departure from his stated aim of analyzing Thomas from the point of view of Jeremias' "laws of transmission" he takes this as an indication that Thomas has abbreviated the parable.

come, they will say, 'Give us back our field.' [4]They take off their clothes in front of them in order to give it back to them, and they return their field to them. [5]*For this reason I say, if the owner of a house knows that a thief is coming, he will be on guard before the thief arrives, and will not let the thief break into his house of his domain and steal his possessions.* [6]As for you, then, be on guard against the world. [7]Equip yourselves with great strength, in case the robbers find a way to get to you, for the trouble you expect will come. [8]Let there be among you a person who understands. [9]*When the crop ripened, he came quickly carrying a sickle and harvested it.* [10]Whoever has two good ears should listen."

Thom 21 consists of a parable (21:1-4) followed by three successive sayings dealing with the theme of defence and vigilance. Two of these, 21:5 (the Thief) and 21:9 (the Reaper), have synoptic parallels.[54] A version of 21:5 occurs in Q's apocalyptic section (Luke 12:39//Matt 24:43), with which Thomas otherwise shows no hint of familiarity.[55] A version of the saying in Thom 21:9 also occurs in Mark 4:29. But there it is formulated more closely to Joel 3:13, perhaps to provide Mark's parable of the Seed Growing Secretly with a more apocalyptically flavored conclusion. Thomas, however, knows neither this parable nor the apocalyptic application of the saying as it is found in Mark.[56] Therefore, the author/editor of Thomas has either surgically removed these two sayings from their synoptic contexts, or he or she has acquired them from an entirely different tradition-historical stream.

The overall structure of Thom 21 speaks for the latter solution. Each of its constituent parts is linked to its adjoining member through the use of interlocking catchwords: ϫⲟⲉⲓⲥ (owner) connects 21:5 to the parable; ⲣⲟⲉⲓⲥ (watch) ties 21:5 to 21:6; and ⲉⲓ (come) links 21:7 with 21:9. The use of this mnemonic device suggests that the cluster was formed not out of complex theological interests, but rather out of a concern for the primarily oral context in which it would have been used and the resulting necessity of committing it to memory.

Thom 26 *Speck and Log* (cf. Luke 6:41-42//Matt 7:3-5, Q)

26 [1]Jesus said, "You see the speck that is in your brother's eye, but you do not see the beam that is in your own eye. [2]When you take the beam out of your own eye, then you will see clearly to take the speck out of your brother's eye."

This well-known saying occurs in Matthew's Sermon on the Mount as well

---

54. I see no connection between 21: 6-7 and Mark 3:27, *contra* Schrage, *Das Verhältnis*, 67.
55. Schrage (*Das Verhältnis*, 67), suggests that Thomas' ϥⲛⲁⲣⲟⲉⲓⲥ (he will be on guard) in 21:5 shows dependence upon Matthew's text (cf. Matt 24:43: ἐγρηγόρησεν [he will be on guard]). To be sure, Matthew's version is generally considered to be a secondary formulation of Q (cf. Luke 12:39)—see Schulz, *Q*, 268, n. 6—but aside from this single word, Thomas and Matthew formulate the second half of this logion very differently, thus calling any direct relationship into question. Since the theme here is "watchfulness," perhaps it should not seem beyond coincidence to find this key word in both the Thomas and Matthean versions.
56. Mark's apocalyptic application of the saying (vs 29) is secondary; see Jülicher, *Gleichnisreden*, 2: 545; Bultmann, *Geschichte*, 186-87; and Suhl, *Die Funktion*, 154-57.

as Luke's corresponding Sermon on the Plain; thus, it comes to the synoptic texts via that very old Sermon tradition taken up and used by Q.[57] Its transmission in the synoptic tradition is therefore closely bound up with the Sermon on the Mount/Plain tradition. This is likely not the case with Thom 26. First, the Thomas version of this saying lacks the reformulation one finds in Luke 6:42//Matt 7:4, a secondary feature that must have accrued already at the level of Q. This, of course, suggests that the Thomas version of the saying derives ultimately from a point in the tradition-history that pre-dates even Q, even though it may have developed features of its own which are themselves quite secondary.[58] Secondly, while Thomas contains individual sayings found within the Sermon tradition (cf. Thom 45, 54, 68–69, and 95), it contains no version of the Sermon itself, lacks most of its content, and presents what it does have scattered in various parts of the collection. If it is unlikely that the author/editor of the Gospel of Thomas would have deliberately dismembered the Sermon tradition in this way, one must assume that Thomas has acquired this saying from a branch of the tradition-history that does not flow through the Sermon, that is, independent from the synoptic tradition.

Schrage's arguments to the contrary fail to convince.[59] To the point that Thomas' word order is closer to that of Luke 6:41 than to Matt 7:3 it must be noted that such things are extremely difficult to track through a translation.[60] Thomas' relative construction ⲡⲥⲟⲉⲓ ⲇⲉ ⲉⲧ2ⲙ̄ ⲡⲉⲕⲃⲁⲗ (but the beam that is in your eye) might just as correctly translate Matthew's τὴν δὲ ἐν τῷ σῷ ὀφθαλμῷ δοκὸν (the beam that is in your eye) as Luke's τὴν δὲ δοκὸν τὴν ἐν τῷ ἰδίῳ ὀφθαλμῷ (the beam that is in your own eye),[61] but renders neither of them literally. Unfortunately the POxy fragments are deficient at this point, so we shall never know whether Thomas' Greek original was closer to Luke or to Matthew here. Neither do those points of contact between Thomas and Matthew prove Schrage's case for dependence. While it may be true that Thomas' ⲡⲉⲕ⁻ (you) in 26:1 seems closer to Matt 7:3 (σῷ [your]) than to Luke 6:41 (ἰδίῳ [your own]),[62] and that Thom 26:2 (ⲉⲛⲟⲩ χⲉ ⲙ̄ⲡ.ⲭⲏ ⲉⲃⲟⲗ 2ⲙ̄ ⲡⲃⲁⲗ ⲙ̄ⲡⲉⲕⲥⲟⲛ [to take the speck out of your brother's eye]) seems closer to Matt 7:5 (ἐκβαλεῖν τὸ κάρφος ἐκ τοῦ ὀφθαλμοῦ τοῦ ἀδελφοῦ σου [to take the speck out of your brother's eye]) than to Luke 6:42b (τὸ κάρφος τὸ ἐν τῷ ὀφθαλμῷ τοῦ ἀδελφοῦ σου ἐκβαλεῖν [to take out the speck that is in your brother's eye]), both of these Matthean details derive from Q, not the redactional hand of

---

57. For the likelihood that the sermon tradition is indeed older than Q itself see Robinson, "LOGOI SOPHON," 94, n. 47.

58. E.g., Q's use of a question to introduce the saying (Luke 6:41//Matt 7:3) would be more primitive than Thomas' statement form (see Bultmann, Geschichte, 97).

59. Schrage, Das Verhältnis, 72.

60. See Sieber, "Redactional Analysis," 72–73.

61. Note that the word order in the Sahidic translations of Matt 7:3 and Luke 6:41 is in this respect identical.

62. Although this too may be disputed; see Sieber, "Redactional Analysis," 72–73.

Matthew.[63] Thus, they do not demonstrate Thomas' dependence upon Matthew, but rather suggest that both Thomas and the synoptic authors share a saying each has inherited from an older tradition.

Thom 31 *Prophet and Physician* (cf. Matt 13:57//Mark 6:4//Luke 4:24)

31 [1]Jesus said, "A prophet is not well received in his hometown; [2]a doctor does not heal those who know him."

Of Mark 6:1-6 Bultmann writes: "It appears to me that we have before us here a prime example of how an idealized scene has been composed around an independent saying."[64] Bultmann then follows Wendling, who knew the Thomas version of the saying already from POxy 1, and suggested that Thomas' double-stich version was probably closer to the original wording of the saying than Mark 6:4.[65] According to Bultmann, Mark must have removed the second stich as a way of softening the saying, adding vs 5 instead.[66] Thus Thomas would seem to present us with a single saying, which, though presently embedded in a secondary apophthegmic context in the synoptic tradition, was judged by both Bultmann and Dibelius, based on form-critical analysis, to have circulated earlier as an independent saying.[67] Such cases provide one of the most important indications that Thomas is based upon a tradition-historical stream independent from, yet parallel to, the synoptic tradition. Indeed, they indicate that the two streams had parted company even before the emergence of the apophthegm as the predominant way of contextualizing the sayings of Jesus in the synoptic tradition.

On the other side, Schrage argues that Thom 31 furnishes yet another instance of Thomas' dependence upon the canonical tradition. He suggests that Thom 31:2 was created by Thomas on the basis of Mark 6:5.[68] But Schrage fails to provide ample motive either for the creation of the second stich or for the separation of the saying from its apophthegmic context in Mark. Grant and Freedman[69] and Gärtner[70] maintain that the second stich is based upon Luke 4:23, which occurs just before the point at which Luke has inserted the prophet saying in his narrative. This, in their view, would indicate that Thomas knew and made use of Luke's text. But the converse is just as easily argued, and is perhaps more plausible. On the assumption that Thomas preserves the more original form of the saying, it seems quite plausible that Luke substituted the proverb in Luke 4:23 for Thom 31:2, crafting it to suit his more polemical purposes in this particular context. This would mean, of

63. See Schulz, *Q*, 147.
64. Bultmann, *Geschichte*, 30.
65. Wendling, *Entstehung des Markus-Evangeliums*, 54.
66. Bultmann, *Geschichte*, 30.
67. Bultmann, *Geschichte*, 30-31; Dibelius, *Formgeschichte*, 106-7; so also Koch, *Die Bedeutung der Wundererzählungen*, 150, n. 14; *contra* Haenchen, *Weg Jesu*, 220.
68. Schrage, *Das Verhältnis*, 76, n. 5.
69. Grant and Freedman, *Secret Sayings*, 149-50.
70. Gärtner, *Theology*, 52.

course, that Luke knew the saying in a form other than that found in Mark 6:4. But this is exactly what Karl Ludwig Schmidt had argued based upon an analysis of the synoptic texts alone, without recourse to Thomas at all![71]

Thom 33:1, 2-3 *Preach from Your Housetops/Lamp under a Bushel*
(cf. Luke 12:3//Matt 10:27, Q; Luke 11:33//Matt 5:15, Q; Mark 4:21//Luke 8:16)

33 [1]Jesus said, "What you will hear in your ear, in the other ear proclaim from your rooftops. [2]After all, no one lights a lamp and puts it under a basket, nor does one put it in a hidden place. [3]Rather, one puts it on a lamp stand so that all who come and go will see its light."

Together with Thom 32 this cluster presents a host of difficulties. Perhaps foremost is the fact that in Thom 32 and 33:2-3 there is a rare instance in which Thomas places in close proximity two sayings occurring together in a synoptic text (cf. Matt 5:14-15), and in the same sequence. This leads Grant and Freedman to the conclusion that Thomas is here dependent upon Matthew.[72] Such a view seems, at least on the surface, to be supported by the fact that Thom 33:1 and 33:2-3 are joined by the catchword ⲙⲁⲁϫⲉ, a word play that works only at the level of the Coptic translation,[73] so that one might conjecture that Thom 33:1 was inserted first by the Coptic translator, and that the original text would then have consisted of Thom 32 followed directly by 33:2-3, exactly parallel to Matt 5:14-15. But there are problems. First, Thom 32 is joined to 33:1 already in the Greek version of Thomas (cf. POxy 1 [•] 36-43);[74] therefore, if 33:1 and 33:2-3 were joined together first at the level of the Coptic, it must be that 33:2-3 was added late to 33:1. A Coptic translator/redactor may have made such an addition for three reasons: 1) the exhortation to open proclamation ties these sayings together, so that the association of 33:1 and 2-3 suggests itself anyway; 2) the scribe might have taken advantage of a clever word play, the humorous side of which should not be overlooked; and 3) the scribe's knowledge of Matt 5:14-15 may have suggested such an association. In any event, relatively late scribal activity is probably the best way to account for the synoptic-like sequence Thom 32 • [33:1] • 33:2-3.[75]

71. Schmidt, *Rahmen der Geschichte Jesu*, 38–41, 158; cf. Sieber, "Redactional Analysis," 22–23. This seems to me preferable to McArthur's solution, which posits Thomas' dependence upon Luke to account for the similarities between the two texts ("Dependence," 287). Snodgrass, ("Gospel of Thomas," 31–32) repeats McArthur's argument.

72. Grant and Freedman, *Secret Sayings*, 143, 94–95.

73. Note that the word for "ear" in 33:1 is spelled exactly as the word for "bushel" in 33:2: ⲙⲁⲁϫⲉ.

74. POxy 1 unfortunately breaks off at this point, so that it is not possible to know whether 33:2-3 was attached to 33:1 already in the Greek text.

75. The possibility is not at all remote (nor does it amount to special pleading, *pace* Snodgrass, "Gospel of Thomas," 25–26). An example of the phenomenon is present in Thom 77:2-3, which owes its present position in the Coptic version to a scribal relocation (so K. H. Kuhn, "Some Observations," 317–23; Toyoshima, "Neue Vorschläge," 235; *contra* Marchovich, "Textual Criticism," 69, who regards the POxy order as secondary).

Apart from the issue of order posed by Thom 32 and 33 (for Thom 32, see pp. 74–75), it is difficult to imagine a synoptic derivation for either. A saying similar to Thom 33:1 occurs also in Q, there combined with the originally independent saying also found in Thom 5:2 and 6:5–6 (Luke 12:2–3//Matt 10:26–27, [= Q]).[76] The notion that the author/editor of Thomas took this cluster from Matthew or Luke (or Q), broke it up, and reduplicated the first half to create the doublet in Thom 5:2 and 6:5–6, would require an elaborate redactional explanation, for which these Thomas sayings offer little evidence. Preferable is the simple explanation that Thomas' author/editor knew these two sayings from traditional circles in which they were not yet combined.[77]

That Thom 33:2–3 was at one time an independent saying is suggested by its separate use by both Mark and Q (Mark 4:21//Luke 8:16; Luke 11:33//Matt 5:15, Q). The dependence of Thom 33:2–3 upon Mark 4:21 (or Luke 8:16a) poses the same difficulties encountered above with Thom 33:1, for Mark (followed by Luke) combines this saying with a version of Thom 5:2/6:5–6 (cf. Mark 4:22//Luke 8:16b). In Q (Luke 11:33//Matt 5:15) a version of Thom 33:2–3 is found in a cluster of sayings about light included in Q's more extensive composition, which Kloppenborg calls the "Q Controversies."[78] If this is, as Kloppenborg argues, a composition of Q, gathering together independent sayings of disparate origin,[79] then it is not necessary to suppose that Thomas' author/editor extracted Thom 33:2–3 from Q; it is quite possible that Thomas drew the saying from the same traditional sources that were available to Q. As for a Matthean or Lukan derivation, Sieber's analysis of the Thomas text turns up no traces of Matthean or Lukan redaction,[80] thus rendering such a thesis wholly speculative. Again, the simplest explanation for the Thomas text is that we have before us an independent tradition.[81]

Thom 34 *The Blind Leading the Blind* (cf. Luke 6:39//Matt 15:14, Q)

34 Jesus said, "If a blind person leads a blind person, both of them will fall into a hole."

In the synoptic tradition a version of this saying was probably to be found

76. For Thom 5:2 and 6:5–6 see pp. 20–23.

77. As Kloppenborg points out, both of these sayings could have stood as originally independent logia (*Formation*, 206–7); there is no reason that Thomas could not have known them as such.

78. Kloppenborg, *Formation*, 134–39.

79. For Luke 11:33//Matt 5:15, Q, as an originally independent saying, see Kloppenborg, *Formation*, 135.

80. Sieber, "Redactional Analysis," 45–47.

81. *Contra* Schrage, *Das Verhältnis*, 83: "Most of the similarities come about undoubtedly between Thomas and Luke, especially Luke 11, that is,the secondary form of the saying as reworked by Luke. That Luke's text here is not the original is indeed demonstrated by the Hellenistic method of building houses that is presupposed in it, and perhaps also the situation of the church's mission which it mirrors." But Kloppenborg (*Formation*, 135, n. 144) shows that none of the elements shared by Luke and Thomas are particularly Lukan, and calls attention to Safrai's more recent work, which calls into question Jeremias' "Bautechnik" argument (Safrai, "Home and Family," 230–35).

already in the primitive Sermon tradition taken up into Q and thence into Matthew and Luke.[82] It therefore presents the same dilemma posed by Thom 26 (see pp. 29–31): either Thomas' author/editor knew the Sermon tradition and deliberately broke it up, scattering its parts throughout his or her collection and discarding some of its sayings altogether; or he or she knew a few of these previously independent wisdom sayings from tradition-historical circles in which they had not yet been gathered together into a discrete collection. As before, I opt for the latter explanation.[83]

Schrage's arguments for Thomas' dependence upon the Sahidic version of Matthew 15:14, are not enough to overturn these tradition-historical considerations.[84] While it is true that the Sahidic version of Matt 15:14 and Thom 34 share the somewhat unusual placement of the conditional marker,[85] the differences between them are far more numerous: 1) Sahidic Matthew uses an adversative ⲁⲉ (but) here, Thomas does not; 2) Sahidic Matthew uses the compound verb ⲭⲓⲙⲟⲉⲓⲧ (to lead), Thomas uses the simple ϭⲱⲕ (to lead); 3) while Sahidic Matthew uses the First Future (ⲥⲉⲛⲁ‾) in the main clause, Thomas uses the Habitual (ϣⲁⲩ‾); 4) Thomas uses the adverb ⲉⲡⲉⲥⲏⲧ (down), Sahidic Matthew does not; 5) in the main clause Thomas locates the subject, ⲙ̅ⲡⲉⲥⲛⲁⲩ (both), directly after the verb, Sahidic Matthew locates it at the end of the sentence. Given these considerable differences (in such a brief saying!), Thom 34's dependence upon the Sahidic version of Matt 15:14 seems quite unlikely. Schrage correctly notes that Matthew and Thomas agree in formulating the saying as a statement, a secondary development over against Luke's question form.[86] But this does not necessarily indicate Thomas' dependence upon Matthew. Given the general tendency within the tradition for questions to be recast as statements,[87] Thomas' secondary indicative form could well be the product of its own tradition history.

Thom 35 *Binding the Strong Person*
(Matt 12:29//Mark 3:27//Luke 11:21–22, Mark/Q overlap)

35 ¹Jesus said, "One cannot enter a strong person's house and take it by force without first tying his hands.[88] ²Then one can loot his house."

82. It is likely that Luke more faithfully preserves the Q position here; so Schulz, *Q*, 472–73; Kloppenborg, *Formation*, 181–82.

83. It may be that the Q pair of sayings in Luke 6:39–40 came to be associated even before their common attachment to the rest of the Q discourse in Luke 6: 41–45 (Schürmann, *Lukasevangelium*, 1.370; Wrege, *Überlieferungsgeschichte der Bergpredigt*, 128–29; Kloppenborg, *Formation*, 182). The second of these sayings does not even occur in Thomas, thus perhaps underscoring how early the Thomas and synoptic tradition-historical streams must have parted ways.

84. Schrage, *Das Verhältnis*, 86–87.

85. Schrage (*Das verhältnis*, 86) notes that the *Conditionalis* (ⲉϥϣⲁⲛ) normally stands first in the conditional clause; both Matthew and Thomas here place it after the subject.

86. Schrage, *Das Verhältnis*, 86. Most agree that Luke preserves the more original Q form of the saying (see Schulz, *Q*, 473).

87. See Bultmann, *Geschichte*, 97.

88. Lit.: "unless he ties his hands."

In both the Markan and Q versions of the Beelzebul controversy (Matt 12:22-30//Mark 3:22-30//Luke 11:14-23)[89] this saying occurs as one of a series of independent sayings that became associated over time with an earlier form of the apophthegm.[90] The fact that its history did not begin with the Beelzebul pericope, of course, means that Thomas may have acquired this saying in any number of ways from the oral tradition. Thus, without the tell-tale signs of the redactional hand of one or another of the canonical evangelists, Thomas' reliance upon the canonical tradition for this saying remains a remote possibility at best. As Sieber shows, Thom 35 bears no such evidence.[91] Moreover, there is no evidence to suggest that Thomas' author/editor knew the Beelzebul tradition at all, or any of the other sayings associated with it in the synoptic tradition. The Thomas parallels to Matthew 11-12 and Luke 11-12 are scattered throughout Thomas, and show no consistent pattern that might indicate influence between Thomas and the synoptics.[92]

Nonetheless, Schrage[93] holds that there is influence from the synoptics at the level of the Coptic translation. Most important in this regard is the fact that Thomas agrees with the Sahidic version of Matthew in using the transliterated Greek ειмнтι (unless). But it is noteworthy that Matthew's Greek text does not use εἰ μήτι (unless) here, but rather, ἐὰν μή (unless). Thus, it is legitimate to ask whether Sahidic Matthew's use of ειмнтι influenced Coptic Thomas' choice of this expression, or vice versa, Matthew's Coptic translator switching from one Greek expression to another under the influence of Thomas. Schrage does not consider the latter possibility. In either case, however, the influence thus isolated would have occurred only in the process of translation, and therefore is irrelevant for the question of dependence in any generative sense. Thom 35 should be regarded as another instance in which Thomas preserves an independent saying in its early, solitary form.

89. That the Beelzebul controversy is another case of Mark/ Q overlap is not disputed (see Laufen, *Doppelüberlieferung*, 126-32); however, whether the saying in question occurred in Q, or only in the version known to Mark, is not yet settled (see Kloppenborg, *Formation*, 125, n. 105).

90. Bultmann, *Geschichte*, 10-12: the original extent of the apophthegm was Matt 12:22-26//Mark 3:22-26//Luke 11:14-15, 17-18a, with a single saying serving as the climax. There are, of course, other views regarding the history of this apophthegm (cf. Schulz, *Q*, 206; Hahn, *Christologische Hoheitstitel*, 298; Wanke, "Kommentarworte," 219), but there is general agreement that Matt 12:29//Mark 3:27//Luke 11:21-22 is an originally independent logion. For a brief summary of the discussion, see Kloppenborg, *Formation*, 121-24.

91. Sieber, "Redactional Analysis," 141-42.

92. So Sieber, "Redactional Analysis," 143. The parallels are as follows: Matt 11:7-8//Thom 78; Matt 11:11//Thom 46; Matt 11:28-30//Thom 90; Matt 12:29//Thom 35; Matt 12:31-35//Thom 44-45; Matt 12:46-50//Thom 99; to Luke 11:9-10//Thom 2, 92, and 94; Luke 11:21-22//Thom 35; Luke 11:27-28//Thom 79; Luke 11:33//Thom 33; Luke 11:39-41//Thom 89; Luke 11:32//Thom 39; Luke 12:3//Thom 5:5, 6:5-6; Luke 12:3//Thom 33; Luke 12:10//Thom 44; Luke 12:13-14//Thom 72; Luke 12:16-21//Thom 63; Luke 12:22-23//Thom 36; Luke 12:32-34//Thom 76; Luke 12:39//Thom 103; Luke 12:49//Thom 10; Luke 12:51-53//Thom 16; Luke 12:56//Thom 91. If there is a pattern here, it is elusive indeed.

93. Schrage, *Das Verhältnis*, 89.

Thom 39:1-2, 3 *The Keys of Knowledge/Serpents and Doves*
(Luke 11:52//Matt 23:13, Q; Matt 10:16b)

39 [1]Jesus said, "The Pharisees and the scribes have taken the keys of knowledge and have hidden them. [2]They have not entered, nor have they allowed those who want to enter to do so. [3]As for you, be as shrewd as snakes and as innocent as doves."

Here one will probably have to reckon with influence upon Thom 39:1-2 from the text of Matthew at some point in the textual transmission of Thomas. While the original wording of Q in this particular passage (Luke 11:52//Matt 23:13) is highly contested,[94] it is generally agreed that "scribes and pharisees" (cf. Thom 39:1: мϕⲁⲣⲓⲥⲁⲓⲟⲥ ⲙⲛ̄ ⲛ̄ⲅⲣⲁⲙⲙⲁⲧⲉⲩⲥ) belongs to Matthean redaction.[95] Its occurrence in Thomas must be explained as due to influence from the Matthean text. Unfortunately the Greek text of POxy 655 is too fragmentary to inform us whether this influence had worked its effect already at the level of the Greek text, or arose first at the level of the Coptic translation. In any case, that we have to do here with a problem of relatively late harmonization, i.e., a text-critical problem, and not a systematic use of Matthew in the composition of the Thomas collection, is shown by the fact that nowhere else in Thomas are these typically Matthean opponents mentioned. For example, the Pharisees also appear in Thom 102, but without their typically Matthean colleagues. If Thomas were intentionally borrowing this *topos* from Matthew one would expect to see it incorporated into Thomas' text more frequently. But in fact, Jesus' opponents in Thomas are quite varied, suggesting no particular pattern at all.[96]

As for Thom 39:3, it provides a good example of how an independent wisdom saying might be applied in different situations, with varying results. In Thomas it serves as a hortatory conclusion to Thom 39:1: ϕⲣⲟⲛⲓⲙⲟⲥ (wise) and ⲁⲕⲉⲣⲁⲓⲟⲥ (innocent) are intended as a contrast to the implicit foolishness and guilt of the opponents. Matthew, on the other hand, in placing it among the mission instructions and by using it in combination with 10:16a, sees it as an exhortation to vigilance in facing impending difficulty. With no redactional evidence to suggest dependence of Thom 39:3 on Matt 10:16b,[97] the Thomas-Matthew parallel is readily explained as an independent use of a common Jewish *mashal*.[98]

94. See Schulz, *Q*, 110; Kloppenborg, *Formation*, 142, n. 175.
95. Schulz, *Q*, 110; Kloppenborg, *Formation*, 142, n. 175.
96. The argument for dependence upon Luke (see Snodgrass, "Gospel of Thomas," 33) is not as compelling. It rests on the supposition that Luke's version using the "keys of knowledge" motif is secondary, a notion not universally shared and not well substantiated (cf. Bussmann, *Studien*, 74).
97. Sieber, "Redactional Analysis," 209.
98. See Bultmann, *Geschichte*, 112.

Thom 41 *Have and Receive*
(Matt 13:12//Mark 4:25//Luke 8:18b; Luke 19:26//Matt 25:29, Mark/Q overlap)

41 [1]Jesus said, "Whoever has something in his hand will be given more, [2]and whoever has nothing will be deprived of even the little that he has."

A textual comparison of these sayings reveals precious little about their relationship to one another. As Schrage points out, when the various Greek originals are translated into Coptic the nuances once evident in the Greek versions are all but obliterated by the less versatile Coptic translation; they all end up looking the same.[99] Thus, if the synoptic texts are any indication, it is difficult to conjecture what exactly lies behind Thomas' Coptic text, let alone offer a judgment about whether Thomas agrees with the redactional hand of one or another of the synoptic evangelists. Thus we are left to decide the matter based on less precise tradition-historical factors.

The fact that this saying occurs in both Mark and Q, used by each independently and in different contexts, indicates that it circulated widely very early on as part of that amorphous body of early Christian oral tradition. Moreover, parallels from contemporary literature indicate that its popularity as an aphorism was not limited to Christian circles.[100] Thus, Thomas' author/editor might have come across this saying through any number of traditional channels. With no hint that he or she was familiar with the particular synoptic forms of the saying, or the synoptic contexts in which we find them, one should assume that it came down to Thomas simply as an independent saying ascribed to Jesus.

Thom 44 *Blaspheming the Holy Spirit*
(Matt 12:31-32//Mark 3:28-29; Luke 12:10, Mark/Q overlap)

44 [1]Jesus said, "Whoever blasphemes against the Father will be forgiven, [2]and whoever blasphemes against the son will be forgiven, [3]but whoever blasphemes against the holy spirit will not be forgiven, either on earth or in heaven."

Matthew follows Mark, who has appended this legal saying to the Beelzebul controversy.[101] By contrast, Luke chooses not to include it there, but uses it instead in his version of Q's Exhortation to Fearless Confession (Luke 12:2–12//Matt 10:26–33), no doubt there derived from Q.[102] That it was used thus independently, and in different ways, indicates that here too we have to do

99. Schrage, *Das Verhältnis*, 96. For example, the saying begins as follows in the various Greek versions: Mark 4:25: ὸς ἔχει (the one who has); Matt 13:12: ὄστις ἔχει (whoever has); Luke 8:18: ὸς ἂν ἔχει (anyone who has). Yet each is rendered ⲡⲉⲧⲉⲟⲩⲛⲧⲁϥ (the one who has) in the the Sahidic version of New Testament.
100. See Schrage, *Das Verhältnis*, 96; examples in Strack and Billerbeck, *Kommentar*, 1. 660-62.
101. Bultmann, *Geschichte*, 11.
102. So Schulz, *Q*, 246-50.

with an originally independent saying.[103] Since there is no evidence to suggest that Thomas has made use of one the three synoptic versions, and not an earlier version available to all in multifarious forms,[104] there is no reason to suppose that Thomas is here directly dependent upon the synoptic texts.

Having said this much, it must be added that Thomas' text here is hopelessly corrupt. The clearly trinitarian tripartite division of the saying represents a relatively advanced stage of theologizing, so that however the saying might have run at some earlier stage in the Thomas trajectory it has by this time been thoroughly re-worked. The similar way in which the saying has been formulated in at least one version of Tatian's Diatessaron[105] suggests that this trinitarian version was crafted first on Syrian soil.

Thom 45 *Grapes and Thorns* (Luke 6:43–45//Matt 7:15–20; Matt 12:34b–35, Q)

45 [1]Jesus said, "Grapes are not harvested from thorn trees, nor are figs gathered from thistles, for they yield no fruit. [2]A good person brings forth good from his storehouse; [3]a bad person brings forth evil things from the corrupt storehouse which is in his heart, and says evil things. [4]For from the abundance of the heart this person brings forth evil things."

It has been argued that Thomas' dependence upon Luke at this point is assured by the fact that both Luke and Thomas share a common order over against Matthew, and unify into a single cluster what Matthew has in two places.[106] The parallel texts align as follows:

Thom	Luke	Matt
	6:43	7:16a
	6:44a	7:16b
45:1	6:44b	7:17–18
45:2–3	6:45a	12:34b
45:4	6:45b	12:35

But the shared order between Thomas and Luke would show dependence of the former upon the latter only if this order could be ascribed to Lukan redaction, and this is not the case. In Luke 6:43–44//Matt 7:16–18 it is Matthew who has reversed the order of these sayings so as to be able to use his reformulation in 7:16a (ἀπὸ τῶν καρπῶν αὐτῶν ἐπιγνώσεσθε αὐτούς [you shall know them from their fruits]) together with his redactional verse 20 to form an *inclusio* around his warnings against false prophets.[107] In the case of

103. Bultmann, *Geschichte*, 11; Schulz, *Q*, 247, n. 483.

104. Schrage (*Das Verhältnis*, 98–99) admits that in this case where Thomas follows Matthew and/or Luke against Mark they are probably following Q, or a related version. Furthermore, Thomas nowhere agrees with Mark when he does not also agree with either Matthew or Luke; such agreements do not demonstrate dependence since they could stem ultimately from a version of the saying common to both Q and Mark.

105. See Haenchen, "Literatur," 166.

106. Schrage, *Das Verhältnis*, 101–2.

107. Schulz, *Q*, 318, agrees that vs 20 is Matthean redaction, noting the use of ἄρα γε (cf. 7:16).

Luke 6:45a, b//Matt 12:34b-35 it is again Matthew who is responsible both for the transpositioning of these sayings and for the reversal of their relative order. Having appropriated this material to fill out his version of the Beelzebul controversy (Matt 12:33–36), Matthew has reversed the original Q order, using 12:34b as the rhetorical response to the question posed in his redactional verse 12:34a.[108] All of this means that with no evidence against the Lukan order one must assume that it derives from Q,[109] and thus may not be used to argue for a special relationship between Thomas and Luke.

If Luke 6:44–45 preserves the original Q order and position of these sayings, it is likely that they were part of the Sermon tradition taken up and used by Q. As already noted, this poses special problems for the proposal that Thomas is dependent upon the synoptic tradition: If Thomas' author/editor knew the Sermon tradition, why has he or she broken it up, scattering some of its pieces randomly throughout his or her collection, omitting others altogether? Without a reasonable explanation for this phenomenon, a separate tradition-history must be posited for Thomas.

Another indication that Thom 45 derives from a tradition-history with non-synoptic roots is that, form-critically speaking, Thomas' version of these sayings is in at least one respect more primitive than its synoptic counterpart, and yet in another more developed. In the synoptic tradition the complex contains also a third element, Luke 6:43//Matt 7:17–18 (= Q), which has no Thomas parallel. The catchword association which joins it to the complex ($\kappa\alpha\rho\pi\delta\varsigma$/ $\delta\acute{\epsilon}\nu\delta\rho\sigma\nu$ [fruit/tree]) indicates that these sayings circulated as a unit already at an oral stage.[110] Since Thomas' version does not have this third saying, it probably derives from circles in which it was not yet attached to the first two.[111] For its part, the superfluos explanation in Thom 45:1 (ⲙⲁⲩϯ ⲕⲁⲣⲡⲟⲥ ⲅⲁⲣ [for they yield no fruit]) shows that the Thomas version too has undergone some amount of tradition-historical development.

Finally, two details in the Thomas tradition may owe something to secondary influence from the synoptic text. The first is the epexegetical comment in 45:2-3: ⲉⲧⲍⲛ̅ ⲡⲉϥⲍⲏⲧ (which is in his heart), against which suspicions are raised in light of Luke's $\tau\hat{\eta}\varsigma$ $\kappa\alpha\rho\delta\acute{\iota}\alpha\varsigma$ (of the heart) in 6:45, which is normally ascribed to Lukan redaction.[112] The second is the close proximity of Thom 44 to Thom 45, which duplicates the order created by Matthew in 12:31-35. Perhaps this reflects a shift as late as the level of the Coptic translation, such as

---

108. So Schulz, *Q,* 318, following Bussmann, *Studien,* 49, and Schürmann, *Lukas-evangelium,* 377, n. 220.

109. So Kloppenborg, *Formation,* 79.

110. Kloppenborg (*Formation,* 182-83) sees them as a pre-Q cluster.

111. Kloppenborg (*Formation,* 182-83) imagines the composition to have proceeded thus: Q 6:([43 + 44] + 45). But if Thomas' cluster, without the saying in vs 43, represents an independent tradition, Kloppenborg's reconstruction is to be adjusted as follows: Q 6:(43 + [44+45]).

112. So Schulz, *Q,* 318, following Schürmann, *Lukasevangelium,* 377; Bussmann, *Studien,* 49, and others.

has occurred in the case of Thom 77:2, but without an extant Greek text against which to compare this order, such a solution remains speculative.[113]

Thom 46 *From Adam to John* (cf. Luke 7:28//Matt 11:11, Q)

46 ¹Jesus said, "From Adam to John the Baptist, among those born of women no one is so much greater than John the Baptist that his eyes should not be averted. ²But I have said that whoever among you becomes a child will recognize the kingdom, and will become greater than John."

Although the sayings in question undoubtedly stem from the same tradition, there is really very little verbal correspondence between the Thomas version on the one hand and the Q version shared by Matthew and Luke on the other. Thus, while some have simply assumed Thomas' dependence here,[114] others have remained skeptical of any direct relationship.[115] Schrage, though less confident about the case for dependence here, does point out two noteworthy details: 1) both Thomas (46:1) and Matthew (11:11a) attach the appositive τοῦ βαπτιστοῦ (the baptist) to "John," an addition generally regarded as secondary over against Luke's (7:28a) more original Q text;[116] and 2) both Thomas (46:1) and Luke (7:28) seem to have abandoned Q's (=Matt 11:11a) semitizing expression ἐγήγερται (there has arisen) in favor of a simple expression using "to be" (ⲙ̄ⲛ̄/οὐδείς ἐστιν [there is no one . . .]).[117]

But these points of convergence are not particularly compelling. The tendency within the tradition to reach for greater clarity is not unique to Matthew; thus, the appositional identification of John as "the Baptist" might easily have occurred simultaneously in separate traditions. Similarly, in a Greek-speaking milieu the gradual movement away from semitizing expressions would not have been limited to one line of tradents. Opting for a form using εἰμί (to be) rather than ἐγήγερται (there has arisen) is a change one might expect to find in disparate quarters. Thus, in the absence of more extensive verbal similarity, it seems prudent here to posit a common ancestry for Q and Thomas in the oral tradition, but nothing more.

Thom 47:2-5 *Divided Loyalties*
(Luke 16:13//Matt 6:24, Q; Matt 9:16-17//Mark 2:21-22//Luke 5:36-39)

47 ¹Jesus said, "A person cannot mount two horses or bend two bows. ²*And a slave cannot serve two masters, otherwise he will honor the one and offend the other.* ³*Nobody drinks aged wine and immediately wants to drink new wine.* ⁴*New wine is not poured into old wineskins, in case they should break, and aged wine is not poured*

---

113. In the POxy 1 version of Thomas, Thom 77:2-3 occurs after Thom 30:1-2. It is not clear which version offers the more original reading.

114. E.g., Grant and Freedman (*Secret Sayings*, pp. 158-59).

115. E.g., Chilton, "The Gospel According to Thomas," 157.

116. Schrage, *Das Verhältnis*, 230; for τοῦ βαπτιστοῦ as secondary see Schulz, *Q*, 230, n. 354.

117. Schulz, *Q*, 129-30; for ἐγήγερται (there has arisen) as deriving from Q, see Schulz, *Q*, 229-30, n. 352.

into a new wineskin, in case it should spoil. ⁵*An old patch is not sewn onto a new garment, since it would create a tear.*"

In Thom 47 a number of sayings are gathered around the theme of choosing between incompatible alternatives. All but the first have synoptic parallels. Since Thom 47:2 is connected to the otherwise unattested saying (47:1) through the catchwords "cannot" (ⲙⲛ̄ ϭⲟⲙ) and "two" (ⲥⲛⲁⲩ), their association around the theme of mutual exclusivity may stem from an early period of oral transmission. In Luke 16:13a//Matt 6:24a (= Q) a version of the saying in Thom 47:2 occurs, of course, without Thom 47:1 but expanded instead with the edifying saying in Luke 16:13b//Matt 6:24b (= Q), which has no Thomas parallel. In view of these circumstances, the presence of two different tradition- historical streams here seems likely.[118]

Arguments to the contrary fail to convince. Snodgrass,[119] for example, argues that Thomas knew and used the synoptic tradition, on the grounds that Thom 47:2 shares with Luke 16:13 the rare word οἰκέτης (servant). Furthermore, he maintains that Thomas' version of this saying presupposes the synoptic version insofar as it includes only the first half of the ἤ . . . ἤ (either . . . or) construction, which the synoptic text presents complete. But both arguments require one to presuppose precisely that which stands in question: Thomas' use of the synoptic texts. For the word used by Thomas (ϩⲙ̄ϩⲁⲗ [slave]) in 47:2 only rarely translates οἰκέτης; far more often the common word δοῦλος (slave) stands behind this Coptic noun, and we might assume that to be the case here. The agreement with Luke thus turns out to be illusory. As for the second point, Thomas' grammatical fragment does indeed seem to presuppose a more complete version in which both halves of the ἤ . . . ἤ construction would have been present. But the fact that Matt 6:24 and Luke 16:13 share this construction indicates that it derives not from their own redactional activity, but from their common source, Q, or from the oral tradition from which Q ultimately stems. Therefore, the grammatical fragment in Thom 47:2 need not lead to the conclusion that Thomas knew the synoptic texts; rather, it simply confirms their *common* heritage in an older tradition which utilized the complete the ἤ . . . ἤ construction.

Versions of the two sayings in Thom 47:4–5 occur also in Mark 2:21–22, par. (though in reverse order). According to Bultmann, they were not originally part of the controversy over fasting (Mark 2:18–20), but were independent sayings added as an expansion perhaps by Mark himself.[120] That Thomas transmits them apart from the apophthegm supports this assessment,

---

118. Aside from the problem of Thom 47:1, the dependence of Thom 47:2 upon Matthew or Luke would require that Thomas had omitted the God and Mammon logion (Luke 16:13b//Matt 6:24b, Q), highly unlikely given the attitude against commercial activity expressed elsewhere in Thomas (see, e.g., Thom 63 and 64).

119. Snodgrass, "Gospel of Thomas," 34.

120. Bultmann, *Geschichte*, 18.

and attests to a separate tradition-history for the cluster in Thomas.[121] Such suspicions are confirmed by the fact that generally Thomas' version seems more primitive: the secondary explanations attached to the sayings ("lest they burst", "lest it spoil it", "because a tear would result") are short and to the point, while Mark's explanations are more elaborate, assuming the worst of his readers. The addition "the new from the old" in Mark 2:21 is very likely Markan redaction.[122] But precisely this is missing from the Thomas version. It is also worth noting that in the case of Thom 47:5, Thomas seems to have misunderstood the figure: it is a new patch on an old garment that causes problems, not an old patch on a new garment! Such garbling attests further to the oral environment out of which the Thomas collection ultimately comes.

More problematic is the saying in Thom 47:3: "No person drinks old wine and immediately desires to drink new wine." Luke adds a similar saying to the end of Mark's controversy over fasting (Luke 5:39), which leads McArthur to conclude that Thomas is dependent upon Luke.[123] But assuming that Luke did not invent this saying, but knew it from the tradition,[124] it is possible that Thomas' author/editor also knew the saying from the tradition, and independently recognized the sense of including it here. Against direct dependence upon Luke is the different position of the saying in Thomas, and the quite different ways in which the saying is formulated in Thomas and Luke.[125]

Thom 54 *Blessed are the Poor* (Luke 6:20b//Matt 5:3, Q)

54 Jesus said, "Blessed are the poor, for to you belongs heaven's kingdom."

The case for seeing Thom 54 as dependent upon the synoptic versions of the first beatitude are not compelling. Schrage, for example, argues that Thomas presents a "mixed text," combining Matthew's $\beta\alpha\sigma\iota\lambda\epsilon\iota\alpha$ $\tau\hat{\omega}\nu$ $o\dot{\upsilon}\rho\alpha\nu\hat{\omega}\nu$ (*heaven's* kingdom)[126] with Luke's use of the second person plural ($\dot{\upsilon}\mu\epsilon\tau\epsilon\rho\alpha$ [yours])[127] in the second half of the saying (cf. Matthew's use of the third person plural $\alpha\dot{\upsilon}\tau\hat{\omega}\nu$ [theirs]) and his lack (with Luke) of the phrase $\dot{\epsilon}\nu$ $\pi\nu\epsilon\dot{\upsilon}\mu\alpha\tau\tau$ (in spirit).[128] But none of these details is necessarily attributable to

121. The transmission of these two sayings as a unit must be very old. The presence of catchwords in both versions ($\pi\dot{\alpha}\lambda\alpha\iotao\varsigma$—$\nu\dot{\epsilon}o\varsigma/\kappa\alpha\iota\nu\dot{o}\varsigma$; ⲁⲥ—ⲃ̄ⲣⲣⲉ/ⲱⲁ̣ⲓ [old–new]) shows that their association probably dates from a period of oral transmission.

122. Gnilka, *Markus*. 1. 113; following Hahn, *Christologische Hoheitstitel*, 362–63.

123. McArthur, "Dependence," 286; so also Schrage, *Das Verhältnis*, 112.

124. Bultmann (*Geschichte*, 18) calls it an independent logion.

125. Especially noteworthy is the omission of anything like Luke's closing comment: "for he says, 'The old is good.'" Snodgrass ("Gospel of Thomas," 34) asserts that the omission is understandable in view of Thomas' gnosticizing proclivities, but does not elaborate. The gnostic motive is far from clear.

126. Cf. ⲧⲙⲛ̄ⲧⲉⲣⲟ ⲛⲙ̄ⲡⲏⲩⲉ (heaven's kingdom) in Thom 54.

127. Cf. ⲧⲱⲧⲛ̄ (yours) in Thom 54.

128. Schrage, *Das Verhältnis*, 118–19. Similarly, Chilton ("The Gospel According to Thomas," 157–58) argues that Thomas uses Matthew's third person formulation in the first half of the logion, but switches then to Luke's second person form in the second half. But Thomas' Coptic may be misleading in this respect. Thomas' ⲍⲛ̄ⲙⲁⲕⲁⲣⲓⲟⲥ ⲛⲉ ⲛ̄ϩⲏⲕⲉ (Blessed are the poor), while not necessarily a vocative construction, is a rather exact translation of

the editorial work of the synoptic evangelists.[129] While βασιλεία τῶν οὐρανῶν is a well-known Matthean phrase,[130] Thomas too consistently avoids the phrase βασιλεία τοῦ θεοῦ (God's kingdom), preferring "heaven's kingdom" or "the kingdom of the Father." Thus, that Thomas and Matthew independently of one another altered an original version of the saying about "God's kingdom" is not at all unlikely. Both apparently shared the Jewish aversion to using the divine name. As for the agreements with Luke, they may well stem from a primitive version of the beatitude shared by both; they do not necessarily suggest any literary dependence of Thomas upon Luke. Their common lack of the Matthean phrase ἐν πνεύματι (in spirit) may certainly be accounted for in this way. Matthew's addition of the phrase is widely recognized as secondary.[131] With their agreement in the use of the second person plural rather than the third, the matter is less assured. The debate about whether the beatitudes would have been cast originally in the third person (Matthew) or the second (Luke) is well represented on both sides.[132] In any event, if this is the only remaining point with any claim to validity, the case for dependence is left to hang on a very thin thread.

When one looks for more positive evidence that Thomas represents an independent tradition, the tradition history of the beatitudes provides some helpful clues. This beatitude is mediated to Matthew and Luke via the Sermon tradition taken up by Q. As has been previously noted (see my comments on Thom 26, 34 and 45 above), Thomas' author/editor seems not to have known this tradition at all. At any rate, he or she did not know it in its Matthean form. Careful examination of the Thomas parallels to this part of the Sermon reveals that Thomas contains parallels to only those beatitudes shared by Matthew and Luke; not one of those added by Matthew turns up in Thomas, astounding if one were to hold that Thomas knew the Matthean Sermon. The evidence that Thomas knew Luke's version is not much stronger. Thomas does not have any version of Luke's third beatitude ("Blessed are you who weep now . . ."), and its parallels to the second and fourth beatitudes are found in another part of the collection (see Thom 68–69) with no apparent connection to Sermon material found elsewhere in Thomas. In addition, there are no Thomas parallels to Luke's woes, the one thing that could possibly link Thomas to Luke's text. All of this speaks against a synoptic derivation for Thom 54 and the other Thomas

---

Luke's μακάριοι οἱ πτωχοί (Blessed are the/you poor). The vocative in Coptic normally employs simply the noun with a definite article, and, thus, like the Greek in Luke's text, is not distinguishable from the third person in such situations.

129. See Sieber, "Redactional Analysis," 25–39.

130. It occurs thirty-two times in Matthew.

131. See Schulz, Q, 77, n. 126.

132. For the originality of Matthew's third person form see Harnack, Sayings, 48–49; Klostermann, Matthäusevangelium, 34; Bultmann, Geschichte, 114; Wrege, Überlieferungsgeschichte der Bergpredigt, 19–20; and Schulz, Q, 77. For the view that Luke's second person form is original, see Bussmann, Studien, 43; Dibelius, Formgeschichte, 248; Manson, Sayings of Jesus, 47; Schürmann, Lukasevangelium, 329–30.

beatitudes. Rather, it suggests that Thomas knew Thom 54 from an independent tradition, in which it still circulated as a solitary, independent saying.

Thom 55/101 *On Hating Family* (Luke 14:26-27//Matt 10:37-39, Q)

55 [1]Jesus said, *"Whoever does not hate father and mother cannot be my disciple,* [2]*and whoever does not hate brothers and sisters, and carry the cross as I do, will not be worthy of me."*

101 [1]*"Whoever does not hate [father] and mother as I do cannot be my [disciple],* [2]and whoever does [not] love [father and] mother as I do cannot be my [disciple]. [3]For my mother [. . .], but my true [mother] gave me life."

The synoptic parallels to these Thomas sayings have come to Matthew and Luke via their shared source, Q. Thus, in order to demonstrate that Thomas knew and used the synoptic versions of the saying, and not that of Q or the older traditions from which it draws, one must show that Thomas reflects the ways in which Matthew and Luke each have edited their Q source. Schrage argues that no matter how one reconstructs the Q document behind Matthew and Luke here, one will always have to admit that Thomas knew at least one of the two gospels.[133] For if one assumes that Luke's οὐ δύναται εἶναί μου (μοι) μαθητής (one cannot be my disciple) derives from Q,[134] ϥΝΑϢϢΠΕ ΑΝ ΕΡΟ ÑΑϨΙΟϹ ΝΑΕΙ ([he] will not be worthy of me) in Thom 55:2 reflects Matthean redaction in Matt 10:37-38; on the other hand, if one views Matthew's οὐκ ἔστιν μου ἄξιος (he is not worthy of me) as the original Q formulation,[135] ϥΝΑϢῩ ΜΑΘΗΤΗϹ ΑΝ ΝΑΕΙ (he cannot become my disciple) in Thom 55:1 is to be seen as dependent upon Lukan redaction in 14:26-27. But this assumes that the apodoses in both of the parallel sayings in Q (or the tradition antecedent to Q) read exactly the same. This is not necessary; it could well be that the Q version read rather like that of Thomas, using οὐ δύναται εἶναί μου (μοι) μαθητής (one cannot be my disciple) in the apodosis of the first saying, but οὐκ ἔστιν μου ἄξιος (he is not worthy of me) in the apodosis of the second. Matthew and Luke, then, each will have altered Q by standardizing the two apodoses in the opposite way, Matthew preferring to use οὐκ ἔστιν μου ἄξιος (he is not worthy of me) in both members, Luke οὐ δύναται εἶναί μου (μοι) μαθητής (one cannot be my disciple).

The same case may be made regarding Thomas' use of ΜΕϹΤΕ⁻ (hate) in Thom 101:1 (reflecting Luke's text), and ΜῩΡΡΕ⁻ (love) in Thom 101:2 (reflecting Matthew's text). If Matthew's version of the saying derives from Q, Thomas agrees with Lukan redaction; but if Luke's derives from Q, Thomas agrees with Matthean redaction. Here, however, one must ask whether the addition of Thom 101:2 belongs to the realm of redactional conflation, or to the creative work going on within the Thomas tradition itself. The final,

---

133. Schrage, *Das Verhältnis*, 120-21.
134. So Schulz, *Q*, 447, following Bultmann, *Geschichte*, 173, Bussmann, *Studien*, 80, and others.
135. So Harnack, *Sayings*, 86.

resolving sentence: "For my mother [gave me falsehood], but [my] true [mother] gave me life" (Thom 101:3) shows that the conundrum created here is intentional, deriving from some esoteric meaning developed within the Thomas tradition.

The other possible connection between Thomas and the redactional work of one of the synoptic evangelists is the fact that Thom 55:2 uses неqсинну мн̄ нецсωне ("his brothers and sisters"), agreeing with Luke 14:26: τοὺς ἀδελφοὺς καὶ τὰς ἀδελφάς (brothers and sisters) against Matthew's simpler text, generally preferred for its strong parallelism.[136] Yet both Matthew and Luke might have altered their source, which likely stood closer to Thomas than to either synoptic text. Matthew will have substituted υἱὸν ἢ θυγατέρα (son or daughter) for τοὺς ἀδελφοὺς καὶ τὰς ἀδελφάς (brothers and sisters) in order to conform his text more closely to 10:34–35, with which he has secondarily joined this cluster to form a speech on discipleship (cf. under Thom 16, pp. 25–26). For his part, Luke will have preserved the Q text in τοὺς ἀδελφοὺς καὶ τὰς ἀδελφάς (brothers and sisters) but expanded it with τὴν γυναῖκα καὶ τὰ τέκνα (wife and children) to fill out the family circle (cf. the similar additions to Mark 10:29 in Luke 18:29b).

If source-critical issues do not demand that one explain Thom 55 and 101 as deriving from their synoptic parallels, other tradition-historical factors point to an independent derivation for the Thomas versions of the sayings. First, there is the overwhelming problem of the Thomas doublet: how is it to be explained that the Thomas author/editor created two different versions of the same saying, including them both as single, independent sayings? This alone seems to rule out dependence on the synoptics. Further, both versions of the saying in Thomas preserve a double-stich parallel structure more tightly than the corresponding versions in Matthew and Luke. Now it may be that an excerpter or gnostic redactor could have had an eye for *parallelismus membrorum*, and thus deliberately created these nice Thomas specimens from the more literarily formulated sayings in Luke 14:26–27//Matt 10:37–39. But if one accepts this, one would then have to suppose that the redactor turned around and immediately ruined his or her own handiwork in Thom 101 by adding the final phrase, which breaks the *parallelismus!* Thus, with no compelling evidence to suggest Thomas' dependence here on the synoptics, it is more reasonable to judge that Thomas' author/editor knew the saying from traditional circles, in which it was formulated variously in a two-stich structure.

Thom 57 *Wheat and Weeds* (Matt 13:24–30)

57 [1]Jesus said, "The kingdom of the Father is like a person who had [good] seed. [2]His enemy came during the night and sowed weeds among the good seed. [3]The person did not let the workers pull up the weeds, but said to them, 'No, in case you go to pull up the weeds and pull up the wheat along with them.' [4]For on the day of the harvest the weeds will be obvious, and will be pulled up and burned."

136. See Schulz, *Q*, 447, n. 326.

Gärtner,[137] Montefiore[138] and Schrage[139] all argue that Thomas' shorter version of this parable is dependent upon that of Matthew, since it seems to presuppose some of the details of the story given only by Matthew, e.g., the actual sowing of the seed (Matt 13:24), the sprouting of the weeds along with the wheat (Matt 13:26), and the plan of the servants to weed out the field (Matt 13:28). Indeed, the apparant gaps in Thomas' narrative may indicate that it is an abbreviation of *some* longer version—but *not necessarily Matthew's* longer version.[140] Closer examination of the language used in those Matthean verses without parallel in Thomas suggests that Matthew himself is responsible for composing them in just this way. Consider the key words occurring in these verses which later become the subject of the Matthean allegorical interpretation of the parable (Matt 13:36–43):[141] σπείρειν (to sow) (13:24,27; cf. 13:37), ἀγρός (field) (13:24, 27; cf. 13:38), θεριστής (reaper) (13:30; cf. 13:39), συλλέγειν (to gather) (13:30; cf, 13:40). The author/editor of Thomas did not know precisely *these* details because they first arose in the way Matthew conceptualized the parable as an allegory. Perhaps Thomas did know a longer version of this parable, and abbreviated it in the telling; but this longer version was not that of Matthew.

Thom 61:1 *Two on a Bed* (Luke 17:34)

61 ¹*Jesus said, "Two will be reclining on a couch; one will die, one will live."* ²Salome said, "Who are you, sir? You have climbed onto my couch and eaten from my table as if you are from someone." ³Jesus said to her, "I am the one who derives from what is whole. I was granted from the things of my Father." ⁴"I am your disciple." ⁵"For this reason I say, if one is ⟨whole⟩, one will be filled with light, but if one is divided, one will be filled with darkness."

A version of Thom 61:1 comes to Luke via the Q apocalypse (Luke 17:22–37//Matt 24:26–28, 37–41; 10:39).[142] Therefore, the mere knowledge of this saying does not demonstrate a knowledge of, and dependence upon, Luke. Since Thomas reproduces no Lukan redactional details,[143] one is left with no evidence that Thom 61:1 is derived from Luke 17:34. Moreover, since there are no other clear Thomas parallels to Q's apocalyptic section in either its Matthean or Lukan form,[144] it is questionable whether Thomas' author/editor

---

137. Gärtner, *Theology*, 45–46.

138. Montefiore, "A Comparison," 228.

139. Schrage, *Das Verhältnis*, 124–25.

140. So Wilson, *Studies*, 91; also Sieber, "Redactional Analysis," 168. The logic of such an argument would require that Matthew created this parable, and thus was Thomas' only possible source for it. This is unlikely; so Beare, *Matthew*, 302–3.

141. The allegory is Matthean; so Jeremias, *Gleichnisse Jesu*, 79–83; Bultmann, *Geschichte*, 202; Cadoux, *Parables of Jesus*, 28–30.

142. Schulz, *Q*, 280–81; Kloppenborg, *Formation*, 154–58.

143. Sieber, "Redactional Analysis," 134.

144. The following provide rough parallels—"synoptic siblings" or "cousins" at best: Thom 3, 51, 113 (cf. Luke 17:22–25//Matt 24: 26–28); Thom 38 (Luke 17:22); Thom 56, 80 (Luke 17:33//Matt 10:39).

was aware of this tradition at all, or of the apocalyptic application of this saying contained therein.

Furthermore, the Q application of this saying is secondary, as comparison of its version with that of Thomas makes clear. The saying was not always apocalyptic in its thrust. It was and is, rather, a straight forward wisdom saying pondering the apparent capriciousness of death. This is obscured by Luke's language ($\pi\alpha\rho\alpha\lambda\eta\mu\phi\theta\dot{\eta}\sigma\epsilon\tau\alpha\iota/\dot{\alpha}\phi\epsilon\theta\dot{\eta}\sigma\epsilon\tau\alpha\iota$ [taken/left]), which is better suited to the notion of being "taken up" in the parousia or of being "left behind" to suffer the impending doom. The Thomas version speaks the simple language of wisdom: "one will die, the other will live"—and so it is with one of life's deepest secrets. The Thomas wording is therefore probably closer to that of the earlier wisdom saying, even though the gnosticizing application of it in Thom 61 also inclines it away from its simple wisdom meaning.

Thom 62:2 *On Secrecy* (Matt 6:3)

62 [1]Jesus said, "I reveal my mysteries to those [who are worthy] of [my] mysteries. [2]*Do not let your left hand know what your right hand is doing.*"

In Matt 6:3-4 the redundancy of 3b and 4a suggests that 3b is a popular maxim on keeping a secret, inserted for color. It is not legal in nature, as is the surrounding material. In Thom 62 the maxim occurs with essentially the same meaning—"keep this a secret"—but attached to a previously unattested saying it is given an entirely new application. It seems best to regard these as two mutually independent uses of a popular *topos*.

Thom 63 *The Rich Person* (Luke 12:13-21)

63 [1]Jesus said, "There was a rich person who had a great deal of money. [2]He said, 'I shall invest my money so that I may sow, reap, plant, and fill my storehouses with produce, that I may lack nothing.' [3]These were the things he was thinking in his heart, but that very night he died. [4]Whoever has ears should listen."

The complex Luke 12:13-21 has many secondary features. Beginning with the parable itself, many details have received embellishment: the wealth of the man is emphasized in vs 18—he already has multiple storehouses (cf. the singular storehouse in Thomas' version), and yet he will build bigger and better ones; in vs 19, $\epsilon\dot{\iota}s$ $\ddot{\epsilon}\tau\eta$ $\pi o\lambda\lambda\dot{\alpha}$ (for many years) seems to enhance the size of the harvest; and in vs 20 the direct address, $\ddot{\alpha}\phi\rho\omega\nu$ (Fool!), together with the divine scolding, makes explicit what the Thomas version leaves to be discerned. Other secondary features include Luke's generalizing conclusion in 12:21[145] and the use of the dominical saying in 12:15 to link the parable to the apophthegm in 12:13-14.[146] Finally, the entire complex in Luke serves as the introduction to the Q speech On Cares (Luke 12:22-31; cf. Matt 6:25-34).

---

145. Bultmann, *Geschichte*, 193; Dibelius, *Formgeschichte*, 258; and Jeremias, *Gleichnisse Jesu*, 110-11.

146. Bultmann, *Geschichte*, 64.

Thom 63 has none of these secondary features. A version of the apothegm to which Luke joins the parable is located elsewhere in Thomas (Thom 72), as is a saying taken up into the Q speech On Cares (Thom 36), with no evidence to suggest that Thomas originally found all three sayings together and broke them up to some tendentious end. Thomas' parable has no generalizing conclusion, nor any of the embellishments noted above. Thus, its derivation from Luke 12:16–21 is all but impossible. Instead, a separate tradition-history must be posited for the Thomas parable, a hypothesis supported by the observation that Thomas has secondary features which may be ascribed to its own distinctive tradition-history, such as the common early Christian hermeneutical conclusion that turns up frequently in Thomas: ⲡⲉⲧⲉ ⲩ̄ⲙ ⲙⲁⲁⲭⲉ ⲙ̄ⲙⲟϥ· ⲙⲁⲣⲉϥ ⲥⲱⲧⲙ̄ (Whoever has ears should listen),[147] and the grouping of this parable with Thom 64–65 to form a cluster that may be older than Thomas itself.[148]

Thom 65/66 The Tenant Farmers/The Rejected Stone
(Matt 21:33–46//Mark 12:1–12//Luke 20:9–19)

65 [1]He said, "A [. . .] person owned a vineyard and leased it to some farmers, that they might work it and he might collect its crop from them. [2]He sent his slave that the farmers might give him the the vineyard's crop. [3]They grabbed him, beat him, and almost killed him. So the slave returned and told his master. [4]His master said, 'Perhaps he did not know them.' [5]So he sent another slave, and the farmers beat that one as well. [6]Then the master sent his son and said, 'Perhaps they will show my son some respect.' [7]But because the farmers knew that he was the heir to the vineyard, they grabbed him and killed him. [8]Whoever has ears should listen."

66 Jesus said, "Show me the stone that the builders rejected: that is the keystone."

This pair of sayings poses several problems. 1) Thomas agrees in a number of features with Matthew or Luke against Mark.[149] Schrage, whose analysis is

---

147. Cf. Thom 8, 21, 24, 65, 92. Its placement here is perhaps related to the textual tradition in U (030), f^{13}, and the minuscule 893, which attach the same logion to Luke 12:21. But one wonders whether these have influenced Thomas, or vice versa (see Wilson, *Studies*, 135; Birdsall, "Luke XII.16ff.," 332–36).

148. For the phenomenon see Jeremias, *Gleichnisse Jesu*, 89–93.

149. Schrage (*Das Verhältnis*, 139–40) has collated the evidence as follows. Regarding Luke and Thomas: 1) Luke 20:9 abbreviates the allusion to Isa 5:1–2, and Thom 65:1 lacks it; 2) both use a similar purpose clause in the sending of the first servant (Luke 20:10; Thom 65:2); 3) in both, the second servant is "beaten" (δείραντες, Luke 20:11; ϩⲓⲟⲩⲉ, Thom 65:3); 4) in both, the ponderings of the owner contain "perhaps" (ἴσως, Luke 20:13; ⲙⲉϣⲁⲕ, Thom 65:4); and 5) both in the purpose clause in the first sending both use the singular "fruit" (καρποῦ, Luke 20:10; ⲡⲕⲁⲣⲡⲟⲥ, Thom 65:2). Regarding Matthew and Thomas: 1) both use the possessive with "servant" in the first sending (αὐτοῦ, Matt 21:34; ⲡⲉϥ-, Thom 65:2); 2) again in the first sending, the substantive "servant" (δούλους, Matt 21:35; ϩⲉⲙϩⲁⲗ, Thom 65:2) is used a second time as the object of the verb in the second sentence; 3) both speak of "killing" in the first sending (ἀπέκτειναν, Matt 21:35; ⲙⲟⲟⲩⲧ-, Thom 65:3); 4) both send the son third, not another group of servants (Matt 21:35; Thom 65:6); 5) both omit Mark's ἀπέστειλαν κενόν (sent him away empty handed) in 12:3 (Matt 12:35; Thom 65:3, 5); and 6) both omit Mark's adjective ἀγαπητόν (beloved) in 12:6 (Matt 21:37; Thom 65:6). But as Sieber ("Redactional Analysis," 234–36) points out, none of these points can be ascribed unequivocally to the

the most comprehensive to date, maintains that two in particular are of such a nature as to indicate that Thomas' author/editor used Luke as a source: ⲛⲁϯ ⲛⲁϥ (that they might give to him) in Thom 65:2 corresponds to δώσουσιν αὐτῷ (that they might give to him) in Luke 20:10, which he regards as a Lukan stylistic improvement;[150] b) both add the word "perhaps" (ἴσως, Luke 20:13; ⲙⲉϣⲁⲕ, Thom 65:4) to the pondering words of the father before the sending of the son (cf. Mark 12:6), which Schrage assigns to a certain Lukan theological interest in softening the possible reproach against God for sending the son in error.[151]

2) Jeremias, among others, has pointed out that from a form-critical point of view Thomas offers a version of the story that is more primitive than any of the three synoptic versions: a) Thomas makes no allusion to Isa 5:1-2 in the introduction (cf. Matt 21:33//Mark 12:1//Luke 20:9 [abbreviated]);[152] b) with respect to the sending of the servants, Thomas' story uses only three messengers, including the son, while both Mark (followed by Luke) and Matthew disrupt this neat "folkloric rule of threes:"[153] Mark adds a third servant to the series, thus bringing the total number of emissaries to four (Mark12:2–5a//Luke 20:10-12), plus an unspecified multitude (12:5b); Matthew creates out of the servants two large groups, perhaps an allegorical representation of the earlier and later prophets;[154] c) Mark allegorizes the figure of the son with υἱὸν ἀγαπητόν (Mark 12:6), as do Matthew and Luke in their own way (cf. Matt 12:39; Luke 20:15),[155] and all three append the quotation from Psalm 118 directly to the parable, further strengthening this allegorical reading;[156] d) all three synoptics include a rhetorical question and answer, which breaks off the narrative and makes the allegory complete (Mark 12:9, par.)[157]

3) Though Thomas' author/editor does not seem to read the parable allegorically, as did the synoptic evangelists, one finds in Thomas a paraphrase of Ps 118:22-23 presented as a separate saying but, surprisingly, following directly upon the Parable of the Tenants (Thom 66). Did Thomas then know the parable in its synoptic, allegorized form, and "de-allegorize" it by removing the quotation from Psalm 118?[158]

But even considering these problems, the evidence still seems to favor of an independent Thomas tradition. First, Sieber identifies a number of redactional

redactional intention of either Matthew or Luke; therefore, they do not demonstrate Thomas' dependence upon the synoptic gospels.
150. Schrage, *Das Verhältnis*, 140, following Jülicher, *Gleichnisreden*, 2. 388.
151. Schrage, *Das Verhältnis*, 140, again following Jülicher, *Gleichnisreden*, 2. 391.
152. Jeremias, *Gleichnisse Jesu*, 68.
153. Jeremias, *Gleichnisse Jesu*, 69; cf. Crossan, "Parable of the Wicked Husbandmen," 460-61.
154. Jeremias, *Gleichnisse Jesu*, 70; cf. 2 Chr, 24:21; Heb 11:37; Matt 23:37; Luke 13:34.
155. Jeremias, *Gleichnisse Jesu*, 70-71.
156. Jeremias, *Gleichnisse Jesu*, 71-72.
157. Jeremias, *Gleichnisse Jesu*, 72.
158. So McArthur, "Dependence," 286; Schrage, *Das Verhältnis*, 143; Snodgrass, "Gospel of Thomas," 30-31.

traits in the Matthean and Lukan versions of the parable,[159] none of which seems to turn up in Thomas. Luke's use of ἵνα δώσουσιν (that they might give) in 20:10 (=ⲛⲁ†, Thom 65:2) is not a case of Lukan redaction, since it is not his habit to use the future indicative with ἵνα (in order that . . .).[160] Nor is ἴσως (perhaps) in Luke 20:13 (=ⲙⲉϣⲁⲕ, Thom 65:4): it merely changes the father's naïveté to uncertainty, hardly in concord with Luke's view of divinely ordained history.[161] In an environment in which one must assume the continued existence of a lively oral tradition, the agreement of two texts on the matter of a few details does not necessarily indicate a relationship of literary dependence. To the contrary, the fact that Thomas and Luke can agree against Mark on details not to be ascribed to Lukan redaction is strongly suggestive of yet another (oral or written) source for the parable, shared by Luke and Thomas but unknown—or at least not used—by Mark.[162]

Secondly, unless one can imagine the author/editor of the Gospel of Thomas moving through the synoptic versions of the parable with the acumen and sensibilities of a modern form critic, consciously removing everything that would appear secondary from a form-critical point of view, the fact that Thomas' version is in every respect more primitive is impossible to explain without the hypothesis of an independent tradition.[163]

Finally, though the sequence Thom 65–66 poses problems, they are not insurmountable. The fact that Thom 66 is a loose paraphrase of Ps 118: 22, as distinct from the more precise synoptic quotations, points toward Thomas'

---

159. "Redactional Analysis," 233. In Matthew's version Sieber identifies the following: ἀκούσατε (Hear!) (21:33); ὅτε (When) (21:34); ὕστερον (Afterward) (21:37); and 21:43, which is a construct based on 21:41; in Luke's version: πρὸς τὸν λαὸν (to the people) and χρόνους ἱκανούς (for a long while) (20:9); ἐξαπέστειλαν αὐτὸν (they sent him away) (20:10); προσέθετο ἕτερον (he sent another), δὲ . . . καὶ (also), and ἐξαπέστειλαν (sent away) (20:11); προσέθετο (he sent), δὲ καὶ (also), and τοῦτον (this one) (20:12).

160. Sieber, "Redactional Analysis," 235; following *BDF* §369, 2; also Schramm, *Der Markus-Stoff bei Lukas*, 163, n. 1.

161. Sieber, "Redactional Analysis," 235, n. 20.

162. Schramm, *Der Markus-stoff bei Lukas*, 150–67.

163. It is difficult to avoid the form-critical problem. Snodgrass' attempt to explain the phenomenon on the basis of the Syriac textual tradition is not compelling ("Parable of the Wicked Husbandmen," 142–44; "Gospel of Thomas," 29–30). Snodgrass argues that the reduction of three servants to two in Sinaitic Syriac Mark 12:4 and Curetonian Syriac Luke 20:12 reveals a tendency in the Syriac textual tradition to harmonize toward the Matthean version of the parable, with its two groups of servants. According to Snodgrass, this, and not form-critical priority, accounts for Thomas' two-servant form. As Koester points out ("Three Thomas Parables," 203, n. 23) to argue that Thomas stands under the influence of Syriac NT textual corruption is anachronistic in the extreme. Thomas' *terminus ad quem* in the second century (see Grenfell and Hunt's dating of POxy 1 in ΛΟΓΙΑ ΙΗΣΟΥ, 6) renders such an hypothesis impossible. Snodgrass' answer to this objection ("Gospel of Thomas," 29, n. 43), that the later Syriac manuscripts reflect a much older "harmonizing tradition," by which Thomas would have been influenced, is special pleading. In any event, the Syriac texts to which Snodgrass points seem much closer to Thomas' version of the parable than to their Syriac Matthean parallels. If one adds this to the fact that Thomas pre-dates all of these manuscripts by at least two centuries, and probably more, it is more plausible to assume that the Thomas version of the parable has influenced these scribes, not that of Matthew.

form-critical priority here as well;[164] thus, it is unlikely that Thom 66 was composed on the basis of the synoptic texts. Nonetheless, this particular shared sequence is too much to ascribe to mere coincidence. Consequently, many have suggested that these two sayings must have circulated together already very early. But this does not necessitate linkage in the sort of allegorical interpretation imposed by Mark.[165] On the other hand, the present position of Thom 66 in Thomas may not be original, but represents a relatively late scribal alteration based on knowledge of the canonical texts, such as has already been detected at various points in this document.[166]

Thom 68-69 *A Collection of Beatitudes* (Luke 6:22-23, 21//Matt 5:10-12, 6, Q)

68 [1]Jesus said, *"Blessed are you when you are hated and persecuted;* [2]*and no place will be found, wherever you have been persecuted."*

69 [1]Jesus said, *"Blessed are those who have been persecuted* in their hearts: they are the ones who have truly come to know the Father. [2]*Blessed are they who go hungry, so that the stomach of the one in want may be filled."*

From a tradition-historical point of view a synoptic derivation for these sayings is unlikely. The synoptic parallels to these beatitudes are all to be found in the Sermon on the Mount/Plain, and were therefore probably mediated to Matthew and Luke via the Sermon tradition taken up by Q. Thus, what has already been said regarding Thom 26, 34, and 54 above, applies here as well: unless Thomas' author/editor deliberately broke up this collection, scattering its parts, using some while omitting others, dependence here upon the synoptics or their sources is unlikely. The separate occurrence of a third member of the beatitude collection in the Sermon tradition (Thom 54; cf. Luke 6:20b//Matt 5:3 [= Q]) further suggests that Thomas did not know this collection in either of its synoptic forms. Rather, Thom 68-69 is a different sort of assemblage, a collection of beatitudes compiled with no apparent editorial concern to regularize their forms,[167] or to combine the various versions into a single saying.

Thus, the arguments for dependence upon the synoptics to be adduced from a close textual comparison is not particularly strong. Thomas, though it records the beatitude on persecution in two different versions, reflects neither Q's ἕνεκεν (on account of) clause,[168] nor the χαίρειν (rejoice) rejoinder (Luke 6:23//Matt 5:12). As for the main body of this beatitude, Matthew and Luke

---

164. The more precise LXX quotations in the synoptic versions are to be considered secondary, as is the addition of Ps 118:23 in Mark 12:11//Matt 21:42b and of the otherwise unknown saying in Luke 20:18.

165. So Wilson, *Studies*, 102; Sieber, "Redactional Analysis," 236; Koester, "Three Thomas Parables," 200; Crossan, "Parable of the Wicked Husbandmen," 458.

166. Cf. my remarks on Thom 32, 33:2-3, and 39, 45, 92:1, 93-94, and 104.

167. Note the second person plural in Thom 68, the third person plural in 69:1, and finally a third person plural in 69:2 using only the relative construction, ⲛⲉⲧϨⲕⲁⲉⲓⲧ (they who go hungry).

168. Sieber, "Redactional Analysis," 33-34.

treat it so differently that it is difficult to know what each owes to its Q source and what each has added editorially. Thus we cannot take much stock in any alleged agreements between Thomas and the redactional activity of either Matthew or Luke here. For example, each of the evangelists uses a series of verbs in this saying, but they agree on only one:

Matthew 5:11	Luke 6:22
ὀνειδίζειν	μισεῖν
διώκειν	ἀφορίζειν
λέγειν (ψευδόμενοι)	ὀνειδίζειν
	βάλλειν (τὸ ὄνομα ὑμῶν)

Now, the Q version also obviously involved a series of verbs, but to identify them on the basis of Matthew and Luke would be quite speculative. Two verbs from these lists appear in Thomas: διώκειν (to persecute)[169] and μισεῖν (to hate).[170] The first is often construed as Matthean on the grounds that Matthew's eighth beatitude (5:10), which he adds to the older Sermon tradition, makes use of the word.[171] But it is equally possible that Matthew composed the eighth beatitude based upon the tradition he had inherited from Q in 5:11, in which case Thomas reflects not Matthew's work, but the older tradition to which he is heir. The second, while it occurs only in Luke's version, is not generally considered Lukan,[172] and thus likewise cannot be used to link Thomas specifically to the synoptic texts. Finally, it is curious that Thomas does not have anything corresponding to the one verb shared by Matthew and Luke (ὀνειδίζειν [to revile]), and hence most certainly to be ascribed to Q. This may serve to confirm what our tradition-historical analysis has already indicated: not only is Thomas unaware of the synoptic texts themselves, it seems to be independent of their source, Q, as well.

Thom 69:2 is perhaps too brief to allow a firm judgment about verbal correspondence. With so few words, naturally most must be shared if any relationship, however remote, is to be detected at all. However, a noteworthy difference between Thomas and the synoptic versions is to be found in the conjunction used in each to introduce the second clause: Thomas uses ϣιⲛⲁ, derived from ἵνα (in order that) in its Greek original, while Q uses ὅτι (for, because). This may mean that Thomas' Greek text actually read quite differently from that of Q, as Kendrick Grobel, among others, has suggested.[173]

---

169. Thom 68 and 69:1 (Coptic ⲁⲓⲱⲕⲉ).
170. Thom 68 (Coptic ⲙⲉⲥⲧⲉ).
171. See Schulz, Q, 453, n. 372.
172. Schulz, Q, 452, notes that Luke uses the word six times, but in each case it has been taken over from traditional material.
173. Grobel, "How Gnostic is the Gospel of Thomas," 373; he translates: "Blessed are they that go hungry in order that they may fill the stomach of him who desires (to be filled)." Cf. Wilson, Studies, 80–81. The translation offered above follows this approach.

Otherwise, the Thomas version manages to avoid reproducing either Matthean[174] or Lucan[175] redaction. This is the strongest argument for Thomas' independence.[176]

Thom 71 A House Destroyed (cf. Matt 26:61; 27:40//Mark 14:58; 15:29; Matt 24:2//Mark 13:2//Luke 21:6; Acts 6:14; John 2:19)

71 Jesus said, "I will destroy [this] house, and no one will be able to build it."

While Thom 71 does not refer explicitly to the temple, its structural similarity to these parallels permits the judgment that it is a version of the so-called temple word and warrants its inclusion among the "twins." The attestation of this tradition in both John and Mark demonstrates that the temple word's tradition-history has more than one branch, and was probably widely known in early Christian circles. It is therefore not surprising to find yet another attestation of the saying, the independence of which is suggested by Thomas' apparent ignorance of either Mark's passion narrative, or John's clearing of the temple scene.

Whether the absence of any reference to the temple in Thom 71 is a secondary feature,[177] or a primitive touch is difficult to decide. The term "this house" certainly appears enigmatic. Gärtner suggests that one understand it metaphorically as an allusion to the world, the "mortal house" from which the gnostic seeks to escape, or perhaps the body, the soul's temporary "house" which must eventually be shed.[178] Gnostic parallels for both images abound.[179] If Gärtner is correct, the Thomas version of the saying is relatively late. On the other hand, οἶκος (house) is frequently used in the sense of a "royal house" or dynasty.[180] Thus, one might understand the saying as more plainly political: it may speak of the destruction of the *Herodian* house. This might explain better the cryptic nature of the saying; such a threat could only have been cast in veiled terms. Of course, after the removal of Agrippa in 44 C.E. such a saying would have been redirected toward another political institution aligned with the Roman occupation. The temple would be a logical target. In this scenario the Thomas version would have to be regarded as the more

---

174. Matthew's hand is to be seen in δικαιοσύνη (righteousness)—so Schulz, *Q*, 77, following Harnack, *Sayings*, 49; Bussmann, *Studien*, 42; Schmid, *Matthäus und Lukas*, 214-15; Strecker, *Weg der Gerechtigkeit*, 151, 157, n. 6; Schürmann, *Lukasevangelium*, 331, n. 41.

175. Luke's hand is to be seen in the use of νῦν (now)—so Schulz, *Q*, 77, n. 135.

176. Sieber, "Redactional Analysis," 35-36.

177. So Wilson, *Studies*, 114-15; Gärtner, *Theology*, 172-73.

178. Gärtner, *Theology*, 171-72. If the latter, Gärtner argues that the saying should be seen as a polemic against the Johannine version of the "temple word," the force of which is to reject the canonical tradition of the resurrection of the body. There is, however, no evidence that Thomas knew the Gospel of John. While it is possible that Thomas has some familiarity with Johannine tradition, this too cannot be proven.

179. See Gärtner, *Theology*, 171-72.

180. *LSJ, s.v., οἶκος* (III).

primitive. All of this is, of course, quite speculative, but no more so than the attempt to read the saying in terms of gnostic theology.

Thom 72 *Jesus as Divider* (Luke 12:13-14)

72 [1]A [person said] to him, "Tell my brothers to divide my father's possessions with me." [2]He said to the person, "Sir, who made me a divider?" [3]He turned to his disciples and said to them, "I am not a divider, am I?"

Luke has the only synoptic parallel to Thom 72 but there is no evidence that Thomas derives its version of the saying from this source. In Luke the saying occurs in a complex in which traditional materials are joined using a modicum of redactional adaptation. It is probably Luke who has brought this chreia together with the Parable of the Rich Fool (Luke 12:16-21) to serve as a kind of introduction.[181] Luke's hand may be seen in vs 15, which forms the transition between our chreia and the parable,[182] and perhaps in the use of τις ἐκ τοῦ ὄχλου (a certain person from out of the crowd) to link the complex with what precedes (cf. Luke 12:1).[183] The fact that Thomas knows nothing of the redactional verse, preserves a simpler introduction,[184] and does not follow Luke's cue in using this chreia to interpret and introduce the parable, which Thomas includes elsewhere (see Thom 63), argues strongly for an independent tradition in Thomas.[185]

Still, some have tried to make a case for viewing Thomas as dependent here upon Luke. Schrage points out that Thomas shares with the Sahidic New Testament the omission of any reference to Jesus as judge, reading simply "who has made me a divider . . .?" But as Tjitze Baarda notes, only one manuscript[186] carries this reading, against the vast majority of Sahidic manuscripts which agree with the Greek text in reading ⲛ̄ⲕⲣⲓⲧⲏⲥ ⲁⲩⲱ ⲛ̄ⲣⲉϥⲡⲱⲣⲝ (judge and divider).[187] Thomas' dependence upon this single Coptic manu-

---

181. Bultmann, *Geschichte*, 21: it is characteristic of Luke to use an apophthegm in this way; the adaptation is accomplished via vs 15.

182. εἶπεν δὲ πρὸς αὐτούς (and he said to them) is a typically Lukan expression; so Fitzmyer, *Luke*, 968.

183. Manson, *Sayings of Jesus*, 271.

184. Cf. Schrage's tortuous assertion (*Das Verhältnis*, 152): Thomas likely shortened the Lukan phrase, since his use of a similar introduction in Thom 79 proves that he did know the Lukan form. If Thomas chose to retain the "crowd" introduction in 79, what offense could be cited as the motive for omitting it in Thom 72? The parallel phrase in Thom 79 logically suggests just the opposite conclusion: its occurrence there assures one that if it had been present in his source for Thom 72, he probably would not have omitted it.

185. Cf. Sieber, "Redactional Analysis," 215. It is worth noting that often in the course of this study it has been found that Thomas presents a saying which Bultmann had identified as originally independent, in its predictable solitary form. Luke 12:13-14, however, is a case in which Bultmann had argued for unitary composition (*Geschichte*, 21). This judgment is also confirmed by Thomas, the saying together with its apophthegmic context occurring in Thom 72 intact.

186. sa 120 (= MS 9 in Horner's apparatus [*The Coptic Version of the New Testament*]) The relevant fragment is Leiden MS Copte 55 (f. 1), a seventh-or eighth-century text on parchment.

187. Baarda, "Luke 12, 13-14," 121.

script hardly seems likely. Moreover, the Coptic New Testament tradition consistently uses ⲣⲉϥⲡⲱⲣⲝ to render μεριστήν (divider), while Thomas uses the synonym ⲣⲉϥⲡⲱϣⲉ (divider), thus suggesting that the two texts do not derive from the same translational tradition at all. All told, Schrage's case here seems especially weak.

Perhaps the most thorough investigation of this saying in all its forms is that of Baarda, who traces its use and development from the first through the fifth centuries (to Augustine). Of particular concern for Baarda is the effective refutation of Gilles Quispel's contention that Thom 72, with its parallel in the newly discovered tenth-century Arabic apologetical document of 'Abd al-Jabbar, is the key to proving the origins of the Gospel of Thomas in the Jewish Christian gospel tradition.[188] But while his arguments against Quispel's position are persuasive, his own position on the origin of the saying is unsatisfactory. He concludes against Quispel: "This saying presents us with the gnostic version of Luke 12, 13-14, just as the Syro-Latin text presents us with the Marcionite version of that Lucan passage."[189] While Baarda does offer a plausible gnostic reading of the form of the saying preserved in Thom 72,[190] he makes no explicit argument to the effect that the Thomas saying in fact *derives from* Luke 12:13-14 and not from an earlier tradition shared by both Thomas and Luke.[191] His suggestion that Jesus himself would have spoken only the word κριτής (judge) and that Luke added μεριστής (divider), upon which Thomas would then be dependent, is purely speculative.[192] If, as Baarda would agree,[193] the only person able to adjudicate in such affairs as the division of inheritance was a κριτής, then the opposite scenario might be imagined just as easily: the original saying referred simply to the indistinct role of μεριστής, causing Luke to "correct" the tradition by adding the more official sounding word κριτής.

In this instance the argument of Quispel and Gershensen[194] has merit. They suggest that behind the word μεριστής is the something like the בעל פלגותא (to make division). The verb פלג (to divide) can be used to refer to the division of inheritances, but also to the introduction of divisive opinions or heresy. Jesus'

---

188. Baarda, "Luke 12, 13-14," 134-56.

189. Baarda, "Luke 12, 13-14," 155.

190. For example, Baarda ("Luke 12, 13-14," 140-41) argues that the omission of κριτής (judge) in Thomas places more emphasis on Jesus' as "divider," the denial of which would fit well within the context of Thomas' theology as a whole (cf. Thom 22, 106). On the other hand, however, the presence of κριτής (judge) in Luke (or Q) may reflect the more apocalyptic christology of the synoptic tradition (so Koester, "One Jesus, Four Primitive Gospels," 171). Otherwise, Baarda ("Luke 12, 13-14," 152) is probably correct (following Schrage, *Das Verhältnis*, 152) in assigning ⲛⲁ ⲡⲁⲉⲓⲱⲧ (the things of my Father) to Thomas redaction, and the omission of the address διδάσκαλε under the influence of Thom 13:5 ("Luke 12, 13-14," 145-46).

191. Nor does he argue that Thomas is dependent upon Marcion and Tatian, as is incorrectly asserted by K. Snodgrass, "Gospel of Thomas," 35.

192. "Luke 12, 13-14," 120-21.

193. "Luke 12, 13-14," 119-20.

194. Quispel and Gershensen, "Meristae," 19-26.

reply is a pun. According to Quispel and Gershenson, the effect of the pun is that Jesus will not divide the inheritance because the Law has already settled the matter, and Jesus will not vere from the Law.[195] Yet I cannot help but hear instead an ironic tone in the double entendre: of course Jesus would not be bothered with so crass a matter as the division of wealth. But was Jesus a schismatic, renegade teacher of the Law? That is another question altogether! After the final rejoinder to the disciples in Thomas' version of the saying one must surely anticipate at least a titter from the implied audience.

Thom 73 *The Harvest is Great* (Luke 10:2//Matt 9:37-38, Q)

73 Jesus said, "The harvest is large but the workers are few, so beg the Lord to send out workers to the harvest."

Schrage considers this saying to be a prime illustration of the dependence of the Coptic version of Thomas on the Coptic New Testament.[196] The degree of verbal correspondence is indeed quite high, and it is striking that both Thomas and the two synoptic versions use the Coptic word ϲⲟⲃⲕ to render what surely must have been ὀλίγοι (few) in the Greek original of all three. As Schrage points out, among the other forty cases in which the Sahidic must translate ὀλίγος, ⲕⲟⲩⲓ is used (never ϲⲟⲃⲕ).[197] But these observations are not probative. If one widens the linguistic data base only slightly (to include, for example, the Coptic Old Testament) one finds that it is not at all unusual to translate ὀλίγος using ϲⲟⲃⲕ.[198] And while there is a high degree of verbal correspondence between these two versions of the saying, in such a brief passage one must reckon with some amount of verbatim agreement if any identity at all is to be recognizable. And the numerous differences between the Coptic texts are not to be overlooked: 1) Thomas places the particle ⲇⲉ (so) before ⲡϫⲟⲉⲓⲥ (the Lord) while both synoptic versions locate δέ after it; 2) Thomas uses the object marker ⲙ̄ (ⲛ̄) before ⲡϫⲟⲉⲓⲥ, while the synoptics omit it; 3) Thomas introduces the final clause with ϣⲓⲛⲁ = ἵνα (so that); the synoptics use ⲭⲉⲕⲁⲥ (Matt) and ⲭⲉ (Luke), which normally translate the Greek ὅπως (so that) in such a context; 4) Thomas, in contrast to the synoptics, does not modify ⲡϫⲟⲉⲓⲥ with ⲙ̄ⲡⲱϩⲥ (of the harvest); 5) nor does Thomas modify ⲱϩⲥ (harvest) in the final clause with the possessive pronoun ⲡⲉϥ⁻ (his), as do both synoptic versions. These last three differences are particularly important, for they likely reflect differences in the Greek texts which underlie these Coptic translations, the sort of incidental differences one would expect to have resulted, not from any deliberate editorial effort, but from the rather capricious processes of oral transmission. This suggests, of course, that Thomas and the synoptics have appropriated this saying from the oral tradition independently of one another.

---

195. Quispel and Gershensen, "Meristae," 24.
196. Schrage, *Das Verhältnis*, 153–54.
197. Schrage, *Das Verhältnis*, 154.
198. See the numerous testamonia listed in Crum, *Coptic Dictionary, s.v.* ϲⲃⲟⲕ.

This suspicion is confirmed by tradition-historical and form critical observations. Bultmann considered the synoptic version of this saying to be a good example of a metaphorical wisdom saying, which received new significance once it was taken up into the early Christian tradition.[199] Its interpretation in terms of early Christian mission activity can be seen already in Q, where it is taken up into Q's Sending of the Seventy (-two).[200] If Thomas had received this saying from the synoptic tradition, one would expect some of this secondary interpretation to have survived the transfer. But this is not the case. In Thomas one encounters the saying without a trace of its secondary literary context in Q, and without a hint of the mission interpretation it received in Q. It is therefore highly unlikely that Thomas knew the saying from Q, or its derivatives in Matthew and Luke. Rather, just as we have seen elsewhere that traditional materials in this Q speech are preserved independently in Thomas (see the comments on Thom 14:4, above), such an explanation seem in order for Thom 73 as well.

Thom 76 *The Pearl Merchant*
(Matt 13:45-46; Luke 12:33-34// Matt 6:19-21, Q)

76 ¹Jesus said, "The Father's kingdom is like a merchant who had a supply of merchandise, and then found a pearl. ²That merchant was prudent; he sold the merchandise and bought the single pearl for himself. ³So also with you, seek his treasure that is unfailing, that endures, where no moth comes to eat and no worm destroys."

Many have tried to find in Thomas' version of the Pearl Merchant a gnostic adaptation of the Matthean version of this parable, found in Matt 13:45-46.[201] Yet, however imaginative and erudite such hypotheses may be, they do not form a solid foundation from which to begin. It is one thing to demonstrate that Thomas' parable is gnostic, it is quite another to demonstrate that it is an adaptation of the Matthean version. For this we need solid evidence of the residue of Matthew's hand in the Thomas version.

Schrage attempts to provide such evidence at several different levels. At the level of the parable's plot, he argues that without Matthew's information that the pearl was "of great value" the action of the merchant in Thomas makes no sense; therefore, Thomas' parable must presuppose a knowledge of Matthew's text.[202] But the value of pearls in antiquity was proverbial;[203] one surely does not need Matthew's remark to motivate the story. At the level of Thomas redaction, Schrage suggests that Thomas' "Father's kingdom" is a gnostic adaptation of Matthew's "kingdom of heaven."[204] But while the parallels he

---

199. Bultmann, *Geschichte*, 103; cf. Jeremias, *Gleichnisse Jesu*, 77, 119.
200. Luke 10:2-12//Matt 9:37; 10:7-16.
201. E.g., Cerfaux and Garitte. "Les paraboles du Royaume," 315; Kasser, *L'Évangile selon Thomas*, 117; Gärtner, *Theology*, 237-38.
202. Schrage, *Das Verhältnis*, 156.
203. See Hauck, "μαργαρίτης," 472.
204. Schrage, *Das Verhältnis*, 157.

assembles from later gnostic texts are impressive, no such programmatic resignification of "kingdom" is evident throughout Thomas. In fact, Thomas himself frequently uses an expression equivalent to Matthew's "kingdom of heaven."[205] In none of these instances does Thomas feel inclined to opt for the 'more gnostic expression.' Furthermore, to suppose that "Father's kingdom" would automatically summon gnostic overtones is itself dubious. Matthew uses a very similar expression in 13:43 ($\beta \alpha \sigma \iota \lambda \epsilon \acute{\iota} \alpha \ \tau o\hat{v} \ \pi \alpha \tau \rho \grave{o}\varsigma \ a\grave{v}\tau \hat{\omega}\nu$ [kingdom of their Father]), where the overtones are apocalyptic, not gnostic. At the level of the Thomas collection itself, Schrage argues that the appending of Thom 76:3 to the parable, with its reference to "treasure," probably indicates that originally Thom 76 was attached by catchword association to the Parable of the Treasure (now found in Thom 109), thus duplicating the order of these two parables in Matthew.[206] This, however, is entirely speculative. Finally, Schrage points to a number of translational similarities between Thomas and the Sahidic version of Matt 13:45–46.[207] But all of these fall within the realm of common Coptic usage, and therefore indicate nothing. Moreover, striking differences between them call into question even the most remote relationship between their respective translational traditions.[208]

On the positive side, several factors weigh heavily in favor of viewing the two versions of the parable as essentially autonomous. First, although the editor's hand is not overpowering in the Matthean version of the parable, there are at least two identifiable redactional elements: 1) the use of $\pi \acute{a} \lambda \iota \nu$ (again) to introduce the parable, which is typical of Matthean style;[209] and 2) the notion that the merchant "sold all that he had," which derives from Matthew's version of the Treasure (13:44).[210] Thom 76, of course, shares neither of these elements, and thus cannot easily be seen as derivative of Matthew's text.

Second, other secondary features from Matthew's version do not appear in Thomas. For example, in Thomas the radically unconventional behavior of the merchant is striking. Here the buyer is no pearl merchant but a common marketer of goods. When he finds the pearl, he sells his entire consignment of merchandise—a going out of business sale of sorts—in order to purchase the

205. Cf. Thom 20, 54, and 114, all of which speak of "Heaven's kingdom." The last example is of particular note, for it is in Thom 114 that Thomas' gnosticizing proclivities become quite strong. Yet even here there is no shift to the 'more gnostic' formulation.

206. Schrage, Das Verhältnis, 157. Matthew's Parable of the treasure is found in Matt 13:44.

207. Schrage, Das Verhältnis, 157: Both Thom and the Sahidic version of Matthew include a dative object after their verbs meaning "to buy"; both lack any reference to the great value of the thing found; Thomas and most of the Coptic versions use the term ογρωμε ñεϣω(ω)τ (lit. "a merchant person") to refer to the merchant, instead of the simple (ε)ϣωτ (merchant).

208. In the Sahidic version of Matthew the merchant is in search of some fine gems (ϩενενεᾶᾶε ενανογογ), not pearls; the two traditions use different words for "to buy": τοογ (Thomas) and ϣωπ (Matthew). Overall, the verbatim agreement of the two versions is rather minimal.

209. Sieber ("Redactional Analysis," 181, 184, after Bultmann, Geschichte, 187 and Jeremias, Gleichnisse Jesu, 197-98) notes the following instances in Matthew 13 in which the idiom is employed: vss 24, 31, 33, and 47.

210. So Hunzinger, "Unbekannte Gleichnisse," 220; Jeremias, Gleichnisse Jesu, 198.

single pearl. However—and here is the parable's distinctive feature, both surprising and radical—this is no investment; rather, he buys the pearl "for himself" (oγωτ, 76:2). It is to him a bauble, an obsession. Against Thomas, the Matthean version seems to have lost this surprising, radical edge.[211] In this case the one who discovers the pearl is a pearl merchant; it is his business to look for pearls, and when he finds one, to buy it. His action is perfectly understandable as an investment. As C. H. Dodd puts it: "To know when to plunge makes the successful financier."[212] This 'conventionalization' of the parable is, in my view, secondary.

Finally, from a tradition-historical perspective, it seems clear that the Matthean and Thomas versions of this parable have traveled along different routes in the early history of their oral transmission. In the Matthean half of the tradition-history it has been paired with the Parable of the Treasure (Matt 13:44),[213] a secondary development not found in Thomas, who preserves a version of the Parable of the Treasure elsewhere (Thom 109). On the Thomas side, a different tradition-history is evident in the secondary appending of Thom 76:3, itself originally an independent *mashal*,[214] as an hortatory conclusion. Thus, though both versions of the parable bear witness to a considerable history of oral transmission, their individual features suggest that each represents a different trajectory within that history.

Thom 79 *Blessed the Womb* (Luke 11:27-28; 23:29)

79 ¹A woman in the crowd said to him, "Blessed are the womb that bore you and the breasts that fed you." ²He said to [her], "Blessed are those who have heard the word of the Father and have truly kept it. ³For there will be days when you will say, 'Blessed are the womb that has not there and the breasts that have not given milk.'"

Here two traditional units are found joined in Thomas, which have landed in two separate literary contexts in the synoptic tradition (Luke 11:27-28 = Thom 79:1-2; Luke 23:29 = Thom 79:3). But one should not privilege the synoptic versions, and assume too quickly that Thomas' editor/author has drawn them out of their synoptic contexts and secondarily combined them. The texts themselves speak against this.

Beginning with Luke 23:29, one may reconstruct at least the following stages in its synoptic tradition-history: 1) it was part of an early Christian prophecy placed on the lips of Jesus;[215] 2) this prophetic speech was given an

---

211. So also Hunzinger, "Unbekannte Gleichnisse," 218; Jeremias, *Gleichnisse Jesu*, 198.
212. Dodd, *Parables*, 86.
213. Jeremias, *Gleichnisse Jesu*, 89-90.
214. Cf. Bultmann's comments (*Geschichte*, 81, 85), regarding the parallel to Thom 76:3 in Luke 12:33-34//Matt 6:19-21, Q. Thom 76:3 is not derived from Luke 12:33-34//Matt 6:19-21, Q, but is an earlier version of this Q cluster, in which the logion in Luke 12:34//Matt 6:21, Q (originally independent—so Bultmann, *Geschichte*, 87) had not yet been drawn to it (*pace* Grant and Freedman, *Secret Sayings*, 167 and Gärtner, *Theology*, 37-38).
215. Bultmann, *Geschichte*, 121-22.

apophthegmic context;[216] and finally 3) Luke included it as an episode in his passion narrative. None of these stages may be detected in Thom 79:1-2: the rest of the prophetic speech, as a whole or in part, does not occur at all in Thomas; the apophthegmic context is missing; and nothing of Luke's redactional hand is to be found.[217] Thus, Thomas' derivation from Luke certainly may not be assumed. By itself, Thom 79:3//Luke 23:29 is an independent saying; there is no reason to suppose that it did not circulate independently in early Christian circles, and was thus capable of a variety of applications.

As for Luke 11:27-28, it was Bultmann's judgment that this apophthegm is an example of unitary composition.[218] This seems to me preferable to Conzelmann's suggestion that vs 28 belongs to Lukan redaction,[219] which would leave vs 27b as the original point of the apophthegm, and the only example in the synoptic tradition in which an anonymous saying functions in this way. If Luke 11:27-28 was, then, a pre-Lukan unit, its appearance in Thomas does not automatically suggest dependence upon Luke. Since Thomas' version has nothing corresponding to Luke's typical introductory ἐγένετο δὲ ἐν τῷ . . . (and it happened that while . . .) in 11:27a,[220] the evidence would seem to suggest that Thomas knew the apophthegm in a pre- or non-Lukan form.

Turning finally to Thom 79 itself, it is noteworthy that 79:1-2 is joined to 79:3 with the catchwords ϩH (womb) and ⲛ̄ⲕⲓⲃⲉ (breasts). This indicates that the two units circulated together already at an oral stage in their tradition-history, where this mnemonic device first acquired its usefulness. Their linking in Thomas, then, is not to be attributed to the redactional work of a Thomas author/editor, but to an earlier stage in the history of the tradition itself.

216. Bultmann, *Geschichte*, 37-38.
217. *Pace* Schrage (*Das Verhältnis*, 165-66), who maintains that Thomas' second person plural in 79:3 (ⲛ̄ⲧⲉⲧⲛ̄ⲭⲟⲟⲥ [you (pl.) will say]) may be explained only on the supposition that Thomas' author/editor knew the Lukan version, whereby the plural address would be directed toward θυγατέρες (daughters) in 23:28 (cf. the singular referent ⲟⲩⲥϩⲓⲙ[ⲉ] [a woman] in Thom 79:1; also ⲛⲁ[ⲥ] [to her] in 79:2). But as Sieber ("Redactional Analysis, 212) notes, this suggests only that Thomas has taken the saying from some (oral or written) source in which a plural antecedent was in view; the options, however, are not limited to Luke. Luke's use of a third person plural rather than a second person formulation makes Lukan derivation unlikely. If there is indeed a syntactical aporia here (the plural could refer to ⲡⲙⲏⲏϣⲉ [the crowd] in 79:1; a lacuna in 79:2 makes the dative object here a matter of conjecture), then it has arisen only because two sayings have been joined without any editorial concern to rectify their contextual differences, a phenomenon we have seen elsewhere in Thomas (e.g., Thom 14 or 68-69). Snodgrass, too, argues that Thomas reflects Lukan redaction ("Gospel of Thomas," 36). But of the Lukan elements he offers, only one is unequivocally Lukan: ἔρχονται ἡμέραι (days will come), and this expression is not paralleled precisely in Thomas (cf. Thomas' ⲟⲩⲛ̄ ϩⲛ̄ϩⲟⲟⲩ = γίνονται ἡμέραι [there will be days]). Rather, the two texts reflect the sort of differences one would expect to result from the process of oral transmission.
218. Bultmann, *Geschichte*, 29-30.
219. *Theology of St. Luke*, 231.
220. So Sieber, "Redactional Analysis," 211-13.

Thom 86 *Foxes Have Holes* (Luke 9:58//Matt 8:20, Q)

86 ¹Jesus said, "[Foxes have] their dens and birds have their nests, ²but a person has no place to lay his head and rest."

The brevity of this saying does not provide much ground for discussing the intertextual relationships of its various exemplars. Matthew and Luke preserve the saying, which each has assuredly drawn from Q, in almost identical verbatim agreement.[221] Neither Matthew nor Luke has likely changed a thing in the tradition they received from Q; therefore, it is simply impossible to show on the basis of content that Thomas made use of Matthew and/or Luke in acquiring this saying. Schrage's learned command of the Coptic texts notwithstanding, his attempt to suggest Thomas' dependence upon the synoptic texts simply falls short.[222]

Tradition-historically, however, the case for an autonomous tradition is quite strong. Originally a saying of secular wisdom ascribed to Jesus,[223] this saying has come down to Matthew and Luke via Q, where it occurs already imbedded in a specific apophthegmic context (Luke 9:57–58//Matt 8:18–20, Q).[224] In Thomas, this secondary context is absent and the saying stands alone in its more typical solitary state. Thus, it is unlikely that Thomas has taken the saying from Matthew or Luke or even from Q. Rather, it derives from another tradition-historical trajectory altogether, in which it was not fitted out as an apophthegm. To be sure, the Thomas version of the saying has itself undergone secondary expansion, in the addition of the phrase ɴϥⲙ̄ⲧⲟɴ ⲙ̄[ⲙⲟ]ϥ (and rest). But this does not prove that Thomas is dependent on the synoptic gospels, only that the Thomas tradition itself was subject to the same kinds of secondary developments one typically also finds in the synoptic tradition.[225]

221. Only the tense of λέγειν in the introductory phrase differs, Matthew using the present, Luke the aorist.

222. Schrage, *Das Verhältnis*, 168–70. Schrage recognizes the problem posed by the close correspondence of the Matthean and Lukan texts. He realizes that if neither evangelist has altered the Q source they share, there is little chance of linking Thomas to them, as opposed to their source, or even to another version of the saying altogether. That leaves him with only the argument that Thomas' Coptic reflects the Coptic of the Sahidic New Testament. But even so Schrage cannot present a strong case. He points out that in only four instances out of forty-seven does the Sahidic New Testament translate the Greek ποῦ with the Coptic ⲙⲁ (place). But this is not convincing. The Greek idiom οὐκ ἔχειν ποῦ (to have nowhere [to do something]) is relatively uncommon, so that the data base is small to begin with. The Thomas and Coptic New Testament versions of this text, each in their own way, attempt to render the Greek literally. The fact that, aside from their both using ⲙⲁ, the two Coptic versions of the saying are really quite different, belies any notion that they come from a common translational tradition.

223. Bultmann, *Geschichte*, 107.

224. So Bultmann, *Geschichte*, 27–28. Luke 9:59–60//Matt 8:21, Q, appears to be a secondary expansion of the apophthegm; Luke fills out the tradition by adding 9:61–62.

225. I see no reason to read the Thomas version of this saying with any particular gnosticizing overtones, *pace* Gärtner, *Theology*, 60–61; Kasser, *L'Évangile selon Thomas*, 104; P. Vielhauer, "ΑΝΑΠΑΥΣΙΣ," 293; and Crossan, *In Fragments*, 241–42. "Rest" here cannot

Thom 89 *Inside and Outside* (Luke 11:39–41//Matt 23:25–26)

89 [1]Jesus said, "Why do you wash the outside of the cup? [2]Do you not understand that the one who made the inside is also the one who made the outside?"

While others have asserted Thomas' dependence upon the synoptics here,[226] once again it is Schrage who has argued in detail for the hypothesis.[227] But his case is not compelling. The similarities between Thomas' Coptic rendering of the saying and that of the Coptic New Testament are not out of the ordinary.[228] Thus, dependence upon the Coptic New Testament is certainly not necessary, and given the considerable differences between the two translations, not very likely. Chief among them is the fact that in the second saying (Thom 89:2; Luke 11:40) Thomas speaks first of the "inside," then of the "outside," while Luke has the reverse order. Schrage explains this as due to Thomas' dependence upon a Greek manuscript tradition in which the saying follows the Thomas sequence;[229] but one is left then with a rather convoluted hypothesis. No doubt if one searches diligently enough through various manuscripts and textual variants, the Coptic version, occasionally the Syriac versions, the Diatessaron, and so forth, one will eventually discover something corresponding to most of Thomas' readings. But at some point the hypothesis begins to loose its strength. In this instance, the simple reversal of elements in a saying is a typical error occurring at the scribal level, and no doubt at the level of the oral tradition as well. In no way does it necessitate Thomas' dependence on 𝔭45 and the like.

A more serious matter is the origin of Thom 89:2//Luke 11:40. Its absence in Matthew raises the question, whether Luke received the saying from Q (out of which Matthew then will have eliminated it) or created the saying redactionally. If the latter, then one could certainly argue that Thomas depends on Luke. But the status of this verse relative to Q is debated. Bultmann thought

---

bear the same connotations as its cognate noun in Thom 50 and 60. Both of these sayings affirm that the Thomas Christian indeed does have a place of "repose," which he/she must strive to find. If "to rest" carried the same significance in Thom 86, then the saying would say the opposite of what one would expect (see my discussion in chapter 5, pp. 133–34). Thus, one should not assign this expansion too hastily to the hand of Thomas; it may well represent a simple variation in an oral rendering of the saying an some pre-Thomas stage of its transmission history.

226. E.g., Grant and Freedman, *Secret Sayings,* 154. But see Sieber, "Redactional Analysis," 250–53.

227. Schrage, *Das Verhältnis,* 170–71.

228. Schrage (*Das Verhältnis,* 171) points out that rarely is the Greek word ποιεῖν (to make) translated into Coptic using ⲧⲁⲙⲓⲟ (to make, in the sense of to create); ⲉⲓⲣⲉ (to make) is much more common. Yet both Thomas and the Sahidic New Testament use the former word here. But in this case the sense in which ποιεῖν is used demands ⲧⲁⲙⲓⲟ, not ⲉⲓⲣⲉ, which does not carry the nuance of "create" in the same way. Likewise, the fact that both Thom 89:2 and the Sahidic version of Luke 11:40 include the resumptive personal pronoun ⲛⲧⲟϥ corresponds to the normal conventions of Coptic.

229. 𝔭45, C, D, G, 251, 291, 482, 700, 716, 1229, 1574, 1675; see Schrage, *Das Verhältnis,* 170–71.

that this cluster of sayings originally ended with this rhetorical question.[230] Something equaling Luke 11:41//Matt 23:26 would have been added secondarily at the level of Q to round out the cluster.[231] Schulz takes the opposite view, arguing that Luke 11:40 comes from the hand of Luke. Aside from the fact that Matthew does not have the saying, he notes the use of ἄφρονες (fools), which occurs elsewhere in the New Testament only in Luke 12:20.[232] While the basis for any decision on this matter will necessarily be thin, I favor Bultmann's solution. To be sure, his explanation for its omission by Matthew is weak, but it is generally agreed that Matthew has redacted this section of Q more extensively than Luke.[233] He may have simply omitted it as distracting to the point he wishes to make in 23:26. Furthermore, if 11:40 is Lukan, then it is peculiar that the one identifiable Lukanism in the saying fails to appear in the Thomas version!

But if the saying comes originally from Q, could Thomas not have borrowed it from this source? This too is unlikely. In Q, the saying occurs as part of a block of material that is highly polemical in tone (Q 11:14–26, 29–36, 39–52), and organized around the theme of the opposition between Jesus and "this generation."[234] The heightened polemic against the Pharisees in Luke 11:39–41//Matt 23:25–26 may therefore stem from its use in Q. But none of this Q polemic directed against the Jewish authorities seems to have found its way into the Thomas version, which does not mention any Jewish groups at all. If Thomas had known the saying in this highly polemical form, either from Q or the later synoptic texts, it would be hard to account for the less polemical Thomas version, since elsewhere Thomas seems to be on no better terms with these authorities (cf. Thom 39 and 102). Had he seen the more polemical version, he would probably have used it. What is more, Q probably had something corresponding to Luke 11:41//Matt 23:26;[235] this too does not appear in the Thomas version, which in at least this respect is more primitive.

Thom 90 *The Yoke* (Matt 11:28–30)

90 Jesus said, "Come to me, for my yoke is easy and my lordship is gentle, and you will find rest for yourselves."

It is often argued that Thomas' shorter version of this saying is the result of gnostic redaction of a synoptic text.[236] But as has been pointed out many times,

---

230. Bultmann, *Geschichte*, 139. Bultmann holds that Matthew likely omitted it because he simply did not understand it.
231. Bultmann, *Geschichte*, 139.
232. Schulz, *Q*, 96.
233. So Kloppenborg, *Formation*, 139–40.
234. See Kloppenborg, *Formation*, 121–48.
235. Bultmann, *Geschichte*, 139.
236. See, e.g., Grant and Freedman, *Secret Sayings*, 173–74; Wilson, *Studies*, 58; Schrage, *Das Verhältnis*, 172–74. Schrage admits that in this instance that there is no real evidence for dependence here upon Matthew, but he opts for this conclusion nonetheless.

once one has shown that Thomas provides a gnosticizing reading of a traditional saying,[237] it does not automatically follow that the original saying has been borrowed from the synoptic text. In a cultural context in which oral tradition must be imagined as playing a far greater role than written documents, one must first presume an oral derivation. Only if Thomas clearly bears the marks of the particular rendition of the saying found (in this case) in Matthew—Matthew's redaction of the saying—can one assert Thomas' dependence upon Matthew. As Sieber has shown, this is simply not the case.[238] First, the saying itself is not a Matthean product; almost all agree that it comes to him from the tradition.[239] If Matthew's hand is to be detected anywhere in it, it would perhaps be in the description of Jesus as πραΰς (gentle) in Matt 11:29b.[240] Yet this entire clause seems quite unknown to Thomas, along with the Matthean context in which the saying has been cast in Matthew 11. Matthew evidently knew the saying as an independent saying, which he used to complete a brief speech drawn from Q (Luke 10:21-22//Matt 11:25-27). But this speech, whose christology would have complemented Thomas' own views, occurs nowhere in Thomas. And while Thomas shares some of the material found elsewhere in this chapter, it is scattered throughout Thomas, and reflects nothing of the canonical order of these sayings.[241] Thus, far from suggesting Thomas' dependence upon Matthew, the evidence from Thom 90 stands rather clearly against this hypothesis.

Thom 91 *Knowing the Times* (Luke 12:56)[242]

91 [1]They said to him, "Tell us who you are so that we may believe in you." [2]He said to them, "You examine the face of heaven and earth, but you have not come to know the one who is in your presence, and you do not know how to examine the present moment."

237. Haenchen (*Die Botschaft*, 72-74) and Vielhauer ("ΑΝΑΠΑΥΣΙΣ") draw attention especially to the theme of ἀνάπαυσις (rest) in the saying as particularly amenable to Thomas' gnosticizing theology (cf. Thom 50 and 60). However, J.-B. Bauer ("Das milde Joch," 101-103, 106) offers an understanding of the parable that is not particularly gnostic, based upon ancient near eastern parallels. Davies (*The Gospel of Thomas*, 39) argues for an interpretation wholly in accord with Jewish wisdom theology. If Thomas is not really a gnostic gospel in the sense of later documents which carry a more characteristic gnostic mythology, there is always a question as to where to locate Thomas' thought. Thom 50 and 60 allow one to conclude, I think, that the notion of ἀνάπαυσις in Thom 90 is not to be read simply as one reads it in Matt 11:28-30; still, the challenge of Thomas is to determine how far it has moved away from related Wisdom traditions (cf. Wis 3:1-4; 4:7; 8:13, 16; Sir 51:26-27) in the direction of a more gnostic way of thinking.
238. Sieber, "Redactional Analysis," 139.
239. The provenance of the logion is debated, but that the saying has a history apart from Matthew is relatively certain—so Betz, "The Logion of the Easy Yoke," 19, siding with Bultmann (*Geschichte*, 171-72) against Dibelius (*Formgeschichte*, 279-81).
240. Barth, "Matthew's Understanding of the Law," 129-31.
241. Sieber, "Redactional Analysis," 139. The parallels are: Matt 11:7-10//Thom 78; Matt 11:11//Thom 46:1; Matt 11:27//Thom 61:3b.
242. Matt 16:2b-3 is probably a late interpolation (B, ℵ, V, X, Y, Γ, Φ, sy^c.s, sa, and bo all omit), though this is debated. If Matthew (and hence Q) did contain the saying, the remarks offered below with respect to Luke's use of the saying may be applied to the Q document as well.

A comparison of Thom 91 and Luke 12:56 shows clearly how, in the course of popular transmission, the tendencies of tradition-historical development might affect the form in which a saying is transmitted variously in different traditional circles. In Luke one can see that it has been fitted with a short introduction, making use of local, almanac-like lore (12:54-55), and then inserted into Luke's long speech on watchfulness and steadfastness in the face of the expected parousia (12:1-13:9). The speech is a Lukan composition based on two earlier Q speeches[243] and including much Lukan special material. Its presence in this context has lent to the saying a decidedly apocalyptic ring.

In Thom 91 the saying has not acquired the secondary introduction found in Luke 12:54-55. Instead, it has been cast in the simplest form of apothegm, or chreia: an interlocutor (here plural) engages the teacher with a simple question or statement requiring a response, in which context the saying is then presented. Here, the application is not apocalyptic but rather christological, insofar as the issue at stake is recognition of Jesus' person, not signs of the apocalyptic end time.[244] Furthermore, while Thomas contains some of the material Luke has included in this speech, they appear scattered throughout Thomas with no apparent relationship to their presentation in Luke.[245]

Whether one of these two applications of the saying is to be considered 'original' is debatable.[246] Both developments are entirely understandable in terms of the history of the tradition, and neither has anything to do with the other. In short, there is no compelling reason to presume dependence of one text upon the other.[247]

Thom 93 *Pearls Before Swine* (Matt 7:6-8)

93 [1]"Do not give what is holy to dogs, for they might throw them upon the dunghill. [2]Do not throw pearls [to] swine, or they might . . . it. . . ."[248]

243. Q 12:2-12 and 12:22-59; so Kloppenborg, *Formation*, 206-223.

244. This application is not necessarily gnostic (*pace* Gärtner, *Theology*, 139-40; Haenchen, *Botschaft*, 64; Schrage, *Das Verhältnis*, 176-77). After all, the issue of the proper recognition of Jesus' person comes up also in the synoptic gospels themselves (cf. Mark 8:27-30 par.)

245. The parallels are: Luke 12:2//Thom 5:1-2; 6:5-6; Luke 12:3//Thom 33:1; Luke 12:10//Thom 44; Luke 12:13-14//Thom 72; Luke 12:16-21//Thom 63; Luke 12:22-23//Thom 36; Luke 12:32-34//Thom 76; Luke 12:39//Thom 21:5; 103; Luke 12:49//Thom 10; Luke 12:51-53//Thom 16.

246. The saying alone (Luke 12:56; Thom 91:2) is understandable as a saying of secular wisdom which criticizes living always for the future while ignoring the present. If this is so, then both in Thomas and in the synoptic gospels the application of the saying should be considered secondary. In each case a secondary context has provided the interpretive key. In Luke (or Q) it is the context that gives the saying its apocalyptic spin. In Thomas, the clause ⲡⲉⲧⲛ̅ⲡⲉⲧⲛ̅ⲙ̅ⲧⲟ ⲉⲃⲟⲗ ⲙ̅ⲡⲉⲧⲛ̅ⲥⲟⲩⲱⲛϥ (You have not recognized the one who is before you.) gives the saying a distinctly christological slant.

247. Sieber ("Redactional Analysis," 219-21) uncovers no redactional traces from Luke (or Matthew).

248. The text is defective. Among proposals for its restoration are the following: "bring it [to naught]!" (Leipoldt, *Das Evangelium nach Thomas*) and "grind it [to bits]!" (Layton, ed. *Nag Hammadi Codex II*).

The case for viewing Thomas as preserving an independent tradition is quite clear. On the one hand, even Schrage admits that at the redaction-critical level there is no evidence that Thomas has made use of Matthew.[249] On the other hand, from a tradition-historical perspective the evidence against a relationship of dependence is overwhelming. Both versions of this saying represent a development of an earlier double-stich wisdom saying, but with results that agree neither in form nor in content. In Matt 7:6 the final μήποτε (lest . . .) clause is a secondary expansion,[250] emphasizing the ingratitude and infidelity of those against whom it polemicizes. In Thom 93, on the other hand, the saying has been expanded with a comment upon each of the two halves, both of which focus on the waste of the object given. Such differences indicate that one has to do here with two streams of tradition, each with its own history.

Thom 96 *The Leaven* (Luke 13:20–21//Matt 13:33, Q)

96 ¹Jesus [said], "The Father's kingdom is like [a] woman. ²She took a little yeast, [hid] it in dough, and made it into large loaves of bread. ³Whoever has ears should listen."

The chief argument for Thomas' dependence upon the canonical texts here has been the fact that Thomas agrees with Matthew in casting the parable's introduction in the form of a statement, rather than a rhetorical question as one finds in Luke.[251] But while it is true that most have followed Bultmann in supposing Luke to have preserved the original introduction to this Q parable,[252] Thomas' agreement with Matthew on this point is not decisive. Bultmann's view is no doubt based upon his judgment that there is within the tradition a *general tendency* to reformulate rhetorical questions as negative statements.[253] That is, even though Matthew has likely recast his introduction to this parable as a statement, this does not belong solely to the redactional hand of Matthew. As Schrage admits, it is entirely possible that Thomas would have similarly reformulated the introduction quite independently from Matthew.[254] Moreover, while it may be a general tendency of the tradition to evolve in this way, Bultmann carefully notes that this cannot be considered a hard and fast rule. One observes the opposite development, for example, in the case of Mark 3:27//Matt 12:29.[255] Thus, it is entirely possible that Matthew

249. Schrage, *Das Verhältnis*, 179. The tentative suggestion that Thomas' use of κοπρια (dunghill) in 93:1 shows the influence of Luke 14:35 simply because the latter is a New Testament *hapax legomenon* is not compelling. Neither do similarities at the level of the Coptic translation provide a foundation for discovering dependence at the point of translation; they pale in comparison with the extensive differences which separate them, in terms both of content and of translational technique.

250. Bultmann, *Geschichte*, 85.

251. Schrage, *Das Verhältnis*, 184; Chilton, "The Gospel According to Thomas," 158.

252. Bultmann, *Geschichte*, 186; see also Schulz, *Q*, 307, n. 330.

253. Bultmann, *Geschichte*, 97.

254. Schrage, *Das Verhältnis*, 184.

255. Bultmann, *Geschichte*, 97.

and Thomas in fact preserve an original indicative introduction here, which Luke has reformulated interrogatively.

There are, on the other hand, more positive indications that Thomas' version of this parable derives from a non- synoptic source. For example, one secondary feature in the Q version not shared by Thom 96 is the extraordinarily large amount of flour ("three measures"), which Jeremias speculates is influenced by Gen 18:6 (MT).[256] More telling may be the context in which each version of the parable is to be found. Here again different traditions have produced different results. On the synoptic side, the tradition has produced what Jeremias refers to as a "double parable,"[257] the Parable of the Leaven having circulated together with the Mustard Seed (Luke 13:18-21//Matt 13:31-32) at least as early as Q. In Thomas its transmission has brought about different results. Here it is part of a small collection of parables (Thom 96-98), which has probably come to Thomas bound together by a common subject matter: "the Father's kingdom." The Mustard Seed occurs independently in Thomas (cf. Thom 20).

Thom 99 *True Relatives* (Matt 12:46-50//Mark 3:31-35//Luke 8:19-21)

99 [1]The disciples said to him, "Your brothers and your mother are standing outside." [2]He said to them, "Those here who do what my Father wants are my brothers and my mother. [3]They are the ones who will enter the kingdom of my Father."

Thomas and Mark share the basic elements of a simple chreia: an independent saying (Thom 99:2; Mark 3:34b-35)[258] preceded by a brief situational introduction (Thom 99:1; Mark 3:31-32).[259] Beyond this Mark's version shows a further degree of development, in that a preliminary rhetorical question has been added to Jesus' response (Mark 3:33),[260] as well as a gesture (Mark 3:34a).[261] But these are not necessarily to be assigned to Markan redac-

---

256. Jeremias, *Gleichnisse Jesu*, 27.
257. Jeremias, *Gleichnisse Jesu*, 89.
258. Cf. Matt 12:49b-50//Luke 8:21.
259. Cf. Matt 12:46-49a//Luke 8:19-20. Bultmann (*Geschichte*, 29) and Dibelius (*Formgeschichte*, 150, n. 80) both hold that an earlier form of the apophthegm circulated with only vs 34b as its conclusion. Verse 35 is secondary, so it is argued, since it stands in tension to vss 31-34, in that not everyone present in this situation might be considered "doers of God's will." If this analysis is correct, then it might be argued that Thomas' version (and Luke's) is a further development based on Mark, since it fuses the two originally distinct logia into a single saying. But for vs 35 to pose problems of this sort one must assume a setting for the apophthegm similar to Mark's, where, on the heels of the Beelzebul controversy, the crowd at the scene must contain both friend and foe. However, Thomas' version serves as a reminder of how artificial this setting really is. In a version such as Thom 99, both Mark 3:34b and 3:35 would be entirely appropriate, since only an elite (ⲙ̄ⲙⲁⲑⲏⲧⲏⲥ) is present. Thus, with no real reason to view vs 35 as secondary, I am inclined to view vss 34b-35 as the original point of the apophthegm, though probably in the multiply attested single-sentence Thomas form (cf. 2 Clem 9:11 and the Gospel of the Ebionites, frg. 5 [Epiphanius, *Haer* 30.14.5]).
260. Cf. Matt 12:48.
261. Cf. Matt 12:49.

tion, for they belong to the sort of elaboration one would expect in the telling of a story. Mark's hand may be seen perhaps in the introduction of a crowd (ὄχλος), which reports the presence of Jesus' relatives "outside": 1) the ὄχλος is first introduced to the scene in Mark redactionally (3:20);[262] 2) it is introduced only with difficulty: not everyone in the crowd (which presumably encompasses everyone mentioned in the scene thus far, including the opponents in the Beelzebul controversy) would fall under the designation ὃς ἂν ποιήσῃ τὸ θέλημα τοῦ θεοῦ (whoever does the will of my father).[263] In Thomas one finds neither the tradition-historical developments nor the redactional elements occurring in Mark. Dependence on Mark, then, seems to be ruled out.

Difficulties arise, however, when one turns to Matt 12:46–50 and Luke 8:19–21. On the one hand, Matthew and Thomas agree on the reading "will of *my father*" (πατρός μου = ⲡⲗⲉⲓⲱⲧ). On the other hand, both Thomas and Luke lack Mark's rhetorical question, and the gesture (Mark 31:33–34). Moreover, Luke has a version of the saying itself that is similar to Thomas' in that both present the gist of it in a single sentence, over against Mark's two-sentence formulation in 3:34b–35 (cf. Luke 8:21). But this should not lead to the conclusion that Thomas has produced a conflation of all three synoptic accounts. Both the reading πατρός μου and the single sentence version of the saying at the end occur independently in 2 Clem 9:11, and in the Gospel of the Ebionites (Epiphanius *Haer.* 30.14.5).[264] These elements, then, could well have come from a parallel tradition, which Matthew, Luke, and Thomas drew upon independently.[265] The same can be said regarding Thomas and Luke lacking Mark's gesture and the rhetorical question. These are secondary features in Mark's account; the less embellished Thomas and Lukan versions must surely derive from a less developed, parallel tradition. Thomas, of course, has its own secondary features, for example, the addition of the final clause: ⲛ̄ⲧⲟⲟⲩ ⲡⲉ ⲉⲧⲛⲁⲃⲱⲕ ⲉϩⲟⲩⲛ ⲉⲧⲙⲛ̄ⲧⲉⲣⲟ ⲙ̄ⲡⲁⲉⲓⲱⲧ (It is they who will enter the kingdom of my Father). But this does not prove dependence upon the synoptic texts. It simply indicates that there was a degree of secondary development in Thomas' parallel tradition-history as well.

Thom 100 *Render to Caesar* (Matt 22:15–22//Mark 12:13–17//Luke 20:20–26)

100 ¹They showed Jesus a gold coin and said to him, "Caesar's people demand taxes from us." ²He said to them, "Give Caesar what belongs to Caesar, give God what belongs to God, and give me what is mine."

262. Regarding vs 20 as redactional see Laufen, *Doppelüberlieferung,* 150, n. 180.
263. Cf. n. 259.
264. So Koester *Synoptische Überlieferung,* 86–88, 109–10.
265. Wilson, *Studies,* 115–16; and Sieber, "Redactional Analysis," 152. It is noteworthy that in Luke's single-sentence version of the logion, only the phrase "hear the word of God and do it" might be considered particularly Lukan (so Conzelmann, *Theology,* 231). But it is precisely here that Thomas, against Luke, agrees with 2 Clem. 9:11 and the Gospel of the Ebionites, frg. 5. This suggests very strongly the existence of a parallel tradition.

Thomas' third clause ⲁⲩⲱ ⲡⲉⲧⲉ ⲡⲱⲉⲓ ⲡⲉ ⲙⲁⲧⲛ̄ⲛⲁⲉⲓϥ (and give me what is mine) probably represents a secondary development over against the synoptic versions of this saying. But this secondary feature neither proves nor suggests that Thomas is dependent upon Mark 12:13–17 or its parallels. For, even if one could be sure that the Thomas version is the result of the redaction of a simpler form of the saying,[266] it would still be necessary to prove that Thomas' editor added the phrase to one of the synoptic versions of the saying, and not to a version available to him or her from the oral tradition. Schrage argues that such evidence may be found in the fact that Thomas, in the query about taxes, uses the word ϣⲱⲙ, which normally translates the Greek word $\phi\acute{o}\rho os$ (taxes). This would mean that Thomas apparently follows Luke, who substitutes $\phi\acute{o}\rho os$ (Luke 20:22) for Mark's $\kappa\hat{\eta}\nu\sigma os$ (taxes) (Mark 12:14). But this is not decisive. The two Greek words are virtually synonyms;[267] thus, a host of possibilities might account for the apparent similarity. The choice of $\phi\acute{o}\rho os$ over $\kappa\hat{\eta}\nu\sigma os$, or vice versa, need not be the result of deliberate redactional alteration, but rather little more than caprice. If we can be sure that Thomas' ϣⲱⲙ (taxes) in fact translates $\phi\acute{o}\rho os$ (and not $\kappa\hat{\eta}\nu\sigma os$),[268] Thomas could still have arrived at his rendition of the saying apart from Luke.

When one considers the question in terms of the broader tradition-historical picture, an autonomous Thomas tradition seems likely. Thomas' text presents us with the simplest form of chreia: a single saying with a brief contextualizing introduction. The synoptic version of this pericope is a much more highly developed apophthegm. It is a controversy dialogue, full of the sort of embellishment and detail a skilled storyteller might provide, yet clearly secondary to the primitive version found in Thomas. Of particular note is the presence of the Pharisees and Herodians (Mark 12:13),[269] Mark's stereo-typical opponents, sent to entrap Jesus in his discourse. In Thomas' version nothing is said of opponents at all.

Thom 107 *The Lost Sheep* (Luke 15:3–7//Matt 18:12–14, Q)

107 [1]Jesus said, "The kingdom is like a shepherd who had a hundred sheep. [2]One of them, the largest, went astray. He left the ninety-nine and sought the one until he found it. [3]After he had toiled, he said to the sheep, 'I love you more than the ninety-nine.'"

---

266. It is not clear how this phrase would reflect the theology of Thomas, even though it has attracted much fanciful interpretation on the basis of this hypothesis. Schrage (*Das Verhältnis*, 190- 91) correctly rejects the interpretation of Grant and Freedman (*Secret Sayings*, 174) and Wilson (*Theology*, 27), who argue that it allows Thomas to cast God here in the role of the gnostic demiurge. As Schrage points out, nowhere in Thomas does one hear of the gnostic demiurge; to detect it here would be entirely speculative.

267. The Coptic word ϩⲱⲧⲉ (taxes) is used to translate either $\phi\acute{o}\rho os$ or $\kappa\hat{\eta}\nu\sigma os$.

268. Though Crum (*Coptic Dictionary*) does not attest an instance in which ϣⲱⲙ translates $\kappa\hat{\eta}\nu\sigma os$, the latter's meaning is so close to $\phi\acute{o}\rho os$ that it would certainly not be out of the question.

269. Luke substitutes the "scribes and chief priests"; Matthew drops the Herodians.

Again the chief arguments for Thomas' dependence on the synoptic versions of this parable come from Schrage.[270] He points out that both Luke and Thomas share the phrase "until he finds (found) it" (Luke 15:4; Thom 107:2). But it is not clear that this phrase derives from Lukan redaction of the parable,[271] and thus it cannot be used to link Thomas specifically with Luke. Likewise, the fact that Thomas and Luke similarly describe the shepherd's ownership of the sheep[272] is not probative, since it is likely that Luke's participial construction comes from Q.[273] On the Matthean side, Schrage argues that the common reference to "seeking" in Matt 18:12 and Thom 107:2 indicates Thomas' knowledge of Matthew. But this detail does not come from Matthew's own pen, but from his source Q,[274] and thus does not prove Thomas' dependence upon Matthew. Schrage also notes that both Thomas and Matthew lack the question $\tau i s$ $\check{\alpha}\nu\theta\rho\omega\pi os$ $\dot{\epsilon}\xi$ $\dot{\upsilon}\mu\hat{\omega}\nu$ (Who among you?). But while this traditional prophetic formulation may well have been in Matthew's Q source,[275] it seems more likely that Luke has borrowed this traditional phrase to provide an effective link between the parable and the Lukan introduction to the parable found in Luke 15:1-3.[276] Thus, its absence in Matthew is probably not redactional, but traditional. Little wonder then that he shares this feature with Thomas.

While Thomas seems consistently to reproduce Q (or the tradition it preserves) rather than Matthew or Luke, it lacks specifically those redactional elements so important to each synoptic version's distinctive character. Matthew's hand may be seen chiefly in the way the entire parable is recast into the legal-sounding *Conditionalis*,[277] a characteristic seen throughout Matthew 18. Thomas retains the declarative/narrative form original to the parable. Luke has added the introduction (15:1-3)[278] and the elaboration upon the shepherd's joy in 15:5-6.[279] Yet these too are missing from the Thomas version.

Finally, both Matthew and Luke provide this parable with a secondary allegorical interpretation: Matthew reads it in terms of God's concern that none might stray from the community (Matt 18:14); Luke in terms of God's joy over new members (Luke 15:7). Both are secondary developments to be

---

270. Schrage, *Das Verhältnis*, 194; cf. Chilton, "The Gospel According to Thomas," 158.

271. Bussmann (*Studien*, 86; *contra* Schulz, *Q*, 388) holds that Luke here preserves the original Q. Schulz's judgment that Luke's own hand may be seen here is based upon the nice parallelism created when this phrase is followed by $\kappa\alpha\dot{\imath}$ $\epsilon\dot{\upsilon}\rho\dot{\omega}\nu$ (and finding) in 15:5. But precisely this parallelism is missing in Thomas.

272. $\check{\epsilon}\chi\omega\nu$ (having) in Luke 15:4 = ⲉⲩⲛ̄ⲧⲁϥ in Thom 107:1.

273. So Schulz, *Q*, 387.

274. Schulz, *Q*, 388, citing Harnack, *Sayings*, 92; Jülicher, *Gleichnisreden* 2. 330.

275. Schulz, *Q*, 387; Schulz notes its traditional nature, and thus surmises that it was not invented, at any rate, by Luke.

276. It is generally agreed that this introduction is Lukan; so Schulz, *Q*, 387, citing Jülicher, *Gleichnisreden* 2. 314-15; Bultmann, *Geschichte*, 209, 360, among others.

277. Schulz, *Q*, 387.

278. See n. 000.

279. Schulz, *Q*, 388.

assigned to the redaction of the evangelists.[280] In this respect, at least, Thomas' non-allegorized version is more primitive, and hardly dependent on Matthew or Luke. Montefiore sees secondary development in the shepherd's direct address of the sheep, reflecting a shift to a gnostic ecclesiastical situation.[281] But since Thomas, unlike Matthew and Luke, includes no explicit interpretation of the parable, it is impossible to know what this particular detail in Thomas might have meant. It may simply serve to heighten the pathos, by providing an emotional rationale for the shepherd's rather irresponsible action.[282]

2. Synoptic Siblings

If one accepts the proposition that most of the synoptic tradition had a history prior to and after its use by the synoptic gospels and that the synoptic texts themselves were therefore not the only source of this material for other early Christian authors, then the assertion that an author or collector like the one who assembled Thomas used the synoptic gospels as sources must be supported with a substantial amount of word-for-word agreement between the texts in question. It is not enough to demonstrate a common structure, or the use of a common figure. There must be some tangible evidence that "a" copied "b." If there is none, one is left to assume that both authors simply had similar backgrounds and thus came to hear the same stories and traditions and write them down independently.

"Synoptic siblings" are Thomas sayings with synoptic parallels which do not stand up to this test for literary dependence. They may share a common outline, perhaps key terminology, but in the end these pairs simply do not show the kind of verbal correspondence that points to the literary dependence of one text upon the other. In many cases the theory of literary dependence is rendered even more dubious by a saying's relationship to a common *topos*, popular among early Christian writers or in the literary and philosophical environment. The more widespread a tradition is, the more one must reckon with the likelihood that two or more early Christian authors made use of it independently.

Thom 3:1–3/113 *The Kingdom Within You/When will the Kingdom Come?* (cf. Luke 17:20–21; Matt 24:23–28)

3 [1]Jesus said, "If your leaders say to you, 'Look, the kingdom is in the sky,' then the birds of the sky will precede you. [2]If they say to you, 'It is in the sea,' then the fish will precede you. [3]Rather, the kingdom is within you and it is outside you."[283]

280. Schulz, *Q*, 389. Jeremias prefers Luke's version as the more the original here (*Gleichnisse Jesu*, 132–34). Yet by his own criteria, the allegorical interpretation should be considered secondary (see *Gleichnisse Jesu*, 64–88).
281. Montefiore, "A Comparison," 233–34.
282. Cf. Jeremias, *Gleichnisse Jesu*, 133.
283. The extant Greek version of Thom 3:1–3 (POxy 654.9–21) reads:

113 ¹His disciples said to him, "When will the kingdom come?" ²"It will not come by watching for it. ³It will not be said, 'Look, here' or 'Look, there.' ⁴Rather, the Father's kingdom is spread out upon the earth, and people do not see it."

Both of these Thomas sayings are closely related to Luke 17:20–21. The final dominical saying in Thom 3:3 ("Rather, the kingdom is within you [cм̅пети2оуи] and it is outside of you.") is likely a variant of Luke 17:21b: "for behold, the kingdom of God is in the midst of you." (ἐντὸς ὑμῶν ἐστιν). But apart from this final clause the two sayings have virtually no verbal correspondence, so that a direct literary relationship between them can be ruled out. Thom 113 is related to Luke 17:20–21 through the notion that one should be wary of those who say of the kingdom, "Lo, here it is," or, "Lo, there," but this is not enough to suggest literary dependence of one upon the other. Each introduces the motif quite differently, and each follows it with a different dominical saying. With both Thom 3 and 113, we have to reckon with a common oral tradition shared at some level with Luke 17:20–21, but nothing more.

In addition, Thom 3:1–2 may share a tradition with Matt 24:23–28, where Matthew augments Mark 13:21–23 (cf. Matt 24:23–25) with a warning against those who would locate the kingdom in a specific place (Matt 24:26). This is comparable to what one finds in Thom 3:1–2, but any generative relationship between the two is unlikely. The Thomas saying is a burlesque of a popular Jewish motif of seeking after wisdom in the furthest reaches of the universe (cf. Job 28:12–15; Bar 3:29–4:1),²⁸⁴ and of speculation about who will be first in the resurrection of the dead (cf. TestJud 25:1–2; 1 QS II, 19–25).²⁸⁵ It is therefore generated out of a popular *topos* with which Matt 24:26 has nothing in common.

Thom 8 *The Wise Fisher* (cf. Matt 13:47–50)

8 ¹And he said, "The human one is like a wise fisherman who cast his net into the sea and drew it up from the sea full of little fish. ²Among them the wise fisherman discovered a fine large fish. ³He threw all the little fish back into the sea, and instinctively chose the large fish."

One may question whether the same parable lies at the base of both texts at all.²⁸⁶ Although attempts to explain Thom 8 as a radically altered gnostic

---

¹Jesus said, "[If] your leaders [say to you, 'Look,] the kingdom is in the sky,' then the birds of the sky [will precede you. ²If they say] that it is under the earth, then the fish of the sea [will enter preceding] you. ³And the [kingdom of God] is within you [and outside (you)]."

284. So Glasson, "The Gospel of Thomas Saying 3," 151–52; Davies, *The Gospel of Thomas*, 41–46.

285. So Lelyveld, *Les logia de la vie*, 124–25.

286. E.g., J.-B. Bauer ("The Synoptic Tradition," 315) argues that Thomas' parable is based not on Matt 13:47–50 or a version thereof but the parable of the pearl in Matt 13:45, and that it draws upon a proverb later quoted by Clement of Alexandria: "Among many small pearls will be a large one, and in a fishing net with many fishes will be the 'beautiful fish'" (Strom. 1.16.3). It is quite possible, however, that Clement's words are inspired by Thom 8 and 76.

adaptation of Matt 13:47–50 have been cleverly conceived, they have proven unconvincing and impossible to place on solid empirical grounds, since they have assumed a fully developed gnostic mythology in Thomas,[287] for which Thomas itself offers little support. One could perhaps conjecture that an earlier parable about making the right choices (Thom 8) has been allegorized in Matthew to herald the coming final judgment (Matt 13:49–50). However, given the widespread attestation of the fisher as a parabolic *topos*,[288] it seems best to assume that the two passages have no more than an "ancestral" relationship: the two traditions use the common *topos* independently.

Thom 11:1 *Heavens Pass Away* (cf. Matt 24:35a//Mark 13:31a//Luke 21:33a; Luke 16:17a// Matt 5:18a, Mark/Q overlap)

11 ¹*Jesus said, "This heaven will pass away, and the one above it will pass away.* ²The dead are not alive, and the living will not die. ³During the days when you ate what is dead, you made it alive. When you are in the light, what will you do? ⁴On the day when you were one, you became two. But when you become two, what will you do?"

It is debatable whether Thom 11:1 and its synoptic parallels should be considered a saying in its own right at all. In Mark and Q it appears simply as a proverbial cliché hyperbolic in character, the point of which is to emphasize the utter durability of that to which it is attached.[289] If Thom 11:1 is a form of this saying at all, in Thomas it has has ceased to function hyperbolically and serves instead as a revelatory saying of the divine emissary. In the end, it may only be said that Thomas, Mark, and Q share a common figure (the passing of heaven and earth). The fact that it was common enough in the early Christian tradition to be used by both Mark and Q, together with the very different ways in which Thomas and the synoptics make use of this figure, make literary dependence quite unlikely.

Thom 22:1–3 *Kingdom and Children*
(cf. Matt 19:13–15//Mark 10:13–16//Luke 18:15–17; Matt 18:2)

22 ¹*Jesus saw some babies nursing. ²He said to his disciples, "These nursing babies are like those who enter the kingdom." ³They said to him, "Then shall we enter the kingdom as babies?"* ⁴Jesus said to them, "When you make the two into one, and when you make the inner like the outer and the outer like the inner, and the upper like the lower, ⁵and when you make male and female into a single one, so that the male will not be male nor the female be female, ⁶when you make eyes in place of an eye, a hand in place of a hand, a foot in place of a foot, an image in place of an image, ⁷then you will enter [the kingdom]."

---

287. E.g., Grant and Freedman, *Secret Sayings*, 127; Lindemann, "Zur Gleichnisinterpretation," 216–19; Schoedel, "Parables in the Gospel of Thomas," 553.
288. Cf. Aesop, Fable 4 (Perry, *Babrius and Phaedrus*, 9–10); Herodotus, *Hist.* 1.141.
289. Cf. esp. Luke 16:17.

Though all of these sayings express a common idea—children as exemplary figures—they are really quite different in the way they present the notion. While Thomas uses the indicative form, all of the synoptic versions use the imperative, presenting the saying as a legal saying. All use the presence of a child as the "occasion" for the saying, but otherwise their settings are different: in Thomas, Jesus happens upon children being suckled; in Mark 10:13-16, par. the children are brought to Jesus in a wave of popular piety; in Matt 18:1-4 a child is not present at all, but must be summoned. Thus, though there is undoubtedly some relationship between these brief chreiai, there turns out to be almost no verbal agreement between Thomas' version and any of the synoptic texts. Literary dependence therefore seems unlikely.

**Thom 25 *Love Your Brother* (cf. Matt 22:39//Mark 12:31//Luke 10:27b;
Matt 19:19; also Gal 5:14; Rom 13:9; Jas 2:8; Did 1:2; Barn 19:5)**

25 ¹Jesus said, "Love your brother like your own soul, ²protect him like the pupil of your eye."

This sort of allusion to or quotation of Lev 19:18 is so common in early Christian and non-Christian Jewish circles[290] that there is no *a priori* reason for assuming that Thomas' author/editor has borrowed Thom 25 from the synoptic gospels. In such circumstances the literal correspondence between Thomas and any of the synoptic versions of the saying would have to be very strong in order to support a thesis of literary dependence. This is not the case. Thomas' version is distinguished from all of the versions listed above in that it less faithfully reproduces the LXX text; and Thomas adds of a second parallel stich: "protect him like the pupil of your eye," which perhaps draws on biblical phraseology.[291]

Thom 32 *The Mountain City* (cf. Matt 5:14b)

32 Jesus said, "A city built upon a high hill and fortified cannot fall, nor can it be hidden."[292]

It has been asserted frequently that Thomas here has created a new saying by mixing elements from Matt 5:14b and 7:24-25.[293] But beyond the common vocabulary—οἰκοδομεῖν (build) (Matt 7:24; cf. POxy 1 [horiz.] 36-37) and πίπειν (to fall) (Matt 7:25; cf. POxy 1 [horiz.] 39-40)—it is not clear how to relate the latter to the discussion of Thom 32. It deals, after all, with houses,

---

290. Strack and Billerbeck, *Kommentar*, 1. 907-8.
291. Cf. Deut 32:10; Ps 17:8; Prov 7:2; Sir 17:22. The second stich would have to be considered secondary from a form-critical point of view. But this, of course, says nothing about the logion's relationship to its synoptic parallels; only that within the tradition-historical stream upon which Thomas draws, the saying developed this secondary characteristic.
292. The extant Greek version of this saying (POxy 1 [horiz.]. 36-41) reads:
Jesus said, "A city built on top of a high hill and fortified can neither fall nor be hidden."
293. See, e.g., Haenchen, *Botschaft*, 38; Schrage, *Das Verhältnis*, 78; Kasser, *L' Évangile selon Thomas*, 66.

not cities. Since such language is also readily applicable to cities,[294] there is no need to conclude that it comes from Matt 7:24-25.

Assessing the relationship of Thom 32 to Matt 5:14b is more difficult. Kasser rightly points out that the combined effect of the parallelism in Thom 32 is awkward[295] . The two concepts are neither opposite nor complementary. Furthermore, structurally the saying seems not to have been conceived as a *parallelismus membrorum*. Rather, "nor can it be hidden" (Coptic: ογλε cνλϣ ϩωπ λν; cf. POxy 1[horiz.] 40-41: οὔτε κρυ[β]ῆναι) seems to have been added almost as an afterthought. If so, then it may be necessary to reckon with relatively late influence from the synoptic text. The original form of the saying in Thomas will have read simply: . . .οὐ πεσεῖν δύναται (cannot fall). A later scribe would have created the οὔτε . . . οὔτε (neither . . .nor) construction and added κρυβῆναι (to hide) from Matt 5:14b. Beyond this, there is no apparent literary relationship between Thom 32 and Matt 5:14b. (On the issue of the proximity of Thom 32 and 33:2-3 [cf. Matt 5:14 and 15], see under "twins," p. 32.)

Thom 36 *What You Shall Wear* (cf. Luke 12:22-30//Matt 6:25-33, Q)

36 Jesus said, "Do not worry, from morning to evening and from evening to morning, about what you are going to wear."[296]

There is no evidence that Thomas' author/editor knew the Matthean or Lukan version of this saying and abbreviated it. First, the very close verbal correspondence between Matthew and Luke throughout the speech "On Cares" makes it relatively certain that both evangelists drew this material from Q. To show, then, that Thomas drew this saying from Matthew or Luke, as opposed to Q, or even from a still older source, one would have to show that Thomas reflects some redactional alteration deriving from the hand of one of the two evangelists. As Sieber has shown, this is not the case.[297] It is obviously a very old tradition, and therefore might have been known to Thomas through a variety of channels. Secondly, the word-for-word correspondence between Thom 36 and the synoptic text here is only slight. Even the longer Oxyrhynchus version shares only a few key words with the synoptic text and it constructs the shared notions quite differently.[298] Finally, Thom 36 should be

---

294. Sieber, "Redactional Analysis," 43-44.
295. Kasser, *L'Évangile selon Thomas*, 66.
296. The extant Greek version of this saying (POxy 655, col 1.1-17) reads:
¹[Jesus says, "Do not worry] from morning [to evening nor] from [evening to] morning, either [about] your [food], what [you will] eat, [or] about [your clothing], what you [will] wear. ²[You are much] better than the lilies, which neither card nor [spin]. ³As for you, when you have no garment, what [will you put] on? ⁴Who might add to your stature? That very one will give you your garment."
297. Sieber, "Redactional Analysis," 63-67. The synoptic versions diverge only on minor points (cf. Schulz, *Q*, 149-52), none of which finds correspondence in Thomas.
298. Cf. POxy 655, col. 1. 3-7: different in Thomas are the use of the μήτε . . . μήτε (neither . . . nor) construction; the use of [τῇ τροφῇ] . . . τῇ στ[ολῇ (food . . . clothing) (cf. τῇ ψυχῇ . . . τῷ σώματι [life . . . body] in Luke 12:22//Matt 6:25, Q); and in lns. 7-8: πολλῷ

considered common secular wisdom, promoting a position familiar especially in Cynic circles,[299] and available to Thomas from many sources, both Christian and non-Christian. For these reasons, it is possible to posit a shared ancestral traditional relationship between these two sayings, but nothing more.

Thom 40 *A Plant Rooted Up* (cf. Matt 15:13)

40 Jesus said, "A grapevine has been planted apart from the Father. Since it is not strong, it will be pulled up by its root and perish."

I agree with Schrage, who sees here only "a loose connection with Matt 15:13."[300] Matthew no doubt picked up this saying from the tradition as an independent saying; there is no reason why Thomas could not have come across a similar saying independently.

Thom 43 *Tree and Fruit* (cf. Luke 6:43–44a//Matt 7:16a, 17–18, Q; Matt 12:33)

43 ¹His disciples said to him, "Who are you to say these things to us?" ²"You do not understand who I am from what I say to you. ³Rather, you have become like the Jews, for they love the tree but hate its fruit, or they love the fruit but hate the tree."

Both Thomas and the synoptics use a (presumably) popular figure here, a metaphor built upon the consistency of the relationship between a tree and its fruit. However, the actual sayings formulated in Thomas and Matthew/Luke respectively are quite different. Thom 43 reproves the sort of person who would accept the benefits (of association with the Jesus movement?), while rejecting either the direct consequences deriving therefrom (they love the tree, but hate the fruit) or its necessary presuppositions (they hate the tree, but love the fruit). The synoptic version, on the other hand, stresses the inevitable connection between what one is (tree), and what one does (fruit).

Beyond these differences, the long tradition-history behind the synoptic version makes it unlikely that Thomas' dependence upon the synoptic gospels here could ever be demonstrated with any degree of certainty. Working backwards from Luke 6:43–44a//Matt 7:16a, 17–18, it is likely that both Matthew and Luke found this pericope already in Q, which in turn probably inherited it

---

κρεί[σσοντ]ές ἐ[στε] (You are much better) (cf. πόσῳ μᾶλλον ὑμεῖς διαφέρετε [Of how much more value are you] in Luke 12:24, and οὐχ ὑμεῖς μᾶλλον διαφέρετε αὐτῶν [Are you not of more value than they?] in Matt 6:26). Noteworthy also is the poetic construction, "from morning until evening and from evening until morning," for which there is no synoptic equivalent. Still, the common order shared by POxy 655 and Q (both mention first food, then clothing, and then a third source of anxiety–in Thomas, one's "stature," in Q, one's life-span) is striking. It is possible that a shared tradition lies somewhere in the background. It is also possible there has been some residual influence from the synoptic text on the Oxyrhynchus version of Thomas, which, for whatever reason, fails to show up in the Nag Hammadi version.

299. See, e.g., Ps.-Diogenes, 7, 32; Ps.-Crates, 9, 30; Seneca, *Ep. mor.* 20.9.
300. Schrage, *Das Verhältnis*, 95.

as part of the Sermon tradition.[301] It is obviously a very old tradition. Thus, any similarities between Thom 43 and its parallel in Matthew and Luke would guarantee nothing more than an ancestral relationship deriving from some point in the saying's long tradition-history. Even the close proximity of Thom 43:3 to 45:1 (cf. Luke 6:44b//Matt 7:16b) could suggest no more than this, since these two sayings were transmitted together already in Q, and probably earlier. The secondary elements to be found in the Thomas version of the saying, but not in the synoptic versions, indicate that the two branches of the tradition must have gone their separate ways early on.[302] They do not necessarily indicate that Thomas knew and used the synoptic text.

Thom 64 *The Supper* (cf. Luke 14:15-24//Matt 22:1-14, Q)

64 ¹Jesus said, "A person was receiving guests. When he had prepared the dinner, he sent his slave to invite the guests. ²The slave went to the first and said to him, 'My master invites you.' ³That one said, 'Some merchants owe me money; they are coming to me tonight. I must go and give them instructions. Please excuse me from dinner.' ⁴The slave went to another and said to him, 'My master has invited you.' ⁵He said to the slave, 'I have bought a house, and I have been called away for a day. I shall have no time.' ⁶The slave went to another and said to him, 'My master invites you.' ⁷He said to the slave, 'My friend is to be married, and I am to arrange the dinner. I shall not be able to come. Please excuse me from dinner.' ⁸The slave went to another and said to him, 'My master invites you.' ⁹He said to the slave, 'I have bought an estate, and I am going to collect the rent. I shall not be able to come. Please excuse me.' ¹⁰The slave returned and said to his master, 'Those whom you invited to dinner have asked to be excused.' ¹¹The master said to his slave, 'Go out on the streets, and bring back whomever you find to have dinner.' ¹²Buyers and merchants [will] not enter the places of my Father."

Though Thom 64 presents yet another version of Q's Parable of the Supper, there is almost no verbal correspondence between Thomas and the versions of the story found in either Matthew or Luke. Even Schrage finds virtually no basis for comparison here.[303] In addition to the notable lack of any textual correspondence, the case for Thomas' independence may be supplemented with the form-critical observation that while both Matthew and Luke present the parable as an allegory for their respective views of salvation history,[304] Thomas preserves the story without any allegorical interpretation at all. In this respect it is to be considered primary. Of course, Thomas' parable shows

---

301. See my similar remarks with regard to Thom 26, 34, 45, 54, and 68-69 under "twins.".
302. The polemical application of the parable ("but you have become like the Jews") in the Thomas version is to be seen as secondary; it indicates that at some point in the Thomas trajectory the logion had been taken up and used in the primitive church's conflict with the synagogue. This is not, however, the way in which Thomas himself uses it. Thomas' own introduction, which introduces the disciples into the scene, represents yet another subsequent stage in this development: the saying is now being used by Thomas Christianity in its quarrel with other Christian groups.
303. Schrage, *Das Verhältnis*, 133-36.
304. So Bultmann, *Geschichte*, 189; Jeremias, *Gleichnisse Jesu*, 65-67.

secondary development of its own, such as the possible addition of a fourth excuse[305] and the interpretive comment added as a conclusion: "Businessmen and merchants will not enter the places of my Father." But these show only that the Thomas version of the parable is also the product of a considerable tradition-history; they in no way suggest the dependence of Thomas upon the synoptic gospels.

Thom 78:1-3 *Why Have You Come Out?* (cf. Luke 7:24-27// Matt 11:7-10, Q)

78 ¹Jesus said, "Why have you come out to the countryside? To see a reed shaken by the wind? ²And to see a person dressed in soft clothes, [like your] rulers and your powerful ones? ³They are dressed in soft clothes, and they cannot understand truth."

Although Thom 78 obviously stems ultimately from the same tradition as the Q passage taken up in Luke 7:24-27 and Matt 11:7-10, the differences between them are enough to suggest strongly that here again we may see two entirely different tradition histories at work. Chief of these is the fact that in Thomas the saying is in no way associated with John the Baptist. If one notes that Thomas elsewhere freely discusses John (see Thom 46), together with the very plastic way in which the tradition in Q has been made to refer to John,[306] it seems very unlikely that Thomas has taken a saying that originally referred to John and recast it to refer now to Jesus.[307] Rather, in Thomas we probably encounter the saying in its more original form. Other differences, though less momentous, serve further to underscore the general autonomy of the Thomas tradition here: 1) Thomas' first question clearly ends with ⲧⲥⲱϣⲉ (countryside) (cf. the ambiguity of the synoptic formulation). 2) Thomas' second question does not include the repetitive "What then did you go out to see?" 3) The respective points scored by Thomas and Q in this second question are quite different. In Q the point is that if you are looking for fine clothes, you are in the wrong place. In Thomas it is that, contrary to popular wisdom, clothes

---

305. Crossan, *Four Other Gospels,* 40-43. Crossan holds that the second invitation/response has been added late. It is distinguished from the other three invitation/response sequences by its use of the past tense in the invitation and the omission of the request to be excused in the invited guest's response. On the other hand, perhaps the first invitation/response is the one that has been added: it corresponds to the interpretive conclusion appended by Thomas (though the Coptic for "merchant" is different in each case, in the Greek original both places would have used ἔμπορος); and without it the three remaining invitation/response sequences correspond to the three excuses for avoiding military service in Deut 24:5-7. If this allusion was intentional, the original parable may have stressed the urgency of accepting the invitation of the Jesus movement, by suggesting that even these sanctioned excuses do not justify avoiding its call.

306. The tradition is associated with John only through the introduction of a generally formulated scene (Luke 7:24a//Matt 11:7a). Coupling it with the sayings in Luke 7:28//Matt 11:11 reinforces this connection , but this is an originally independent tradition, as its separate attestation in Thomas indicates (Thom 46). All of this, of course, is included in the larger Q composition, Luke 7:24-35//Matt 11:7-19, which deals with the relationship of John and Jesus. Thus, it is possible that it was in Q that the saying first came to be used in reference to John.

307. Cf. R. Cameron, "'What Have You Come Out to See?'" 44-45.

do not "make the person." 4) Thomas does not include a third question regarding Jesus as prophet. Since Thomas elsewhere takes up this question explicity (see Thom 52) it is not likely that he would have deliberately omitted it had he known the synoptic text. Since it does not have this question, Thomas also does not preserve anything like Luke 7:27//Matt 11:10, Q.5) Thomas does not couple this tradition with that preserved in Thom 46.

These differences notwithstanding, Schrage still inclines in favor of a synoptic derivation even here.[308] But the case is especially slim. To this end he notes that in Coptic, Thom 78:1 agrees with the Sahidic and Bohairic translations of Matt 11:7 and the Sahidic of Luke 7:24 in using the definite article with the word for "wind" (ⲡⲧⲏⲩ)) But such changes are all too common in translations, and in view of the very different ways in which this clause is otherwise formulated in Thomas and the synoptics,[309] this detail appears as nothing more than a coincidence. He also notes that Thomas follows Matthew (and Luke in the Sahidic) in omitting anything like Luke 7:25's "and live in luxury" ($\tau\rho\upsilon\phi\hat{\eta}$ $\dot{\upsilon}\pi\acute{a}\rho\chi o\nu\tau\epsilon\varsigma$). But most agree that this belongs to Lukan redaction of Q;[310] its absence, therefore, is an indication of Thomas' greater antiquity, not of its dependence on the Coptic New Testament tradition. Finally, he also notes that Thom 78:2a agrees with Luke 7:25 (and the Sahidic translation of Matthew) in inserting "clothes" to clarify the more elliptical expression found in the Greek original of Matt 11:8. Indeed, the move probably represents a Lukan improvement of the more original version of the text found in Matthew (= Q),[311] but it is the sort of improvement anyonw would have made for the sake of clarity and thus cannot prove that Thomas knew and used Luke's similar text. It certainly does not indicate, contrary to Schrage, that Thomas is dependent for this detail on the Coptic New Testament tradition, since Thomas' word choice (ⲱⲧⲏⲛ) is quite distinct from that of Matthew and Luke (ϩⲃⲥⲱ).

Since there is nothing to indicate Thomas' dependence on the synoptic tradition here, and a number of reasons to doubt such an hypothesis, again it seems prudent in this case to assume Thomas' basic autonomy vis à vis the synoptic gospels.

Thom 95 *Lend Without Return* (cf. Luke 6:34–35a)

95 [1][Jesus said], "If you have money, do not lend it at interest. [2]Rather, give [it] to someone from whom you will not get it back."

While Luke 6:34–35a is, in its present form, a Lukan composition,[312] its exhortation to lend freely probably rests upon a similar tradition in the Q

---

308. Schrage, *Das Verhältnis*, 162.

309. Thomas uses ⲕⲓⲙ (to move/be moved) with ϩⲓⲧⲛ̄ to form a passive construction; Sahidic Matthew and Luke use a circumstantial construction.

310. So Schulz, *Q*, 229, n. 344.

311. So the concensus indicated by Schulz, *Q*, 229, n.343.

312. So Schulz, *Q*, 130–31, following Wernle, *Frage*, 62–63; Schmid, *Matthaus und Lukas*, 229; Bultmann, *Geschichte*, 100.

Sermon (cf. Matt 5:42); therefore, this attitude toward lending among early Christians is probably not a Lukan invention. Short of this it would be impossible to demonstrate that Thom 95 is literarily dependent here upon Luke. Rather than suppose that Thomas has distilled a concise, negatively formulated prohibition from Luke's weaving, rhetorical style, one would sooner suspect just the opposite. As a legal saying, the Thomas version is to be preferred for its brevity and precision.

Thom 103 *Knowing the Danger* (cf. Luke 12:39//Matt 24:43, Q)

103 Jesus said, "Blessed is the person who knows where the robbers are going to enter, so that [he] may get up, bring together his domain, and prepare himself before they enter."

Thomas and Q share here a common figure, and even apply it to the same end: as an admonition to watchfulness. Yet in each stream the figure has received a different traditional form. In Q it occurs as a prophetic admonition;[313] in Thomas it is formulated as a beatitude. Therefore, a common oral tradition might be posited, but a judgment of literary dependence would be groundless.[314]

Thom 104 *The Bridegroom* (cf. Matt 9:15b//Mark 2:20//Luke 5:35)

104 [1]They said to Jesus, "Come, let us pray today, and let us fast." [2]Jesus said, "What sin have I committed, or how have I been undone? [3]Rather, when the bridegroom leaves the wedding chamber, then let people fast and pray."

Whether the "weak echo"[315] to Mark 2:20, par. in Thom 104 is strong enough to warrant its listing here is perhaps debatable; nonetheless, it is included for the purpose of consideration. As with other "siblings," the gist of the saying is the same in both versions, but a lack of verbal correspondence makes literary dependence of one upon the other unlikely.

But McArthur has noticed that while Mark's version of the saying is applied only to the question of fasting, Luke seems to have added to this the question of prayer (cf. Mark 2:18//Luke 5:33); hence, both Luke and Thomas include a saying about prayer, which raises the possibility of a relationship between these two texts.[316] However, as Sieber points out, the use of ποιεῖν δεήσεις meaning "to pray" is not characteristic of Lukan vocabulary (Luke prefers προσεύχεσθαι);[317] therefore, one should not assume that the addition of

---

313. Bultmann, *Geschichte*, 125.
314. Schrage (*Das Verhältnis*, 193) sees no possibility for making such an argument. He posits simply a "free reworking of New Testament figures." Of course, that Thomas has taken the "thief" metaphor from the New Testament and not, for example, from Q or an even earlier oral tradition, is nowhere proven.
315. The characterization is Schrage's (*Das Verhältnis*, 193).
316. McArthur, "Dependence," 286; so also Schrage, *Das Verhältnis*, 193; Snodgrass, "Gospel of Thomas," 37.
317. Sieber, "Redactional Analysis," 97. I am not persuaded by Sieber's further observation

"prayer" here derives from Lukan redaction. But there are other factors which raise the suspicion that the text of Thomas is dependent upon Luke. 1) It is doubtful that Thom 104:3//Mark 2:20 ever existed as an independent saying apart from Mark 2:18–19 or some other context, such as Thom 104:1–2. Bultmann sees Mark 2:19b-20 as an expansion of 2:19a, perhaps added by the author of Mark himself, to reflect a shift in the practice of the early church.[318] The independent occurrence of a version of Mark 2:20 in Thom 104:3 would require a modification of this view, so that Mark 2:20 is now to be seen as a previously independent saying. 2) A second question arises over the gist of the saying, and its appropriateness in Thomas. In both the synoptic and Thomas versions the image of the bridegroom's departure seems to imply conscious reflection on the death of Jesus, a theme in which Thomas otherwise shows almost no interest. Both also counsel fasting and prayer, which Thomas elsewhere consistently opposes (cf. Thom 6 and 14:1–2).[319]

For these reasons Thom 104:3 is to be considered an example of relatively late development in Thomas based upon a knowledge of the synoptic texts, perhaps added to accommodate a shift in the position of the Thomas community on such matters, or, more likely, the adoption of the document by a group that did not agree with the position of Thom 6 and 14 (such as a group of Egyptian monks). It may be conjectured that such a group sought to relativize this radical position on popular piety by relegating it to the remote past.

Thom 109 *The Hidden Treasure* (cf. Matt 13:44)

109 [1]Jesus said, "The kingdom is like a person who had a treasure hidden in a field but did not know it. [2][At] death he left it to his [son]. The son [did] not know (about it). He took over the field and sold it. [3]The buyer went plowing, [discovered] the treasure, and began to lend money at interest to whomever he wished."

One might question placing this parallel here among the "siblings," and not the "cousins" below. For while Thom 109 and Matt 13:44 share a common situation—a treasure hidden in a field—the two parables develop it quite differently. The fact that a rabbinic parable makes independent use of the same *topos* indicates that Thomas need not have relied upon Matthew for the basic idea.[320] The figure was probably quite common in Jewish lore.

---

that Thom 6 and 14 also mention prayer and fasting together (Sieber, "Redactional Analysis," 98). If Thom 104:1 were to be seen as an analogous formulation, one would also expect the third member of the triad that occurs in Thom 6 and 14, i.e., almsgiving.

318. Bultmann, *Geschichte,* 17–18.

319. Sieber's point ("Redactional Analysis," 98) that the third person plural subject here is non-specific, and therefore could refer to "outsiders," or opponents, rather than Thomas "insiders," seems to me too sophistic. It is doubtful that the tradition would portray Jesus as giving bad advice to anyone, even his opponents.

320. Cf. Midr. Cant. Rab. 4.12.1.

3. Synoptic Cousins

According to the definition of "cousins" given above (cf. p. 18) the following are sayings which have no parallel in the synoptic tradition, but which, in terms of their traditional form and content, are indistinguishable either chronologically or topically from sayings found in the synoptic tradition. Before proceeding with their analysis some clarification of what is at stake is in order.

First, most prior investigations of this material have focused on the question of its possible "authenticity" vis-à-vis the historical Jesus.[321] This is not the issue here (it will be addressed in chapter 9, below). Such a distillation of the Thomas tradition is to be avoided, at least initially. In searching for pearls there is a tendency to avoid asking what the collection as a whole might tell us about the unfolding development of the Jesus movement, a question which offers a far better chance of being answered than that of the authenticity of specific sayings of Jesus. The question I wish to pose presently may be formulated in this way: Does Thomas contain sayings which, though without parallel in the synoptic gospels, may nonetheless derive from the early stages of the Jesus movement? If so, then this must be given due weight in considering the larger question of whether the Thomas tradition derives from an early Christian tradition that is essentially independent of the synoptic gospels.

Second, the term "*synoptic* cousins" should not mislead. It does not intend to suggest "synoptic-like," as though the synoptic tradition is to be taken as the standard for measuring whether or not a saying may lay claim to a relatively early place in the Jesus tradition. One need only point to the Pauline and Johannine traditions to remind one that the problem of Christian origins is more than simply the problem of synoptic origins, and that the Jesus of Q, or Mark, and later of Matthew and Luke is the "*syn-optic*" view of but one family of texts and traditions. There are many cousins to this tradition that are also part of the problem of Christian origins. In the opinion of many, Thomas belongs to this extended family. Yet, like a long lost relative wishing to attend the family picnic, its pedigree must somehow be verified. In addition to "synoptic twins" and "siblings," the category "synoptic cousins" offers a means of doing this. These "cousins" are sayings which compare well with acknowledged members of the family—the synoptic tradition, but also the Johannine and Pauline traditions as well—in terms of form and content.

Finally, many of the sayings I have designated "synoptic cousins" below have been treated previously by Haenchen[322] and others, in terms of their gnostic meaning. Their inclusion here does not mean implicitly to dispute such an interpretation, but to challenge the notion—often taken for granted—that what is "gnostic," or "gnosticizing" is late and/or irrelevant to the dis-

---

321. E.g., J.-B. Bauer, "Echte Jesusworte," 108–50; Hunzinger, "Unbekannte Gleichnisse," 209–20.
322. See Haenchen, *Botschaft, passim.*

cussion of Christian origins. The goal in the following analysis is this: to mediate the strangeness of each of these sayings by showing compatibility with material readily accepted as belonging to the stuff of early Christian tradition—for the most part synoptic, Johannine, and Pauline traditions.

Thom 4:1 *A Place for Old and Young*

4 ¹*Jesus said, "The person old in days will not hesitate to ask a little child seven days old about the place of life, and that person will live.* ²For many of the first will be last, ³and will become a single one."³²³

The notion of the old asking advice from the young does not seem too distant from Mark 10:13–16. The notion of a τόπος τῆς ζωῆς (place of life) does not occur in the New Testament, but John, of course, speaks of a τόπος (place) to which the disciples are to be borne away (14:2–7); and, ζωή (life) is central to the theology of John. (Regarding Thom 4:2–3, see above under "synoptic twins.")

Thom 5:1 *Knowing the Obvious.*

¹*Jesus said, "Know what is in front of your face, and what is hidden from you will be disclosed to you.* ²For there is nothing hidden that will not be revealed."³²⁴

The proper recognition of revelation is a concept well known from the Johannine tradition: cf. John 1:12, 14; 3:1–21; 8:19; et al. (For 5:2 see above under "synoptic twins.")

Thom 6:1–4 *Against Hypocrisy*

¹*His disciples asked him and said to him, "Do you want us to fast? How should we pray? Should we give alms? What diet should we observe?"* ²*Jesus said, "Do not lie,* ³and do not do what you hate, ⁴because all things are disclosed before heaven. ⁵For there is nothing hidden that will not be revealed, ⁶and there is nothing covered that will remain without being disclosed."³²⁵

The questions in 6:1 regarding the practice of piety concern topics familiar from the New Testament (cf. Matt 6:16–18; Luke 11:1–4//Matt 6:5–13, Q; Matt 6:2–4); and the the answer given in 6:2–4 need not seem anomolous in

---

323. The extant Greek version of Thom 4 (POxy 654.21–27) reads:
¹[Jesus says], "A [person old in] days will not hesitate to ask a [little child seven days] old about the place of [life, and] that person will [live]. ²For many of the [first] will be [last, and] the last first ³and [will become one]."
324. The extant Greek version of Thom 5 (POxy 654.27–31) reads:
¹Jesus says, "[Know what is in front of] your face, and [what is hidden] from you will be disclosed [to you. ²For there is nothing] hidden that [will] not [be] brought to light, ³and (nothing) buried that [will not be raised]."
325. The extant Greek version of Thom 6 (POxy 654.32–40) reads:
¹[His disciples] ask him [and] say, "How [should we] fast? [How should] we [pray]? How [should we give alms]? What [diet should we] observe?" ²Jesus says, "[Do not lie, ³and] do not do [what] you [hate, ⁴because all things are apparent before] truth. ⁵[After all, there is nothing] hidden [that will not be brought to light]."

early Christian circles. Its intent is to oppose hypocrisy,[326] a theme well known in the early church (e.g., see Matt 6:1–8, 16–18). (For Thom 6:5–6, see above under "twins.")

Thom 12 and 13 *James as Leader/Thomas and Jesus* (cf. Matt 18:1–5// Mark 9:33–37//Luke 9:46–48; Matt 16:13–23//Mark 8:27–33//Luke 9:18–22)

12 [1]The disciples said to Jesus, "We know that you will leave us. Who is going to be our leader?" [2]Jesus said to them, "No matter where you are, you are to go to James the Just, for whose sake heaven and earth came into being."
13 [1]Jesus said to his disciples, "Compare me to something and tell me what I am like." [2]Simon Peter said to him, "You are like a just angel." [3]Matthew said to him, "You are like a wise philosopher." [4]Thomas said to him, "Teacher, my mouth is utterly unable to say what you are like." [5]Jesus said, "I am not your teacher. Because you have drunk, you have become intoxicated from the bubbling spring that I have tended." [6]And he took him, and withdrew, and spoke three sayings to him. [7]When Thomas came back to his friends, they asked him, "What did Jesus say to you?" [8]Thomas said to them, "If I tell you one of the sayings he spoke to me, you will pick up rocks and stone me, and fire will come from the rocks and devour you."

Both sayings are reminiscent of episodes from the synoptic tradition, but there is insufficient textual coincidence to suggest a literary relationship. That Thom 12 depends upon Mark 9:33–37, par.[327] is out of the question; the two traditions simply share the question of leadership. It has been argued that Thom 13 is an expanded version of the recognition scene at Caesarea Philippi.[328] Both traditions share the general question of Jesus' identity, the character Peter (in a relatively minor role in Thomas) and the use of dialogical structure. But there were a number of such traditions circulating in early Christianity. In addition to these one may also point to John 6:60–69 and ApJas 5.31–6.11. None of these traditions resemble another so closely as to warrant the hypothesis of literary dependence. Rather, I am inclined to agree with Ron Cameron that, while all are certainly related to a common tradition or typology, it is a tradition that "circulated freely and independently of all four gospels of the NT."[329]

Thom 14:1–3 *Fasting, Prayer, Alms*

14 [1]*Jesus said to them, "If you fast, you will bring sin upon yourselves, [2]and if you pray, you will be condemned, [3]and if you give alms, you will harm your spirits.* [4]When you go into any region and walk about in the countryside, when people take you in, eat what they serve you and heal the sick among them. [5]After all, what

---

326. Cf. chapter 5, p. 147.
327. As suggested, e.g., by Grant and Freedman, *Secret Sayings*, 130–31.
328. E.g., by Kasser, *L' Évangile selon Thomas*, 47; Gärtner, *Theology*, 125; Haenchen, "Literatur," 315.
329. Cameron, *Sayings Traditions*, 87.

goes into your mouth will not defile you; rather, it is what comes out of your mouth that will defile you."

The remarks offered above on early Christianity's critique of popular piety with regard to Thom 6:1-4 apply here as well. (For Thom 14:4-5 see above under "synoptic twins.")

Thom 17 *What no Eye has Seen*

17 Jesus said, "I will give you what no eye has seen, what no ear has heard, what no hand has touched, what has not arisen in the human heart."

This saying was so widespread in antiquity one could hardly argue that it is an authentic saying of Jesus.[330] However, that a saying like this could have been attributed to Jesus early on is shown by its similarity to Luke 10:23-24//Matt 13:16-17, Q, as well as the mysterious saying in 1 Cor 2:9. Otto Piper suggests that Thom 17 may have come from an early collection of Jesus' sayings known also to Paul.[331] Koester goes further in suggesting a source shared by Paul, the Gospel of Thomas, Q, and Dialogue of the Savior (140.1-4).[332] As with other "cousins," its presence in Thomas suggests an early Christian derivation for Thomas that is independent of the synoptic gospels.

Thom 21:6-7 *On Guard Against the World*

21 ¹Mary said to Jesus, "What are your disciples like?" ²He said, "They are like little children living in a field that is not theirs. ³When the owners of the field come, they will say,'Give us back our field.' ⁴They take off their clothes in front of them in order to give it back to them, and they return their field to them. ⁵For this reason I say, if the owner of a house knows that a thief is coming, he will be on guard before the thief arrives, and will not let the thief break into his house of his domain and steal his possessions. ⁶*As for you, then, be on guard against the world.* ⁷*Prepare yourselves with great strength, so the robbers cannot find a way to get to you, for the trouble you expect will come.* ⁸Let there be among you a person who understands. ⁹When the crop ripened, he came quickly carrying a sickle and harvested it. ¹⁰Whoever has two good ears should listen."

The notion that one must remain vigilant against the world is strongly reminiscent of elements in Johannine thought (e.g. John 15:18-21). (For Thom 21:1-6, 8-10 see above under "synoptic twins.")

Thom 24 *The Person of Light*

24 ¹His disciples said, "Show us the place where you are, for we must seek it." ²He said to them, "Whoever has ears should listen. ³There is light within a person of light, and it shines on the whole world. If it does not shine, it is dark."

---

330. See the numerous versions of it collected by Stone and Strugnell (*The Books of Elijah*, 42-73).

331. Piper, "The Gospel of Thomas," 21.

332. Koester, "Gnostic Writings," 244-50; see also Robinson, "Kerygma and History," 42-43; Koester, *Ancient Christian Gospels*, 58-59. Koester notes a further parallel in the Prayer of the Apostle Paul (25-29); see *Ancient Christian Gospels*, 59, n. 1.

The secondary introductory question posed by the disciples is the present-oriented equivalent of Peter's future-oriented question in John 13:36.[333] The answer seems odd because it is a *non sequitur*. But as an independent saying, it seems quite comparable to other early gospel materials. 24:2 is a common early Christian hermeneutical admonition,[334] and 24:3 seems quite comparable to Matt 6:22–23 and Luke 11:34–35.[335]

Thom 27 *Fasting and Sabbath*

27 [1]"If you do not fast from the world, you will not find the kingdom. [2]If you do not keep the sabbath a sabbath, you will not see the Father."[336]

"Fasting from the world" is to be understood in the same vein as Thom 21:6–7,[337] and hence stands in a similar relationship to Johannine thought. In the second clause it is not clear how one is to "keep the sabbath a sabbath." Is a stricter legal observance of the sabbath being required? Or is this a circumlocution for a new (looser?) interpretation? The text does not tell us. At any rate, that this topic belongs to the subject matter of early Christian discourse is certain (cf. Mark 2:23–28, par.; Mark 3:1–6, par. ; Luke 14:5//Matt 12:11–12, [= Q?]).

Thom 29 *Flesh as Poverty*

29 [1]Jesus said, "If the flesh came into being because of spirit, that is a marvel, [2]but if spirit came into being because of the body, that is a marvel of marvels. [3]Yet I marvel at how this great wealth has come to dwell in this poverty."[338]

The relationship between flesh and spirit is, of course, a well-known Pauline theme (see, e.g., Gal 5:16–24; Rom 8:2–9); no doubt it came up in Johannine circles as well (cf. John 3:6). In these instances, as in Thomas, it arises in relation to the question of the genesis of human being.

Thom 38 *Too Late*

38 [1]Jesus said, "Often you have desired to hear these sayings that I am speaking to you, and you have no one else from whom to hear them. [2]There will be days when you will seek me and you will not find me."[339]

333. Cf. also John 14:1–6.
334. Cf. Mark 4:9, 23; Matt 11:15; 13:9, 43b; Luke 8:8b; 14:35b; Rev 2:7a, 11a, 17a; 3:6, 13, 22; 13:9.
335. Cf. also John 8:12; 12:35–36; 2 Cor 4:6.
336. The extant Greek version of Thom 27 (POxy 1 [vert.].4–11) reads:
[1]Jesus says, "If you do not fast from the world, you will not find the kingdom of God. [2]If you do not keep the sabbath a sabbath, you will not see the Father."
337. The implications of this notion of vigilance against the world is to be taken up in more detail as the subject of chapter 6.
338. POxy 1 (horiz.) 22 preserves only a fragment of this saying:
[3]". . . comes to dwell in this] poverty."
339. The extant Greek version of Thom 38 (POxy 1 [vert.].11–21) reads:
[1][Jesus says, "Often you have desired to hear these sayings of mine], and [you have no one else from whom to hear (them). [2]And [there will come days when you will seek me and you will not find me]."

Thom 38:1 is comparable to Luke 10:23–24//Matt 13:16–17, Q. Thom 38:2 would be very much at home in John (cf. 7:33–34; 8:21; 13:33; 16:19).[340]

Thom 47:1 *Mounting Two Horses/Stretching Two Bows*

47 [1]*Jesus said, "A person cannot mount two horses or bend two bows.* [2]And a slave cannot serve two masters, otherwise he will honor the one and offend the other. [3]Nobody drinks aged wine and immediately wants to drink new wine. [4]New wine is not poured into old wineskins, in case they should break, and aged wine is not poured into a new wineskin, in case it should spoil. [5]An old patch is not sewn onto a new garment, since it would create a tear."

A simple double-stich wisdom saying, Thom 47:1 goes well with 47:2–5, which has clear synoptic parallels. (For 47:2–5, see above under "synoptic twins.")

Thom 48 *Making Peace*

48 Jesus said, "If two make peace with each other in a single house, they will say to the mountain,'Move from here!' and it will move."

While the last part of this saying ("they will say to the mountain . . .") is closely paralleled in the synoptic tradition,[341] it seems best to treat the whole of Thom 48 as a new saying. "Moving a mountain" is by itself not an independent saying but a proverbial cliché to be attached to any activity, character trait, etc., whose limitless potential one wishes to praise. It is similarly used in Thom 106. Though elsewhere in the Jesus tradition only faith seems to have attracted this figure,[342] its application to peacemaking does not seem out of place in an early Christian context. Paul places a high premium on peace within the household (1 Cor 7:15),[343] and in Q's mission speech the "peace" that goes into a house seems also to have a powerful, almost numinous quality to it (Luke 10:5–6//Matt 10:12–13).

Thom 51 *When will the "Rest" Come?*

51 [1]His disciples said to him, "When will the rest for the dead take place, and when will the new world come?" [2]He said to them, "What you are looking forward to has come, but you do not know it."

Though the ἀνάπαυσις (rest) motif is often treated in terms of its relation to later gnostic systems,[344] one should not assume that this is its primary significance here.[345] Of chief importance in the saying is the polemic against

---

340. There is probably no relationship between 38:2 and the apocalyptic saying in Luke 17:22.
341. Cf. Mark 11:23//Matt 21:21b; also Matt 17:20b.
342. Cf. also 1 Cor 13:2.
343. Even though Thomas elsewhere does not—cf. Thom 16, 55, and 101! It may be that in Thom 48 "house" is not necessarily meant to connote a literal familial context, but rather some form of inner-group relationship.
344. So Haenchen, *Botschaft*, 72–74; Vielhauer, "ΑΝΑΠΑΥΣΙΣ."
345. Cf. Heb 3:7–4:13; Matt 11:28–29.

deferring the soteriological goal until some future time, a theme carrying much weight in the Gospel of Thomas (cf. esp. Thom 3 and 113), but also found within the synoptic tradition (cf. Luke 17:20–21; Mark 9:12–13//Matt 17:11).

Thom 53 *True Circumcision*

53 [1]His disciples said to him, "Is circumcision useful or not?" [2]He said to them, "If it were useful, their father would produce them already circumcised from their mother. [3]Rather, true circumcision in spirit has become profitable in every respect."

Circumcision was certainly under discussion in Christian circles very early on—the Pauline examples require no further comment: Rom 2:25–29 (esp. vs 28!); 3:1–8; 1 Cor 7:17–19; Galatians, *passim;* and Phil 3:3. There is no reason why such a saying might not have been attributed to Jesus very early indeed.

Thom 58 *Blessed the Laborer*

58 Jesus said, "Blessed is the person who has toiled[346] and found life."

The saying shares both its subject matter (suffering, persecution) and its form (beatitude) with Matt 5:10; Luke 6:22//Matt 5:11, Q. Lest the $\zeta\omega\acute{\eta}$ (life) motif seem to suggest lateness, cf. Jas 1:12, whose author must have known some form of this saying.

Thom 62:1 *Knowing the Secrets*

62 [1]*Jesus said, "I disclose my mysteries to those [who are worthy] of [my] mysteries.* [2]Do not let your left hand know what your right hand is doing."

Thom 62:1 forms a precise conceptual parallel to Mark's parables theory (Mark 4:10–12, par.).[347] (For Thom 62:2, see above under "synoptic twins.")

Thom 74 *The Cistern*

74 He[348] said, "Lord, there are many around the drinking trough, but there is nothing in the well."

While there are no New Testament or other early Christian parallels to this particular saying, so that according to the criteria set out above there is nothing to recommend it, it is worthy of consideration here on purely form-critical grounds. It is a simple saying of secular wisdom; many such sayings were ascribed to Jesus early on. There is nothing to suggest that Thom 74 is not also an example of this phenomenon.

---

346. The Coptic reads ϩιсе, which can mean either "to toil" or "to suffer." For the latter meaning cf. Wis 3:15; Sir 51:26–27; Matt 11:28–30.

347. Note the use of $\mu\upsilon\sigma\tau\acute{\eta}\rho\iota o\nu$ (mystery) in both texts.

348. The saying is not explicitly attributed to Jesus. It may be that Thom 74 forms a dialogue together with Thom 73 and/or 75.

Thom 81 *Riches and Power*

81 ¹Jesus said, "Let one who has become wealthy reign, ²and let one who has power renounce (it)."

While the second clause of this wisdom-like admonition could perhaps be read simply in terms of the synoptic critique of wealth and position (e.g., Mark 10:17–23, par.), the first clause is more problematic. But if one reads ⲣ-ⲣⲣⲟ (to reign) here in the peculiar sense of ruling found in Thom 2, it may be construed as exactly parallel to the second clause: just as the powerful renounces power, so too should the wealthy learn "to reign," i.e., learn to live according to the insights one has gained from these sayings (Thom 2), which inevitably entails the renunciation of wealth (Thom 95).[349] Already in Paul's day early Christians were using "reigning" as a metaphor for arriving at special theological insight (cf. 1 Cor 4:8).[350]

Thom 82 *Near the Fire*

82 ¹Jesus said, "Whoever is near me is near the fire, ²and whoever is far from me is far from the kingdom."

As an I-saying this declaration may be considered here on form-critical grounds.[351] Though in terms of content there is really nothing like it this in the early Christian corpus,[352] Bauer argues convincingly for seeing a hellenistic proverb behind this saying.[353] Therefore, it could easily be viewed as another example of the attribution of popular secular wisdom to Jesus. Finally, the subject matter is not without parallel in the synoptic tradition.[354]

Thom 92:2 *Then and Now*

92 ¹Jesus said, "Seek and you will find. ²*In the past, however, I did not tell you the things about which you asked me then. Now I am willing to tell them, but you are not seeking them.*"

The periodization of the teaching activity of Jesus put forth in this I-saying is a concept not foreign either to the synoptic (cf. Luke 24:44–49) or Johan-

---

349. So Bauer, "Echte Jesusworte," 124–26; Haenchen, *Botschaft*, 57.

350. For a discussion of the relationship between the concept of "reigning" in Thomas and the tradition behind 1 Cor 4:8 see Robinson, "Kerygma and History," 43–4; Koester, *Ancient Christian Gospels*, 60.

351. The fact that Jeremias includes it as an authentic saying of Jesus (*Unbekannte Jesusworte*, 64–71), citing the antithetic structure and Semitic style he sees as characteristic of Jesus' sayings, bears witness at least to its formal similarities to the early Jesus tradition. See also Higgins, "Non-Gnostic Sayings," 303; Piper, "The Gospel of Thomas," 21; J.-B. Bauer, "Echte Jesusworte," 122–24.

352. The age and provenance of Origen's version of the saying (*In Jerem. hom. lat.*, 20.3) is unknown: *Que iuxta me est, iuxta ignem est; qui longe est a me, longe est a regno;* "Whoever is near me is near the fire; whoever is far from me is far from the kingdom." It could derive from the Gospel of Thomas itself. For a discussion see Jeremias, *Unbekannte Jesusworte*, 64–66.

353. J.-B. Bauer, "Echte Jesusworte," 122–24.

354. Cf. Mark 9:49; 12:34.

nine (cf. John 11:54; 12:36b; 14:25–26; 16:4–5, 12–15, 22–28) traditions. (For Thom 92:1, see p. 19.)

Thom 97 *The Empty Jar*

97 [1]Jesus said, "The kingdom is like a woman who was carrying a [jar] full of meal. [2]While she was walking along [a] distant road, the handle of the jar broke and the meal spilled behind her [along] the road. [3]She did not know it; she had not noticed a problem.[355] [4]When she reached her house, she put the jar down and discovered that it was empty."

Without entering into an extensive discussion about the meaning of the parable at this point, it is difficult to make a judgment about how it might compare to other early Christian traditions.[356] It is, of course, a parable, and since it is safe to say that parables were both spoken by Jesus and attributed to him very early in the tradition, there is no reason to consider this parable particularly late. If, as Jeremias argues,[357] it warns against false security, in that one is enjoined to remain attentive lest the kingdom slip away, one might consider it comparable to Luke 11:24–26//Matt 12:43–45, Q.[358]

Thom 98 *The Assassin*

98 [1]Jesus said, "The Father's kingdom is like a person who wanted to put someone powerful to death. [2]While still at home, he drew his sword and thrust it into the wall to find out whether his hand would go in. [3]Then he killed the powerful one."

As a parable Thom 98 would be quite at home formally in the early period of the development of the Jesus tradition. If it is about preparing sufficiently for the task that is to come, then in terms of content it compares well with Luke 14:28–32.[359] Bruce Malina, on the other hand, has argued that the parable is primarily about revenge; the central element is the fact that the weak is able in the end to kill "someone powerful."[360] The element of reversal thus links it to many other parables in the Jesus tradition. The violent imagery of the parable may be disturbing, but it is not without parallel even within the synoptic tradition.[361]

---

355. Or: "she had not understood how to toil." Both the grammar and the vocabulary of the Coptic is ambiguous.

356. Various interpretations of the parable have been suggested. Bauer ("Echte Jesuworte," 137) offers a Naassene interpretation. Cerfaux and Garitte ("Les paraboles du Royaume," 326) also think it has a gnostic meaning.

357. Jeremias, *Gleichnisse Jesu*, 175.

358. The fact that Higgins ("Non-Gnostic Sayings," 303), Quispel ("Thomas and the New Testament," 15), and Jeremias (*Gleichnisse Jesu*, 175) all hold it to be an authentic saying of Jesus perhaps testifies at least to its formal similarity to the early Jesus tradition.

359. Jeremias, *Gleichnisse Jesu*, 195; also Hunzinger, "Unbekannte Gleichnisse," 209–20 (but for the wrong reasons; see Higgins, "Non-Gnostic Sayings," 304–5).

360. Malina,"A Parable of Vengeance," unpublished paper presented *in absentia* to the Jesus Seminar, March 2, 1990 in Sonoma, CA.

361. E.g., Mark 12:1–12, par. (cf. Thom 65); Luke 14:31–32.

Thom 102 *The Dog in the Manger*

102 Jesus said, "Damn the Pharisees, for they are like a dog sleeping in the cattle manger, for it neither eats nor [lets] the cattle eat."

Here a popular hellenistic proverb[362] has been assigned to Jesus, a phenomenon well attested in early Christian circles. Its polemical use in this case against the Pharisees gives it a distinct early Christian touch. Its thrust, of course, is quite similar to Thom 39:1 (par. Luke 11:52//Matt 23:13, Q).

Thom 112 *Flesh and Soul*

112 [1]Jesus said, "Damn the flesh that depends on the soul. [2]Damn the soul that depends on the flesh."

The $\sigma\acute{\alpha}\rho\xi/\psi\upsilon\chi\acute{\eta}$ (flesh/soul) dichotomy in this saying may be comparable to the $\sigma\acute{\alpha}\rho\xi/\pi\nu\epsilon\hat{\upsilon}\mu\alpha$ (flesh/spirit) schema discussed above in relation to Thom 29. The enigmatic nature of the dialectic created by the tautological reversal in its two halves should not exclude it. John's Jesus frequently utters enigmatic sayings, whose hermeneutical clues only insiders are expected to know.[363]

Summary

The above analysis of synoptic "twins," "siblings," and "cousins" in Thomas is intended to show that in terms of material content, there is little evidence to suggest that the Gospel of Thomas is literarily dependent upon the synoptic gospels. In the case of "synoptic twins," a tradition-historical analysis and comparison of the Thomas and synoptic versions of individual sayings has consistently indicated that here we have to do essentially with two independent tradition-historical streams. The presence in Thomas of a large number of "synoptic siblings," for which literary dependence upon the synoptic gospels is excluded by their widely divergent wording, and "synoptic cousins," which demonstrate that Thomas' author/editor had access to early Christian traditions apart from the synoptics, serves greatly to strengthen this hypothesis.

I have chosen to speak here of the Gospel of Thomas as an "independent" tradition. At the same time, in the course of this analysis it has become necessary from time to time to point out places in Thomas where the wording of the synoptic gospels seems to have had an influence on the present form of the text. Thus, it may prove helpful to clarify just what is meant by the term "independent" as it is used to describe the Thomas tradition.

First, it must be borne in mind that for most of the text of Thomas we must

362. Cf. Lucian, *Tim.* 14; *Ind.* 30.
363. The best example, perhaps, is the Nicodemus discourse in John 3. Nicodemus never knows what is really being discussed in 3:3 or 3:13; to the Johannine community, he represents the outsider who cannot understand what it is that has excited the Johannine community.

rely upon a single exemplar, itself the end product of a long period of textual transmission, which included translation from Greek to Coptic, and this during a time when the synoptic gospels were growing ever more popular and influential. If one is to learn anything from the textual transmission of the synoptic gospels themselves, it is that there is a marked tendency toward harmonization among parallel gospel texts, a tendency which John Horman suggests is particularly strong among the Coptic translations.[364] Given these conditions, it is almost inconceivable that the Thomas manuscript upon which we rely for most of this text could have passed through any number of scribal hands without being subjected to the effects of harmonization toward one or more of the synoptic gospels.

Throughout the analysis offered in this chapter I have pointed out those places in the surviving text of Thomas where I suspect this sort of textual corruption has in fact taken place. First, there are the four instances in which Thomas' order may have been affected by the tendency to harmonize: Thom 32 followed closely by 33:2-3 (cf. Matt 5:14b-15); Thom 44 grouped together with 43:3 and 45:1-4 (cf. Matt 12:31-35); the sequence Thom 65-66 (cf. Mark 12:1-11, pars.); and the sequence Thom 92:1, 93-94 (cf. Matt 7:6-7). These instances will be dealt with in greater detail in the next chapter. For now, however, there are two observations to be made about them. First, these sayings have no catchwords to connect them to the sayings that surround them. In the case of Thom 44 and 66 this is clear. As for Thom 33:2-3, it is connected to 33:1 by a pun that works only in Coptic—ⲙⲁⲁϫⲉ means either "ear" or "basket"—and is thus not to be considered a genuine catchword. Thom 94 shares with 92 the word ϣⲓⲛⲉ (to find), but this is not necessarily a catchword, since 94 and 92 are essentially the same saying (a catchword is intended to help one to remember two different sayings in sequence, not to repeat a single saying!). Thus, unlike most of the rest of the collection, the order of these sayings does not reflect an oral heritage. This simply serves to underscore the likelihood that they are examples of relatively late literary tampering. Second, it is to be observed that three of the four have only Matthean parallels, while the fourth has a Marcan parallel found also in Matthew. This may suggest a special relationship between Matthew and Thomas, a Coptic scribe perhaps having been influenced by familiarity with the Gospel of Matthew, occasionally altering Thomas to conform more closely to the canonical text.

In addition, the following instances of possible scribal corruption have been noted in the above discussion:

Thom 32: ⲟⲩⲁⲉ ⲥⲛⲁϣ ϩⲱⲡ ⲁⲛ (nor can it be hidden)[365] seems to be an afterthought that brings the saying into closer conformity with Matt 5:14b.

---

364. Horman, "The Parable of the Sower," 328-29, 335-37.
365. οὔτε κρυ[β]ῆναι ("nor can it be hidden") in the POxy version of the saying.

Thom 39:1: ⲙⲫⲁⲣⲓⲥⲁⲓⲟⲥ ⲙⲛ̄ ⲛ̄ⲅⲣⲁⲙⲙⲁⲧⲉⲩⲥ (Pharisees and scribes) corresponds to Matthean redaction in Matt 23:13.

Thom 45:3: ⲉⲧ₂ⲛ̄ ⲡⲉϥ₂ⲏⲧ (which is in his heart) corresponds to Lukan redaction in Luke 6:45.

Thom 104:1, 3: Thomas' reference to both prayer (ⲱⲗⲏⲗ) and fasting (ⲛⲏⲥⲧⲉⲩⲉ) may reflect Luke 5:33 (cf. Mark 12:18).

Thom 104:3: The allusion to the death of Jesus is unusual here in Thomas; together with the copulative ⲁⲗⲗⲁ (but) joining 104:3 to 104:2, this casts suspicion on Thom 104:3 (cf. Luke 5:33-35).

These several instances represent the best evidence for the dependence of Thomas upon the synoptic gospels. It may therefore seem to do less than full justice to them to lump them together and dispose of them with a single blow as examples of scribal harmonization; that is, until their testimony is put in perspective. First, given the extensive amount of material shared by Thomas and the synoptics, this very small number of cases where synoptic redaction can be detected in Thomas is hardly enough to suggest that Thomas is thoroughly dependent for its traditions upon the synoptic gospels. If this were the case, the number would be much higher and the parallels much more consistent. This failing, the small number of cases that have been identified must be otherwise accounted for.

Secondly, it is impossible that Nag Hammadi Codex 2, and the many copies of Thomas which stand between our extant Thomas manuscripts and the original, were immune to the almost universal phenomenon of scribal error, especially that of harmonization. That the present text of Thomas has such text-critical commonplaces is to be expected; it is only a matter of identifying where they occur. Since the text as a whole does not rely upon the synoptic tradition, it is reasonable to assign the handful of instances in which influence from a synoptic text is likely, to the phenomenon of textual harmonization.

In consequence of this it is not entirely accurate to speak of the Gospel of Thomas as an "independent" tradition, for over the course of two to three centuries of textual transmission it is scarcely imaginable that the synoptic tradition did not come to affect the text of Thomas in some way, especially during the period in which the canonical gospels were experiencing great popularity and gradual ascendency. It may therefore be preferable to speak of the Thomas tradition as an *autonomous,* rather than independent tradition. Indeed, it would be foolish to speak of any early Christian tradition as absolutely "independent" from other perspectives at work in the early Christian movement and their respective texts. Nonetheless, as the analysis in this chapter has shown, Thomas is not linked to the synoptic gospels in any generative way. In this sense the Gospel of Thomas is to be considered the representative of an autonomous early Christian tradition.

3

Thomas and   A Question
the Sayings Tradition   of Form

If the first test for literary dependence is the detection of a consistent pattern of influence of one text on another, the second is the discovery of a relatively high degree of shared order in the sequence in which each text presents this shared material. An important pillar of the hypothesis of Markan priority is the fact that Matthew and Luke follow Mark's lead in ordering the pericopae all three have in common. Likewise, the Q hypothesis is supported by the residual cases of shared order among the Q sayings included by both Matthew and Luke. On the other hand, one of the long-standing difficulties attending the hypothesis of John's direct dependence upon Mark or any of the synoptic gospels is the fact that John presents the events that both traditions share in a narrative sequence that seldom reflects the synoptic order. As we address the question of Thomas' relationship to the synoptic texts, then, it seems pertinent to inquire: does the order in which Thomas presents its sayings reflect in any way the order in which the same material is presented in the synoptic gospels?

The Question of Order

There is no better way to adjudicate the question of order than simply to compare the respective sequences in which Thomas and the synoptic gospels present the sayings they share. I have listed in Figure 1 all of the discrete sayings in Thomas for which there are synoptic parallels. For purposes of comparison, I have placed them in the order in which one finds them in Thomas,[1] giving their synoptic counterparts in running parallel columns to

---

1. I follow the Coptic order, even though it is suspect in some instances, e.g., Thom 77:2–3, which in POxy 1 occurs after Thom 30:1–2. We must allow for a small percentage of error.

the right. Instances of shared order are readily apparent wherever one finds consecutive texts occurring in the correct order in any of the synoptic columns.

Figure 1

Sigla: Brackets [ ]: rough parallels.
Bold type: instances of approximate shared order.

Thom	Matt	Mark	Luke
2:1 (Twins)	7:7		11:9 (Q)
3:1–3 (Siblings)			17:20–21
4:1 (Cousins)	[19:13–15]	[10:13–16]	[18:15–17]
	[18:3]		
4:2 (Twins)	19:30	10:31	13:30
	20:16		
5:2 (Twins)		4:22	8:17
	10:26		12:2 (Q)
6:1–4 (Cousins)	[6:16–18]		
	[6:2–4]		
	[6:5–13]		[11:1–4] (Q)
6:5–6 (Twins)		4:22	8:17
	10:26		12:2 (Q)
8:1–4 (Siblings)	13:47–50		
9:1–5 (Twins)	13:3–9	4:2–9	8:4–8
10 (Twins)			12:49
11:1 (Siblings)	5:18		16:17 (Q)
	24:35	13:31	21:33
12:1–2 (Cousins)	16:13–20	8:27–30	9:18–22
13:1–8 (Cousins)	16:13–20	8:27–30	9:18–22
14:1–3 (Cousins)	[6:1–8,16–18]		
14:4 (Twins)			10:8–9
14:5 (Twins)	15:11, 18	7:15, 18	
16:1–4 (Twins)	10:34–36		12:51–53 (Q)
17 (Cousins)	[13:16–17]		[10:23–24] (Q)
20:1–4 (Twins)	13:31–32	4:30–32	13:18–19
21:5 (Twins)	24:43		12:39 (Q)
21:9 (Twins)		4:29	
22:2 (Siblings)	18:3	[10:15]	[18:17]
24:3 (Cousins)	[6:22–23]		
25:1–2 (Siblings)	22:39	12:31	10:27
26:1–2 (Twins)	7:3–5		6:41–42 (Q)
31:1 (Twins)	13:57	6:4	4:24
32 (Siblings)	**5:14b**		
33:1 (Twins)	10:27		12:3 (Q)

33:2-3 (Twins)	**5:15**		11:33 (Q)
			8:16
		4:21	
34 (Twins)	15:14		6:39 (Q)
35:1-2 (Twins)	12:29	3:27	11:21–22(Q/Mk.)
36 (Siblings)	6:25-33		12:22-30 (Q)
38:1 (Cousins)	[13:16-17]		[10:23-24] (Q)
39:1-2 (Twins)	23:13		11:52 (Q)
39:3 (Twins)	10:16b		
40:1-2 (Sibling)	15:13		
41:1-2 (Twin)	13:12	4:25	8:18b
	25:29		19:26(Q)
43:3 (Siblings)	7:16a, 17-18		**6:43-44a** (Q)
	12:33		
44:1-3 (Twins)	**12:31-32**	3:28-29	
			12:10 (Q)
45:1 (Twins)	**7:16b**		**6:44b** (Q)
45:2 (Twins)	**12:35**		**6:45a** (Q)
45:3-4 (Twins)	**12:34b**		**6:45b** (Q)
46:1 (Twins)	11:11		7:28 (Q)
46:2 (Twins)	18:3	10:15	18:17
47:2 (Twins)	6:24		16:13 (Q)
47:3 (Twins)			**5:39**
47:4 (Twins)	**9:17**	**2:22**	**5:37-38**
47:5 (Twins)	**9:16**	**2:21**	**5:36**
48 (Cousins)	[21:21]	[11:23]	
54 (Twins)	5:3		6:20b (Q)
55:1-2 (Twins)	10:37-39		14:26-27 (Q)
57:1-4 (Twins)	13:24-30		
58 (Cousins)	[5:10, 11]		[6:22] (Q)
61:1 (Twins)			17:34a
62:1 (Cousins)	[13:10-13]	[4:10-12]	[8:9-10]
62:2 (Twins)	6:3		
63:1-4 (Twins)			12:16-21
64:1-12 (Sibling)	22:1-14		14:15-24 (Q)
65:1-8 (Twin)	**21:33-41**	**12:1-9**	**20:9-16**
66 (Twins)	**21:42**	**12:10-11**	**20:17-18**
68:1 (Twins)	5:10-12		6:22-23 (Q)
69:1 (Twins)	5:10-12		6:22-23 (Q)
69:2 (Siblings)	5:6		6:21a (Q)
71 (Twins)	26:61	14:58	
	27:40	15:29	
	24:42	13:2	21:6
72:1-3 (Twins)			12:13-14

73 (Twins)	9:37–38		10:2 (Q)
76:1–2 (Twins)	13:45–46		
76:3 (Twins)	6:19–20		12:33 (Q)
78:1–3 (Siblings)	11:7–9		7:24–26 (Q)
79:1–2 (Twins)	11:27–28		
79:3 (Twins)	23:29		
86:1–2 (Twins)	8:20		9:58 (Q)
89:1–2 (Twins)	23:25–26		11:39–41 (Q)
90:1–2 (Twins)	11:28–30		
91:1–2 (Twins)	16:3b		12:56
92:1 (Twins)	7:7		11:9 (Q)
93:1–2 (Twins)	7:6		
94:1–2 (Twins)	7:7		
95:1–2 (Siblings)	5:42(?)		6:34–35a(Q?)
96:1–3 (Twins)	13:33		13:20–21 (Q)
99:1–3 (Twins)	12:46–50	3:31–35	8:19–21
100:1–4 (Twins)	22:15–22	12:13–17	20:20–26
101:1–2 (Twins)	10:37–39		14:26–27 (Q)
103 (Siblings)	24:43		12:39 (Q)
104:3 (Siblings)	9:15	2:20	5:35
106:2 (Siblings)	17:20b	11:23a	
	21:21b		
107:1–3 (Twins)	18:12–14		15:3–7 (Q)
109:1–3 (Siblings)	13:33		
113:1–4–(Siblings)			[17:20–21] (Q?)

As may be seen from this simple listing of parallels, there are only five sequences in which the ordering of sayings in Thomas approximates synoptic arrangement of the same material:

1) Thom 32, 33:2–3   (cf. Matt 5:14b-15)
2) Thom 43:3–45:4   (cf. Matt 12:31–35//Luke 6:43–45, Q)
3) Thom 47:3–5   (cf. Matt 9:16–17//Mark 2:21–22// Luke 5:36–39)
4) Thom 65–66   (cf. Mark 12:31–35, par.)
5) Thom 92:1; 93–94   (cf. Matt 7:6–7)

Collectively they comprise only a small percentage of the total number of discrete sayings in the Gospel of Thomas—hardly the foundation for a theory of literary dependence. Still, if one supposes instead that Thomas represents an independent tradition, they must be accounted for.

The similar (though inverted) order shared by Thom 47:3–5 and Matt 9:16–17//Mark 2:21–22//Luke 5:36–39 does not necessarily indicate that Thomas is dependent upon the synoptic text. In the synoptic tradition Matthew and Luke have clearly taken the cluster from Mark, who probably did not create the material himself. Rather, these sayings derive ultimately from the early

Christian sayings tradition, perhaps oral,[2] where they quite plausibly would have been linked already, due to their similar form and content.[3] Thus, their appearance together in Thomas is due, not to literary dependence upon Mark, but to a common heritage of oral tradition. Given the form-critical and tradition-historical evidence outlined in the previous chapter, which argues against Thomas' dependence upon the synoptic gospels in this case,[4] this latter alternative seems more likely. It seems all the more so when one observes that Thomas and the synoptic texts do not really share the same order here. Rather, in Thomas the synoptic order is reversed. But this is exactly the sort of difference one would expect to find resulting from the somewhat capricious processes of oral transmission.

With respect to Thom 32, 33:2–3 and 65–66, I have already presented arguments for why these clusters could not have been composed on the basis of the synoptic text, even though their present form may be the result of a relatively late harmonization in the course of the text's manuscript transmission.[5] This seems the best way to account for the synoptic-like sequence found in Thom 92:1, 93–94 (//Matt 7:6–7) as well. Matthew certainly did not create from whole cloth the saying used in 7:6; he has taken it from the tradition and combined it with Luke 11:9–10//Matt 7:7–8 (Q) to fill out this section of the Sermon on the Mount. The order thus created in 7:6–8 is his creation, and the similar sequence in Thom 93–94 should therefore be considered suspect. However, it is unlikely that Matthew's influence on the text of Thomas is to be located at the compositional stage; the form-critical evidence summarized above for Thom 92:1,[6] 93,[7] and 94[8] argues strongly against this. It is also difficult to explain why Thomas' author/editor would have created two versions of Matt 7:7b (cf. Thom 92:1 and 94).

As for Thom 43:3–45:4 (par. Matt 12:31–35//Luke 6:43–45, Q), it has already been pointed out that the corresponding order between Thomas and Luke is misleading, since Luke's order derives from Q and therefore cannot be taken as evidence for Thomas' dependence upon Luke. If there is a relationship to Luke here, it may well derive from a common dependence on Q, or on a tradition older still.[9] Nonetheless, questions are raised by Thom 44, which

2. Bultmann (Geschichte, 107) regards these as examples of secular wisdom taken up and ascribed to Jesus. Gnilka (Markus, 1: 114) considers them to come from the tradition, but holds that 21–22a is earlier than 22b. Haenchen (Weg Jesu, 115) calls vss 21–22 a Wanderspruch, that is, a saying that originally circulated independently from Mark.

3. For the phenomenon, see Bultmann, Geschichte, 86–88. Bultmann himself did not think that the two sayings would have come together in this way. Rather, he argues that perhaps vs 22 was formed on analogy to vs 21. However, Bultmann did not have the evidence of Thomas to consider.

4. See the discussion of Thom 47 under "Twins" in chapter 2. Note, however, the peculiar case of Thom 47:3, which may reflect scribal corruption incorporating Luke 5:39.

5. For Thom 65–66 see pp. 48–51; for Thom 32, 33:2–3 see p. 32.

6. See p. 19.

7. See p. 66.

8. See p. 19.

9. See pp. 76–77.

parallels Matt 12:31-32, a Markan saying (cf. Mark 3:28-29) used by Matthew to introduce his version of this Q complex (Matt 12:31-35). But again, that Thom 43:3-45:4 was composed on the basis of Matthew here is not likely: 1) Thom 43:3 and Matt 12:33 are only "siblings" at best;[10] 2) Thomas has no parallel to Matt 12:34a, while Matthew has nothing here corresponding to Thom 45:1 (but cf. Matt 7:16b); and 3) within this cluster of sayings the respective ordering of the logia in Thomas and Matthew is quite different. Under the assumption of literary dependence upon Matthew, nothing short of a deliberate scrambling of Matthew's order could account for Thomas' text. But such an explanation seems strained in view of the corresponding order shared by Thomas and Q (Thom 45:1 ● 45:2 ● 45:3 = Luke 6:44b ● 45a ● 45b [= Q]), and the reliance upon older sources which this suggests. Therefore, it seems best to conclude that the present position of Thom 44 within this cluster is also the product of a later scribal hand under the influence of the similar cluster in Matthew.

These exceptions, then, do not seriously detract from the fact that in the vast majority of cases Thomas' author/editor has arranged his or her material differently from the synoptic gospels. If a common order is the second test of literary dependence of one text upon another, Thomas fails this test as well.

Thomas' Organizing Principle

Proponents of the thesis that Thomas depends upon the synoptic gospels have not ignored the problem posed by Thomas' unique ordering of the traditions allegedly derived from the synoptic texts. Under such a theory, Thomas will have intentionally rearranged the synoptic tradition to reinterpret it by forming new combinations which, when read through the proper theological lens, may be recognized as gnostic. For example, Grant and Freedman, who regard Thomas as dependent upon the canonical gospels, regard Thomas' peculiar arrangement of the text as a deliberate attempt to scramble and in this way reinterpret the synoptic tradition, the results of which are to be read in terms of Naassene theology.[11] Thus, it is necessary at this point to say something more about the principles at work in the ordering of material in Thomas and the implications these might have for the question of Thomas' relationship to the synoptic texts.

It has often been noticed that the Gospel of Thomas contains a number of catchwords, that is, a series of words serving to link successive sayings.[12] Now, since for most of this text we are dependent today upon a late Coptic translation, it is *prima facie* likely that many such catchwords will have been washed away over the course of its transmission history and lost, especially in

10. See p. 76.
11. *Secret Sayings, passim,* but esp. 102-8.
12. Many have pointed out this phenomenon; perhaps the earliest was Garitte in "Le premier volume," 63-64.

the course of translating from Greek to Coptic. Nonetheless, the pervasiveness of catchword associations within Thomas is underscored by the very large number of them that have survived even the translation into Coptic. When one adds to this list certain instances in which a Greek catchword may still be detected behind two different words or phrases in the present Coptic text, the list of catchwords in Thomas becomes quite extensive indeed. A complete list of catchword associations in Thomas is assembled in Figure 2.

Figure 2: Potential Catchwords in Thomas

Note: Catchwords are taken from the Coptic text; Greek equivalents from the Greek *Vorlage* are provided in parentheses. Where the POxy fragments make use of another word altogether this has been noted.

Prologue • Thom 1	ϢⲀϪⲈ (λόγος)
Thom 1 • 2	ⳅⲈ/ⳅⲒⲚⲈ (εὑρίσκειν)
Thom 3:4 • 3:5	ⲤⲞⲞⲨⲚ̄ (γνωρίζειν)
Thom 3:4 • 4:1	ⲱⲚⳅ (ζῆν) and ϢⲎⲢⲈ (παῖς)[13]
Thom 5:1 • 5:2 • 6:6	ⳅⲱⲠ (οὐ φανερός)[14]
Thom 5:1 • 6:4, 6	ϬⲱⲗⲠ ⲈⲂⲞⲗ (ἀποκαλύπτειν)
Thom 7 • 8	ⲢⲱⲘⲈ (ἄνθρωπος)
Thom 8 • 9	ⲘⲞⲨⳅ (πλήρης/πληροῦν)
Thom 8 • 9 • 10	ⲚⲞⲨϪⲈ (βάλλειν)
Thom 9 • 10	ⲈⲒⲤ ⳅⲎⲎⲦⲈ (ἰδού)
Thom 11:2 • 11:3	ⲘⲞⲞⲨⲦ (νεκρός)
Thom 11:3a,b • 11:4 (?)[15]	ⲈⲒⲢⲈ (ποιεῖν)
Thom 12 • 13	ⲀⲒⲔⲀⲒⲞⲤ (δίκαιος)
Thom 18:2 • 18:3	ⲀⲢⲭⲎ (ἀρχή) and ⳅⲀⲎ (τέλος)
Thom 18:3 • 19:4	ϤⲚⲀϪⲒ †ⲠⲈ ⲀⲚ Ⲙ̄ⲘⲞⲨ (οὐ γεύσεται θανάτου)
Thom 20:1, 2 • 21:1 • 22:2	ⲦⲞⲚⲦⲚ̄/ⲈⲒⲚⲈ (ὁμοιοῦν, or ὅμοιός ἐστιν)
Thom 21:3 • 21:5	ϪⲞⲈⲒⲤ/ϪⲈⲤ⁻ (κύριος)
Thom 21:2 • 22:1	ϢⲎⲢⲈ ϢⲎⲘ/ⲔⲞⲨⲈⲒ (παῖς)
Thom 21:5 • 21:6	ⲢⲞⲈⲒⲤ (γρηγορεῖν)
Thom 21:5 • 21:7	ⲈⲒ (ἔρχεσθαι)
Thom 22:3 • 22:7	ⲂⲱⲔ ⲈⳅⲞⲨⲚ ⲀⲦⲘⲚ̄ⲦⲈⲢⲞ (εἰσέρχεσθαι εἰς τὴν βασιλείαν)
Thom 22:5 • 23:2	ⲞⲨⲀ ⲞⲨⲱⲦ (εἷς μόνος)
Thom 25 • 26	ⲂⲀⲗ (ὀφθαλμός) and ⲤⲞⲚ (ἀδελφός)
Thom 26 • 27	ⲚⲀⲨ (βλέπειν[16]/ὄψεσθαι)

13. Note that Attridge ("Greek Fragments," 115) restores the Greek text of POxy 654.18 as υἱοί rather than παιδία.
14. Note that Attridge ("Greek Fragments," 115) restores the Greek text of POxy 654.28 as τὸ κεκαλυμένον, but οὐ φανερόν might possibly fit here as well.
15. In Thom 11:4 ⲈⲒⲢⲈ may translate γίνεσθαι rather than ποιεῖν.
16. Note: POxy 1.1 has διαβλέπειν rather than βλέπειν.

Thom 27 ▪ 28	κοcмοc (κόσμος)
Thom 28 ▪ 29	capϫ (σάρξ) and ϩωπ (κρύπτειν)
Thom 33:3 ▪ 35	вωк εϩογν (εἰσέρχεσθαι)
Thom 47:1 ▪ 47:2	мῆ бом (οὐ δύνασθαι) and cnaγ (δύο)
Thom 47:3 ▪ 47:4	нрπ (οἶνος)
Thom 47:3 ▪ 47:4 ▪ 47:5	вϻϻε/ϣλει (νέος) and λc (παλαιός)
Thom 48 ▪ 50	ϫоос (εἰπεῖν)
Thom 50 ▪ 51	αναπαγcιc (ἀνάπαυσις)
Thom 51 ▪ 52	νετμοογτ (οἱ νεκροί)
Thom 53:2 ▪ 53:3	cῆῆε (περιτομή) and ϻωφελει/6ῆ ϩнγ (ὀφειλεῖν)
Thom 55 ▪ 56	αϫιοc/ ῆπϣλ (ἄξιος)
Thom 57 ▪ 58	ρωμε (ἄνθρωπος)
Thom 59 ▪ 60	νaγ (ἔρχεσθαι)[17]
Thom 59 ▪ (60)[18] ▪ 61 ▪ 63	моγ (ἀποθνῄσκειν)
Thom 61:1 ▪ 61:2	6λο6 (κλινή)
Thom 61:5 ▪ 63:2	моγϩ (πληροῦν)
Thom 63 ▪ 64 ▪ 65	ρωμε (ἄνθρωπος)
Thom 64 ▪ 65	ϩмϩαλ (δοῦλος)
Thom 68 ▪ 69	ϫιωκε (διώκειν)
Thom 68 ▪ 69:1 ▪ 69:2	маκαριοc (μακάριος)
Thom 73 ▪ 74	ϫоειc (κύριος)
Thom 74 ▪ 75	ϩαϩ (πολλοί)
Thom 77:1 ▪ 78	ει (ἔρχεσθαι)
Thom 78:3 ▪ 79:2	ме (ἀλήθεια)
Thom 79:1 ▪ 79:2 ▪ 79:3	ειλ (μακάριος), ϩн (κοιλία) and κιве (μάστος)
Thom 83 ▪ 84	ϩικων (εἰκών) and оγωνϩ евоλ (φανεροῦν)
Thom 84:2 ▪ 85:1	ϣωπε (γίνεσθαι)
Thom 85:1 ▪ 85:2	αϫιοc/ ῆπϣλ (ἄξιος)
Thom 88 ▪ 90	ει (ἔρχεσθαι)
Thom 96 ▪ 97	cϩιме (γυνή)
Thom 96 ▪ 97 ▪ 98 ▪ 99[19]	тмῆτερο ῆπειωτ [εcтῆτωн] (ἡ βασιλεία τοῦ πατρὸς [ὁμοιοῖ])
Thom 97 ▪ 98	нει (οἶκος) and ειме (γνωρίζειν)
Thom 99 ▪ 101:1, 2 ▪ 101:3	маλγ (μήτηρ)
Thom 100 ▪ 101:3	† ([ἀπο]διδόναι)
Thom 103 ▪ 104	ει (ἔρχεσθαι)

17. The connection exists only if αγναγ has been omitted by haplography at the beginning of Thom 60.

18. Thom 60's connection to this series is through моγоγτ (ἀποκτείνειν) rather than моγ (ἀποθνῄσκειν).

19. Omits εcтῆτωн from the formula.

Thom 105 ● 106	ϣΗΡΕ (υίός)
Thom 107 ● 109	ΜΝΤΕΡΟ (βασιλεία)
Thom 109 ● 110 ● 111:3	ϨΕ/ ΕΙΝΕ (εὑρίσκειν)
Thom 110 ● 111:1 ● 111:3	ΚΟϹΜΟϹ/ ΚΑϨ (κόσμος)
Thom 113 ● 114	ΕΙ (ἔρχεσθαι) and ΜΝΤΕΡΟ (βασιλεία)

To assess the significance of this feature of Thomas' structure it is important to recognize that the use of catchwords is itself an organizing principle, with its own internal logic. Its nature is essentially mnemonic: a catchword in saying "A" calls to mind a similar word in saying "B," something in saying "B" suggests something in saying "C" that is to come, and so on. The significance of such a pattern in Thomas may be assesed variously. For example, an editor might have organized the collection in this way to facilitate its memorization. The utility of this for the street preacher, who would compose his or her speeches ad hoc in the busy collonades of the agora, is obvious.[20] Alternatively, one could well imagine an editor assembling these sayings simply as he or she remembered them, catchwords triggering the recollection of each new saying. In this case the catchwords will not have been part of any conscious design on the part of the editor, but simply the result his or her own process of remembering. The occasional gaps where no catchwords are to be found suggest the latter.[21] This may also mean that the order within clusters of Thomas logia was already determined at an oral stage in the tradition, before the sayings had been written down in the Gospel of Thomas.[22] At any rate, catchword association is the principle upon which the sayings in the Gospel of Thomas were originally collected. This observation is important in that it exposes as ill-founded the attempt to explain Thomas' own order as an intentional scrambling, reversal, confusion, or conflation of the more familiar synoptic order, on the supposition that Thomas' author/editor set out to use the tradition to create a text that was more congenial to his or her own theological point of view. The order of Thomas' sayings is largely a function of its genre, not its theology.

Logoi Sophon and the Development of Early Christianity

Apart from the issue of order, the question of Thomas' genre has further implications for the question of Thomas' relationship to the synoptic gospels. The Gospel of Thomas, of course, is not formally unique; there are many other examples of the sayings collection in antiquity. The first attempt to describe this genre and assess the implications of its early Christian use was

20. Epicurus' letter to Herodotus (Diogenes Laertius, 10. 35-37) illustrates the uses to which such a collection might be put once memorized, and also the pedagogical rationale for encouraging the memorization of sayings (esp. 36). See the interpretation of Betz, "Sermon on the Mount," 10-15.

21. E.g., in Thom 14-17; 70-72; 91-95.

22. So Vielhauer, Geschichte der urchristlichen Literatur, 623.

the programmatic essay by James M. Robinson, "ΛΟΓΟΙ ΣΟΦΩΝ. Zur Gattung der Spruchquelle Q."[23] Published originally as his contribution to the Bultmann *Festschrift*, this was his attempt to work out the implications of Bultmann's treatment of the sayings of Jesus in the synoptic tradition under the heading "Logien (Jesus als Weisheitslehrer)."[24] Robinson began by looking at the synoptic sayings collection, Q, within the context of other Jewish and early Christian sayings collections, and in this way sought to clarify and carry forward Bultmann's association of the synoptic logia with the Jewish *meshalim*, or proverbs.[25] Using the vocabulary native to the genre, λόγοι or λόγια (words or sayings), to identify and track examples of the genre, Robinson sought first to trace its development forward into the world of early Christian literature. The path leads, according to Robinson, to the Gospel of Thomas, whose *incipit* identifies it as such a sayings collection: "These are the secret sayings (ⲛ̄ϣⲁϫⲉ, = Greek λόγοι) that the living Jesus spoke. . . ." The *incipit* of another Nag Hammadi tractate, the Book of Thomas the Contender (138.2), similarly identifies it. In Thomas the Contender one can observe the transformation of the sayings genre into a genre more typical of Gnosticism: discourses with the resurrected Lord, in which the esoteric interpretation of traditional material becomes ever more important. The end point of this development Robinson finds in the Pistis Sophia, where traditional sayings are juxtaposed freely with esoteric interpretation in the context of a post-resurrection discourse.[26]

Robinson then follows the history of the genre from Q backwards by noting remnants of it in smaller early Christian sayings collections, such as the collections embedded in Did 1:3–5,[27] and Mark 4:1–34.[28] Ultimately he traces it through the late Jewish sayings collections contained in the Testaments of the Twelve Patriarchs,[29] the Apocalypse of Adam,[30] and the Similitudes of Enoch,[31] to what he considers to be its roots in Jewish wisdom literature, in particular the collections of λόγοι in Prov 22:17–24:22, from whose superscription, λόγοι σοφῶν, or "Sayings of the Sages," Robinson derives his own designation for the genre.[32]

Robinson thus sketches out both forwards and backwards the literary trajectory upon which Q is to be located. He therefore finds it to stand in morphological continuity with other Jewish and early Christian sayings collections on the one hand, and Thomas and other collections—some with

---

23. Revised version in English in Robinson and Koester, *Trajectories*, 71–113. References are to this version.
24. Bultmann, *Geschichte*, 73–113.
25. Robinson, "LOGOI SOPHON," 73–74.
26. Robinson, "LOGOI SOPHON," 76–85.
27. Robinson, "LOGOI SOPHON," 86–87; note the designation λόγοι (words) in 1.3.
28. Robinson, "LOGOI SOPHON," 91–95.
29. Robinson, "LOGOI SOPHON," 106–7.
30. Robinson, "LOGOI SOPHON," 107–8.
31. Robinson, "LOGOI SOPHON," 108–9.
32. Robinson, "LOGOI SOPHON," 109.

marked gnosticizing proclivities—on the other. By tracing the trajectory in this way Robinson has also made it possible to gauge the theological potential of the genre. Its manifestation in the Gospel of Thomas and the Book of Thomas the Contender on the one hand, and its disappearance in what was to become orthodox Christianity on the other, Q having been defused and embedded in the Markan outline by Matthew and Luke, illustrates at once the gnosticizing proclivity of the genre, and the consequent orthodox criticism of its continued use.[33]

In this foundational essay Robinson did not comment upon the significance of his study for the question of Thomas' relationship to the synoptic gospels.[34] It was left to Helmut Koester to draw its implications for this question closer to the surface. In his article "GNOMIA DIAPHOROI: The Origin and Nature of Diversification in the History of Early Christianity," published originally in 1965, a year after Robinson's study,[35] Koester addresses the significance of Robinson's *logoi sophon* thesis for the discussion of Thomas' relationship to the synoptic gospels:

> A direct consequence of [Robinson's] study for our question can be formulated in this way: the *Gospel of Thomas* continues, even if in a modified way, the most original gattung of the Jesus tradition—the *logoi sophon*—which, in the canonical gospels, became acceptable to the orthodox church only by radical critical alteration, not only of the form, but also of the theological intention of this primitive gattung. Such critical evaluation of the gattung, *logoi*, was achieved by Matthew and Luke through imposing the Marcan narrative-kerygma frame upon the sayings tradition represented by Q.[36]

Thus, in Koester's view the fact that Q and Thomas share a literary genre is not inconsequential for the discussion of Thomas' origins. In tracing the

33. Robinson, "LOGOI SOPHON," 113. It is instructive to note in this connection that Paul recognizes the potential of wisdom to develop into a form of gnosis in 1 Corinthians. The wisdom background of 1 Corinthians 1–4, and the opponents dealt with there, is well known (see, e.g. Dupont, *Gnosis;* Wilkens, *Weisheit und Torheit;* Hurd, *Origins of 1 Corinthians;* Horsley, "PNEUMATIKOS vs. PSYCHIKOS"). Throughout this letter Paul struggles against the notion that this special category of revealed wisdom has somehow elevated certain members of the Corinthian community above the common herd. In this context wisdom has become a kind of gnosis. Indeed, it is in this letter that Paul introduces the slogan "Knowledge (γνῶσις) puffs up, but love builds up" (1 Cor 8:2)—a seeming poke at the pseudo-wise in Corinth who would eat meat that had been offered to idols, thus creating needless controversy in the community. Paul mistrusts this Corinthian wisdom theology precisely because of its proclivity toward gnosis. It may be that this mis-trust of the wisdom tradition was one reason Paul did not often appeal to the tradition of Jesus' sayings (see Patterson, "Paul and Jesus").

34. But see Robinson, "LOGOI SOPHON," 113, n. 95. In a more recent discussion of the thesis ("On Bridging the Gulf," 165–66) Robinson reveals that part of the impetus for his work had come from his opposition to the view made popular by Kümmel in the 13th edition of his *Einleitung in das Neue Testament* (1963). Kümmel asserts that Thomas is not a real sayings collection, comparable say to Q, but rather a different sort of collection developed to present Jesus in the role of the gnostic revealer figure, a view that has since become important in the more recent arguments of Dehandschutter against an independent Thomas tradition ("L'Évangile de Thomas").

35. Reprinted in Koester and Robinson, *Trajectories*, 114–57. References are to this reprint.

36. Koester, "GNOMAI DIAPHOROI," 135.

development of the sayings tradition directly from Q through Thomas, Robinson had provided the conceptual framework for understanding not only how Thomas might be related to some of the earliest stages in the history of the synoptic tradition, but also why it makes little sense to speak of Thomas' derivation from the synoptic gospels at all. Insofar as the synoptic gospels absorb and defuse the sayings tradition by embedding it in a biographical narrative, they represent a critical detour from the literary and theological development traceable in a more direct line from Jewish and early Christian sayings collections, such as Q, to the Gospel of Thomas. In other words, any continuity between Thomas and the early stages of the Jesus tradition is not to be traced through the synoptic gospels, but rather directly to the collections of sayings used as sources by the synoptic evangelists.

At this point Koester holds back from offering a more precise source-critical hypothesis for Thomas, saying only that Thomas must incorporate small collections of sayings also taken up in part by Q, but perhaps also available to Mark and Luke. Thus, this sketch of the literary and theological trajectory from Q to Thomas does not lead to an overly simplistic corollary source hypothesis, positing Thomas' dependence upon Q. Koester formulates his more nuanced position geographically:

> Thus, Thomas does not use Q, but he does represent the eastern branch of the gattung, *logoi,* the western branch being represented by the synoptic *logoi* of Q, which was used in western Syria by Matthew and later by Luke.[37]

Hence the identity of Thomas' own sources is left vague. It is enough to say that Thomas represents a development of the early Christian sayings tradition, and hence lies on a tradition-historical trajectory that runs parallel to, but relatively unaffected by, the development of the narrative gospel form. Q was ultimately pulled into the wake of the predominance of the narrative gospel form; Thomas, for whatever reason, was not.

In a second programmatic essay, on the nature and extent of diversity within early Christianity, Koester supplemented this thesis with a comparative analysis of various form-critical categories shared by Thomas and the synoptic tradition, in an effort to work out more precisely the way in which the development from early sayings collections to the sort of theological presentation one finds in Thomas might have actually proceeded.[38] Comparing first prophetic and apocalyptic sayings, parables, and I-sayings in both traditions, Koester notices in Thomas the conspicuous absence of the sort of apocalyptic expectation one is accustomed to finding in such sayings in the synoptic tradition. Among prophetic and apocalyptic sayings, for example, there are no parallels to the traditional apocalyptic images of Mark 13, nor to the Son of

---

37. Koester, "GNOMAI DIAPHOROI," 136.
38. Koester, "One Jesus." Reprinted in Robinson and Koester, *Trajectories,* to which subsequent references will be made.

Man sayings, typical of Q's apocalyptic expectation.[39] Rather, one finds in Thomas a type of eschatological preaching about the kingdom, which emphasizes its presence in the words of Jesus, a concept which Koester holds to be very close to the original proclamation of Jesus himself.[40] Likewise, the parables in Thomas are not allegorized or given secondary conclusions, which would draw them into the service of traditional apocalyptic themes. Rather, they speak of finding the presence of the divine in Jesus' words.[41] And in Thomas' I-sayings, Jesus speaks not as the apocalyptic judge who is to come on clouds of glory but as the revealer, whose word brings life.[42]

The emphasis on Jesus' words found in each of these categories is perhaps best seen in the category of sayings most typical of the genre *logoi sophon*, Thomas' wisdom sayings. Koester points out that like wisdom sayings in general, many of Thomas' sayings express the simplest of self-evident truths (e.g., 47:1: "No one can serve two masters"), or general admonitions to virtuous or prudent behavior (e.g., 39:3: "Be wise as serpents, and innocent as doves"). As words of self-evident wisdom they do not require the validation of a particular person whose authoritative status is confirmed by the kerygma or by being assigned a role within a particular mythological scheme (such as the notion of the Son of Man or the imminence of apocalyptic judgment). The word itself carries its own weight, since it is derived from the realm of human experience.

Yet there are wisdom sayings in Thomas which carry the form beyond this limited sphere. Thomas is not a simple book of proverbs; alongside its proverbial sayings are sayings whose esoteric and/or gnosticizing content is far from self-explanatory. Nonetheless, insofar as Thomas does not abandon the wisdom genre *logoi sophon*, but instead presents these more abstruse sayings of revelation alongside, and often simply appended to, sayings of the proverbial form, it shows a continued allegiance to the word as divine revelation. Koester underscores this point by calling attention especially to those logia in which the modulation from wisdom to gnosis is accomplished in concord with the theme of seeking and finding, e.g., in Thom 2:

1Jesus said, "Let one who seeks not stop seeking until he finds. 2When he finds, he will be disturbed. 3When he is disturbed, he will marvel, 4and will reign over all."[43]

---

39. Koester, "One Jesus," 168–70.
40. Koester, "One Jesus," 171–75. Koester argues that the absence of apocalyptic eschatology in Thomas is not the result of a purging of apocalyptic from the Thomas tradition. Rather, Thomas presupposes a stage in the tradition before the eschatological sayings contained any apocalyptic expectation of the Son of Man. Koester sides with Vielhauer in claiming that the most primitive stage of the synoptic tradition did not yet contain this christological development (Vielhauer, "Gottesreich and Menschensohn;" and "Jesus und der Menschensohn;" both reprinted in Vielhauer, *Aufsätze*.)
41. Koester "One Jesus," 175–77.
42. Koester "One Jesus," 177–79.
43. Koester "One Jesus," 183; cf. Thom 42.

Here the seam between the wisdom admonition (cf. Thom 94) and the gnosticizing expansion is clearly evident,[44] so that the modulation from wisdom to gnosis is relatively transparent. But even more striking is the way in which the wisdom orientation has pulled the gnostic element into its orbit, so that the gnostic revelation does not simply come from, and rest upon, the authority of the revealer; rather, it comes as a result of a positive response to the admonition to seek and find. In Thomas the disclosure of knowledge is always self-disclosure. Koester writes:

> It is only here that the tradition of wisdom sayings takes its characteristic turn into gnostic theology. Throughout the tradition of these sayings their truth does not depend upon the authority of Jesus. Whether the wisdom saying envisages man's being in general, or whether it discloses man's spiritual nature and origin, its truth is vindicated whenever he finds this truth in himself.[45]

In this way, then, Koester shows how Thomas' theology is related to, and may have developed from, early Christian eschatological preaching about the kingdom (without its characteristic apocalyptic turn in the synoptic gospels). He also shows how such preaching might have modulated into Thomas' own theological bias via the *logoi sophon* genre, and how the wisdom admonition can have evolved into self reflection on the nature of the world and human being in the world. These are not developments which are to be traced through the specific form of early Christian proclamation found in the synoptic tradition; their roots lie deeper than this. Koester's synthesis of the Thomas tradition's place among the various streams of early Christian thought warrants quotation in full:

> The basis of the *Gospel of Thomas* is a sayings collection which is more primitive than the canonical gospels, even though its basic principle is not related to the creed of the passion and resurrection. Its principle is nonetheless theological. Faith is understood as belief in Jesus' words, a belief which makes what Jesus proclaimed present and real for the believer. The catalyst which has caused the crystallization of these sayings into a "gospel" is the view that the kingdom is uniquely present in Jesus' eschatological preaching and that eternal wisdom about man's true self is disclosed in his words. The gnostic proclivity of this concept needs no further elaboration.
>
> The relation of this "saying's gospel," from which the *Gospel of Thomas* is derived, to the synoptic sayings source Q, is an open question. Without doubt, most of its materials are Q sayings (including some sayings which appear occasionally in Mark). But it must have been a version of Q in which the apocalyptic expectation of the Son of man was missing, and in which Jesus' radicalized eschatology of the kingdom and his revelation of divine wisdom in his own words were dominant motifs.
>
> Such a version of Q is, however, not secondary, but very primitive. At least

---

44. Koester "One Jesus," 183, n. 4.
45. Koester "One Jesus," 184.

Paul's debate with his opponents in 1 Corinthians seems to suggest that the wisdom theology which Paul attacked relied on this understanding of Jesus' message. These opponents propagated a realized eschatology. They claimed that divine wisdom was revealed through Jesus. And at least one saying which Paul quotes in the context of his refutation is indeed found in the *Gospel of Thomas* 17 (1 Cor 2:9).

This would prove that such sayings collections with explicit theological tendencies were in use quite early, and not only in Aramaic-speaking circles in Syria; that the source "Q," used by Matthew and Luke, was a secondary version of such a "gospel," into which the apocalyptic expectation of the Son of man had been introduced to check the gnosticizing tendencies of this sayings gospel; and that the *Gospel of Thomas*, stemming from a more primitive stage of such a "gospel," attests its further growth into a gnostic theology.[46]

By looking at the whole of the Gospel of Thomas, its form, its genre, and not just at individual sayings in Thomas which happen to have synoptic parallels, Robinson and Koester changed the terms of the Thomas debate in two ways. First, since the earlier discussion tended to focus on those sayings in Thomas most like the synoptic sayings, perhaps uncritically accepting the synoptic tradition as the standard for making judgments about the age and possible authenticity of a given logion,[47] it seldom addressed those sayings most typical of Thomas' own theological orientation. Thus, the discussion never really came to address the fundamental question raised by the position that Thomas is the product of an independent tradition: How is it that a gospel like Thomas, with its brand of gnosticizing theology, can have developed directly out of the preaching of Jesus and its continuation in the earliest proclamation of the church? In the 1966 Colloquium on Gnosticism held in Messina, Torgny Säve-Söderbergh could still address critically the entire field of Thomas research with the probing question: "Were Gnostic faith and 'orthodox' Christianity opposed entities or even different to start with? Were Gnostic ideas acceptable to the first congregation and were they, originally, incompatible with the preaching of Jesus?"[48] Koester's 1965 answer to this question anticipates Säve-Söderbergh's critique:

> The crucial problem of Gnosticism . . . is not how to relate second century Gnostic writings to subsequent developments—as important as this task may be— but how to interpret early forms of Gnosticism with respect to their roots in early Christian and Jewish theology. Here, it seems, the *Gospel of Thomas* occupies a uniquely decisive position, since we can see in it a distinctive reinterpretation of originally eschatological sayings and their terminology. The question is not only that of various stages in the growth of the tradition, so as to distinguish between an older "synoptic Palestinian" core and later gnosticizing accretion. We are rather

---

46. Koester "One Jesus," 186–87.
47. So e.g., J.-B. Bauer, "Echte Jesusworte;" R. McL. Wilson, *Studies;* Hunzinger, "Unbekannte Gleichnisse;" and Higgins, "Non-Gnostic Sayings."
48. Säve-Söderbergh, "Gnostic and Canonical Gospel Traditions," 557–58.

confronted also with the "gnosticizing proclivity" of the gattung *Logoi* itself, i.e. in its oldest and most primitive states.[49]

Thus, by focusing on Thomas as a whole, especially its genre, Robinson and Koester were able to locate Thomas within the earliest stages of the development of early Christianity. Its literary and theological "home," so to speak, was not in the second or later centuries, but in the first.

Second, the work of Robinson and Koester has rendered inadequate that part of the Thomas debate that attempted to prove Thomas' dependence on the synoptic gospels by providing a theological explanation for the Thomas form of the saying over against its synoptic parallel based on the highly developed gnostic systems from the second century and later. To those who argued for this method of interpreting Thomas the excerpt thesis made sense because the theological motives they imagined to be at work in Thomas' text first arose relatively late, and thus formed a radical break with Christianity as it had developed in its first three or four generations. Again, if one takes the synoptic gospels as the standard, such a radical break almost demands the sort of literary mutilation presupposed by this theory. But what many early studies failed to see was that Thomas itself presents a fundamental and decisive challenge to this view of Gnosticism and early Christianity. Insofar as Robinson and Koester were able to demonstrate a continuity, both literary and theological, between Thomas and Jewish and early Christian sayings collections, they showed that there really is no radical break between early Christianity and the emergence of Gnosticism. This realization—hinted at also in Säve-Söderbergh's question—is not really very new. The adequacy of such labels as "gnostic" and "orthodox" when dealing with the problem of earliest Christianity was called into question already in 1934 by Walter Bauer.[50] It is not incidental that Koester frames his remarks in "GNOMAI DIAPHOROI" in terms of Bauer's insights.[51] Thomas is probably the most dramatic illustration of the inadequacy of traditional categories to which Bauer pointed, for its own brand of gnosticizing theology can be drawn into direct continuity with the earliest layers of the Jesus tradition. The position that Thomas depends on the synoptic gospels, to the extent that it relies on the assumption of a break between (early) Christianity and (late) Gnosticism, fails to grasp the challenge to this assumption posed by Thomas itself.

Summary

When approached from the point of view of form, Thomas thus presents one with a number of indications that its sources are the oral and/or written traditions generally available to early Christian gospel writers, not simply the

---

49. Koester, "GNOMAI DIAPHOROI," 137.
50. W. Bauer, *Rechtgläubigkeit und Ketzerei;* ET: *Orthodoxy and Heresy.*
51. Cf. Koester, "GNOMAI DIAPHOROI," 114.

canonical texts themselves. First is the fact that Thomas presents its sayings in a sequence that is almost entirely divorced from that in which one finds them in the synoptic texts. Second, attempts to explain Thomas' different order in terms of a deliberate, theologically motivated redaction of the synoptics fail to grasp the significance of Thomas' genre as it informs our understanding of this text. The order of Thomas' sayings is motivated not by an elaborate theological system, gnostic or otherwise. Rather, its organizing principle is the very pragmatic technique of using catchwords to link successive sayings together. Finally, to the extent that Thomas' genre itself implies a theological orientation in Gnosticism or speculative wisdom, the work of Robinson and Koester has shown that such an orientation does not mean that a writing is necessarily late or derivative. Rather, Thomas' genre and the theological significance it carries form a point of continuity between Thomas and the earliest stages of the Jesus tradition, especially other sayings traditions. Hence, Thomas belongs on a trajectory that does not pass through the synoptic gospels at all, but proceeds along a parallel course with its own literary and theological roots planted deeply in the fertile soil of earliest Christianity.

To the historian of early Christianity this means that with Thomas we are afforded yet another lens through which to view the development of the Jesus tradition and its social setting, the Jesus movement. Thomas is the offspring of an autonomous stream of early Christian tradition. By looking at the way in which it treats the tradition, how it selects from the tradition, what it prefers, what it emphasizes, it stands to broaden our understanding of the variety of early Christian thought and experience within its first few generations—provided we can locate it within this geographical, theological, and social diversity. It is to this task of location that Part Two of this study is devoted.

The Gospel of Thomas

and the Historical Development of Early Christianity

4

The Date and Provenance
of the Gospel of Thomas

A Time
and a Place

It is now possible to proceed to the problem of Thomas Christianity, and its place within the overall historical development of the early church. But preliminary to this task there remain two questions: When was the Gospel of Thomas written, and where?

The Date of the Gospel of Thomas

Dating the Gospel of Thomas is not an easy task. To be sure, there are general chronological boundaries within which one must work, but they are wide indeed. The fact that Thomas is not dependent upon the synoptic gospels is informative insofar as it means that these texts, the latest (Luke) having been written perhaps near the end of the first century, do not offer a *terminus a quo* for Thomas. But this only widens the parameters within which we may work; it does not in itself suggest a date for Thomas.[1] It simply indicates that Thomas could have been assembled any time after the origin of the Jesus movement. As for a *terminus ad quem*, the manuscript tradition itself provides one limiting factor. The oldest manuscript evidence for Thomas is POxy 1, which Grenfell and Hunt assigned an approximate date of 200 C.E. on the basis of the script and the level at which the fragment was uncovered at Oxyrhynchus.[2] If one

---

1. *Pace* Davies (*The Gospel of Thomas*, 145), who offers this as one argument for dating Thomas before 70 C.E. But the fact that Thomas is not dependent upon the synoptic gospels does not mean that it was written before them. To argue so would be to assume that the synoptic gospels were almost immediately so prominent among early Christians that after their appearance nothing could have been written independently of them. This, however, is a dubious assumption. As Koester has shown (*Synoptische Überlieferung*), one must count on an active oral tradition well past the composition of the synoptic texts and on into the second century.

2. Grenfell and Hunt, ΛΟΓΙΑ ΙΗΣΟΥ, 6.

assumes for the moment that the Gospel of Thomas comes not from Egypt, but Syria (a full treatment of the question of provenance will be offered presently) then the actual *terminus ad quem* can be pushed back. We may allow a generation for the growth in popularity of the book, such as would result in its wider dissemination, and yet another for the popularity to reach Egypt. This brings us to the middle of the second century. Grenfell and Hunt themselves placed the *terminus ad quem* at 140 C.E.[3]

The parameters thus established, one is left to locate Thomas somewhere within a range of more than 100 years. To narrow this range into a meaningful period of time poses a multitude of problems. At the heart of the difficulty is the general instability of the gospel tradition in its early years. One may take the Gospel of Mark as illustrative of the problem.[4] It is generally agreed that both Matthew and Luke made use of the Gospel of Mark in the composition of their respective gospels. But Luke, oddly, does not contain anything corresponding to Mark 6:45–8:26, a section which Matthew, for his part, includes. To account for this large omission many have supposed that Luke simply did not have this section in his version of Mark. This would mean, of course, that in the earliest years of its transmission history, the Gospel of Mark already existed in at least two different versions: a Mark^{Mt} and a Mark^{Lk}. But the history of Mark does not stop there. In the recently discovered fragment of Clement of Alexandria's letter to Theodore, Clement tells his friend of yet two more versions of Mark known to him in Alexandria near the end of the second century: a "Secret Mark" intended only for those who had been initiated into the higher mysteries of the Alexandrian church, and an edited version of this secret gospel created by Carpocrates (who flourished in the Alexandria in the first half of the second century) and used in Clement's day by the Carpocratians. Finally, citing several places in the canonical version of Mark wherein textual residue from the Secret Gospel of Mark is to be found, a growing number of scholars has come to the opinion that our canonical Mark is not that

3. Grenfell and Hunt, ΛΟΓΙΑ ΙΗΣΟΥ, 16. Their reasoning was as follows: "The primitive cast and setting of the sayings, the absence of any consistent tendency in favor of any particular sect, the wide divergences in the familiar sayings from the text of the Gospels, the striking character of those which are new, combine to separate the fragment from the 'apocryphal' literature of the middle and latter half of the second century, and refer it back to the period when the Canonical Gospels had not yet reached their pre-eminent position." Grenfell and Hunt's instincts turned out to have been good. Their comments were not outdated after the entire text of Thomas surfaced at Nag Hammadi fifty years later. Many scholars, however, have chosen to elevate Grenfell and Hunt's *terminus ad quem* to the position of *terminus a quo*, and thus take the middle of the second century as the date of the Gospel of Thomas; so Puech, "Gospel of Thomas," 305; Wilson, *Studies,* 7 (at least on into the second century); Piper, "*The Gospel of Thomas,*" 21; Gärtner, *Theology,* 271–72; Haenchen, "Literatur," 155; Cullmann, "Das Thomasevangelium," 327; Leipoldt, *Das Evangelium nach Thomas,* 17; Vielhauer, *Geschichte der urchristlichen Literatur,* 621. But it is arbitrary simply to assign Thomas the latest possible date allowed by the manuscript evidence. Were such a procedure to be used to date the canonical gospels, only John, by virtue of p52, could reasonably lay claim to a first century date.

4. The following points summarize Helmut Koester's thesis regarding the Secret Gospel of Mark; see his article "History and Development."

early version of Mark used by Matthew, but rather a recension that derives (by way of abbreviation) from the Secret Gospel of Mark to which Clement refers.[5] Thus, all told, by the end of the second century there may have been as many as five different versions of the Gospel of Mark circulating among various early Christian groups.

While Mark's variegated history might be the easiest to trace, similar well-known examples of textual instability from the Pauline corpus,[6] from the Gospel of John,[7] the Apocryphon of John,[8] and other early Christian writings are enough to dispel the notion that, once written, a text's authority could shield it from the creativity of subsequent curators. Thus, when dating an ancient text, one should always be as clear as possible about *which version* of the text one means to date. As a simple collection of sayings, the Gospel of Thomas poses problems of this nature, but on a much larger scale. Without having to look after the narrative integrity of the text and its overall aesthetic quality, each new curator of the Thomas collection—and perhaps many simultaneously—could easily have added new sayings as he or she came across them, or sloughed away outmoded sayings as their relevance to new situations in the life of the sage became questionable. Thus, a collection such as the Gospel of Thomas would quite naturally have been a cumulative product, whose content no doubt changed from generation to generation.

How, then, is one to date such a text? The usual method for dating a text is to focus on particular sayings or traditions whose content suggests a time frame. Such a procedure, however, could clearly mislead the student of Thomas. For example, there are sayings in Thomas (e.g., Thom 54 and some of Thomas' parables) which may well come from the verbal repertoire of Jesus himself;[9] this does not mean, however, that the entire collection could thus be considered an apostolic transcript! For at the other extreme there are sayings which have no doubt been added to the collection quite late (e.g. Thom 7),[10] conceivably as late as the third or fourth century. Likewise, such sayings are also not necessarily relevant for dating the collection as a whole.[11] However,

5. So Koester, "History and Development;" Schenke, "Mystery of the Gospel of Mark;" Cameron, *Other Gospels,* 68–69; Meyer, "The Youth in the *Secret Gospel of Mark,*" 129–53; and Crossan, *Four Other Gospels,* 91–110.

6. E.g., the deutero-Pauline interpolation in 1 Cor 14:33b-36; the problem of Romans 16; the interpolation in 1 Thess 2:13–16; and the vexing problem of the multiple letter fragments that comprise 2 Corinthians.

7. E.g., John 7:53–8:11, and the suspected "ecclesiastical redaction" responsible for John 21 and other passages.

8. The four exemplars of this tractate that survived antiquity give evidence of two distinct versions: a long (NHC 2, 1 and 4, 1) and a short recension (BG 8502, 2 and NHC 3, 1).

9. At a recent meeting of the Jesus Seminar Thom 54 received a "red" vote (= clearly represents the voice of Jesus). Thom 98, the Parable of the Assassin, received a "pink" vote (= probably represents the voice of Jesus). See Patterson, "Outside the Bible," 5.

10. Jackson (*The Lion Becomes Man*) has argued that Thom 7 was coined by a second-century Egyptian encratite.

11. These considerations are aptly pointed out and developed in Neller, "Diversity in the Gospel of Thomas."

bracketing out these extremes there are a number of considerations relative to Thomas as a whole which make it possible to suggest an approximate period within which at least the torso of this collection was assembled.

First, as Koester has argued, the collection must come from a period in which particular communities were still appealing to the authoritative position of particular apostles as a way of guaranteeing the reliability of its traditions.[12] The *incipit* and the title certainly function in this way. But one might also point to Thom 12, which appeals to James, and to Thom 13, which appeals to the authority of Thomas, to illustrate the feature. In this sense the Gospel of Thomas is comparable to Matthew, in which the authority of Peter is asserted (Matt 16:13-20), or perhaps to the deutero-Pauline epistles, which appeal to Paul's authority in like manner. All of these texts derive from the last decades of the first century C.E.

It should also be noted that Thomas does not appeal to the authority of Thomas or James simply because they are "apostles." Thomas never treats the "the twelve" as a rarefied concept, a venerated group. The authority of each apostle is not taken for granted by virtue of the status earned simply through being part of "the twelve." In Thom 13, for example, Thomas' answer is held up as exemplary, but those of Peter and Matthew are deprecated as inadequate.[13] The text thus dates to a period in which authority was still *personal,* or dependent upon a leader's personal charisma and powers of persuasion, and not yet *apostolic* properly speaking. The latter depends upon a nostalgia, in which "the apostles" have become venerated figures in the community's foundational stories, a view not shared by Thomas (cf. esp. Thom 43, 51, and 52). All of this would suggest a date close to Paul, who feels no compunction about maligning the reputation of an apostolic leader when he feels so compelled (cf. Gal 2:11-12), or to Mark, who often portrays the "disciples" as simple dunderheads. By contrast, at the end of the first century Luke can smooth over all of these difficulties to portray a single, harmonious, apostolic church guided and unified by the Holy Spirit.

It might be objected, however, that such arguments could be used to date Thom 13 itself, with its pro-Thomas and anti-Petrine stance, to this early rough and tumble period of unsettled rival claims, without necessarily sug-

---

12. Koester, "Introduction (to the Gospel of Thomas)," 40–41.

13. Koester makes the same point with respect to what he views as competing claims in Thom 12 and 13, arguing that Thom 13 was added to supplant the claims behind Thom 12. But I cannot agree that James is to be included in the polemic. If this were the case, it is not likely that Thom 12 would have been included or retained in the collection at all. Still, supposing that there were some unknown reason for retaining it, such as for the purpose of setting up a straw man to be knocked down by Thom 13, one would have to explain why it is that Thom 13 takes the trouble to undermine the authority of Peter and Matthew, but makes no direct mention of James, who could have easily been slipped in along side these two with a foolish response of his own. This lacking, it seems best to assume rather that Thom 12 and 13 represent parallel but not necessarily competing claims. Those who used this document likely esteemed them both, and assigned each a place of importance in their myths of origin. (Cf. Koester, *Introduction*, 2. 152–53, where his position is moderated somewhat.)

gesting an early date for the collection as a whole, which might simply have incorporated these earlier elements. Yet this does not seem to be the case with Thom 13. Its links with the Prologue (Thomas' preeminence) and Thom 114 (Peter's censure) indicate that Thom 13 is not isolated in its predilections or its willingness to make them explicit. Furthermore, the way in which these sayings enclose the collection as a whole suggests that they are not part of that older stratum of sayings taken up into the collection from an earlier period, but belong rather to a later (perhaps the latest) redaction of the collection, from which it takes its name. The superfluity of Thom 13 over against the claims already laid down in Thom 12 suggests this secondary status for Thom 13 as well. This means that the basic Thomas collection was already in existence when the Prologue, Thom 13, and Thom 114 were added, presumably still in that early period of jostling personal claims to authority. Precisely when this Thomas layer was added, or how extensive it was, may never be known. One might perhaps speculate that it coincided, more or less, with the martyrdom of James in 62 c.e.,[14] which will have called forth a reassessment of the older structure of authority implied in Thom 12. But this must remain a guess, since the tradition of authority laid down in Thom 12 could have survived James himself through the selection of a successor, thus presenting the distinct possibility that a James-Thomas rapprochement came somewhat later.

To these may be added a number of observations relative to the genre in which the Gospel of Thomas is cast, the sayings collection. The sayings collection as a literary form belongs to the earliest period of Christian literary activity, as evidenced by Q. Another example of the genre may be the collection of parables in Mark 4. The fate of these two examples of the genre is instructive: neither survived as an independent document; rather, each was absorbed into the more biographical genres favored by Christians in the latter part of the first century. This suggests a climate in the later period of Christian origins that was not as favorable to the literary form in which we find Thomas as was the earlier period. As one moves into the second century the biography-like gospels such as one finds in the New Testament come more and more to dominate the scene. To the extent that the sayings collection survived, it did so primarily among emerging gnostic groups, which tended to recast it in the form of a dialogue between the resurrected Lord and his former students (perhaps explaining why it was shunned by non-gnostic groups).[15] At any rate, the collection we know as the Gospel of Thomas must have its origins before the end of the first century, when such collections were still thought useful.[16]

---

14. According to Josephus (*Ant.* 20. 197–203) James was martyred under the high priest Ananus the Younger, who took advantage of the absence of a procurator after the death of Festus, but before the arrival of his successor, Albinus, thus in 62 c.e. (cf. the discussion in Pratscher, *Der Herrenbruder,* 227–60).

15. So Robinson, "LOGOI SOPHON," 113.

16. Stevan Davies (*The Gospel of Thomas,* 145) also argues that within the corpus of Christian literature Thomas' form is closest to that of Q, and therefore that the two should be dated similarly. But it is not simply these two documents' form that suggests that they be dated

Finally, Koester has argued that the relative antiquity of Thomas may be seen also in its use—or lack of use—of christological titles.[17] Koester argues that in contrast to other documents from Nag Hammadi, Thomas exhibits a singular lack of any use of the christological titles "lord," "messiah/Christ," or "Son of Man,"[18] such as had become widespread in early Christianity as early as the Pauline writings and the canonical gospels. Koester invites comparison with other early sayings collections such as Q, which he has long argued originally did not include sayings identifying Jesus with an apocalyptic Son of Man.[19] Kloppenborg's recent redaction critical study of Q[20] confirms and strengthens Koester's argument on this point. Kloppenborg has shown that the formative layer of Q comprises a series of wisdom speeches, in which the sayings of apocalyptic doom and of prophetic judgment against "this generation," with their characteristic Son of Man Christology, do not play a role. In Koester's view, it is to this early, formative layer of Q that Thomas should rightly be compared. This, of course, suggests an early date for Thomas.

Provenance

It was Puech[21] who first drew attention to the fact that the particular name for the apostle Thomas found in the Prologue to the Gospel of Thomas, Didymus Judas Thomas (ⲇⲓⲇⲩⲙⲟⲥ ⲓ̈ⲟⲩⲇⲁⲥ ⲑⲱⲙⲁⲥ), is associated especially with Christianity as it developed in eastern Syria, in the area around Edessa. The tradition of referring to Thomas as Judas Didymus Thomas, or Judas Thomas (as opposed to simply Thomas, or Thomas Didymus in the West) occurs most notably in the third-century Acts of Thomas, whose Prologue similarly reads "Judas Thomas, who is also called Didymus" ('Ιούδας Θωμᾶς ὁ καὶ Δίδυμος; cf. AcThom 11: "Judas Thomas" ['Ιούδας ὁ καὶ Θωμᾶς]).

---

comparably; sayings collections are relatively common in the ancient world, and they come from a variety of periods, not just the middle of the first century (see Kloppenborg, *Formation*, 263-316). Thus, its form alone does not suggest a date for Thomas. Rather, it is the fate of this form *within early Christian circles* that is decisive. For the apparent reluctance of early Christians to make much use of the sayings collection after the first century and their growing preference for biographical or dialogical forms (a preference seen only in its nascent stages in Thomas—see, e.g., Thom 13, 72, and 79) means that we are not likely to find Christians creating from scratch a document such as Thomas much later than the final decades of the first century. The sayings collection may reemerge later in the second century, as it seems evident that Justin Martyr and the writer of 2 Clement each made use of some sort of gospel florilegium. But these sayings are clearly derived from the canonical gospel texts, and are thus secondary, and not original compositions. As Part I of this study has sought to demonstrate, this is not the case with the Gospel of Thomas.

17. Koester, "Introduction (to the Gospel of Thomas)," 40; see also his *Introduction*, 2. 152-53.

18. In Thom 86 son of man is not titular; so Koester, "One Jesus," 170-71, n. 34.

19. Koester builds upon the work of Vielhauer, who argues that sayings about the Son of Man were absent from the earliest layers of the synoptic tradition (Vielhauer, "Gottesreich und Menschensohn;" and "Jesus und der Menschensohn;" both reprinted in Vielhauer, *Aufsätze*.

20. Kloppenborg, *Formation*.

21. Puech, "Gospel of Thomas," 286.

Puech thinks the parallel so striking as to suggest a literary relationship between the Gospel of Thomas and the Acts of Thomas, and points out several places where he thinks that the latter might be dependent upon the former: AcThom 136 (cf. Thom 2); 147 (cf. Thom 22); 170 (cf. Thom 52); and others where it perhaps comments on Thomas' content: AcThom 14 (cf. Thom 37) and 92 (cf. Thom 22).

Though Puech himself does not develop these observations into a thesis concerning the provenance of the Gospel of Thomas,[22] most have taken the preponderance of the "Judas Thomas" tradition in the East as decisive for locating the Gospel of Thomas there.[23] The only serious challenge to this convention has come from Barbara Aland, who offers (primarily) three arguments against Syrian provenance: 1) If Thomas was originally written in Greek, one would have to name a bilingual environment as its place of origin. Edessa, in the second century, Aland maintains, was almost entirely Syriac-speaking.[24] 2) Aland argues that the name "Judas Thomas" must have originated earlier than the Gospel of Thomas (she assumes a 140 C.E. date for Thomas), and in non-gnostic circles (she assumes that Thomas is gnostic), and must have been more widespread than just eastern Syria.[25] 3) Aland disputes Puech's theory that the Acts of Thomas made use of the Gospel of Thomas. The parallels to which Puech points are rough, and the ocurrence of the name Judas Thomas in both documents is simply not enough to warrant such a theory.[26]

A.F.J. Klijn, in a 1972 article, "Christianity in Edessa and the Gospel of Thomas: On Barbara Ehlers', Kann das Thomasevangelium aus Edessa stammen?" has made answer to Aland's objections. In response to Aland's charge that Edessa was not a bilingual environment, Klijn points to recent studies showing the use of Greek on a much greater scale than was granted by Aland.[27] In the Sevenster *Festschrift* he shows that the name Judas Thomas indeed belongs distinctively to eastern Syria.[28] Finally, on the matter of Puech's thesis that the Acts of Thomas made use of the Gospel of Thomas,

22. Puech, "Gospel of Thomas," 287: "If this be so [that the Acts of Thomas is dependent upon the Gospel of Thomas], it might allow us to determine approximately at least the date of the composition of our gospel [Thomas], if not its place of origin."

23. Wilson, *Studies*, 10 ("suggests a Syrian origin"); Gärtner, *Theology*, 271-72 (accepts Puech's argument as indicating a Syrian origin); Koester, *Introduction*, 2. 151-52; Layton, *Gnostic Scriptures*, 360-64, 377; Crossan, *Four Other Gospels*, 23-26. Guey offers an argument for Syrian provenance based upon the "gold coin" in Thom 100 ("Comment le 'denier de César'," 478-79). Quispel has argued persistently for a relationship between Thomas and several documents of eastern Syrian Christianity—see esp. Quispel, "The Gospel of Thomas and the New Testament;" "L' Évangile selon Thomas et les Clémentines;" and "L'Évangile selon Thomas et le Diatessaron," (all reprinted in Quispel, *Gnostic Studies*) and Quispel, *Makarius.*

24. Aland, "Kann das Thomasevagelium aus Edessa stammen?" 303-4.

25. Aland, "Kann das Thomasevangelium aus Edessa stammen?" 304-7.

26. Aland, "Kann das Thomasevangelium aus Edessa stammen?" 307-8.

27. Klijn, "Christianity in Edessa," 72-74.

28. Klijn, "John XIV 22 and the Name Judas Thomas."

Klijn correctly concedes Aland's argument: the parallels to which Puech points are certainly not enough to prove dependence.[29] But it is enough that Puech's evidence suggests at least that the two documents stand in a common line of tradition, a tradition whose continuity in the East we might then trace through association with the figure of Judas Thomas: the Old Syriac (sy[s.(c)]) readings of John 14:22; the Prologue to the Book of Thomas the Contender (138.2); the Abgar legend as preserved by Eusebius (*Hist. eccles.* 1.13.11); and in the *Sermones de fide* (7.11.3) of Ephraem. If a gospel were to be associated with Judas Thomas, it seems quite likely that it would be in eastern Syria.

But this holds true only for the final (Thomas) phase of the collection. Using the same logic of assigning a collection to that region associated with its patron apostle, the initial (James) phase of the collection should probably be assigned to Jerusalem and its surroundings.[30] It might be conjectured, then, that at some point (after the death of James?) the group that used the collection migrated East, to eastern Syria.[31] Whether it brought with it the new orientation towards Thomas' authority, and thus introduced it to Syria, or encountered it first in Syria as an indigenous tradition, would be difficult to determine.

Summary

While the cumulative nature of the sayings collection understandably makes the Gospel of Thomas difficult to date with precision, several factors weigh in favor of a date well before the end of the first century: the way in which Thomas appeals to the authority of particular prominent figures (Thomas, James) against the competing claims of others (Peter, Matthew); its genre, the sayings collection, which seems to have declined in importance after the emergence of the more biographical and dialogical forms near the end of the first century; and its primitive christology, which seems to presuppose a theological climate more primitive even than the later stages of the synoptic sayings gospel, Q. Together these factors suggests a date for Thomas in the vicinity of 70–80 C.E. As for its provenance, while it is possible, even likely, that an early version of this collection associated with James circulated in the environs of Jerusalem, the Gospel of Thomas in more or less its present state comes from eastern Syria, where the popularity of the apostle Thomas (Judas Didymos Thomas) is well attested.

29. Klijn, "Christianity in Edessa," 77; cf. Davies, *The Gospel of Thomas*, 18–21.
30. Pratscher (*Der Herrenbruder*, 74–77) argues that James would have had charge of the Jerusalem circle from about 44 C.E.
31. The reason for this migration can only be speculated. Perhaps the martyrdom of James itself motivated the group to leave Jerusalem. Or it may have left this area along with the many other refugees, who moved out of harm's way at the outbreak of the Jewish war.

5

Thomas **A Social-Historical**
Christianity **Description**

The Gospel of Thomas is the product of an autonomous tradition. Of this one may be sure. Put in the most general terms, it belongs to the same period of Christian writing that produced the canonical gospels. Of this, too, one may be confident. As such, it stands as a relatively new and independent witness to the complex and obscure period of Christian origins. Whatever we may learn about the persons who used and championed it, about their relationship to other early Christian groups, and about their theology will be of obvious value in the continuing endeavor to understand the elusive reality of Christian beginnings. In the four chapters comprising Part II of this study, then, I wish to make a start toward understanding the Thomas tradition as an historical phenomenon; I wish to begin exploring *Thomas Christianity*. Ultimately the task will be to integrate Thomas Christianity into our overall picture of the development of early Christianity, and to make adjustments based upon the new information that Thomas provides. Something along these lines will be attempted in Chapter 6. But first, it is necessary to begin with a clearer understanding of what Thomas Christianity is all about. For this we must turn to the Gospel of Thomas itself, to see what it reveals about the sort of person who might have produced this collection, or the type of people who might have identified with and laid claim to its traditions. To this task the present chapter is devoted.

The task thus described is, more or less, an historical one, and admittedly one whose legitimacy is not to be taken for granted. Following the lead of theorists in the field of literary criticism, exegetes too have begun to raise questions about the often facile way in which early church historians are wont to move between texts and contexts, and to draw conclusions about the social reality behind these texts. It is therefore necessary now to be clear about *why* one should expect that a particular text might be able to inform the historian about the social context in which it was written and used, and *how* such information is to be wrung from the text in question. Both are particularly important in the case of Thomas, or for that matter of any religious text, whose purpose is not really to supply historical information but to develop and promote a particular religious understanding of life and the world.

From Text to Social Reality: A Matter of Hermeneutics

The expectations one has of a text for rendering up historically valuable information must be bound up closely with its genre. The type of document one wishes to examine, be it a poem, a biography, or a shopping list, will of course delimit both the prospects for finding historically relevant material as well as the methods by which one goes prospecting. Speaking strictly in terms of its genre, the Gospel of Thomas does have prospects. It is a sayings collection.[1] As such, there is an air of utility about it that allows one to expect a relatively close relationship between this text and its social context. In contrast, say, to a work of literary fiction, whose fantasies may well render the connections between it and its social context more obscure, the Gospel of Thomas as a sayings collection may be considered a literary toolbox, or perhaps a quiver full of arrows to be drawn forth and used when the proper situation should arise, be it the instruction of new recruits or the parry and jab of philosophical debate. The place for the sayings collection was in the classroom or on the street; this was its Sitz im Leben.[2] Either type of situation imparts to the text an implicit hermeneutic that allows one to assume that the "speaker" in this text stands firmly behind its content, and that the "audience" is called upon to respond in some way, taking seriously what the text requires.[3] The relationship, of course, will be particularly close between the text and those who champion it.

This principle is not compromised by the Prologue and Thom 1, as if these introductory words were to impute to *every* saying that follows an oblique

1. So Robinson, "LOGOI SOPHON," 75-80. More recently Kloppenborg has attempted to render Robinson's preliminary designations more precise in terms of ancient sayings collections. He refers to Thomas as a chreia collection (*Formation*, 291), but also treats it as a gnomologium (cf. pp. 296, 301, 302, 305-6).
2. For the use of chreia collections in education, as well as for purposes of philosophical propaganda, see Kloppenborg, *Formation*, 311-13. The setting of the gnomologium was chiefly educational (Kloppenborg, *Formation*, 299-301). See also Betz's remarks concerning the purpose of the *Kyriai Doxai* of Epicurus in "Sermon on the Mount," 10-15.
3. So Kloppenborg, *Formation*, 305-6, 315. In this sense the distinction between oral and written tradition made by Kelber (*The Oral and the Written Gospel*, esp. 14-15) is somewhat overdrawn. The function of the sayings collection is practical, not literary in nature: teachers or street preachers could commit such collections to memory—taking advantage of the catchword arrangement—and thus have a store of tradition upon which to draw as the need arose. For this reason, in distinction from narrative gospels, the sayings collection cannot be said to presuppose the distance from social context that Kelber argues typifies written, over against oral, tradition.

gnostic interpretation that supersedes its obvious meaning.[4] Neither the Prologue nor Thom 1 speaks of a "gnostic" or even "secret" *interpretation* of the sayings in Thomas; it is the *sayings themselves* that are secret, not their interpretation.[5] To be sure, the fact that this interpretation is to be "sought" (Thom 1) means that the full significance of each saying may not be readily transparent on a first reading. Therefore, Kloppenborg justifiably speaks about the opening lines of Thomas in terms of a certain hermeneutic of "penetration and research" similar to what one finds at work in the Pythagorean *symbola*.[6] But he also makes it clear that the difference between this and the "hermeneutic of obedience" implied in other sayings collections is only a matter of degree:

> There is no absolute dichotomy between the hermeneutics of "penetration and research" and "obedience" since the latter, as Sirach shows, is not a matter simply of the reception and memorization of traditional sayings, but also of reflection on their hidden meaning and implications (cf. Sir 39:1-3). The goal of this mode of wisdom is to produce those who, through their assimilation of the sapiential ethos, become exponents of that ethos and sources of new wisdom. The difference between this and the hermeneutic prescribed by the Pythagorean *symbola* and the *Gos. Thom.* is one of degree: the deliberate use of obscure sayings only highlights the need for penetration and enlightened exegesis. And the result of the hermeneutical process is represented not simply as assimilation of a sapiential ethos, but as the acquisition of immortality.[7]

The converse of this, of course, is that the highlighted need for penetration and enlightened exegesis does not supplant the need to assimilate the ethos that informs the collection as a whole. To presuppose that the Gospel of Thomas requires nothing of its audience would be to make the unwarranted assumption that Thomas' gnosticizing form of theological reflection, unlike other types of religious thought, is not to be accompanied by a corresponding praxis.

From Text to Social Reality: Further Problems

Given these grounds for expecting that there is some concrete relationship between the Gospel of Thomas and its social context, the second question remains: How does one exploit this relationship to prompt the text to reveal something about the persons who formulated and used its traditions? The degree to which such an endeavor is possible depends upon the material content of the tradition to be examined. For example, a problem presents itself when one considers a saying such as Thom 83:

4. *Contra* Haenchen, *Botschaft*, 37-38.
5. The opening words of the Gospel of Thomas read: naei ne ñϣaϫe eϩHn; "These are the secret [*or* hidden] *words.* . . ."
6. Kloppenborg, *Formation*, 305-6.
7. Kloppenborg, *Formation*, 306.

[1]Jesus said, "Images are visible to people, but the light within them is hidden in the image of the Father's light. [2]He will be disclosed, but his image is hidden by his light."

It would be difficult to reconstruct the social history of a text based solely on this sort of abstruse saying. To be sure, once the basic lines of a social history have been sketched it may be possible for others using social-anthropological methods to see how this sort of material also relates to the text's social history. But as a starting point such material will not do. On the other hand, there are many sayings in the Gospel of Thomas which hold distinct possibilities, e.g., Thom 95:

[1][Jesus said], "If you have money, do not lend it at interest. [2]Rather, give [it] to someone from whom you will not get it back."

This saying is very concrete and straightforward about the action it recommends. Thus, from a social-historical point of view, it might be considered quite valuable indeed.

The task, then, is to develop a method for finding and evaluating material which may have worth for matters of social-historical interest so that the text of Thomas may speak for itself on these matters. This is important, for the fact that so much of Thomas' material consists of uninterpreted wisdom sayings and parables, which might be read in any number of ways, or cryptic sayings of a metaphysical nature, whose social-historical implications are far from transparent, means that it is very easy to approach the text with a hypothesis about the Thomas "community" in mind, and then produce a reading of the text which confirms these suspicions.

In my view, two previous attempts to describe the Thomas "community" lend themselves to criticism on this score. In his study, "Thomas-Gospel and Thomas-Community: A New Approach to a Familiar Text," Bruce Lincoln begins with the supposition that since (later) Edessene religious communities were characterized by stratification according to levels of initiation, the Thomas community must have also been so characterized.[8] With this as a working hypothesis he proceeds to divide various of Thomas' sayings into four different groups, each corresponding to a different level of initiation in the Thomas community. Were it not for the fact that the Gospel of Thomas itself never mentions levels of initiation, nor any readily recognizable procedures for initiation, and does not itself offer any indication that some sayings might be addressed to novices, others to "perfects" (cf. the fourth-century *Liber Graduum*), still others to various stages in between, Lincoln's groupings would be quite convincing. The problem is that they are his groupings, not those of Thomas.

In a more recent study, Karen King approaches the problem of social history in the Gospel of Thomas by suggesting how a community might have

8. Lincoln, "Thomas-Gospel," 67–68.

made use of various Thomas sayings for purposes of social formation.[9] On the assumption that the Gospel of Thomas was used by a cohesive group living in community together, the readings King offers are often quite convincing. But the notion that Thomas was used by this sort of community is itself an un-reflected assumption, without solid grounding in the text. Consequently problems arise when sayings such as Thom 42, or Thom 16 are encountered,[10] which raise the possibility that this is not the sort of group one should associate with Thomas. Sayings such as Thom 14:4, and Thom 86, which similarly challenge the notion that the Thomas community was a settled community in the normal sense, are not brought into the equation at all.

Identifying the Relevant Material

In addressing this dilemma of how to identify material in Thomas that will be of use to the social historian it is necessary to return to the methods in which modern social-historical investigations of the sayings tradition have their roots: form criticism.[11] From a form-critical point of view, such things as legal sayings and community rules, wisdom sayings, and parables, or Thomas' numerous esoteric sayings should not be considered of equal value for the purposes of the social historian. The use of esoterica for such matters is obviously problematic. But no less so would be the untempered use of para-bles, whose rhetoric and artistry often leave one with a devastating general impression of a world turned upside down, but with little directive about what is to be done about it. Likewise, wisdom sayings of the aphoristic sort tend to tease the brain into a different way of viewing the world,[12] but they do not indicate very concretely a behavior commensurate with this new world view. Even sayings of a more proverbial nature are not much help: their wisdom is so conventional it is difficult to capture from them anything of the distinctive values and ethos of their tradents. Only legal sayings, or community rules, which presumably *address directly the behavior of the group that has coined and/or transmitted them,* are clear enough to yield up the sort of information about Thomas Christianity that is the focus of this chapter.[13]

But legal sayings are not always easy to recognize. Rudolf Bultmann, whose treatment of *Gesetzesworte und Gemeinderegeln* (Legal Sayings and Church Rules) remains a standard, is not much help; he declines to offer either a formal or material definition of them in his major form-critical work, *Die*

9. King, "Kingdom in the Gospel of Thomas."
10. King, "Kingdom in the Gospel of Thomas," 70.
11. See especially Theissen, "Sociological Interpretation," 177; "Zur Forschungsgeschicht-lichen Einordnung," 4–7.
12. For this view of aphorisms see Crossan, *In Fragments,* 1–36, esp. 4–6, 25.
13. Here the brief observations of Koester relative to the Thomas "community" form a basic point of departure ("One Jesus," esp. 184–85). It is methodologically significant that Koester offers his comments on the Thomas community only within the context of his discussion of *legal sayings* in Thomas.

Geschichte der synoptischen Tradition.[14] It may be helpful, then, to lay out at least a working definition of the sayings I have in mind.

A formal definition of legal sayings is useless as a starting point, for one of the problems with deciding what might be considered under this category is that most of its typical forms are to be found in other types of sayings as well. For example, its most characteristic grammatical form, the imperative, is also found frequently in proverbial wisdom sayings; the warnings that may follow as a form of enforcement are also quite typical of prophetic sayings. It is better, then, to begin with a material definition, and then describe the range of typical forms that one might expect to find within it. In what follows I will consider legal sayings to be those sayings which identify a concrete behavior or practice (including attitudes) as either desirable or undesirable, in such a way that they function to regulate the behavior of those who hear or read them as authoritative. Their most typical forms are:

1. The use of the imperative form, either positively or negatively (e.g., Thom 12:2; 25; 6:2-4; 36; 42; and 100). They may also be formulated conditionally, where the prodosis defines the conditions under which the imperative in the apodosis is to apply (e.g., Thom 14:4 and 95).

2. Warnings, which typically consist of two parts: a) a particular behavior or practice is identified; b) this behavior or practice is judged by associating it with an undesirable consequence (e.g., Thom 14:1-3; 27:1, 2; 45; 55; and 101).

3. Rewards, which typically consist of two parts: a) a particular behavior or practice is identified; b) this behavior or practice is judged by associating it with a desirable consequence (e.g., Thom 99 and 114:3).

4. The implicit indictment, in which a particular behavior or practice is indicted implicitly by placing it in juxtaposition to a commonly esteemed opinion, such that the behavior or practice is identified as 'wrong-headed' or nonsensical (e.g., Thom 53 and 89).

In the description of Thomas Christianity that follows, I will begin with legal sayings thus defined. Only after Thomas' legal sayings have been used to sketch out each facet of a basic social description of Thomas Christianity will it be possible then to draw in wisdom sayings, parables, and occasional prophetic and I-sayings to help fill in and further refine particular aspects of the picture already drawn in rough form using legal material.

Thomas Christianity: A Social Description

The ethos and behavior that a religiously motivated group of persons chooses to embrace is closely related to the way it sees itself in relation to the world around it—what Vincent Wimbush has styled its "response to the world."[15] In the Gospel of Thomas the "world" is important. One's relation-

---

14. Bultmann, *Geschichte*, 138-61.
15. Wimbush, *Renunciation Towards Social Engineering*, 3. Wimbush appropriates the term for exegetical purposes from Wilson, *Magic and Millenium*, 16-30.

ship to the world and the response one offers based upon a correct perception of that relationship are tied directly and unequivocally to the prospects for salvation:

"If you do not fast from the world, you will not find the kingdom."

Thom 27:1

But what does it mean to "fast from the world"? In one sense it is no doubt necessary to speak here of a state of mind, a certain attitude toward the world that results from theological reflection. The Thomas Christian is imbued with a knowledge that elevates him or her above the world, beyond its effects (Thom 111). But though the Gospel of Thomas may speak of a kind of superiority, even of revulsion of the Thomas Christian toward the world,[16] in reality the world is still present, and still a problem, challenging in every minute his or her claim to be above its influence. The intersection of *realia* and *theologica*, and the response it evokes from Thomas Christianity, is perhaps expressed metaphorically in Thom 21:

[1]Mary said to Jesus, "What are your disciples like?" [2]He said, "They are like little children living in a field that is not theirs. [3]When the owners of the field come, they will say, 'Give us back our field.' [4]They take off their clothes in front of them in order to give it back to them, and they return their field to them. [5]For this reason I say, if the owner of a house knows that a thief is coming, he will be on guard before the thief arrives, and will not let the thief break into his house of his domain and steal his possessions. [6]As for you, then, *be on guard against the world.* [7]Prepare yourselves with great strength, so the robbers cannot find a way to get to you, for the trouble you expect will come. [8]Let there be among you a person who understands. [9]When the crop ripened, he came quickly carrying a sickle and harvested it. [10]Whoever has two good ears should listen." [Emphasis mine.]

The Gospel of Thomas speaks frequently of realizing the presence of the "kingdom" here and now.[17] However, these wisdom sayings, together with the imperative (italics) which provides for them a hermeneutical key, are appended as a block to the difficult parable in Thom 21:1-4[18] to reinforce the

16. Cf. also Thom 56 and 80. Haenchen's existential understanding of these sayings is to be followed ("Anthropologie des Thomas-Evangeliums," 210–11).

17. See esp. Thom 3 and 113.

18. The precise meaning of this parable has yet to be settled. Smith speculates that behind it may lie a baptismal rite, whose presence is suggested more strongly by Thom 37 ("The Garments of Shame," esp. 235–36 for Thom 21:1-4). But one must wonder about the procedure of using fourth- and fifth-century materials to explain elements in the Gospel of Thomas. In Thomas, Smith may well have discovered the theological roots of a fifth-century Christian baptismal liturgy, but it would be highly questionable, from a methodological standpoint, to conclude from this that he has discovered a fifth-century baptismal liturgy in Thomas. If this were the case, one would have to explain the troubling fact that baptism itself is never mentioned in Thomas, even obliquely. In light of this, Davies' thesis (*The Gospel of Thomas*, 136) that the Gospel of Thomas is part of a post-baptismal instruction seems quite unfounded. Grant and Freedman (*Secret Sayings*, 141) hold that the saying refers to stripping off the body and leaving the world behind (i.e. at death). But it must be asked whether the

bare fact that the world is still, and always will be present for the Thomas Christian, offering a perpetual assault, against which he or she must defend.[19] This is their predicament. The world lurks ever present in the shadows, like a thief in the night waiting for the lights to go out, brigands on the highway waiting for a hapless traveler, or the reaper who comes at just the right moment with sickle in hand.[20] In the Gospel of Thomas the world is portrayed as a threat, and the hearer is exhorted always to be aware of the danger. But how does this intersection of *theologica* and *realia* translate into actual behavior? How does one *be* vigilant towards the world? For this it is necessary to turn to sayings in Thomas that express more concretely the way in which this anticosmic ideology manifests itself in the behavior of the Thomas Christian.

1. Wandering and Homeless

(a) Legal Sayings

There are two legal sayings in the Gospel of Thomas which indicate that Thomas Christianity gave a positive value to wandering and homelessness: Thom 42 and Thom 14:4.

Thom 42 is the shortest, most tersely formulated saying in the entire Thomas collection:

ⲡⲉⲭⲉ ⲓ̅ⲥ̅ ⲭⲉ: ϣⲱⲡⲉ ⲉⲧⲉⲧⲛ̅ⲡ̅ⲁⲣⲁⲅⲉ.

It is most commonly translated:[21]

Jesus said, "Be (or become)[22] passers-by."

But its brevity invites speculation. Consequently, perhaps more than any saying in Thomas it has inspired the most creative of conjectures and pro-

---

interpretive sayings added in 21:5-10 allow for such finality—21:5 seems to imply that this is an encounter one expects to survive. At any rate, 21:5-7 do underscore the siege mentality behind 21:1-4; it is enough to say that 1) the owners are a threat, 2) their threat is somehow associated with the world, and 3) the threatening world is to be guarded against with vigilance (cf. also Thom 103).

19. Crossan (*In Fragments*, 62) agrees that this is the significance of Thom 21:5-7. He speculates that the vigilance motif is more natural to this particular application of these sayings than to the apocalyptic use to which they have been put in the synoptic tradition (cf. Luke 12:39-40//Matt 24:43-44, Q).

20. This interpretation of "The Reaper" (21:9) may strike the reader as odd, but it seems to me best to interpret it here in light of the sequence building through 21:1-8, in which the various characters arriving unexpectedly on the scene seem to embody the threat to the Thomas Christian. Here the reaper arrives unexpectedly; is this not also a threatening image? It need not be associated with the glorious eschatological harvest of Mark 4:26-29.

21. So, e.g., Guillaumont, et al., *The Gospel According to Thomas*, 25; Wilson, *Studies*, 104; Kasser, *L'Évangile selon Thomas*, 71 ("Soyez passants."); Jeremias, *Unbekannte Jesusworte*, 107 ("Seid Vorübergehende"); Haenchen, *Botschaft*, 50 ("Werdet Vorübergehende"); Robinson, *Nag Hammadi Library*, 131; Kloppenborg, et al., *Q—Thomas Reader*, 139.

22. The Coptic word ϣⲱⲡⲉ allows for either "be" or "become." In either case the verb is rendered in the imperative, as would be the normal sense of ϣⲱⲡⲉ followed by the circumstantial (ⲉⲧⲉⲧⲛ̅⁻); see Till, *Koptische Grammatik*, 171, § 332).

posals regarding its meaning and significance. The discussion to date, however, calls for critical review.

In his ground-breaking translation of Thomas into German in 1958, Johannes Leipoldt rendered the saying: "Werdet, indem ihr vorübergeht."[23] William Schoedel supplied an English version reflecting this understanding of the text: "Come into being as you pass away."[24] While such a translation is certainly defensible in terms of the Coptic grammar,[25] the understanding of the saying that informs this translation is essentially theological—acceptable, provided, of course, that the theology is at home within the Gospel of Thomas. This is not the case. In the Gospel of Thomas, it is the world (Thom 56), the cosmos (Thom 11:1, 111:1) that passes away, not the Thomas Christian, who is immortal (Thom 1; 11:2; 18:3; 19:4; 85:2 111:2). Furthermore, neither does the Thomas Christian come into being; paradoxically he or she exists already before coming into being (Thom 19:1).[26] Such a translation, while grammatically possible, is therefore to be rejected.

Taking another tack, Joachim Jeremias sought to enrich the logion's meaning by probing beneath the Coptic, through its Greek precursor, finally to reach bedrock in a semitic original.[27] Of particular interest to Jeremias is the final word: ⲡⲁⲣⲁⲅⲉ, which he proposes transliterates a Greek substantive participle, παράγοντες (passers-by),[28] thus yielding an earlier Greek version of the saying which would have read γίνεσθε παράγοντες (Be passers-by).[29] Now, it is true that in one instance οἱ παράγοντες (those who pass by) is used by the LXX to translate the Hebrew הָעֹבְרִים; ("those who pass by"),[30] so that it would be reasonable to conclude that an original semitic version of this saying could have used some form of the root עבר. This is what Quispel suggests,[31] and it is undoubtedly what Jeremias has in mind when he invites comparison to the Talmudic tradition (*b. Sanh.* 70a and 103b), where עֹבֵר comes to have the technical meaning "wanderer."[32] Thus, Jeremias proposes that the original version of this saying meant "Be wanderers."[33]

Titze Baarda, too, quests after a semitic original for this saying, but suggests that rather than עֹבֵר ("wanderer") the original version might have used the

---

23. Leipoldt, "Ein neues Evangelium," col. 487; also in *Das Evangelium nach Thomas*, 37. Leipoldt is followed closely by J.-B. Bauer, "Echte Jesusworte," 111.
24. In Grant and Freedman, *Secret Sayings*, 147; so also Gärtner, *Theology*, 243.
25. One need not take the construction using ϣⲱⲡⲉ ("be" or "become") as imperatival (cf. n. 22). The two verbs may be taken as distinct, with the circumstantial converter (ⲉⲧⲉⲧⲛ̄-) indicating simultaneity and/or instrumentality.
26. So Baarda, "Jesus said, Be Passers-by," 181, n. 18.
27. See esp. Jeremias, *Unbekannte Jesusworte*, 107–110.
28. This is no doubt the reasoning behind the translation in the *editio princeps* (Guillaumont, et al., *The Gospel According to Thomas*) as well.
29. German: "Seid Vorübergehende."
30. Ps 128 (129):8; so Baarda, "Jesus said, Be Passers-by," 203, n. 117.
31. Quispel, *Makarius*, 20–21.
32. Jeremias, *Unbekannte Jesusworte*, 110, n. 250.
33. Jeremias, *Unbekannte Jesusworte*, 110. German: "Seid Wanderer."

word עִבְרִי ("Hebrew"). Recalling that in Gen 14:13 the LXX uses the Greek word περατής ("traveler") to render עִבְרִי ("Hebrew"), he concludes:

> If we were to assume that the Greek version of logion 42 read γίνεσθε περαταί might it then be possible that the Coptic "Be *passers-by*" is based, in the last analysis, on a Semitic text, "Be *Hebrews*"? If this is so, the next question is what the phrase might mean.[34]

Baarda explains the saying then in terms of an instance in Philo in which "the name 'Hebrew' was allegorized to mean *migrant* from the objects of sense-perception to those of the mind."[35] Finally, by linking the saying with Thom 43[36] he constructs a dialogue in which Jesus exhorts the disciples to "Be Hebrews" (in the Philonic sense), thus causing their dismay (43:1) and Jesus' subsequent scolding: "Rather, you have become like the Jews. . . ."[37] The merits of this last suggestion may be debated. However, it is all rather academic, for Baarda never explains why, arbitrarily, he is moved to substitute עִבְרִי ("Hebrew") for עבֵר ("wanderer") at the level of the semitic original (if indeed one may legitimately speak of such an original at all), or, working back from the Coptic text, how one might arrive at περαταί (Philo's cerebral Hebrews) from ⲡⲁⲣⲁⲅⲉ/παράγοντες ("passers-by").[38] The saying that Baarda reconstructs simply does not exist.

If one sets aside for the moment all speculation based on theology (gnostic, Alexandrian, Rabbinic, or Islamic!), the quest for a semitic original of this saying, and any attempt to link 42 to its neighbors,[39] Thom 42 can stand on its own. First, we must work with what we have—a Coptic version of the saying and evidence to suggest that it is translated from a Greek original.[40] If one takes ϣⲱⲡⲉ with the circumstantial (ⲉⲧⲉⲧⲛ̄⁻) as an imperative, there are two

---

34. Baarda, "Jesus said, Be Passers-by," 195.

35. Baarda, "Jesus said, Be Passers-by," 195. The passage in Philo (*De migr. Abr.* 20) is discussed by Baarda on p. 193. He suggests that the gnostic sect known as the Peratae (Hippolytus, *Ref.* 5.16.1 and 5.16.4) may have been familiar with this Philonic tradition. He nobly admits, however, that "there is not a shred of evidence (at least as far as I can ascertain) that the Alexandrian allegorical interpretation of the name was also current among Palestinian Jews." (195).

36. The suggestion is arbitrary. Thom 43 by itself forms a chreia understandable in its own right. To begin with a question from the disciples is rather typical of Thomas (cf. Thom 6, 12, 18, 20, 24, 37, 51, 52, 53, 99, 113).

37. Baarda, "Jesus said, Be Passers-by," 196.

38. I find no instance in which the Coptic transliteralism ⲡⲁⲣⲁⲅⲉ is used to render the Greek περεῖν/περατής.

39. In addition to Baarda's suggestion regarding Thom 42–43, see also Meerburg's hypothesis regarding Thom 42's relationship to Thom 37–41 (*De structur van het Koptisch Evangelie naar Thomas* [Maasrtricht, 1964] 112, 118, as cited by Baarda, "Jesus said, Be Passers-by," 196, n. 145.)

40. There is no direct evidence for an antecedent semitic version. Jeremias and Quispel are drawn to this hypothesis by the possibility that the saying might have been originally uttered in Aramaic by Jesus. But in view of the paucity of evidence for the use of Aramaic in the first century, even in a remote place such as Galilee, even this assumption is currently under critical review.

reasonable possibilities for reconstructing the latter: γίνεσθε παράγοντες[41] and γίνεσθε παρερχόμενοι.[42] For both παράγειν (intransitive) and παρέρχεσθαι the most common meaning is "to go (or pass) by."[43] The meaning of the saying is not illusive; it simply enjoins the reader/hearer to become one who "passes by," who does not stay in one place. The imperative here is to "Become itinerants."[44]

The second legal saying to come under consideration here is Thom 14:4. It will be discussed again in connection with the question of how Thomas Christians supported themselves, but it warrants attention here as well for what it implies about the wandering activity of the Thomas "community":

> [4]When you go into any region and walk about in the countryside (χώρα), when people take you in, eat what they serve you and care for[45] the sick among them.

"When you go into any region and walk about in the countryside"—these are the circumstances under which the rules which follow are to apply. Meyer's rendering of the conditional (ⲉⲧⲉⲧⲛ̄ϣⲁⲛ⁻) captures the sense here with "when," for the fact that a rule was necessary to cover such exigencies implies that this was a situation in which Thomas Christians frequently found themselves. They were much on the move; they were itinerants.

Of course, Thomas Christians did not invent this saying, as its independent occurrence in the synoptic tradition clearly indicates.[46] Gerd Theissen noticed it there as part of Q's larger "Sending Out" narratives,[47] which form a central pillar in his thesis that the Jesus movement was characterized by a group of wandering radical preachers.[48] While its parallel occurrence here in Thomas generally confirms Theissen's notion that the early sayings tradition affirmed the ideal of radical itinerancy, it may also suggest a few necessary adjustments. For example, Burton Mack has noticed a tendency among scholars to link Theissen's radical wandering ethos with early Christian apocalyptic preaching, whereby taking up the life of the itinerant becomes the appropriate response to the imminent appearance of the reign of God.[49] Mack challenges this notion on the grounds that if one accepts the thesis of Kloppenborg, that

---

41. In the Sahidic New Testament the transliteral form ⲡⲁⲣⲁⲅⲉ is used to render παράγειν eleven times (so Baarda, "Jesus said, Be Passers-by," 192, n. 120).
42. In the Sahidic New Testament ⲡⲁⲣⲁⲅⲉ is used to render παρέρχεσθαι five times (so Baarda, "Jesus said, Be Passers-by," 192, n. 122.
43. *LSJ*, *s.v.* παράγω and παρέρχομαι.
44. This, of course, is not altogether different from what Jeremias proposes; however, I wish to make it clear that such a reading does not depend upon the somewhat tenuous procedure of reconstructing a semitic original for the saying. There is no evidence that Thomas ever existed in a semitic version (Hebrew or Aramaic), and to speak of an oral "original" is becoming ever more problematic (see, e.g., Kelber, *Oral and Written Gospel*, 30.)
45. Or: "heal"; the Coptic simply transliterates θεραπεύειν, which means either "to heal" or simply "to care for" the sick (*LSJ*, *s.v.* θεραπεύω).
46. Luke 10:8–9; Matt 10:5–8; also 1 Cor 10:27.
47. Matt 10:5–15//Luke 10:1–12, Q.
48. Theissen, "Wanderradikalismus," 92–94; *Sociology*, 10–11.
49. Mack, "The Kingdom that Didn't Come," 620–21.

the earliest layer in Q (i.e., Q^1) did not contain the words of apocalyptic and prophetic judgment characteristic of Q's later development (i.e., Q^2),[50] and if one locates the Sending Out discourse at the level of Q^1 (as Kloppenborg does),[51] the instructions for itinerants found in this Q scene must have been motivated originally not by apocalyptic fervor but by something else. The fact that part of these instructions also find their way into Thomas, which, like Q^1, is not grounded in an apocalyptic world view, confirms Mack's point. Mack also challenges the idea that such instructions were originally associated with a "mission" *per se*, noting that the general impression of a group of early Christian missionaries sent out to address a Jewish world in trouble also derives from Q^2, not Q^1.[52] This hunch, too, is borne out by Thom 14:4. The material found in Luke 10:8–9//Matt 10:5–8, Q occurs here independently, without the larger context of Q's Sending Out discourse. Hence, originally the ideal of radical itinerancy was not necessarily linked with an early Christian "mission" at all but rather had more the quality of a permanent manner of living, a life-style advocated by the Jesus movement.

Finally, however, Mack argues that on inspection the Sending Out discourse in Q^1 has much more to do with the behavior of those who receive wayfarers, rather than with that of the itinerants themselves:

> If it were not for the fiction of Jesus saying "Behold, I send you out as lambs in the midst of wolves," the main body of instruction could easily be read as written from the perspective of house groups interested in a network of cordial relations with other house groups.[53]

Mack concludes: "Apparently radical itinerancy was not the only way, or not the way at all, in which the reign of God was talked about, practiced and announced by the tradents of Q^1."[54] This may be a reasonable inference from the material in Q^1, but it is certainly not true of the sayings tradition in general[55] or of the Thomas tradition in particular. Thom 14:4 clearly reflects the point of view of the itinerants themselves; it has nothing to do with those who would receive them. It may be that we are looking here at two different formulations of a common itinerancy tradition, one written reflecting the situation of settled communities that might receive itinerants (Matt 10:5–15//Luke 10:1–12, Q^1), the other reflecting the situation of the itinerants themselves (Thom 14:4). The bifurcation of the tradition thus reflects the bifurcation of roles in the Jesus movement proposed by Theissen, wherein the wandering itinerants would have been supported by those living more con-

50. Kloppenborg, *Formation*, esp. 102–245.
51. Kloppenborg, *Formation*, 192–97.
52. Mack, "Kingdom that Didn't Come," 621.
53. Mack, "Kingdom that Didn't Come," 623.
54. Mack, "Kingdom that Didn't Come," 623.
55. *Pace* Richard Horsley, *Sociology*, esp. 44. Horsley rejects the itinerancy thesis altogether, proposing instead that the Jesus movement was interested more in local community renewal (see esp. 106). Horsley does not devote attention to the Thomas side of the sayings tradition.

ventional, settled lives in the villages of rural Palestine and Syria.[56] The latter is reflected especially in Thom 14:4, which assumes that this wandering activity typically occurs in the χώρα, i.e. the rural countryside, including the small villages that populated the interstices between the larger metropolitan centers, precisely the areas Theissen imagines to have been the most congenial to the practice of wandering radicalism.[57]

(b) Wisdom Sayings

There is one wisdom saying that seems to speak directly to the social situation of the homeless wanderer. It is the lament over homelessness found in Thom 86, already familiar to most readers from its synoptic counterpart in Luke 9:58//Matt 8:20, Q. Its Thomas version reads:

> [1]Jesus said, "[Foxes have] their dens and birds have their nests, [2]but a person[58] has no place to lay his head and rest."

The temptation to invest Thomas' version of this saying with gnostic soteriological overtones is to be resisted here.[59] It makes sense, after all, in terms of the wandering existence that is mandated by Thom 42 and reflected in Thom 14:4. To be sure, the use of the term "rest" (ṀΤΟΝ = ἀναπαύειν) in the final clause could in some contexts carry gnosticizing connotations, as its cognate noun perhaps does at least in Thom 50 and 60.[60] But in Thomas, the extent of whose gnosticizing character is not yet fully charted, one must refrain from imputing a gnostic meaning to every detail. If "rest" is to be understood as referring to that final state of redemption to be achieved by the gnostic soul, the saying states exactly the opposite of what one would expect, for in the soteriological sense Thomas Christians do indeed have a place of repose, which they must strive to discover (Thom 50, 51, and 60). Thus, "to rest" in Thom 86 must carry another meaning altogether. In view of the itinerancy reflected in Thom 42 and 14:4, one might simply assume that these itinerants occasionally became weary. Theissen relates the Q version of this saying (Matt

---

56. Theissen, *Sociology*, 13–14.

57. Theissen, "Wanderradikalismus," 98–100; cf. Robinson, "On Bridging the Gulf," 137.

58. The Coptic here reads πϣΗΡε . . . Ṁπρωμε, lit. "son of man." But most scholars agree that it is not intended here as a title for Jesus, but rather the semitizing idiom meaning simply "person" or "human being" (see esp. Koester, "One Jesus," 170–71, n. 34).

59. So Strobel, "Textgeschichtliches zum Thomas-Logion 86," 223; *contra* Gärtner, *Theology*, 60–61; Kasser, *L'Évangile selon Thomas*, 104; Vielhauer, "ΑΝΑΠΑΥΣΙΣ," 293; and Crossan, *In Fragments*, 241–42.

60. The use of the term in these two sayings is esoteric enough to suggest the effect of Thomas' general gnosticizing proclivity. With Thom 90 the case is not so clear. In view of the wisdom background of this saying, it is advisable to look rather to this history of religions orientation to explain its significance in this case (see, e.g., Wis 3:1–4; 4:7; 8:13, 16; Sir 51: 26–27). More problematic is its use in Thom 51. On the one hand, the polemic here against the notion of a future "rest" casts a critical eye toward views such as those espoused in Heb 3:7–4:13, but what the author/editor has in mind by the "rest" that has already come is not fully clear.

8:20//Luke 9:58) to the phenomenon of itinerancy behind the synoptic tradition;[61] I see no reason to suppose that it has any other significance in Thomas. It is a lament that befits the plight of the wandering itinerant, whose request for a place to stay has been turned down or whose welcome in the home of a host has expired.

As with the wandering radicalism Theissen has described elsewhere in early Christianity, the radical lifestyle of Thomas Christianity involves more than just itinerancy. The wandering life it calls for is part of a pattern of socially radical behavior with many aspects, which together comprise its response to the world. To assemble the composite picture it is necessary to look also at other features of Thomas' radicalism.

2. Cutting Family Ties

Some of the same traditions Theissen uses to demonstrate the presence of what he terms a "lack of family ethos" in the synoptic sayings tradition are present also in Thomas.

(a) Legal Sayings

The tradition preserved in Thom 55 will already be familiar from its independent synoptic parallel.[62] Its position on familial relations is plain[63] and severe:

> [1]Jesus said, "Whoever does not hate father and mother cannot be my disciple, [2]and whoever does not hate brothers and sisters, and carry the cross as I do, will not be worthy of me."

In Thom 101 one finds a doublet to this saying, here attached to its paradoxically formulated converse:

> [1]"Whoever does not hate [father] and mother as I do cannot be my [disciple], [2]and whoever does [not] love [father and] mother as I do cannot be my [disciple]. [3]For my mother [. . .],[64] but my true [mother] gave me life."

Thom 101:2 should not be taken as a softening of the statements in Thom 55 and 101:1. Rather, it reinforces the practice of leaving real family concerns

---

61. Theissen, *Sociology*, 10; "Wanderradikalismus," 83; *pace* Horsley (*Sociology*, 44) who thinks that the saying is addressed in Q to more than just the itinerants. But Q 9:58, following directly upon vs 57, certainly indicates that homelessness is in view.

62. Cf. Luke 14:26//Matt 10:37, Q.

63. *Contra* Horsley (*Sociology*, 44–45), who disputes that the synoptic versions of the tradition support Theissen's thesis. But Horsley's case is strained. First he must suppose that Matthew's toned down version of the saying is original, thus flying in the face of virtually all scholarship on this tradition (see Schulz, *Q*, 446, n. 321). Second, he must view Luke's radical formulation as an hyperbolic illustration of "counting the cost," the subject under discussion in Luke 14:28–32. But while this may explain Luke's understanding of the saying (vss 28–32 are unique to Luke) it is irrelevant for our appraisal of it's significance apart from this setting. Horsley does not comment on what the independent saying might have meant in Q, in Thomas, or in the common tradition to which all were heir.

64. This lacuna cannot be filled in with certainty.

behind by redefining what "family" means to a dedicated member of the group. This is accomplished in 101:3, which resolves the antithetical opposition of vss 1 and 2 by speaking of a "true mother," who may legitimately become the focus of familial attachment, in distinction from natural parents.[65] Crossan regards this redefinition of family as a function of Thomas' gnosticizing theology.[66] Indeed it is, but not simply in the sense that the reference to one's "true mother" here is to be taken as a gnostic mythologization of the tradition. Rather, it is an expression of the anticosmic attitude that is endemic to Thomas' gnosticizing proclivity, which demands that traditional family ties be replaced by family ties newly defined so as to reflect the relatedness of those who lay claim to these traditions. Thom 99 has exactly the same effect, though here without recourse to the esotericizing of the tradition seen in 101:

> [1]The disciples said to him, "Your brothers and your mother are standing outside." [2]He said to them, "Those here who do what my Father wants are my brothers and my mother. [3]They are the ones who will enter the kingdom of my Father."

If "Those here who do what my Father wants" is self-referential for Thomas Christians, then it is clear that the resignification of family in Thomas is not simply, or even primarily, a matter of mythological speculation, but rather a phenomenon of social formation. Thomas Christians see themselves as familial in their relatedness to one another, replacing original family ties with new familial bonds based upon a common code of conduct.

(b) Wisdom Sayings

Theissen has speculated on the sort of reaction that such a decision to leave family behind and take up the life of the wanderer would have evoked at home, especially in cases where this would have had an economic impact on the life of the family, such as when older siblings would leave the family business, trade, or farm.[67] It is unlikely that Thomas Christians would have been welcomed as heroes and heroines at home after having made such a decision. It is perhaps in this vein that one should read the familiar saying in Thom 31:

> [1]Jesus said, "A prophet is not acceptable in his hometown; [2]a doctor does not heal those who know him."

It may be that this was the way Thomas' version of the Rejected Stone (Thom 66) was applied as well.[68]

The lengths to which families might have gone to oppose the recruitment of sons and daughters to the itinerant life is not known, but if the example of Thecla in the fictitious romance, the *Acts of Paul and Thecla,* may be taken as

---

65. Meyer, "Making Mary Male," 556.
66. Crossan, *In Fragments,* 136.
67. Theissen, *Sociology,* 12.
68. The saying in Thom 66 is regarded in Thomas as a separate logion apart from Thom 65 (see ch. 3, pp. 48–51).

realistic in this aspect, it is not going too far to include Thom 68 and 58 in this cluster as well. It is difficult to imagine that a family's reaction to a group that recruits a son or daughter to a life of itinerancy, which demands not only separation from family but also its redefinition would have been anything but bitter opposition, directed against both the recruit (Thom 31, 58) and the group (Thom 68).[69]

(c) Other Sayings

In addition to these legal and wisdom sayings, there are a handful of sayings in the Gospel of Thomas of various form-critical classification that might be related to this set of traditions. The first, Thom 105, is cast in the form of a prophetic saying:

> Jesus said, "Whoever knows the father and the mother will be called the child of a whore."

Of course it is difficult to know exactly what this slightly odd saying might have meant among Thomas Christians. However, in view of what has been said about the Thomas attitude toward families, it might be possible to read it as referring to outsiders who have refused to join the group because of familial obligations, and thus failed to recognize the verity of the new familial definitions proposed by Thom 55, 99, and 101.

The second is a short discourse composed of two I-sayings, and a con-

---

69. The Coptic text of Thom 68 poses a number of difficulties for the translator: ⲡⲉϫⲉ ⲓ̄ⲥ̄ ϫⲉ ⲛ̄ⲧⲱⲧⲛ̄ ϩⲛ̄ⲙⲁⲕⲁⲣⲓⲟⲥ ϩⲟⲧⲁⲛ ⲉⲩϣⲁⲛⲙⲉⲥⲧⲉ ⲑⲩⲧⲛ̄ ⲛ̄ⲥⲉⲣ̄ⲇⲓⲱⲕⲉ ⲙ̄ⲙⲱⲧⲛ̄ ⲁⲩⲱ ⲥⲉⲛⲁϩⲉ ⲁⲛ ⲉⲧⲟⲡⲟⲥ ϩⲙ̄ ⲡⲙⲁ ⲉⲛⲧⲁⲩⲇⲓⲱⲕⲉ ⲙ̄ⲙⲱⲧⲛ̄ ϩⲣⲁⲓ̈ ⲛ̄ϩⲏⲧϥ. I am in agreement with Toyoshima ("Neue Vorschläge," 239) that Haenchen's thesis ("Spruch 68 des Thomas-evangeliums," 19–29), which maintains that the negative particle has been misplaced in the second clause, so that the saying originally read something like Clement of Alexandria *Strom.* 4.41.2, stretches one's credulity. Toyoshima (239) himself translates: "Kein Platz wird gefunden werden, wo ihr verfolgt würdet" ("No place will be found where you have been persecuted"). The saying refers, in his view, to a future end time in which there will exist no place where Thomas Christians will be persecuted. But this seems to presuppose an eschatological world view not found in the Gospel of Thomas. Preferable is Leipoldt's rendering: "Ihr seid selig, wenn sie euch hassen und euch verfolgen und keinen Platz finden werden an dem Ort, an dem sie euch verfolgen" ("Blessed are you when they hate you and persecute you and no place will be found in the place, in which they persecute you") (*Das Evangelium nach Thomas*, 45). This corresponds closely to Lambdin's translation: "Wherever you have been persecuted they will find no place" (in Robinson, *The Nag Hammadi Library*, 134). Here ⲧⲟⲡⲟⲥ ("place") might be understood in conjunction with Thomas' conclusion to Thom 64, where ⲧⲟⲡⲟⲥ bears a soteriological connotation (cf. Cameron, "Parable and Interpretation," 18). The sentence would then mean something like: those who live in the places where you have been persecuted will not be saved. It is clear at least from ϩⲙ̄ ⲡⲙⲁ ⲉⲛⲧⲁⲩⲇⲓⲱⲕⲉ ⲙ̄ⲙⲱⲧⲛ̄ ϩⲣⲁⲓ̈ ⲛ̄ϩⲏⲧϥ (in the place in which you have been persecuted) that the group knows of particular places where its members have been persecuted. I see no reason to assume (*contra* Gärtner, *Theology*, 248, and Haenchen, "Spruch 68," 28) that Thom 68 does not speak of actual persecution; had Thom 69:1 been intended to replace the "persecution" of Thom 68 with a certain "persecution in the heart," Thom 68 would likely have been dropped from the collection.

cluding prophetic warning. Though the I-sayings in Thom 16 may originally have carried a force of their own, here one is invited to read them, prefixed as they are to the concluding prophetic saying, in terms of the familial dissention brought about by Jesus in the past—and by extension, the activity of the Thomas movement in the present.

[1]Jesus said, "Perhaps people think that I have come to cast peace upon the world. [2]They do not know that I have come to cast conflicts upon the earth: fire, sword, war. [3]For there will be five in a house: three will be against two and two against three, father against son and son against father, [4]and they will stand alone."

3. Willful Poverty and Begging

(a) Legal Sayings

Thom 14:4 spells out how it is that these Thomas wanderers are to support themselves while on the road:

When you go into any region and walk about in the countryside ($\chi\omega\rho\acute{\alpha}$), when people take you in, eat what they serve you and care for[70] the sick among them.

These instructions are quite simple: one performs a service (care for the sick), and then takes what comes. This is the same sort of itinerant "begging of a higher order" that Theissen describes at the center of the wandering radical ethos.[71] Unlike the parallel synoptic injunctions found in Mark, there is no mention here of preaching,[72] and unlike Q's version there is no word of peace;[73] yet from Thom 33 and 48 one may *perhaps* judge that these too were services offered.

The Thomas version of "Render to Caesar" (Thom 100) compliments the injunctions in Thom 14:4:

[1]They showed Jesus a gold coin and said to him, "Caesar's people demand taxes from us." [2]He said to them, "Give Caesar what belongs to Caesar, give God what belongs to God, and give me what is mine."

While 14:4 addresses itself to the beggars, Thom 100:2 is aimed at their potential supporters. Jesus here becomes the prototypical beggar. He refuses to sympathize with the interlocutors' longing for 'less government' and demands instead *support also for himself;* and this with an authority and at a level on a par with state levies on the one hand and the Temple tax on the other![74] The resulting donation probably seldom matched the weight of the claims. But whatever the results, one can easily sense the usefulness of a tradition such

70. Or: "heal;" see n. 45.
71. Theissen, "Wanderradikalismus," 94.
72. See Mark 6:12; cf. Matt 10:7; Luke 9:2.
73. See Luke 10:5–6; cf. Matt 10:13.
74. See p. 149, n. 117.

as this to beggars within the Jesus tradition who sought to live from voluntary donations.[75]

With this sort of policy on making a living, it is obvious that the Thomas movement was not out to get rich. On the contrary, its members were called upon to be willfully impoverished:

1[Jesus said], "If you have money, do not lend it at interest. 2Rather, give [it] to someone from whom you will not get it back."

Thom 95

It is justifiable to ask about the potential audience of this saying. Of course, it could function quite easily in the same manner as Thom 100. But with lending practices like these, lenders would soon become beggars, an outcome which in the long run would not be to the benefit of the itinerants since they would eventually lose their constituency. This saying, often considered only in terms of its prohibition of usury, really requires much more from the hearer— do not lend your money, but give it to one from whom you *will not get it back.* The saying requires nothing less than the divestment of all one's assets.[76] It seems best, then, to regard this as a minority ethic, which in practical terms can be taken in full seriousness only by the itinerant radicals themselves.[77]

Finally, in Thom 36, one finds that also in matters of fashion Thomas counsels a decorum befitting the beggar's existence:

Jesus said, "Do not worry, from morning to evening and from evening to morning, about what you are going to wear."[78]

75. Rudolph, *Gnosis,* 265.

76. Rudolph (*Gnosis,* 270) agrees that the saying counsels against property.

77. *Pace* Horsley (*Sociology,* 45), who argues that such measures would have been applicable to the entire constituency of the Jesus movement. But his appeal to Acts 4:32–37 is not probative. Aside from the obvious problem of Acts' historical reliability, one must say that the pooling of possessions described there is really much different (and much less risky!) than what is counseled here.

78. The extant Greek version of Thom 36 (POxy 655, col 1.1–17) reads as follows:

1[Jesus says, "Do not worry], from morning [to evening nor] from [evening to [morning, either [about] your [food], what [you will] eat, [or] about [your clothing], what you [will] wear.

2[You are much] better than the lilies, which neither card nor [spin].

3As for you, when you have no garment, what [will you put] on?

4Who might add to your stature? That very one will give you your garment."

There is no certainty with respect to the question of which version of the saying is more original. One may not simply assume that the Greek version is earlier; although Thomas was written originally in Greek, the extant Coptic version may well derive from a Greek version which is itself more primitive than that which survived at Oxyrhynchus. Many have viewed the Coptic version as a condensation of the Greek (e.g., Schrage, *Das Verhältnis,* 91; Sieber, "A Redactional Analysis," 67) on the supposition that the Coptic thereby focuses more on the concept of "clothing," a theme important elsewhere in Thomas (cf. Thom 21 and 37). But the Coptic version of Thom 36 does not directly mention clothing (cf. ⲱⲧⲏⲛ in Thom 37); only in POxy 655 is this connection made explicit (cf. ἔνδυμα, col 1.11–12, 16). Hence, one could well

Wilson makes much of the fact that Thom 36, unlike Luke 12:22-31//Matt 6:25-33, does not mention any assurances that God will see to it that clothes are provided. This suggests to him that Thomas here exhibits what a "distinctly Gnostic" disregard for the body.[79] But Thomas' failure to mention any comforting provision of this sort could take on this level of significance only under the assumption that Thomas made use of Q's speech, and with conscious intention omitted Luke 12:27-28//Matt 6:28-30, an assumption which the evidence will not support. Rather, in view of the radical ethos that we have been tracking in the Gospel of Thomas, it is preferable not to read too much into this saying, but to view it simply as sound policy for an itinerant beggar not to give much thought to dressing fashionably.

(b) Wisdom Sayings

There are a number of wisdom sayings in Thomas that could be mustered to support this sort of willful impoverishment and beggarly form of life. Of interest first is Thom 54, a beatitude:

Jesus said, "Blessed are the poor, for to you belongs heaven's kingdom."

The Coptic Ⲍ̄ⲚⲘⲀⲔⲀⲢⲒⲞⲤ ⲚⲈ Ⲛ̄ⲌⲎⲔⲈ is no doubt a translation of the Greek μακάριοι οἱ πτωχοί, commonly rendered "Blessed are the poor." But this term πτωχοί/πτωχός is a curious one for our purposes: in hellenistic literature generally speaking it does not commonly carry the connotation of simple poverty as it is often assumed to have in the New Testament. Rather, it usually means more specifically "beggar."[80] Now, whether beggars were called πτωχοί because they were usually poor, or whether πτωχός was a term sometimes applied to the poor because they were thought of as always begging, is a question that for now may be left unanswered. For our purposes it is enough to note this possibility within the connotative range of πτωχός, and to suggest that in view of what has been learned thus far about the mendicancy of the Thomas "community" a more appropriate translation here would perhaps be "Blessed are the beggars." In any event, for Thomas Christianity the saying is self-referential; the poverty of the radical existence its adherents have chosen makes this conclusion unavoidable.

Other wisdom sayings help to compensate for the various aspects of deprivation attendant upon the mendicant life. Are these itinerants poor? That it no disgrace, for it is by choice that they have forsaken the wealth of the world (Thom 110). Are they hungry? Then it is to their advantage, a source of

---

argue that vss 3-4 in the Greek version are a late expansion designed to inhance this connection. Whether vs 2 might also belong to such an expansion is unclear. It may represent scribal harmonization (cf. Matt 6:26b, 30//Luke 12:24b, 28).

79. Wilson, *Studies*, 68-69. It is difficult to determine Wilson's precise meaning here. Is docetism the issue (for which evidence is completely lacking in Thomas), or simply asceticism?

80. *LSJ*, s.v. πτωχός; so also Hauck, "πτωχός, κτλ.," 886-87.

blessing (Thom 69:2).[81] Are they without fine clothing? Of what use are such things in the higher pursuit of life's wisdom (Thom 78)? Are they weak, without (political) power? This too is by design (Thom 81).[82] In this way wisdom sayings will have been used to support and encourage Thomas Christians in their willfully marginalized existence.

(c) Parables

There are two sets of parables in Thomas which may be related to this theme of willful poverty. The first cycle consists of Thom 63, 64, and 65, and has to do with rejecting involvement in activity aimed toward material gain.

Thomas on Material Gain

Thom 63
[1]Jesus said, "There was a rich person who had a great deal of money. [2]He said, 'I shall invest my money so that I may sow, reap, plant, and fill my storehouses with produce, that I may lack nothing.' [3]These were the things he was thinking in his heart, but that very night he died. [4]Whoever has ears should listen."

Thom 64
[1]Jesus said, "A person was receiving guests. When he had prepared the dinner, he sent his slave to invite the guests. [2]The slave went to the first and said to him, 'My master invites you.' [3]That one said, 'Some merchants owe me money; they are coming to me tonight. I must go and give them instructions. Please excuse me from dinner.' [4]The slave went to another and said to him, 'My master has invited you.' [5]He said to the slave, 'I have bought a house, and I have been called away for a day. I shall have no time.' [6]The slave went to another and said to him, 'My master invites you.' [7]He said to the slave, 'My friend is to be married, and I am to arrange the dinner. I shall not be able to come. Please excuse me from dinner.' [8]The slave went to another and said to him, 'My master invites you.' [9]He said to the slave, 'I have bought an estate, and I am going to collect the rent. I shall not be able to come. Please excuse me.' [10]The slave returned and said to his master, 'Those whom you invited to dinner have asked to be excused.' [11]The master said to his slave, 'Go out on the streets, and bring back whomever you find to have dinner.' [12]Buyers and merchants [will] not enter the places of my Father."

Thom 65
[1]He said, "A [. . .] person owned a vineyard and leased it to some farmers, that they might work it and the he might collect its crop from them. [2]He sent his slave that

---

81. I follow Meyer in adopting the reading of this saying proposed by Grobel ("How Gnostic is the Gospel of Thomas?" 373): "Blessed are they that go hungry in order that they may fill the stomach of him who desires." Meyer (in Kloppenborg, et al, *Q—Thomas Reader*, 146) translates: "Blessed are they who are hungry, that the stomach of the one in want may be filled."

82. The first stich of this saying poses problems. But if one reads ⲣ ⲣⲣⲟ here in the peculiar Thomas way of "ruling" (as in Thom 2), then it is possible to view the first stich as parallel in meaning to the second (so Bauer, "Echte Jesusworte," 124–26; also Haenchen, *Botschaft*, 57): just as the powerful renounces power, so too should the wealthy learn to "rule," i.e., live by the insights gained in contemplating these sayings (Thom 2), which inevitably entails the renunciation of wealth (Thom 95).

the farmers might give him the vineyard's crop. ³They grabbed him, beat him, and almost killed him, and the slave returned and told his master. ⁴His master said, 'Perhaps he did not know them.' ⁵He sent another slave, and the farmers beat that one as well. ⁶Then the master sent his son and said, 'Perhaps they will show my son some respect.' ⁷Because the farmers knew that he was the heir to the vineyard, they grabbed him and killed him. ⁸Whoever has ears should listen."

In view of the admonition in Thom 95 to give up all claims to wealth, Thom 63 may be read quite simply in terms of the folly of investing one's money, here in a (probably absentee[83]) farming operation. The story is likely based upon a common wisdom motif (cf. Sir. 11:18–19), which opposed generally this sort of devotion to achieving for oneself material and financial security. Its relevance here, in light of such sayings as Thom 95 and 54, need not be elaborated.

In Thom 64 one is presented with the single instance in this collection where a parable is given an explicit interpretation, and it accords well with what has been said thus far about Thomas' attitude toward wealth and its accumulation. At the end of Thomas' version of the Parable of the Great Supper is the interpretive comment: "Buyers and merchants [will] not enter the places of my Father." Ron Cameron[84] has recently provided excellent information about the significance of using the peculiar language "buyers[85] and merchants"[86] in this hermeneutical conclusion. These were the stereotypical "wheelers and dealers, hucksters, and hustlers" of the ancient world, "bent on greed and corruption, trafficking in sophistry, pandering to deceit."[87]

Now by any normal standards the excuses offered by Thomas' guests are really quite acceptable, even honorable, especially in view of the last-minute nature of the whole affair in Thomas. Would a person in the midst of closing a deal on a house drop everything at once—the dinner is already prepared and waiting!—just to provide conversation at a dinner party for a few out-of-town guests? Would an honorable person neglect preparations for a friend's wedding celebration and run off to a feast next door? The 'acceptability' of these activities is perhaps underscored by the occurrence of excuses similar to three of Thomas' four in Deut 20:5–7. There, three conditions under which a person might be excused from battle are given: when one has 1) purchased a house and not yet had the opportunity to dedicate it; 2) planted a vineyard

---

83. It is notable that Thomas portrays the act as a financial investment on the part of a rich person, who *puts his money to use* by sowing, etc.; in other words, he must buy the seed, and probably the land as well. A person already engaged in farming would have saved plenty of seed from the previous year's crop for replanting; only an entrepreneur would start with a capital investment.

84. Cameron, "Parable and Interpretation," 18–19.

85. Cameron ("Parable and Interpretation," 18) proposes that the Coptic ⲛ̅ⲣⲉϥⲧⲟⲟⲩ translates the Greek καπήλοι; he renders the term "traders."

86. Cameron ("Parable and Interpretation," 18) proposes that the Coptic ⲛⲉϣⲟⲧⲉ translates the Greek ἔμποροι.

87. Cameron, "Parable and Interpretation," 18; see esp. n. 39 for references and discussions.

without yet having had the opportunity to collect from its fruit; or 3) married and not yet been able to consummate it. Of course in the parable there is nothing at stake so weighty as a Holy War; how much more would such excuses suffice to free one from a simple dinner invitation. Whatever the relationship between Thomas' story and Deut. 20:5-7,[88] it seems clear that these would not normally have been viewed as lame excuses. Yet in Thomas' view they are. They are the excuses of the untrustworthy, of charlatans, of 'hucksters' trying to get out of something; that is the implication of the name-calling in Thomas' interpretive conclusion to the parable. And to the Thomas way of thinking they are indeed lame excuses, for these are not worthwhile activities. The first excuse probably involves collecting on a line of credit (cf. Thom 95); the second and fourth excuses involve investment in property (cf. Thom 63). The third excuse ("My friend is to be married, and I am to arrange the dinner") is less clearly problematic within the Thomas scheme, yet even here one should remember that this too would probably have involved a considerable outlay of funds, and all for the folly of a feast.[89]

The third parable in this cycle is Thom 65, the Parable of the (Rebellious) Tenants. Crossan is correct in identifying the point of this parable as a lament over the terrible effects of greed; but I cannot follow him in identifying the tenants as the primary villains in the story.[90] His view rests upon the notion that Thomas' version pits a "good man" against a group of evil tenants. But such a reading is not supported by the text. The Greek adjective applied to ογωмε (person) in 65:1 is obscured by a lacuna, and may be transcribed thus: ñхρн[. . .]с.[91] With room for two letters in the lacuna, plus a third indistinct letter before the sigma, one is presented with two possibilities for completing the word: хρн[сто]с (good), the usual choice, or хρн[стн]с (i.e. a creditor or usurer[92]), which is equally possible, and in my view more probable.[93] The person thus described is, after all, an absentee landlord,[94] a creditor of those to

---

88. The parallels between Thomas' second excuse and the first excuse in Deut 20:5, and Thomas' fourth excuse and the second excuse in Deut 20: 6 are quite close; the parallel between Thomas' third excuse and the third excuse in Deut 20: 7 is more remote. The third excuse in Luke's version of the story (Luke 14:20) is closer to Deut 20:7, but whether this reflects an earlier (pre-Thomas) version of the story, originally modeled more closely upon the Deuteronomy passage, or is the result of Luke's editing of an earlier version of the story to bring it more into conformity with the LXX text, is debatable. Thomas' first excuse is not paralleled in Deut 20:5-7 at all. It may be that it, together with the final interpretive comment, constitute Thomas' redaction of the story. But cf. Crossan's arguments (*Four Other Gospels*, 41-42) for viewing Thomas' second excuse, not the first, as redactional.

89. Cf. Thom 69:2, as translated by Grobel (see n. 81).

90. Crossan, *Four Other Gospels*, 53-54.

91. Guillaumont, et al. (*The Gospel According to Thomas*, 38) print ñхρн|ст|ос in the *editio princeps*, the dot beneath the omicron indicating only that some ink is visible here, but not necessarily enough to suggest one letter over another. In fact, the ink is but a trace on the edge of the lacuna, not enough to suggest a letter. For all practical purposes, the omicron should be located inside the brackets, thus indicating the lacuna (so Layton, *Nag Hammadi Codex II*, 78).

92. *LSJ, s.v.* χρήστης.

93. So also Dehandschutter, "La Parabole de vignerons homicides," 218.

94. For the social-historical situation of absentee land ownership in first-century Palestine,

whom he rents and hardly a sympathetic character in the rural areas of Palestine and Syria. Given what has already been said about Thomas' attitude toward the quest for wealth and profit, it seems preferable to see in the landlord a bit of the villain as well. The tragedy here is a double one: the absentee landlord is rewarded for his greed with the death of his son; the tenants' desire to hold on to the produce leads to their debasement by their violent actions, first against the innocent servants, and then against the son. The story has no winners, all are ruined by the desire for the land and its produce.

The second set of parables is related to the motif of willful poverty in a similar way, in that they are all about persons who, in the course of working for a living, make a choice which makes very bad business sense, but very good "Thomas sense."

Thomas on Earning a Living

Thom 76

¹Jesus said, "The kingdom of the Father is like a merchant who had a supply of merchandise, and then found a pearl. ²That merchant was prudent; he sold the merchandise and bought the single pearl for himself. ³So also with you, seek his treasure that is unfailing, that endures, where no moth comes to eat and no worm destroys."

Thom 107

¹Jesus said, "The kingdom is like a shepherd who had a hundred sheep. ²One of them, the largest, went astray. He left the ninety-nine and sought the one until he found it. ³After he had toiled, he said to the sheep, 'I love you more than the ninety-nine.'"

Thom 8

¹And he said, "The human one is like a wise fisherman who cast his net into the sea and drew it up from the sea full of little fish. ²Among them the wise fisherman discovered a fine large fish. ³He threw all the little fish back into the sea, and easily chose the large fish. ⁴Whoever has two good ears should listen."

The first is Thom 76, the Parable of the Merchant. Though Robert W. Funk names it "The Pearl Merchant,"⁹⁵ leading one to think perhaps of the merchant who is in the market for pearls in Matthew's parallel to our text (13:45–46), the most important thing to notice about the Thomas version of this story is that the merchant is not a pearl merchant at all, but a dealer in general "merchandise."⁹⁶ This being the case, his action is most dramatic—he holds a "going out of business sale" to buy a single pearl. This is not an investment. He buys it "for himself" (ⲚⲀϤ), but in so doing leaves himself broke, with no way to make a living. Only to the Thomas way of thinking is he "wise" (ⲤⲀⲂⲈ):

upon which the plot of this parable is based, see Hengel, "Das Gleichnis von den Weingärtnern."

95. Funk, *New Gospel Parallels*, 2: 161.

96. So Jeremias, *Gleichnisse Jesu*, 198.

"Buyers and merchants [will] not enter the places of my Father" (Thom 64:12).

The shepherd in Thomas' Parable of the Lost Sheep (Thom 107) is similarly wise: he leaves ninety-nine sheep unattended and searches for a single one which has strayed. Jeremias calls attention to the fact that in Thomas the stray sheep is the largest, which together with the shepherd's affectionate words to the sheep at the conclusion of the parable indicates why the shepherd would do such a thing: this sheep was his favorite.[97] But while this may explain the shepherd's action, it does not justify it.[98] Any shepherd would recognize the foolhardiness of such an act and the impulsiveness of leaving the others standing unguarded in the field while wandering off to find the stray. No single sheep (no matter how large!) is worth risking the safety of ninety-nine others. Far from justified, the shepherd here stands doubly convicted: not only is he stupid, he has also allowed his petty affection for the largest sheep to take precedence over sound shepherding. Yet it is precisely this aspect of Thomas' telling of the story that allows one to see it in continuity with the overall Thomas position on earning money. Like the merchant in Thom 76, the shepherd's action is exemplary: it demonstrates his willingness to pursue that one thing which he values most highly, even though it may appear as foolish when measured against the normal standards of the workaday world.[99]

The third member of this cluster, Thomas' Parable of the Wise Fisher (Thom 8), is to be read in this manner as well. Matthew's fisher (Matt 13:47–50) is a good one, sorting out the bad fish and keeping all of the good ones. Thomas' fisher, on the other hand, does a very foolish thing. He throws *all* the fish back, both good and bad, keeping only the one large fish.[100] But in so doing he demonstrates an exemplary Thomas attitude of disregard for the

97. Jeremias, *Gleichnisse Jesu*, 133.
98. *Contra* Jeremias (*Gleichnisse Jesu*, 133), who argues that Thomas ruins the gist of the parable by making it worthwhile for the shepherd to run after this particular sheep.
99. This interpretation seems to me preferable to that of Petersen ("The Parable of the Lost Sheep"), who sees here a parable about salvation history, wherein the tiring of the shepherd reflects the tiring of God in the pursuit of beloved Israel (cf. Isaiah 43). There is no evidence for a salvation history motif elsewhere in Thomas; reading it in here thus seems arbitrary. The manner in which Schnider ("Das Gleichnis vom verlorenen Schaf") arrives at a gnostic interpretation of this parable, by assigning cosmic roles to each of the characters (the sheep = the gnostic lost in the world; the shepherd = the gnostic redeemer) also seems highly arbitrary in view of the absence in Thomas of any systematic gnostic mythology within whose scheme such an interpretation could make sense.
100. So Jeremias, *Gleichnisse Jesu*, 199–200. Hunzinger ("Unbekannte Gleichnisse," 218–19) argues conversely that Thomas' fisher has acted wisely. In his view, the fisher catches sight of the big fish, not "among" the smaller fish in the net, but "beneath" them, i.e., still swimming free in the water below. He therefore releases the smaller fish so as to catch the large fish. The question turns on how to translate ⲛ̄ϩⲣⲁⲓ ⲛ̄ϩⲏⲧⲟⲩ in 8:2, which is ambiguous (Crum, *Coptic Dictionary*, s.v. ϩⲣⲁⲓ). One must rely upon the context in this case. Hunzinger's translation would make the fisher a more skillful one, but it is not clear how this reading squares with Thomas as a whole, especially Thom 76 and 107, with which it shares so many features. Jeremias' reading at least has the virtue of continuity with these parables and other Thomas sayings that assign little value to pursuing a profession.

wisdom of the practical world of securing a living, while striving after a single treasured prize.[101]

These three parables have one thing in common: their characters all place the pursuit of one prized thing over the everyday common sense involved in making a living. But what is that one prized thing that is to be sought? What is it that stands above the necessity of making a living, of securing house and home, food and clothing? Haenchen argues that Thom 107, 76, and 8 are all about the gnostic quest for the self, that divine spark to be reunited with the godhead.[102] But the Gospel of Thomas itself never specifies what is to be sought. For example, does the injunction to seek and find in Thom 2 refer back to Thom 1 (i.e., seek the interpretation of these words) or forward to Thom 3 (i.e., seek after the kingdom)? In Thom 92:1 one is again exhorted to seek, but the content or nature of the information that Jesus holds at bay (Thom 92:2) is not revealed. What does the pearl represent? the sheep? the fish? Since Thomas does not tell us, we simply cannot know. But perhaps this is not the point. What links these three parables is not a single thing that is to be sought, nor even seeking itself—only in Thom 107 is searching a motif—but rather choosing, and the fact that in making the right choice the logic, priorities, and values of the world are rejected or ignored. To those who labor under the necessity of securing an adequate standard of living these characters are fools, but to the Thomas Christian, who wanders from house to house asking for a handout, they have seen the light.

This manner of undermining the priority of wealth and property by reversing the conventional system of values is perhaps to be found in one of Thomas' most problematic parables as well, Thom 109 (The Hidden Treasure), a parable of ignorance and accident. It was Cerfaux who first drew attention to the fact that Thomas' Hidden Treasure parable is probably a version of a story found also in *Midr. Cant. Rab.* 4.12.1:[103]

> R. Simeon b. Yohai taught: [The Egyptians were] like a man who inherited a piece of ground used as a dunghill. Being an indolent man, he went and sold it for a trifling sum. The purchaser began working and digging it up, and he found a treasure there, out of which he built himself a fine palace, and he began going about in public followed by a retinue of servants—all out of the treasure he found in it. When the seller saw it he was ready to choke, and he exclaimed, "Alas, what have I thrown away."[104]

101. This interpretation is to be preferred to the gnostic interpretation of Lindemann ("Zur Gleichnisinterpretation," 216–18), which is based upon a redactional analysis that assumes Thom 8 is a secondary melding together of Matt 13:45–46 and 47–50. Similarly Schoedel's gnostic interpretation is based on the assumption of Thomas' dependence upon the synoptic gospels ("Parables in the Gospel of Thomas," 553). It is also arbitrary in that it imposes upon the parable categories borrowed from later Valentinian Gnosticism (e.g., ⲡⲣⲱⲙⲉ = the Valentinian Primal Man).

102. Haenchen, *Botschaft*, 47–48.

103. Cerfaux and Garitte, "Les paraboles du Royaume," 314; so also Jeremias, *Gleichnisse Jesu*, 28.

104. The translation is that of Maurice Simon in Freedman and Simon, *Midrash Rabbah: Song of Songs*, 219–20.

The story is used here in a way that might be considered quite conventional: it plays upon the conventional wisdom that anyone would greatly regret having passed up so golden an opportunity. The lazy person receives his or her just recompense in the ironic turn of events after the sale.

In Thomas, however, the story is told quite differently:

[1]Jesus said, "The kingdom is like a person who had a treasure hidden in his field but did not know it. [2]And [when he] died he left it to his [son]. The son [did] not know (about it either). He took over the field and sold it. [3]The buyer went plowing, [discovered] the treasure, and began to lend money at interest to whomever he wished."

                                                                                        Thom 109

Like the rabbinic tale, this is a story about one person's ignorance and another's luck.[105] But unlike the rabbinic version, Thomas' does not focus at all upon the natural irony of the story—that point at which the previous owner discovers his or her error. As far as Thomas is concerned, the son simply goes his merry way, and is never heard from again. Instead, the focus falls upon the person who discovers the treasure: "He began to lend money at interest to whomever he wished." This final comment really invites one to read the parable anew, in light of the reversal of values we have been tracing throughout Thomas. In so doing it stands the story on its head—and its moral as well. For to the Thomas way of thinking, the finder, far from lucky, has fallen into that despised activity in Thomas, usury (cf. Thom 95). As for the son, his ignorance and disinterest in cultivating the field turn out to have been his blessing, for he has successfully escaped the treasure's corrupting influence. That this is the thrust of Thomas' retelling of the story is further suggested by the fact that Thomas follows the parable immediately with Thom 110: "Jesus said: 'Whoever finds the world and becomes rich, let him renounce the world'"—an apt rejoinder to the parable as a whole.[106]

The persons for whom this tradition spoke were homeless beggars. They wandered about the countryside without money, depending upon handouts for such necessities as food and clothing. In their repertoire of sayings they held a number with which to justify the life they had taken up, wisdom sayings and parables that speak of the foolishness of life's pursuits and the wisdom of giving it all up to go for that which they have chosen for themselves.

---

105. This distinguishes it from the recurring theme of "seeking and finding" in Thomas (contra Haenchen, Botschaft, 47–48); as in Thom 8 and 76, the discovery here is quite accidental.

106. Thom 109 has been troublesome in that it appears to liken the kingdom to the activities of two ignorant fools, the father and his son (see, e.g., King, "Kingdom in the Gospel of Thomas," 56). But the final line of the parable, together with Thom 110, really invite one to view the parable in terms of Thomas' reversal of values: to the Thomas way of thinking, the father and son were the fortunate ones, and the finder was the fool.

4. Relativizing Piety and Purity

(a) Legal Sayings

The radicality of Thomas Christianity extends also to the realm of religious piety. Such traditional disciplines as fasting, prayer, alms giving, dietary regulations are all explicitly rejected in Thom 14:1-3:

> ¹Jesus said to them, "If you fast, you will bring sin upon yourselves, ²and if you pray, you will be condemned, ³and if you give alms, you will harm your spirits."

The basis for this radical position is to be found in Thom 6. There a general admonition against hypocrisy in 6:2-4 is focused specifically on the question of pious observance by the addition of an artificially constructed introduction, produced no doubt on the basis of 14:1-3:[107]

> ¹His disciples asked him and said to him, "Do you want us to fast? How should we pray? Should we give alms? What diet should we observe?" ²Jesus said, "Do not lie, and do not do what you hate, because all things are disclosed before heaven."

If one thinks of Jesus' response here ("do not do what you hate") as a kind of "Golden Rule,"[108] it will appear as somewhat of a *non sequitur*. But this is a misreading of his answer that does not give due attention to its relationship to the question that prompts it. "Do not do what you hate" calls attention to the transparent hypocrisy ("for all things are plain in the sight of heaven") of going through the motions of pious observance without the proper motivation.[109] This is not so much an outright rejection of pious observance as it is an extreme intensification of it to the point that no one is really able to measure up to its demands. Who does not hate to fast? The result is that pious observance is placed under such stringent requirements that no one is able to comply with them; piety is thus rejected *de facto*.[110] Ultimately this line of reasoning leads to the rejection of piety and ritual purity altogether, including dietary laws (Thom 14:4), matters of ritual washing (Thom 89), even initiation (Thom 53). For Thomas, all of these things pale in significance when compared with what one actually thinks, feels, and does with conviction.[111]

---

107. Form-critically Thom 6 is a simple chreia, composed of an originally independent legal saying (6:2-4) which has been supplied with a secondary introduction (6:1). 6:5-6, a wisdom saying, was also originally an independent saying (see chapter 2, pp. 20-22) probably added to the chreia later. The similarity of Thom 6:1 to Thom 14:1-3 is striking, but may be accounted for form-critically in that 6:1 is a secondary formulation designed to steer 6:2-4 in the direction of the specific question of pious observance. In formulating the disciples' question here, the tradents no doubt drew upon items having to do with pious observance already known to them through the tradition, viz., Thom 14:1-3.

108. So Crossan, *In Fragments*, 52-53; Funk, *New Gospel Parallels*, 108-9.

109. So Rudolph, *Gnosis*, 263.

110. Theissen calls attention to this phenomenon in his treatment of the Jesus movement (*Sociology*, 78-80).

111. Of course all of this is contradicted by Thom 104:3; but this is one of a handful of

This sort of radical intensification is behind Thom 27:2 as well:

"If you do not keep the sabbath a sabbath, you will not see the Father."

This saying does not stand in opposition to the general position on popular piety traced in Thomas thus far. While it is admittedly difficult to discern exactly what this saying might have meant to Thomas Christians, since it does not itself spell out what a "sabbatical" sabbath is, in light of what has already been said about the tendency in Thomas to shun uninspired pious observance, it is best to read this saying as a protest of sorts against piety without substance.[112]

(b) Wisdom Sayings

There are at least two wisdom sayings in the Gospel of Thomas that buttress its position on the practice of traditional piety. Thom 6:5–6 is appended to 6:1–4 to reinforce the idea that a hypocritical piety does not go unobserved. Similarly Thom 14:5 is added to 14:1–4 to provide a rationale for the elements in its accompanying sayings having to do with fasting and dietary practice.[113]

(c) Other Sayings

There is but one other saying in Thomas that comes under consideration here, since it further illustrates the iconoclasm of Thomas Christianity, and in a slightly different vein. Thom 52 is the following chreia:

[1]His disciples said to him, "Twenty-four prophets have spoken in Israel, and they all spoke of you." [2]He said to them, "You have disregarded the living one who is in your presence, and have spoken of the dead."

It is striking here that the disciples' comment is not viewed as a compliment. This much must be gathered from the reproachful tone in Jesus' reply, which disparages the prophets in favor of the superiority of Jesus.[114] Perhaps this relativizing of the prophets is not intended to be absolute. Nevertheless, it seems clear that in Thomas there is no interest in associating Jesus with the venerable tradition of the prophets; his "living" presence represents a clean break with the "dead" past.

5. The Deprecation of Officialdom

(a) Legal Sayings

On the matter of the Thomas Christian's response to Roman and Jewish officials the Gospel of Thomas is for the most part silent. Under legal sayings it

---

examples in Thomas where one must reckon with relatively late secondary influence from the synoptic text (see chapter 2, pp. 80–81).

112. So Rudolph, *Gnosis*, 263.

113. Rudolph, *Gnosis*, 263.

114. J.-B. Bauer, "Echte Jesusworte," 128–30; Haenchen, *Botschaft*, 66.

might be appropriate to mention briefly Thom 100, already considered above under "Willful Poverty and Begging" because of its relevance to the question of support for the "community" ("and give me what is mine"). What is noteworthy here is the ambiguity of the answer Jesus offers, an answer much more ambiguous than that offered in the synoptic version of the story. There (Mark 12:13-17, par.) the ploy of asking: "Whose likeness and inscription is this?" and the subsequent correct answer: "Caesar's." (Mark 12:16, par.) could be construed as lending a conciliatory tone to the saying "Render unto Caesar the things that are Caesar's" (Mark 12:17, par.). In Thom 100 there is nothing comparable to Mark 12:16 in reducing the ambiguity of Jesus' comment; the question is left open: What things then belong to Caesar?[115] along with its parallel dilemmas: What things belong to God? and What things belong to Jesus? As for the last, I have already that that the third question is to be answered with support for the Thomas mendicants.[116] But what about the first two? Since the Gospel of Thomas does not instruct one in how to answer them, it is left to the exegete to surmise how someone giving ear to the beggar's pitch might have done so. Given the choice of paying or not paying his or her Roman taxes, obviously most people living under Roman occupation in Palestine and Syria in the first century would have preferred not to.[117] To be sure, the ambiguity of the saying makes it unlikely that it would have ignited a riotous tax rebellion. Still, there remains something subversive about suggesting to taxpayers the notion that one may determine for oneself what belongs to whom.

(b) Other Sayings

Another saying that seems to be of relevance for mapping Thomas Christianity's response to officialdom is the enigmatic I-saying in Thom 71:

Jesus said, "I will destroy [this] house, and no one will be able to build it [. . .]."

On the one hand, this may be the Thomas version of the Temple word known from the canonical tradition (cf. Matt 26:61; 27:40//Mark 14:58; 15:29; Matt 24:2//Mark 13:2//Luke 21:6; Acts 6:14; and John 2:19). But even if this is the case, the canonical parallels do not help to interpret its peculiar form here. In Thomas, where the death of Jesus does not occupy a prominent place, it is not possible to allegorize the saying as the author of John has done (cf. John 2:19–22). Nor is there in Thomas an eschatological end time in view, which could

115. One can imagine how the tradition came to include something like Mark 12:16 to help clear up precisely this ambiguity.
116. See pp. 137–38.
117. For a discussion of the tax system in Palestine, and the bind in which it placed the people, see Theissen, *Sociology*, 42–45. The problem was created by two competing tax systems, that of the Romans and that of the Temple. In Thomas' three-stich version of this saying it seems entirely plausible that the second stich ("Give to God what belongs to God") originally referred to the Temple tax system, thus undermining it just as the Roman system is here undermined.

absorb the saying into its apocalyptic mythology (cf. Mark 13:2). In Thomas one is left with the Temple as a Jerusalem institution, whose destruction the Thomas movement perhaps applauds with this familiar saying. Whether they would have opposed the Temple for reasons related to their stance on popular piety or for political reasons related perhaps to their stance on paying taxes,[118] it is difficult to say; the text does not tell us. It is probably a dubious procedure to try to separate these two issues too cleanly. Paying the tithe, after all, was a political act supported and enforced within the structure of piety (cf. Matt 18:11–12).

On the other hand, there may be other possibilities. The enigma of this saying, of course, is in Thomas' use of "house" rather than "Temple," as in the canonical gospels. To what might this refer? Might it have in mind the house as "home," so that we should consider it among those sayings dealing with itinerancy, or perhaps among those which reject conventional family relationships? Or might it refer to some more prominent "house," for example the king's house, the house of David, occupied in the early years of the Jesus movement by an illegitimate Herodian "house"? If the latter were the case, we could consider it here alongside sayings that thwart the powers that be. For those who spent their days among the rural folk in the χώρα ("countryside"; cf. Thom 14:4), a veiled attack on the Herodians would be readily explicable. The brutality of Herodian rule, especially in the rural districts, is well known.[119] And this would not be the only place where the Thomas tradition strikes out at kingship. Thom 78 reads:

> [1]Jesus said, "Why have you come out to the countryside? To see a reed shaken by the wind? [2]And to see a person dressed in soft clothes, [like your] kings and your powerful ones? [3]They are dressed in soft clothes, and they cannot understand truth."

The tradition is of course familiar from the synoptic parallels in Matt 11:7–9//Luke 7:24–26 (Q). But here, rather than John it is presumably Jesus himself whose example stands in contrast to that of the "kings and powerful ones," subverting the conventional wisdom "clothes make the person." This is subversive wisdom, but with a sharp political edge. It is reminiscent of the critique of kingship commonly found on the lips of the Cynic philosophers of the period.[120]

---

118. Cf. n. 117. If Thomas Christians spent much time in the χώρα (countryside) (cf. Thom 14:4), they would have been sensitive to the problems that the Temple tax posed for rural folk at times (cf. Josephus, *Ant.* 20. 181, and 206–7; and *Vita* 12.) The centrality of the Temple in the tensions which stood between city and country in first century Palestine is treated by Theissen in "Die Templeweissagung Jesu."

119. See, for example, the discussion in Horsley and Hanson, *Bandits, Prophets, and Messiahs*, 30–43; see also Horsley, *Sociology*, 83–90.

120. Cf. Diogenes Laertius 2.25; Lucian, *Dem.* 41 and *Perig.* 17–19; Epictetus, *Disc.* 1.24.7; and Ps.-Crates 23.

6. Minimal Organization

Finally, in addition to inquiring how these Thomas Christians comport themselves to the world around them we might ask how they relate to one another. In other words, how did they organize themselves? If we begin as usual with legal sayings, it becomes plain that an analysis of this aspect of the Thomas tradition has precious little material with which to work.

(a) Legal Sayings

The only legal saying in the Thomas tradition that concerns itself directly with internal organization is Thom 12:2. The fact that there is so little in Thomas having to do with such matters is itself not insignificant. If one is to judge on the basis of the amount of material in Thomas devoted explicitly to organizational matters, one would have to conclude that the group that identified with and used this document was not very highly organized. This, of course, can only be a suspicion, since it is based on an argument from silence. But a careful analysis of Thom 12:2 strengthens this suspicion:

> ²Jesus said to them, "No matter where you are, you are to go to James the Just,[121] for whose sake heaven and earth came into being."

Meyer's rendering of ⲚⲦⲀⲦⲈⲦⲚⲈⲒ ⲘⲘⲀⲨ as "No matter where you are" perhaps does not convey the notion of itinerancy as clearly as the Coptic. But the use of ⲈⲒ (to go) here means not simply that they *are* somewhere, but that they have *gone* somewhere. In other words, the Thomas Christians are dispersed, and this saying provides for a central figure of authority to whom the wanderers might go for advice or perhaps the adjudication of disputes—although the manner and extent of the James-based authority is here not fully specified.[122] Of course, this tallies with what has already been said about the itinerant life that characterized the Thomas movement. Itinerants are mobile by definition. Moreover, it is hardly likely that these itinerants roved the countryside in large bands; they were beggars, not brigands, and beggars must of necessity work alone or in relatively small groups. Thus it is not surprising that there is little in Thomas that provides for community organization or structure: there is no Thomas community *per se*, but rather a loosely structured movement of wanderers.[123]

---

121. James the brother of Jesus (cf. Mark 6:3; Matt 13:55; Gal 1:19) was known as James the Just in antiquity (Eusebius, *Hist. eccles.* 2.23.4–7).
122. It is interesting that Paul's relations with Jerusalem as described in Galations seem to presuppose the system of authority laid down in Thom 12. In Gal. 1:18–19 Paul seems to have been billeted by Peter, but it was James he really needed to see. In the second visit (2:1–10), it falls to James, Peter and John (in that order?) to certify what Paul wishes to accomplish. Finally, in the dispute at Antioch (2:11–14) it appears to have been those sent from James who have clout enough to oppose Paul, and essentially to bring his activity there to a close.
123. King ("Kingdom in the Gospel of Thomas," 72) is resistent to the notion that Thomas

(b) Monachos Sayings

Pertinent to this discussion are a number of non-legal sayings which seem to make reference to the singleness of those who identified with this text. Most important are those sayings which employ the technical term ΜΟΝΑΧΟC.[124] The beatitude in Thom 49:1 is one of them:

> Jesus said, "Blessed are those who are alone (ΜΟΝΑΧΟC) and chosen, for you will find the kingdom."

The shift to direct address in the second clause directs the saying onto the movement which identifies with this text, and thus makes it a self-referential statement—these Thomas Christians *are* the "alone and chosen." But what do these terms imply about Thomas Christians? The notion of election or chosenness is common as a soteriologically significant claim; but the significance of the term ΜΟΝΑΧΟC, in addition to the soteriological twist it is given here, is chiefly *social-historical*. Aelred Baker has noted that most historians of monasticism agree that the derivation of μόναχος (monk) from μόνος in the sense of "alone" is to be taken seriously in terms of the social-historical origins of the concept.[125] The occurrences of the term elsewhere in Thomas would seem to

---

Christians were itinerant individuals. This, she assumes, would not be compatible with her thesis that the parables in Thomas have largely to do with defining who is inside the community and who is not. But King reflects too little on how one might *describe* the Thomas "community" based upon clues in the text, or how her thesis would be affected if the Thomas "community" were conceived differently from the settled group she imagines. In fact, a Thomas movement, as described here, would not be incompatible with King's thesis: its identity would still be a matter for self-questioning, no matter how loose its organization, and the parables might well have played a role in this matter of self-definition. Even Greco-Roman Cynics, who seem to have avoided all forms of organization as a matter of principle, argued among themselves about who was a true Cynic and who was not. King's statement "we [do not] see in the Gospel of Thomas the 'rugged individualist' of the philosopher type" is therefore unwarranted, and certainly does not reflect the text.

124. I do not agree with Klijn ("The 'Single One' in the Gospel of Thomas," 271–72) that ΜΟΝΑΧΟC in Thom 16, 49, and 75 is to be considered synonymous with ΟΥΑ ΟΥΩΤ (single one) (cf. Thom 4, 22, and 23) or simply ΟΥΑ (one) (cf. Thom 11, 22, and 106). The latter terms must indeed translate something like the emphatic form εἷς μόνος (single one) and εἷς (one) respectively, which the Coptic translator did not know as technical terms. But this does not allow one to assume with Klijn that ΜΟΝΑΧΟC and ΟΥΑ ΟΥΩΤ represent the same word in the translator's *Vorlage*—even under the very remote possibility (*pace* Klijn) that the Coptic Thomas is a translation of a Syriac version—on the grounds that in Thom 16, 49, and 75 he would have been trying to render a term unknown to him with a word already familiar to his readers. Had this been the case, one would expect that the translator would have taken care to use ΜΟΝΑΧΟC throughout so as to avoid leaving the impression that in some cases his text was speaking of those monastic figures familiar to fourth century Copts and in others not, when his *Vorlage* was using the same word throughout. More reasonable would be to assume that the translator had two different terms in his Greek *Vorlage*, one of which he recognized as a technical term (μόναχος) and thus simply transliterated, the other of which he did not so recognize (εἷς μόνος, or εἷς), and hence translated it with ΟΥΑ ΟΥΩΤ or simply ΟΥΑ. Removing Thom 16, 49, and 75 from consideration does not significantly affect his thesis regarding the gnosticizing metaphysics behind the term ΟΥΑ ΟΥΩΤ, with which I find myself largely in agreement.

125. Baker, "'Fasting to the World,'" 293, n. 14.

indicate that this general statement is accurate with respect to μόναχοι within the Thomas movement as well: in Thom 16 ΜΟΝΑΧΟC is applied to those who have broken away from family and become solitary in having adopted the radical Thomas lifestyle.[126] In Thom 75 it has become the designation for those who "enter the bridal chamber." The sense in which ΜΟΝΑΧΟC is used here is not clear from Thomas itself, since neither the nature of a "bridal chamber" ritual nor the requirements for participating in it are spelled out. But in the later Syrian romance, the Acts of Thomas, it is clear that only the sexually abstinent are allowed to enter the bridal chamber.[127] Thus, ΜΟΝΑΧΟC in the Gospel of Thomas very likely carries with it the connotation of sexual asceticism as well.[128]

Another saying which refers to the aloneness of the Thomas Christian is Thom 30. Following the reconstruction of the original text offered by Attridge,[129] it reads as follows:

[Jesus said], "Where there are [three], they are ⟨without God⟩, and where there is but [a single one], I say that I am with [him].

If Attridge is correct in his reconstruction, the directly antithetical way in which this saying is formulated over against the tradition found in Matt 18:20 and elsewhere[130] is striking. The presence of Jesus is guaranteed not in numbers, or community, but in the singleness of an individual. It is this manner of living that is most highly prized in Thomas, not the confines of a highly organized community.

7. Women Disciples in Thomas

One of the most notorius sayings in the Gospel of Thomas in Thom 114:

[1]Simon Peter said to them, "Make Mary leave us, for females do not deserve life." [2]Jesus said, "Look, I will guide her to make her male, so that she too may become a living spirit resembling you males. [3]For every female who makes herself male will enter heaven's kingdom."

---

126. Cf. Meeks, "The Image of the Androgyne," 196, n. 138.

127. AcThom 12; cf. Baker, "Early Syriac Asceticism," 400. In later Syrian tradition the Syriac for this term (*yihiydaya'*) came to mean "virgin" (so Baker, "Syriac and the Origins of Monasticism," 348-50.)

128. Meyer, "Making Mary Male," 557-58.

129. Attridge, "The Original Text of Gos. Thom, Saying 30." Attridge's reading of POxy 1 (horiz.). 23-27, achieved with the use of ultraviolet light, produces the following transcription (with his consequent restoration):

23   [λέγ]ει ['Ι(ησοῦ)ς· ὅπ]ου ἐὰν ὦσιν
     [τρ]ε[ῖς,] ε[ἰσὶ]ν ἄθεοι· καὶ
25   [ὅ]που ε[ἷς] ἐστιν μόνος
     [λ]έγω· ἐγώ εἰμι μετ αὐ-
27   τ[οῦ.]

Attridge explains the tautology in the Coptic translation by supposing that the alpha privative (i.e., the α in ἄθεοι) in line 24 had fallen out of the MS used by the Coptic translator, who attempted then to make sense of εἰσὶν θεοί (they are gods) in this sentence.

130. Cf. also 2 Cor 13:1; 1 Tim 5:19; Heb 10:28; 1 John 5:7-8.

The first and most obvious point to be made here is that the very existence of the legal saying at the end of this dialogue (114:3) presupposes that there were women in the group.[131] To be sure, the saying itself makes its point in a way that assumes the androcentric bias of its day. Women may be part of this group only if they negate what is female and 'unworthy' and 'make themselves male.' Nonetheless, this saying provides the clearest evidence in all of the early Christian sayings tradition for women disciples in the Jesus movement. Critical analysis yields futher insights.

Marvin W. Meyer has shown with great erudition that the conceptual framework of this saying is the notion, popular especially among second- and third-century gnostic groups, that femaleness is the focus of passion, earthliness, and mortality, and hence must be transcended or transformed if one is to return to the original state of primal perfection.[132] In Thomas we may well be seeing the fledgling beginnings of this type of anthropological speculation within Christianity. But more important for the present discussion are the practical implications of such a view in the social-historical sphere. How could a woman "make herself male"? Is this really a rule? Is it actually to be fulfilled?

Elizabeth Castelli has pointed to a motif in early Christian women's ascetic practice that may prove helpful in answering this question, viz. the phenomenon of male impersonation, or actual "androgenization" of women under severe ascetic circumstances.[133] Accepting the life of asceticism meant cropping the hair close, accepting male dress, and in extreme cases, physical emaciation to the extent that female bodily functions and characteristics all but disappear. Most of the sources Castelli uses to document the phenomenon are too late to be of direct help in explaining Thomas, and it remains to be seen how early this type of ascetic practice among women in the early church might be traced.[134] But if one is to discover an origin for this practice somewhere in the early church (as the title of Castelli's article implies), should not one look precisely to Thomas, where, if the two beatitudes in Thom 79 are read along

131. So Rudolph, *Gnosis*, 271; Walls, "References to the Apostles," 270.
132. Meyer, "Making Mary Male," esp. 563–67.
133. Castelli, "Virginity and its Meaning for Women's Sexuality," 75–77.
134. There are several examples of women impersonating men in the Apocryphal Acts: Thecla in the *AcPaulThecla* 3.25, 40; Mygdonna in the *AcThom* 114; and Charitine in the *AcPhil* 44. To these Christian sources one might add the case of the fictitious female philosopher described by Lucian in *Fug.* 27: "hair closely clipped in the Spartan style, boyish-looking and quite masculine." In his treatment of Thom 114, Meyer ("Making Mary Male," 562–63) makes brief mention of the phenomenon of male impersonation but he does not follow up its implications. Cf. also Meeks, "The Image of the Androgyne," 196. Discussing the significance of the term *monachos* in the Gospel of Thomas, Meeks writes of Thecla: "The virgin Thecla, for example, could be taken as the very model of a female who 'makes herself male,' represented in the story by her wish to cut her hair short and her donning of men's clothing, thus becoming what the Gospel of Thomas would call a *monachos*—not only a celibate, but also one who must break all ties to home, city, and ordinary society, becoming a wanderer."

side 114:3, a view of women's asceticism emerges that is very like that reflected in the tracts describing the ascetic practices of women in later Christian circles:

> ¹A woman in the crowd said to him, "Blessed are the womb that bore you and the breasts that fed you." ²He said to [her], "Blessed are those who have heard the word of the Father and have truly kept it. ³For there will be days when you will say, 'Blessed are the womb that has not conceived and the breasts that have not given milk.'"

Although the final beatitude speaks of virgins (presumably virgins within the Thomas group), it speaks of the virginal state in a rather roundabout way. That is, what seems to be important is not abstinence from intercourse as the sign or basis of one's virginal status. Rather, the beatitude speaks specifically about the functions of the female body, as though the highest state to which a woman might aspire would be one in which her body did not function as a female body—she "becomes male."

If this ascetic reading of Thom 79 at first sight seems farfetched, it may be helpful to reflect upon the question, under what circumstances women would have been able to take up the wandering life required of the Thomas Christian. Castelli draws attention to the fact that rape and assault were problems with which virgins had to cope, sometimes in very dramatic ways, even after the office of virgin had become regularized within the church.[135] The problem will have been infinitely greater in a situation of itinerancy. One thinks, for example, of the perils encountered by Xenophon's heroine Xanthipe in the *Ephesaica*, who is forced to travel alone in search of her lost husband Habracomes. The entire plot of the *Ephesaica* revolves around the question whether, under these circumstances, Xanthipe will be able to preserve her virginity. In using this motif Xenophon probably plays on common fears that were grounded in very real conditions on the road in hellenistic antiquity. It would have been difficult for a woman to live the itinerant life unmolested by the various characters inhabiting highway and byway. Disguise as a man would have offered at least some protection from these dangers.

Summary

Thomas Christianity positioned itself over against the world, and in so doing it rejected the world and its standards in every way. Theologically, this anticosmic ideology expressed itself in the gnosticizing proclivity of the Gospel of Thomas. Sociologically, it expressed itself as a way of living in but not of the world. The world values the security of house and home, of family, and of means; those in the Thomas movement rejected it. The world values engage-

---

135. Castelli, "Virginity and its Meaning for Women's Sexuality," 87.

ment in traditional religious piety, and respect for authority; Thomas Christians did not. Their itinerant mode of existing in the world represented the Thomas Christians' radical protest against the world.

In a 1973 article entitled "Wanderradikalismus. Literatursoziologische Aspekte der Überlieferung von Worten Jesu im Urchristentum," Gerd Theissen broke new ground in the study of early Christianity by using methods borrowed from the field of sociology. The resulting thesis about early Christian social behavior has subsequently come to take up an important place in the present discussion of Christian origins. Theissen's thesis is that characteristic of the persons who first collected and transmitted the sayings of Jesus was a particular style of living, which placed a premium on leaving behind house and home, family, and profession to take up the life of the wandering preacher. It was a radical form of existence—Theissen calls it *Wanderradikalismus*.[136]

If Robinson, Koester and others have argued correctly, that the Gospel of Thomas presents us with an example of the ancient Christian tradition of collecting sayings and ascribing them to Jesus,[137] it it is clear that Theissen's thesis has significance for the discussion of the social-historical context of the Thomas tradition as well. Theissen himself, however, did not argue this. Rather, he assumed that Thomas is a gnostic gospel and that the tendency among gnostics would be to disarm the sayings tradition of its original radical norms by "spiritualizing" its radicality, so that none of its demands need be taken seriously in terms of actual behavior. Thus, Theissen did not see Thomas as relevant to his thesis, save for the evidence it might provide for the domestication of the radical sayings tradition in the third or fourth Christian generation, as its locus shifted from a rural to an urban milieu.[138]

To focus in this way on Thomas as a gnostic gospel, and to impose on it a set of assumptions about the social life of gnostic groups, led Theissen to draw too dark a line between Thomas and other sayings collections, with which Thomas, despite its gnosticizing proclivity, stands in direct continuity. To demonstrate this continuity was Robinson's achievement in "LOGOI SOPHON."[139] Robinson, however, has acknowledged the need for some sort of sociological supplement to his thesis, which was sketched out originally in terms of the history of ideas, and has recently raised precisely this objection to Theissen's view of Thomas. Robinson argues that there is no reason to suppose such a "radical sociological-geographical jolt" between Thomas and other early Christian sayings collections, such as Q. If Thomas is located in Syria, it is easy to imagine a group of Thomas itinerants having wandered there from Palestine without having to entertain any major changes, such as learning a new language or making other cultural adjustments. Unlike other areas of early

---

136. Theissen, "Wanderradikalismus," 86; more will be said about Theissen's thesis in the following chapter.
137. See chapter 3, pp. 102–9.
138. Theissen, "Wanderradikalismus", 103.
139. See chapter 3, pp. 102–4.

Christian mission activity, such as Asia Minor or Egypt, where the indigenous tongues of rural peoples would have formed a linguistic barrier driving most missionary activity into the cities, where Greek served as the *ligua franca*, in Syria the Jesus movement could have carried on in the rural areas more or less as it had done before in Palestine.[140] In addition, noting especially the work of Kendrick Grobel, who pointed out the danger of assuming too quickly that Thomas has "spiritualized into vapor" the literal force of its traditions,[141] Robinson suggests that Theissen's contrast between the "conduct radicalism" of Q and the "epistemological radicalism" of Thomas has been similarly overdrawn.[142] If one accepts the proposition that as a sayings collection, the Gospel of Thomas presents its precepts as injunctions to be taken seriously, there is no inherent reason to suppose that Thomas should be read any less literally than, for example, Q.

Thus, in spite of Theissen's reluctance to view Thomas as another witness to socially radical ethos he associates with the early Christian sayings tradition, it is not remarkable to find that Thomas Christianity too had adopted this form of existence as its ideal. Already in 1968 Koester had drawn attention to this kind of ethos in Thomas, attributing it to early Christian roots that go deeper still:

> The disciples [in the Gospel of Thomas] are wanderers who have no home (Saying 42). They heal the sick and accept what is set before them (Saying 14b). If, in this way, they imitate Jesus' own experience of homelessness (Saying 86)—and indeed, this motif was destined to have a powerful influence upon Syrian Christianity—then Jesus' radical divorce from the accepted Jewish interpretation of the law has become a new set of religious rules. They have become test cases for the separation from this world and time. Otherworldliness is the new ideology.[143]

Koester's remarks confirm how needless is the assumption that Thomas' gnosticizing proclivity tended to defuse the radicality of an ethos of wandering homelessness. To the contrary, the anticosmic ideology of Thomas is complemented by, indeed entirely bound up with, the radical life style associated with the early Christian sayings tradition. Far from diffusing the social radicalism of the early sayings tradition, Thomas' gnosticizing proclivity finds its concrete expression in the socially radical ethos of Thomas Christianity.

---

140. Robinson, "On Bridging the Gulf," 137.
141. Grobel, "How Gnostic is the Gospel of Thomas?" 373; quoted in Robinson "On Bridging the Gulf," 137.
142. Robinson, "On Bridging the Gulf," 138.
143. Koester, "GNOMAI DIAPHOROI," 140-41.

6

Thomas Christianity
and Itinerant Radicalism

Be
Passers-By

Since Theissen published his ground-breaking work on the sociology of Palestinian Christianity in the late 1970s,[1] his fundamental thesis about the
emergence and character of the Jesus movement has become the center of a
lively debate about the very nature of earliest Christianity, and it continues to
fuel scholarly discussion.[2] Owing to the great similarity of what I have just
described as "Thomas Christianity" to Theissen's social description of the
sayings tradition in general, I have already alluded to Theissen's proposals in
some detail in the previous chapter. But now that the entire picture of Thomas
Christianity's social radicalism is more clearly in view, it is useful to draw back
and ask what such an assessment of Thomas Christianity might contribute to
an understanding of the movement of wandering radicalism in earliest Christianity. To this question the present chapter is devoted. But first it will be
helpful to review the basic structure of Theissen's thesis.

1. A number of Theissen's early essays on the subject are published in his *Studien zur
Soziologie des Urchristentums*. The results of these studies were summarized in *Soziologie der
Jesusbewegung*. The latter work is made available to American audiences in 1978 (*Sociology*).
2. The extent to which Theissen's thesis has shaped the discussion is perhaps best
illustrated by the fact that Richard Horsley in 1989 (*Sociology*, esp. 13–64) would devote almost
an entire book to its refutation. There is not space here to devote a full discussion to the
various critiques of Theissen's position which have been offered through the years. While
many critical assessments have brought the thesis into clearer focus, I am not persuaded by the
more thoroughly critical stance of Mack ("The Kingdom that Didn't Come," 620–23) and
Horsley (*Sociology*), who would call into question the very existence of wandering radicalism as
a phenomenon within early Christianity. Their critiques focus too narrowly on the question of
Q and the Q community, and ignore for the most part the broader swath Theissen's own work
cuts through a wide range of early Christian literature. And neither takes into account the
Thomas material discussed in the previous chapter. This above all else convinces me of the
correctness of Theissen's basic proposal. The following analysis reveals my own criticisms of
Theissen's work and suggests a number of correctives to the overall thesis.

Theissen's Thesis

According to Theissen, the social formation that characterized earliest Christianity can be described in terms of the interplay of three different roles at work in the primitive church: wandering charismatics, local sympathizers, and the Son of Man. To support this hypothesis he undertakes a "role analysis" that focuses successively on each of these three roles.

1. Wandering Charismatics

The first and most striking role Theissen describes is that of the wandering charismatic. Wandering charismatics, in Theissen's view, were among the earliest participants in the Jesus movement, and included the likes of Peter, Stephen, Paul, Barnabas, and other less illustrious figures, such as Lucius from Cyrenaica or Agabus the prophet.[3] This itinerancy was not an institutional form of life, but was based upon a call to discipleship and office in the early church over which the itinerant had no control.[4] It was characterized by homelessness,[5] turning away from family,[6] shunning of wealth and possessions,[7] and rejection of any means of protection on the road.[8] The picture Theissen offers is one of the itinerant preacher who wanders from place to place offering preaching and healing in exchange for hospitality.[9]

2. Local Sympathizers

Beggars need donors upon whom they can rely for support. But of course, in order to be in a position to offer support, one cannot subscribe to the same sort of unconventional ethos advocated by the wandering charismatics, or at least not in full. Shelter can only be offered by those who have not left house and home behind, food by those who have money to buy it, or land upon which to grow it. Theissen thus posits the existence of a second type of early Christian alongside the wandering charismatics, viz., local sympathizers.[10] Such local sympathizers would have existed in a kind of mutually supportive relationship with the wandering charismatics, supporting their basic needs of food and shelter in exchange for their gifts of preaching and care for the sick.

Theissen substantiates this thesis in three areas of inquiry: regulations for

3. Theissen, *Sociology,* 9.
4. Theissen, *Sociology,* 8.
5. Theissen, *Sociology,* 10–11. Note esp. Theissen's comments relative to Mark 1:16–20; 10:28–31; Matt 8:20; 10:5–15; 10:23; 23:34; Acts 8:1.
6. Theissen, *Sociology,* 11–12; note esp. Theissen's comments relative to Mark 10:29–30; 1:20; 6:4; 3:32; Matt 8:22; 19:10–11; 16:17; 10:24; Luke 14:26; 8:19–21; 11:27–28; 12:52–53.
7. Theissen, *Sociology,* 11–14; note esp. Theissen's comments relative to Mark 10:17–22, 25; Matt 10:10; 6:19–21, 25–34; 10:42; Luke 16:13, 19–31; 6:24; 10:5–15.
8. Theissen, *Sociology,* 14; note esp. Theissen's comments relative to Matt 5:39, 41; 10:17–23.
9. The thesis was worked out originally in the 1973 article "Wanderradikalismus." This important article was made available to American audiences in 1976 as "Itinerant Radicalism."
10. Theissen, *Sociology,* 17–23.

behavior, the structure of authority, and the procedure for accepting and rejecting members in early Christian groups. In the first area, he points out that it may not have been as easy for local sympathizers to behave as freely with regard to the law and conventional wisdom as did the wandering charismatics. Thus he calls attention to the sort of contradictions one finds throughout the synoptic gospels on the subject of the law:

> Some communities wanted to see the law fulfilled down to the smallest detail (Matt. 5.17ff.) instead of criticizing it (Matt. 5.21ff.). They felt that scribes and Pharisees were legitimate authorities (Matt. 23.1ff.) instead of morally corrupt groups over which one could only throw up one's hands in horror (Matt. 23.13ff.). They recognized the temple and its priesthood through sacrifice (Matt. 5.23), paying the temple tax (Matt. 17.24ff.) and accepting priestly declarations of wholeness (Mark 1.44), instead of rejecting its cultic practices (Mark 11.15ff.). They accepted patterns of fasting practised around them (Matt. 6.16f.) and had a positive attitude towards marriage and the family (Mark 10.2ff.; 10.13ff.).[11]

Theissen thus suggests that there was among early Christians a two-tiered system of norms, one set of norms applicable to the more radically oriented wandering charismatics, and another, less severe set followed by those living more conventional lives in established communities, who knew of the radical ethos of the wanderers, but could subscribe to it only to a limited degree.[12]

As for the structure of authority among early Christian groups, Theissen here notices another sort of contradiction. On the one hand there is in Matthew a tradition which assigns authority "to bind and loose" to a community (Matt 18:18), while at the same time another assigns it to Peter (Matt 16:19), whom Theissen considers to have been a wandering charismatic. Similarly, one may contrast Matt 23:8-12, which suggests an egalitarian structure of shared authority, with Matt 23:34, which recognizes the authority of certain Christian "prophets and wise men and scribes."[13] According to Theissen, these apparent contradictions may be explained if one imagines small communities whose leadership fell under the authority of wandering charismatics. Such a system would have been small and uncomplicated enough to function as a communal, egalitarian form of decision making during the extended periods in which the wandering authorities were absent. Theissen hypothesizes:

> At first, wandering charismatics were the authorities in the local communities. In any case, local authorities were unnecessary in small communities. Where two or three were gathered together in the name of Jesus (Matt. 18.20), a hierarchy was superfluous. Problems were resolved either by the community as a whole or by wandering charismatics who happened to arrive. . . . The less the structures of authority in local communities had come under the control of an institution, the greater was the longing for the great charismatic authorities. And conversely, the

11. Theissen, *Sociology,* 18-19.
12. Theissen, *Sociology,* 19.
13. Theissen, *Sociology,* 20.

greater the claim of these charismatics to authority, the less interest there was in setting up competing authorities within the communities.[14]

Yet as such communities grew in size, becoming more complex and demanding more reliable and consistent forms of leadership, this older structure gradually became obsolete. As Theissen points out, there inevitably arose the need to establish local authorities who quite naturally found themselves in competition with the wandering charismatics.[15] More will be said of this development presently.

Finally, Theissen points to a discrepancy in the manner in which early Christian groups accepted or rejected members. As a rite of initiation, baptism seems to have been decisive in local communities (Matt 28:19; Didache 7), yet there is no rite of initiation for wandering charismatics (with the exception of Matt 28:19), and Paul (whom Theissen considers a wandering charismatic) certainly does not regard baptism one of his primary responsibilities (1 Cor 1:17). Similarly, Matt 18:15–17 describes procedures by which someone might be expelled from the community. Yet these measures, in Theissen's view, apparently did not apply to wanderers, who were subject only to "the judgment of God" (Did 11:1).[16] The implication seems to be that there are two different sets of rules for two different sets of people, wandering charismatics on the one hand and local sympathizers on the other.

Thus Theissen argues that in each of three areas the record of the tradition suggests the existence of two different groups in early Christianity. There is a stricter, more radical set of norms to be applied to the wandering charismatics, a looser set of standards for local people.[17] The texts indicate on the one hand an abdication of individual authority within local groups, and yet at the same time the veneration of wandering authority figures. And they describe procedures for becoming part of a Christian group which do not seem to apply to important apostolic figures such as Paul. In each case, Theissen argues, the double standard indicates the existence of two distinct roles: wandering charismatics and local sympathizers.

3. The Son of Man

The third role discussed by Theissen is that of the Son of Man. He divides the sayings about the Son of Man into two groups: sayings about the earthly Son of Man, and sayings about the heavenly Son of Man whose power and role

---

14. Theissen, *Sociology*, 19–20.
15. Theissen, *Sociology*, 19–20.
16. Theissen, *Sociology*, 21.
17. Horsley (*Sociology*, 39) objects to such a differentiation of roles on the grounds that it tends to "domesticate" the Jesus movement, segregating its social radicalism off into a small band of itinerants, leaving the larger number of Jesus folk to settle into normal lives. Whether this is Theissen's purpose is debatable; however, the argument does not in any event stand or fall on the purity of Theissen's motives, whatever we might guess them to be. And Horsley does not suggest an alternative reading of such texts as Mark 10:17–31, par. (esp. Matt 19:21), or Did 9:3–6. It is quite clear especially in the latter that "prophets" engage in a style of living that differs from that of the communities which support them.

attain cosmic proportions. The first group contains both sayings of an "active" form, in which the Son of Man is assertive in abrogating the norms of the world around him (Matt 12:28: breaking the sabbath; Matt 11:18-19: rejecting fasting; Matt 9:6: forgiving sins by his own authority), and sayings of a "passive" form, in which the Son of Man is rejected by the world, and as a result suffers even death (Mark 8:31; 9:31; 10:45). Thus, in both an active and a passive way he is an outsider, distinguishing himself from the world by rejecting its norms (active), and being distinguished from the world by its rejection of him (passive). In the second group of sayings about the heavenly Son of Man, this dichotomy is transcended. In these sayings Jesus is seen as the outsider transformed. As the eschatological judge who is to come unexpectedly to gather the elect and reject his enemies (see Mark 14:62; 13:27; Matt 24:27; 13:41) his views must be accepted, and rejection of his person and authority is no longer possible.[18]

But Theissen goes on to notice that such statements are not found only in reference to the Son of Man. They also describe the role of the disciple in the synoptic gospels. Just as the Son of Man transcends the norms of his environment (especially with regard to traditional piety), so too the disciples transcend those norms (see, e.g., Mark 2:18-22, 23-28). If the Son of Man lived the life of the homeless vagabond, so do they (Matt 8:20; Mark 10:28). If the Son of Man was persecuted, so are they (Matt 10:19). Finally, even his claim to heavenly authority in administering justice in the world to come has become their own (Matt 19:28).[19] To explain this curious correspondence Theissen introduces what he terms a structural homologue—a correspondence between the structure of social reality and the structure of religious beliefs held by those engaged in it[20]—between the figure of the Son of Man in the synoptic texts and the disciples who continued in the tradition begun by Jesus:

> Evidently the images of the Son of man christology had a significant social function. Above all in the figure of the Son of man, early Christian wandering charismatics were able to interpret and come to terms with their own social situation: within small groups of believers they were regarded as authorities and appointed new norms and rules; within society as a whole they were despised and persecuted outsiders. A resolution of the conflict between the role of the outsider and that of the authority was expected in the future. At that time the whole of society would recognize the authority of the wandering charismatic. The ambivalence of the sayings about exaltation and those about humiliation in the Son of man christology is a structural homologue of an inevitable conflict of roles for the early Christian wandering charismatics.[21]

Thus, in Theissen's view, just as the Son of Man rejected social convention, so too the wandering charismatics now live socially marginal lives; just as the Son

---

18. Theissen, *Sociology,* 25.
19. Theissen, *Sociology,* 26-27.
20. Theissen, *Sociology,* 26, n. 8, citing the work of Goldmann, "Soziologie der Literatur."
21. Theissen, *Sociology,* 27.

of Man was rejected by the world, so too are they now rejected; but just as the Son of Man will one day be vindicated, so too will the wandering charismatics be confirmed in the status to which they have aspired, judging the world against the new ethos around which their early Christian communities were beginning to take shape.

Thomas and Wandering Radicaism

When one compares Theissen's social-historical overview of early Christianity with the view of Thomas Christianity sketched above, part of it looks familiar, but part of it does not. First, concerning the relationship of Theissen's wandering charismatics to local sympathizers, on the one hand the role of the itinerant, the wandering radical, is amply attested. Thomas Christians too are homeless vagabonds (Thom 42, 86), who have given up possessions (Thom 95, 54, 36, et al.) and family ties (Thom 55, 99, 101). Like the wandering charismatics described by Theissen, they have rejected conventional piety and its attitudes (Thom 6, 14, 53, et al.), and seem resistant to stringent organization (see ch. 3, pp. 151-53). On the other hand, there is little in the Gospel of Thomas that would reflect the correlating, yet often conflicting role of the local sympathizers. Thom 14:4 indeed indicates that the Thomas Christians were engaged in a type of itinerant begging, preaching, and caring for the sick in exchange for whatever might be offered in the way of food. But unlike the texts examined by Theissen, there is nothing in Thomas that actually *supports* or *justifies* the option of settled living. Nor is there any sign of competing loyalties in Thomas, some sayings addressing settled communities, others favoring the wanderers. How is one to account for this curious situation?

First, the greater significance assigned to the role of local sympathizers in the synoptic texts is probably due to their having been written in the social context of settled local communities. Theissen's own analysis provides a cogent explanation for the prominence that the "local sympathizer viewpoint" has achieved in these sources. It is inevitable that in communities in which local leaders had begun to attain a level of control, thus supplanting the leadership role of the wandering radical, the wandering ethos would soon be supplanted by an ethos more congenial to the social situation of the local sympathizers.[22] That this sort of "changing of the guard" was indeed taking place within synoptic Christianity is confirmed by a closer source-critical analysis of the synoptic materials upon which Theissen himself draws.[23] It is notable that of the Q material used in Theissen's analysis, almost all of it

---

22. Theissen, *Sociology*, 19-20.
23. Theissen is criticized for his lack of attention to source-critical matters by Stegemann ("Vagabond Radicalism," 152-53). However, Stegemann's own results, from a source-critical point of view, are far from satisfactory; see n. 26.

reflects the orientation of the wandering charismatics.[24] Consequently, this leaves almost all of the material having to do with the life of settled communities either to Mark or to Matthean or Lukan special material. The resulting stratification suggests a gradual development in early Christianity from an early period dominated by a wandering radical ethos (Q) to a later period of settling down, producing the localized communities whose views are reflected in the synoptic gospels themselves.[25] Furthermore, the fact that Q seems to be interested primarily in the role of the wandering charismatic, while the synoptic gospels give more prominence to material reflecting a settled existence, suggests that the conflicting ethical standards plotted by Theissen in the synoptic tradition arose in the second and third generations of the Jesus movement, after persons within it began to settle down and to attract less radical recruits to their numbers. In the course of these developments the wandering radicals, of course, did not simply disappear. Many must have tried to maintain their way of life even in the face of gradual attrition. The presence of the wandering tradition in Mark and in Matthean and Lukan special material shows both that these communities shared as part of their heritage a wandering tradition, and that they continually must have had to come to terms with the awkward circumstance that they had ultimately turned away from it, while others had not.[26]

24. Theissen uses only one Q saying to help document the phenomenon of settled communities: Matt 23:34 (//Luke 11:49); by contrast the following Q texts are aligned, in Theissen's view (see his remarks relative to each in Sociology, 10–14), with the wandering radical ethos: Matt 8:20 (//Luke 9:58); Matt 10:5–15 (//Luke 10:1–12); Matt 23:34 (//Luke 11:49); Matt 8:22 (//Luke 9:59); Luke 14:26 (//Matt 10:37); Luke 12:52–53 (//Matt 10:35); Matt 10:10 (//Luke 10:4); Matt 6:19–21 (//Luke 12:33–34); Luke 16:13 (//Matt 6:24); Luke 6:24 (Q?); Matt 6:25–32 (//Luke 12:22–30); Luke 10:5–6 (//Matt 10:11–13); Matt 6:33 (//Luke 12:31); Matt 5:38 (//Luke 6:29); Matt 5:41 (Q?).

25. Such a conclusion would be consistent with the results of Hoffmann's work relating to the sending-out passages in Q (Studien zur Theologie der Logienquelle, 237–63). Hoffmann concludes that already to an extent in Mark, and certainly in Matthew and Luke, the radicality of the mission instructions has been undercut (esp. pp. 261–62). This may also serve to account for what Mack observes about the Mission Discourse in Q, viz., that it reflects more the perspective of those who would be asked to provide hospitality than of those who would seek it ("The Kingdom that Didn't Come," 619–23.) One must remember that we only have Q strained through the sieve of later (settled) synoptic Christianity. Still, the existence of Luke 11:49//Matt 23:34 in Q, which Theissen identifies with settled community life, may indicate that the process of settling down may have begun already at a point corresponding to the latter stages of the development of the Q tradition.

26. Stegemann ("Vagabond Radicalism," 164–67) attempts to show, by stratifying Theissen's thesis source-critically, that the wandering ethos belongs not to Q, but to the imagination of the Lucan redactor, who looks back on an earlier period with unrealistic nostalgia. He is, in my view, mistaken. Of the Lucan material he cites to prove his point, four passages derive from Mark, and therefore cannot be used to argue for any special Lucan interest: Luke 18:22 (=Mark 10:21); 18:29 (=Mark 10:29); 5:20 (=Mark 2:5); 5:28 (=Mark 2:14). Only in the last is there any grist for the mill: Luke 5:28 adds to Mark 2:14 the words καταλιπὼν πάντα (left everything). A fifth passage comes from Q: Luke 14:26 (=Matt 10:37). That leaves Luke 12:13–33 and 14:33. The first cannot really be considered a Lucan creation: 12:13–14=Thom 72; 12:16–21=Thom 63; and 12:22–31=Matt 6:25–34, Q. Thus, when one applies to Stegemann's own thesis the rigors of source criticism which he so aptly commends to Theissen, only Luke 14:33 is left to support it, and that is not enough.

Perhaps the most telling illustration of the attitude that has developed within the synoptic tradition toward the radical lifestyle of the wanderers is the way each of the synoptic gospels treats the story of the Rich Young Man (Matt 19:16-30//Mark 10:17-31//Luke 18:18-30). Taking Mark's presentation of the story first, Bultmann recognized already its composite nature. A self-contained apophthegm is found in Mark 10:17-22,[27] in which the call to radical existence is extended, only to be rejected by the rich young man because "he had great possessions." The point has been made: wealth is a hindrance to those who would take up the radical life of discipleship. The rest of the sayings that have attached themselves thematically to this original story, trailing off through vs 31, all make sense in terms of the basic moral of the story, all except one, that is. Verse 23 forms an appropriate summary of the story, as does its doublet in vs 24b. The Eye of the Needle (vs 25) is likewise appropriate, applying the metaphor to drive home more forcefully the point of vss 23 and 24b. Verses 28-30 form a parallel examination of the other side of the proposition: for those who do give up house and home, possessions, land, and family, the reward shall be great indeed (vs 31).

In the midst of this extensive defense of wandering radicalism, vss 26-27 stand out. First, their sense in the present context is strained. The question: "Then who can be saved?" seems to presuppose a general condemnation of humankind, while the apophthegm in vss 17-21, and the sayings in vss 23-25 condemn only those whose possess great wealth. Furthermore, the question is posed by the disciples (note vs 24) as though concerned about the implications of the young man's rebuke for their own situation. Yet it is precisely these disciples who have left home, family, and possessions behind, and taken up the wandering life that the apophthegm requires (vss 29-31!); in the context of the story, nothing has been said that would reflect badly upon their situation. But perhaps most importantly, vss 26-27 seem out of place in that they cut in precisely the opposite direction from everything else in the pericope. Here the radical requirements of discipleship are completely removed, the radical life rendered unnecessary and superfluous. In the midst of a tradition that champions the life of the homeless, cast-away disciples, Mark has introduced two verses that make it possible for group members to exist comfortably in the community without feeling inferior to those who would still embrace the radical life. In Mark's version of the pericope, the radicals have no advantage—the question in vs 26 implies that everyone stands equally in need of the pardon that only God can supply.

Turning briefly to Luke, it need only be pointed out that he makes no significant changes to Mark: Luke incorporates vss 26-27 (Luke 18:26-27) without difficulty and with no particular concern to enhance the role of the wandering radical or to repristinate the radical tradition.[28]

---

27. Bultmann, *Geschichte*, 20.
28. *Pace* Stegemann, "Vagabond Radicalism."

Matthew's version is more interesting for the addition of one small detail: rather than following Mark to the letter in penning Jesus' reply to the young man in 19:21 (Mark 10:21), Matthew departs from Mark's opening phrase ("You lack one thing . . .") and writes instead: "If you would be perfect . . ." (εἰ θέλεις τέλιος εἶναι). Though there is a tendency among more recent interpreters to resist the implications of this introduction, the possibility cannot be dismissed that in 19:21 Matthew delineates a two-tiered ethic. The "perfect" are called to the radical life; as for the rest, "with God all things are possible." This reluctance is most surprising in Eduard Schweizer,[29] who elsewhere argues persuasively that the Matthean community does not have its own hierarchical structure, but rather is serviced by a number of wandering prophets and teachers, such as one finds referred to in the Didache (chapters 11–13), or other early Christian documents of Syrian origin, such as the Pseudo-Clementine letters and the Gospel of Thomas(!).[30] For Matthew, there is still a place for the wandering radical. But their calling is special, not a necessary requirement for everyone who wishes to associate with the community. After all, Matthew does not omit Mark 10:26–27 (=Matt 19:25–26).

The synoptic gospels are written from the perspective of settled communities. They look upon the wandering radicals perhaps with some amount of nostalgia and respect. Perhaps persons in their respective communities had themselves been social radicals, itinerants in an earlier time. But now they have settled, and for whatever reasons the role of the wandering radical has been relativized. If it is recognized at all, it has become the ethos of a special type of individual, not of the community as a whole. This is not true for the Thomas group. There is no evidence to suggest that it has settled down or begun to compromise the wandering tradition of social radicalism in any way.[31] There is no competing set of ethical standards, no undermining of the radical lifestyle. If in the synoptic gospels we see the effects of a process of settling down in early Christianity, *in the Gospel of Thomas, we encounter the product of the continuing tradition of wandering radicalism.*

But is this possible—indeed, is it likely? In assessing this thesis it should be recalled that though Thomas' traditions must ultimately derive from early Palestinian Christian circles, the Gospel of Thomas as we now have it is Syrian in origin, and thus belongs to the development of a branch of Christianity about whose earliest stages little is known. Yet even without the new information that the Gospel of Thomas provides, the great historian of early Syrian Christianity, Arthur Vööbus, had already surmised that the origins of Christianity in the East must lie in an early Palestinian mission with a strong

---

29. Schweizer, Matthew, 388.
30. Schweizer, Matthew, 178–84, esp. 183–84.
31. I do not agree with Theissen ("Wanderradikalismus," 103) that Thomas' gnosticizing tendencies indicate that here we have a modulation of an earlier *Handlungs-radikalismus* (radicalism of behavior) into an *Erkenntnisradikalismus* (radicalism of ideas). (See the discussion in chapter 5, pp. 156–57)

ascetic element.[32] It was in response to this suggestion by Vööbus that Georg Kretchmar sought to flesh out more concretely the origins of Syrian asceticism in terms of its relationship to Palestinian Christianity.[33] Kretchmar identifies several exemplary second and third century sources, such as the Pseudo-Clementine letter *Ad virgines,* where a group of itinerants who preach, teach, and work miracles and exorcisms is the topic of concern and discussion,[34] the Acts of Thomas, whose hero, Thomas, is a wandering missionary, homeless and poor,[35] and Origen's *contra Celsum,* in which the apologist discusses certain wandering prophets who were active at that time in Palestine and Phoenicia.[36] From such examples Kretchmar argues that it was in the eastern reaches of Christian influence, Palestine and Syria, that the continuing tradition of early Christian asceticism took an itinerant form. His procedure is to trace backward what Theissen would later trace forward, their studies intersecting in the Didache and the synoptic gospels.[37] The Didache is important for Kretchmar, since it helps him locate the origins of this type of early Christian asceticism in the period before there was any clear break between the synagogue and the church,[38] i.e., in "the discipleship of Jesus in the post-Easter period."[39] Of course, in turning to the Didache and the synoptic gospels, Kretchmar must rely for this crucial portion of his work upon sources which, in their final form, reflect the point of view of settled communities, not wandering radicals. Had he known of the Gospel of Thomas, he might have found precisely the "missing link" he was looking for.[40] It demonstrates that in the latter part of the first century there was a group of wandering radicals in Syria, who, when judged by the nature and age of the Jesus tradition they carried with them, must have ultimately come from out of the same primitive Christian circles which gave rise to the synoptic gospels themselves.

In his contribution to the 1983 conference on Gnosticism held in Springfield, Missouri, James M. Robinson sought to explain in more practical terms how it is that the itinerant lifestyle of the early Jesus movement might have come to influence the development of eastern Christianity. Robinson argues

---

32. Vööbus, *History of Asceticism,* 14–15. Vööbus posited an original connection between these early Christian ascetics and the Essenes. Had he known the nature of the traditions in Gospel of Thomas, one wonders if he would have inclined in this direction. The Essene hypothesis seems to me unlikely, owing to the very strong apocalyptic element in Essene thought, an element that is not nearly so strong in much of the more ascetic literature of Syrian Christianity.

33. Kretchmar, "Ein Beitrag."

34. Kretchmar, "Ein Beitrag," 33–34; he cites *Ad virgines* 1.12.1–2 and 2.1.3.

35. Kretchmar, "Ein Beitrag," 34–35; see esp. AcThom 61, 107 (syr.), 136, 139, and 145.

36. Kretchmar, "Ein Beitrag," 36; see esp. *Celsum* 7.8.

37. Theissen ("Wanderradikalismus," 86) viewed his contribution as a continuation of the work begun by Kretchmar.

38. Kretchmar, "Ein Beitrag," 47.

39. Kretchmar, "Ein Beitrag," 49: "*in der Nachfolge Jesu in der nachosterliche Zeit*"; the rest of the article (pp. 49–67) develops this hypothesis.

40. It is not clear why Kretchmar did not avail himself of the Gospel of Thomas, which would have been available to him from 1957 on.

that if the tradition of wandering radicalism was to continue and expand beyond the bounds of Palestine itself, and if we are to understand this as a movement carrying on its activities primarily in the small towns and villages of the countryside, then linguistic factors alone will have left the itinerants but one direction to go: east, to Syria, precisely the route followed by Thomas Christianity. Only in this region will they have been able to move out of the Greek speaking cities and into the surrounding countryside, where the predominating local dialects were similar enough to those of Palestine itself to make communication between the itinerants and their potential supporters easy. In an area such as Asia Minor, by contrast, the movement would have been limited to the cities, where Greek as the *lingua franca* would have facilitated comfortable interchange, while the obstacle of mastering the local dialect would have hindered its activities, and appeal, in the outlying areas.[41]

Vööbus and Kretchmar argue that to account for the itinerant asceticism one finds in later Syrian Christianity, one must look for its roots in early Palestinian Christianity. From the other side of the problem, Robinson suggests that if the itinerant radicalism of the early Jesus movement was to continue and expand, it would have had to turn east, to Syria. The Gospel of Thomas, with its roots in the same tradition of itinerant radicalism found in early synoptic Christianity on the one hand, and its final Syrian provenance on the other, provides the connection Vööbus, Kretchmar and others had sought, and thus represents an important chapter in the vexing problem of the origins of Syrian Christianity. At the same time it provides, so I have argued, one of the later chapters in the history of the itinerant radicalism of the early Jesus movement. While in the gradually domesticating communities of synoptic Christianity the wandering radical ethos gave way to a more conventional code of conduct, in Thomas Christianity the wandering radicalism of the Jesus movement continued to define its way of living in the world.

Wandering Radicalism, Christology, and Jesus

Another part of Theissen's social-historical sketch of early Christianity that finds no correspondence in Thomas Christianity is the role of the Son of Man. Comparison of Thomas and synoptic Christianity on this score also reveals something about the nature of early Christian wandering radicalism.

Of course, the term "son of man" is not used in the Gospel of Thomas in the titular sense.[42] Instead there are other christological notions at work, most prominently Jesus speaking as Wisdom or in the role of Wisdom's prophet (Thom 4, 5, 40, 52, 67, 74, 90, 94), and the closely related role of Jesus as the heavenly revealer (Thom 11, 15, 19, 22, 24, 28, 43, 57, 61, 62, 77, 83, 88, 92). Now, even though Thomas does not share with the synoptic gospels the

41. Robinson, "On Bridging the Gulf," 137–38.
42. So Koester, "One Jesus," 170, n. 34; also 171–72.

christological characterization of Jesus as the Son of Man, we have seen that much of what Theissen relates to the structural homologue that he argues exists between the Son of Man and the disciples, is paralleled in Thomas as well: the transcending of norms (Thom 99, 101, 6, 14, 53, etc.), claims to authority (Thom 12), and the life of homelessness (Thom 42, 14:4), poverty (Thom 95, 54), and persecution (Thom 58, 68). The fact that these features of the wandering radicals' existence can turn up in a context in which Jesus was not thought of in terms of the mythological figure of the Son of Man indicates that there is nothing about these features that relates them intrinsically to this christological category. Thus, while in the synoptic tradition this socially radical mode of living developed into a kind of structural homolgue between the radicals themselves and the figure of the Son of Man, the radical comportment of the Jesus movement must actually pre-date the emergence of this psychological construct for coping with the stress accompanying this lifestyle. It may even belong originally to a different kind of correspondence, viz., that which exists between teacher and students, between master and disciples. Whether this relationship is to be thought of as historical, under the hypothesis that Jesus himself was the first wandering radical, who passed the wandering ethos and the reins of authority to his immediate successors, the Jesus movement,[43] or whether this entire picture of Jesus as a wandering radical is a literary fiction, is a question deserving careful consideration. One indication of its historicity is that two independent traditions (the Thomas and synoptic traditions) have preserved it, even though they differ widely in their respective christological views, neither of which seems endemically related to the phenomenon of wandering radicalism itself.

Apart from wandering radicalism, an element in Theissen's structural homologue between the role of the Son of Man and that of the wandering charismatics that does *not* find a place in the Gospel of Thomas is the notion that the disciples will share with the Son of Man in his future glory, sitting in judgment with him over the twelve tribes of Israel (Matt 19:28).[44] This, of course, belongs specifically to the mythological notion of the Son of Man and his role as judge (cf. Matt 25:31–46), so that its absence in Thomas, which does not share this christology, is in no way surprising. However, Thomas bears witness to a similar parallel phenomenon, in which the disciples acquire for themselves a portion of the christological role assigned to Jesus in the Gospel of Thomas, viz. that of the heavenly revealer:

[1]Jesus said, "Whoever drinks from my mouth will become like me; [2]I myself shall become that person, [3]and the hidden things will be revealed to him."

Thom 108[45]

43. So Koester, "GNOMAI DIAPHOROI," 90–91.
44. Theissen, *Sociology*, 27.
45. See also Thom 3, 13, and 70.

The implications of this kind of identification of the Thomas Christian with Jesus as revealer are really quite remarkable. Unlike the synoptic disciples or Paul, who must wait for the apocalyptic end of time to assume their anticipated role as co-judge with Jesus, the Thomas Christian claims the role of the revealer immediately. In Thomas there is no eschaton, no second coming, no future revelatory event that will set the world straight once and for all. The revealer is/was present in Jesus, and the association of the Thomas Christian with Jesus has made him or her the agent of revelation as well.

Summary

A social description of the Gospel of Thomas strengthens Theissen's thesis that the Jesus movement was at least partly shaped by the prominent role played in its early development by wandering radicals. But while in the synoptic tradition one sees their influence only through the veil of the more pressing interests of the communities in which those texts were written, in Thomas one encounters the tradition of wandering radicalism more clearly. As the communities of synoptic Christianity gradually settled into a more conventional style of living, Thomas Christianity did not. It continued the tradition of marginal social behavior as an expression of its negative evaluation of the world and of its hope in a salvation gained through careful attention to Jesus' words. If in synoptic texts one must read the tradition largely through the lens of "local sympathizers," in the Gospel of Thomas one reads it through the lens of the "wandering charismatic."

The third of Theissen's roles, that of the Son of Man, is notably absent from the Gospel of Thomas. Instead, Thomas understands Jesus in terms of another christological category altogether: the heavenly revealer, familiar to modern students of speculative Jewish Wisdom and Gnosticism. Yet, just as in Theissen's view the wandering charismatics of the synoptic tradition could interpret their own experience of rejection and hope for redemption in terms of the fate of the Son of Man, so Thomas Christians seem to have understood themselves as in some sense heir to Jesus' divine agency as the revealer (Thom 108). And originating with neither tradition, but presupposed by both is a concept of discipleship that involves a socially radical style of living. This social radicalism must therefore antedate both Thomas and the synoptics, and hence be rooted deeply in the origins of the Jesus movement itself.

7

Itinerant Radicals and Settled Communities

The Beginnings of Conflict

Thus far I have argued two things about those who created and used the Gospel of Thomas. First, by way of social description (Chapter 5) I have argued that Thomas Christianity was characterized by a socially radical ethos, which included much time on the road, if not a thoroughly itinerant life style altogether, severance of family ties and responsibilities, a kind of willful poverty which required the Thomas Christian to beg for food and shelter, a relativizing of codes of purity and the conventions of piety, including prayer, fasting, and the giving of alms, a certain cynical attitude over against the powers that be (emperors, kings, and the like), a predilection for minimal organization and openness to participation by women in the group. Thus, these social radicals are not altogether unlike the wandering charismatics that Theissen has argued propagated the sayings tradition in general. Second, I have tried to show by comparing the results of Theissen's study and those of my own that while the evidence of synoptic Christianity suggests that in such circles one may detect a shift in focus away from wandering radicalism toward a more conventional, settled way of life, in Thomas one may detect no such shift, the focus remaining on the socially radical ethos which characterized the synoptic side of things only in an earlier phase of its development (Chapter 6). If Thomas and the synoptic gospels are roughly contemporaneous documents, then the two traditions represent two different perspectives on the development the Jesus movement as it unfolded in the latter part of the first century. The synoptic gospels represent for the most part the perspective of those working out Christian existence in the context of settled communities, with all the issues and problems associated with the social location thus implied. This can be seen not only in the recasting of traditions originally formulated with a more socially radical existence in view, but also in the development and use of materials more directly suited to local problems, such as controversy dialogues or other pieces representing various local apologetical interests. Thomas, on the other hand, represents for the most part the perspective of those who did not settle, but continued to travel from community to community trying to exercise the authority that historically would have belonged to such wanderers in the earliest days of the Jesus movement.

This interpretation of the evidence has obvious implications. Most importantly, it must be supposed that as local communities formed and grew in size, and thus demanded ever greater forms of local organization, the leadership provided in an earlier time by the occasional visit of a wandering preacher would have gradually begun to fail to meet all the needs of a local group. Where would a group meet; who would provide the space? If a meal were involved, who would secure its provision? How would inevitable disputes among members of the group be resolved? Who would speak for the group in disputes with local authorities suspicious of the new social experiment taking place within their judicatory? Such needs could not be met by occasional passers-by; they would require local leadership. Moreover, as local leaders emerged, there would be the inevitable question of how these new leaders were to relate to the itinerants. Could authority be shared or divided amicably, or would hierarchy be the only answer to competing loci of authority? The competition may well have been keen, with no clear rules for how such conflicts were to be worked out.

This, of course, is but an hypothesis; it must be tested. In this chapter I intend to do that by looking more broadly at early Christianity in the late first century to see whether the process as I have described it may be confirmed in the documents of this period. I will focus on three cases in which it may be seen that: 1) during this period settled communities were visited from time to time by itinerant social radicals, whose authority among local folk, while under review, is still in evidence; and 2) the alternate claims to authority of local leaders and itinerant social radicals had come into conflict during this period. Of the three cases, one (Didache 11-13) reflects more the perspective of local leaders in this quandary. A second (James) reflects more the perspective of the social radicals. The third is a series of documents (3 and 2 John) which both tells the story of such a dispute and participates in its resolution, 3 John working from the side of the social radicals, 2 John from the side of a local leader. In each case I will argue that the communities involved are in the midst of a shift in the locus of authority, from wandering radicals to newly emerging local leaders.

Didache 11-13

We begin with the clearest case of conflict between local authority and itinerant radicals: Didache 11-13. Already at the end of the last century Harnack had pointed out that these chapters presuppose a type of early Christian wanderer, who goes from place to place relying upon the support of local communities to survive.[1] Harnack noted that these wanderers were not chosen by local congregations, but rather apparently relied for their calling upon "a divine mandate or charisma.[2] He also noticed that the didachist seems to know of three different sorts of wandering radicals: apostles (ἀπόστολοι), prophets (προφῆται), and teachers (διδάσκαλοι).[3] Even though Harnack tended to think of the Didache more as belonging to the second century than the first[4] he nonetheless was inclined to regard these figures as having ancient antecedents from the very earliest period of the early Christian movement.[5] Of course today, when the similarities between the Didache and Barnabas, or the Shepherd of Hermas, are no longer taken as proof that the Didache is literarily dependent upon these documents,[6] the trend is to date the Didache much earlier, at least by the end of the first century or the beginning of the second,[7] and in the case of Jean-P. Audet, as early as 50–70 C.E.[8] This, together with the growing consensus that the Didache is of Syrian provenance,[9] make this text of utmost importance for our thesis.

It has long been noted that the chapters in question (11–13) do not form a unity. Audet, for example, regards 13:3, 5–7 as a later gloss.[10] Schille has offered a very complex redactional history of these chapters based upon the different sorts of rules he claims to have identified within them.[11] Particularly compelling, however, are a series of observations offered by Kurt Niederwimmer in 1977.[12] Niederwimmer notices a number of aporia in the text of Didache 11–13 which suggest the presence of more than one redactional layer here. For example, he points out that with 11:3 a new section seems to begin, but that it does not continue on into chapter 12, where a new type of wanderer is introduced, viz., travelers without any particular charismatic claim. Then, after this interruption, chapter 13 returns redundantly to the subject of prophets, even though this topic seems to have been handled in full already in chapter 11. This resumption of the theme of prophets cannot be accounted for by supposing that chapter 12 is a later interpolation, breaking up an earlier

---

1. Harnack, *Lehre der zwölf Apostle*, 93–137.
2. Harnack, *Lehre der zwölf Apostle*, 96.
3. Harnack, *Lehre der zwölf Apostle*, 98–110.
4. Harnack, *Lehre der zwölf Apostle*, 158–59.
5. Harnack, *Lehre der zwölf Apostle*, 98–103.
6. See, e.g., Vielhauer, *Geschichte der urchristlichen Literatur*, 735.
7. So, e.g., Rordorf and Tuilier, *La doctrine*, 91–97, esp. 96; Koester, *Introduction*, 2:158; Vielhauer, *Geschichte der urchristlichen Literatur*, 737.
8. Audet, *La Didachè*, 187–206; esp. 199.
9. So, e.g., Adam, "Erwägungen zur Herkunft der Didache"; Audet, *La Didachè*, 206–10; Rordorf and Tulier, *La doctrine*, 96–99; Koester, *Introduction*, 2.158; Vielhauer, *Geschichte der urchristlichen Literatur*, 737.
10. Audet, *La Didachè*, 105–8, 457–58.
11. Schille, "Das Recht der Propheten und Apostel"; see, however, its critique by Niederwimmer, "Zur Entwicklungsgeschichte des Wanderradikalismus," 48–49, n. 8.
12. Niederwimmer, "Zur Entwicklungsgeschichte des Wanderradikalismus."

unity consisting of 11:1-12; 13:1-7, since chapter 13 is itself connected to 12:3-5 via the catch phrase πᾶς ... θέλων καθῆσασθαι πρὸς ὑμᾶς (all who want to settle among you), and thus presupposes the new subject matter introduced in chapter 12. Finally, there appears to be a discrepancy between the two different discussions in chapters 11 and 13 insofar as the discussion in chapter 11 treats the matter of teachers, apostles and prophets, while in chapter 13 only teachers and prophets are discussed—apostles are not mentioned at all.[13]

To account for all of these peculiarities, Niederwimmer argues that these three chapters have incorporated an earlier, traditional set of rules having to do with prophets and apostles (11:4-12), which the didachist has appropriated for his or her community. According to Niederwimmer, the didachist's hand may be seen in the redactional transition from the previous section (11:1-2), the introduction to the traditional material (11:3), and two redactional additions to deal alternatively with non-charismatic (12:1-5) and charismatic (13:1-3, 5-7) wanderers who wish to settle within the community. 13:4, in his view, is a later gloss.[14] Thus, the material in Didache 11-13 having to do with the community's dealings with wanderers is derived primarily from two different sources: 11:4-12, from a traditional source known to the didachist and 12:1-5, 13:1-3, 5-7, from the hand of the didachist him or herself.

Elsewhere I have offered observations relevant to the redactional history of this part of the Didache that would suggest a similar division of the material, though for different reasons.[15] Proceeding from the conclusion, based on papyrological considerations, that the scribe responsible for P. Lond. Or. 9271 (the 'Coptic Didache')[16] was reproducing a text of the Didache that ended with 12:2a, I have argued on structural and stylistic grounds that there may have been an ancient version of the Didache that ended at 12:2a, and furthermore, that this would represent an earlier version of the text than has come down to us through the 11th century manuscript Hierosolymitanus 54. If this is so, then the material on wanderers would be divided in roughly the same way that Niederwimmer has suggested, even though the redactional history of the section would have to be conceived somewhat differently. If 11:4-12 is still to be considered traditional, we may conclude that the didachist originally prefixed it with 11:1-2, to deal with the question of teachers, and 11:3, as a transition to the older material. He or she also would have supplied 12:1-2a as a conclusion. A second redactional phase would then be characterized by the addition of 12:2b ff., a phase called forth by the greater need to deal with refugees.[17]

13. Niederwimmer, "Zur Entwicklungsgeschichte des Wanderradikalismus," 148-51.
14. Niederwimmer, "Zur Entwicklungsgeschichte des Wanderradikalismus," 150-52.
15. Patterson and Jefford, "A Note on *Didache* 12:2a."
16. For the text see Lefort, *Les Pères apostoliques en copte*, 32-33 (Texte). For a description of the fragment, see C. Schmidt, "Das koptische Didache-Fragment," 81.
17. This arrangement has the advantage of explaining the discrepancy in the "offices" that are presupposed alternatively in chapters 11 and 13. If one assumes that the didachist is responsible for both 11:1-2 and 11:3, and then the subsequent inclusion of 11:4-12, it

At any rate, in Didache 11–13 we are presented with two different moments in the history of this community's attempt to deal with the question of itinerants. Both stand to reveal something about the nature of the relationship between wanderers and the communities that supported them.

Beginning with 11:1–12:2a, it goes without saying that the fact that the didachist has seen fit to address this question at all indicates that the relationship between wanderers and the communities that supported them had become problematic. There are three points to be made about the resulting conflict and what it can tell us about the interplay of wandering radicals and local communities during this period:

1) That the didachist has taken it upon him or herself to legislate on behalf of the community regarding the matter of wandering radicals shows that the focus of authority in this community lies not with wandering radicals, but with local leaders. I cannot agree with Theissen's assessment that here the authority of the wanderers is still superior to that of the local authorities.[18] From the point of view of the Didache, they do not really belong to the community; the text always addresses their situation as that of a third party. In effect, the text discusses with other "insiders" what is to be done about these "outsiders." To be sure, they are to be accorded every honor (11:11c) and they do have their privileges (11:4), but it is not to be overlooked that it is the community, through its own regulating document, that grants these privileges, reserving at the same time the right of the community to judge these outsiders and to rescind their "accreditation" at any time (11:4–12). Whatever authority the wandering radicals may have had at one time, it now persists in form only.

2) That the legislation consists of guidelines for checking out the legitimacy of a wanderer's claim to be a teacher, apostle, or prophet, shows that from the community's point of view, it is the behavior of the wandering radicals that has called into question and made problematic the relationship that exists between the radicals and the community. With teachers, questions had arisen as to the correctness of things taught (11:2). With apostles, the problem has been that some have worn out their welcome (11:5), or asked for money in addition to the day's rations to which they are entitled (11:6). As for prophets, the problem has apparently been the abuse of 'speaking in a spirit' to order a meal (τράπεζαν; 11:9),[19] or to ask for money. Such grievances would be justified, for

---

becomes clear that he or she was thinking of three types of possible frauds: teachers (11:1–2), apostles (11:3, 4–6), and prophets (11:3, 7–12). In chapter 13 (as in chapter 15) there is no longer any question of apostles; only prophets and teachers are mentioned. If one supposes, as does Niederwimmer, that 11:1–3 and chapter 13 both come from the same hand, this would be difficult to explain. Even if one might argue that 11:4–12 is from a traditional source, as Niederwimmer does, this still would not explain the discrepancy, as the didachist's introduction in 11:3 presupposes the existence of both apostles and prophets. In the present arrangement this discrepancy poses no difficulty, since chapter 13 derives not from the didachist who created 11:1–3, and either created or added 11:4–12, but a secondary redactor who added 12:2b ff.

18. Theissen, *Sociology*, 9.

19. The term has interesting implications. It can refer to a meal dedicated to a God, and

by the wandering radicals' own self-definition such things would have been problematic. They are supposed to wander (Thom 42), to get along without a permanent home (Thom 86); thus, suspicions would justifiably be raised when an itinerant stayed in one place too long. They are supposed to live without money (Thom 95); likewise, asking for it would call their legitimacy into question. They are supposed to live on the food that "is put before them" (Thom 14:4); thus, to ask for more than bread for the trip at hand,[20] or to request lavish meals would have been questionable behavior.

However, one suspects that not everything dealt with here by the didachist would be considered a legitimate grievance by *both* sides. Interesting in this regard are the rules imposed upon teachers in 11:1-2. From the point of view of the community, some teachers had overstepped their authority, presenting a certain ἄλλη διδαχή (contrary teaching), not acceptable to the community at large. If one recalls the point made above regarding Thom 108 and the potential problems inherent to the conviction of a wandering radical that he or she had become the recipient of special revelation, it is easy to understand how a community would come to impose such conservative restrictions on teaching.[21] Of course, from the wandering radicals' point of view, it is difficult to imagine their accepting this complaint as legitimate or these restrictions as justified. From 11:7 one may conclude that there had already been similar attempts to restrict the speech of prophets, a measure which the didachist here opposes unless a prophet should show him or herself to be a fraud by some unacceptable behavior. Evidently the authority of prophets is still somewhat stronger in the view of the didachist than that of teachers.

3) The need to invoke the code of hospitality with respect to the wandering radicals suggests that this community, or perhaps other communities known to the didachist, had initially dealt with these grievances simply by refusing to take in wanderers altogether. The didachist opposes this and introduces criteria by which a teacher, apostle, or prophet might be judged, and if guilty, ignored (11:2, 12: μὴ αὐτοῦ ἀκούσητε [do not listen to him]). But the itinerant cannot be refused the right of hospitality. Thus, even though much of the real authority that the wanderers once had is now gone, they still command enough traditional respect, at least among some in the community, to retain the basic right to receive hospitality. In the other cases to be examined below, the dispute over this issue will come up again.

Turning now to Didache 12-13, we find ourselves at an entirely different point in the history of this community's experience with the wanderers. A new problem has arisen: the need to deal with refugees. As distinct from the strictly

---

thus a lavish spread of foods, including meats. Or it can carry the general connotation of a fairly elaborate feast (see *LSJ, s.v.* τράπεζα).

20. One thinks also of Q's (Luke 10:4//Matt 10:9) prohibition against carrying a bag (πήρα), in which the beggar would carry provisions for sparse days ahead.

21. Note how 11:1 restricts the content of teaching to that which appears in chapters 1-10.

itinerant, these are people seeking a permanent home. One thinks perhaps of the stre of refugees out of Palestine that would have been produced by the Jewish war, or later by the revolt of bar Kochba. Both the settled communities and the wanderers who depended upon them would have been displaced by such events; thus, it is perhaps not surprising that one finds among the refugees being addressed both normal refugees with no claim to any special status (12:3–5), and prophets and teachers who have lost their base of support (13:1–7).

Looking specifically to chapter 13 and the measures taken on behalf of prophets and teachers (as noted earlier, apostles are no longer part of the picture), the generosity of the community's attitude is striking in comparison to the air of suspicion that dominates chapter 11. The matter of a meal is no longer cause to question a prophets' legitimacy (cf. 13:1–3!). And nothing is said regarding correct teaching. These problems now all belong to the past. One might perhaps conclude that this new period had seen a resurgence in the popularity and authority of the wandering radicals at the expense of local leaders, so that no one would dare raise the sort of questions raised earlier in chapter 11.[22] But if this were the case, one would have to explain why chapter 11 was retained at all. Rather, it is more likely that in this later episode in the history of relations between itinerants and the didachist's community the power and authority of the wanderers has declined even further. In fact, they seem to have been all but replaced or neutralized altogether. This much is clear from the new material introduced in chapter 15, concerning a new set of local offices: bishops and deacons. Of highest significance is the way in which these new offices are placed in direct competition with the old guard: "for they also minister to you the ministry of the *prophets and teachers*, . . . they are your honorable ones, together with the *prophets and teachers*" (15:1, 2). The community has by now developed its own secure pattern of leadership, which it views as equally legitimate to the old guard. The prophets and teachers can now be allowed to inhabit the community without fear that the community will be misled or swindled. The presence of bishops and deacons assures that their influence will be relatively limited, and this all the more in view of the fact that none of the limitations placed upon teachers and prophets in chapter 11 are really rescinded. The new material in chapter 13 honors them, but in so doing it makes them objects of nostalgia, reminding the community of its past. It is clear, however, that real authority now lies with the new order.

Whether one should properly call the wandering teachers, apostles and prophets known to the didachist "Thomas Christians" is probably an unanswerable question. We simply cannot know what these early Christians were

---

22. Schille takes this approach, arguing that over the course of time local leaders were losing ground, and eventually had their right to test the prophets rescinded ("Das Recht der Propheten und Apostel," 99–103; cf. the critique in Niederwimmer, "Zur Entwicklungsgeschichte des Wanderradikalismus," 148–49).

reading or using as their focus of theological reflection about their situation. We learn of them only through the document of one community they visited; their own self-conception and theological orientation is not known to us. But their situation is probably typical of wandering radicals trying to hold onto the older role of wandering teacher or prophet in the face of ever greater trends toward local organization within the settled communities they visited. Inevitably their authority, if not also their respect, would fall victim to the new order, perhaps raising questions about the value of continuing with the wandering radical life. Its hardships were taxing, and if the rewards were too few, it would not be surprising to find wanderers succumbing to the pressure and settling down to a more conventional existence.

The Epistle of James

Another document of early Christianity in which one might expect to find the marks of the wandering radical tradition is the Epistle of James. It has often been observed that aside from the gospels themselves, James, of all the other New Testament writings, seems to have the closest contact with and interest in the sayings tradition. Dibelius pointed to three different sorts of similarities that tend to link James and the sayings tradition: 1) formal similarities,[23] 2) similarity in style,[24] and 3) a set of shared general convictions, including an "ethical rigorism whose pithy injunctions warn against the world and a worldly attitude and exhort to peace, meekness, and humility."[25] Moreover, such similarities cannot be accounted for by assuming that the author of James was simply drawing sayings material from the synoptic gospels, since at least in the case of 5:12, James offers a form of a saying that is more primitive than its synoptic counterpart,[26] thus suggesting that its author may have had access to the sayings tradition apart from its presentation in the synoptic gospels, from circles in which the tradition was still relatively young and fluid.[27] Thus, if the phenomenon of wandering radicalism is to be associated

23. Dibelius, *James*, 28: "In part, Jas contains paraenesis made up of sayings, and the words of Jesus were collected in the same way, connected to one another only externally (by means of catchword association) or not connected at all. Thus, these collections of sayings which are incorporated into the Gospels of Matthew and Luke have the same literary character as, for example, Jas 1 and 5."

24. Dibelius, *James*, 28. Specifically Dibelius mentions the following: the use of short, pointed imperatives; the recurrence in James of certain fixed groups of metaphors, such as of soil and plants (5:7; 3:12), of moths and rust (5:2-3), and of watching and waiting (5:9), all familiar from the synoptic tradition.

25. Dibelius, *James*, 28, n. 88: "Especially noteworthy are the following points of contact: The man who is making his plans in Jas 4:13 reminds one of the parable of the rich farmer in Luke 12:16-21; the admonition to action rather than mere hearing in Jas 1:22 is similar to the parable at the conclusion of the Sermon on the Mount; Jas 3:18 reminds one of Matt 5:9; the warning against judging in Jas 4:11 calls to mind Matt 7:1; the admonition to humility in Jas 4:10 resembles Matt 23:12=Luke 14:11, 18:14."

26. Dibelius, *James*, 29; cf. Schenke and Fischer, *Einleitung*, 2.234.

27. Cf. Dibelius, *James*, 29: "it must be assumed that Jas is familiar with the Jesus-

particularly with the sayings tradition, one should expect to find some evidence of its effect in James more than in any other non-gospel text within the New Testament corpus.

But it is not easy to divine the specific concerns of the author of this epistle. The fact that it is not really an epistle at all, but a paraenetical collection fitted with a catholicizing epistolary introduction (1:1) excludes any discussion of its specific social-historical setting.[28] Nonetheless, the writer was a real person, who had real concerns for the developing church he or she surveys. Dibelius suggests that one way to get beyond the generalizing nature of the paraenesis in James and to speak about the real concerns of the author is to pay close attention to the selection of material throughout the letter, noticing what themes tend to recur and dominate within it.[29] Now, if there is one theme that could be said to dominate the tone of this letter, it is the denigration and condemnation of the rich. This may be said not only because of the frequency with which the theme crops up (1:9-11; 2:5-12; 5:1-6; and the illustration in 2:2-4), but also because of the intensity of the fervor and rancor with which the author spits out his contempt for the wealthy (esp. 5:1-5).

But why should a leader in the early church feel so ill-disposed toward the wealthy? Would not the young local communities have sought the sponsorship of wealthier patrons just as did other clubs and groups of the period? Perhaps not, if, as Dibelius argues, its ideology was so bound up with that form of Jewish piety he refers to as the "ardor of the poor," if the early Christians were poor and remained poor and were proud to be poor because the poor alone could be seen not to have compromised towards success within the economic world of their gentile overlords.[30] But if this ideology is of primary concern to the author of James, it is surprising that only in 2:5 does one find anything like a glorification of the status of being poor, and here it is not simply the poor who are "chosen" of God, but the πτωχοὶ τῷ κοσμῷ (poor with respect to the world).[31]

No, much more prominent and to the point is his attitude toward the rich: they persecute (2:6), they blaspheme (2:7), they have cheated (5:4), and killed

---

tradition;" also Schenke and Fischer, *Einleitung*, 2.234, who speak of an "intellectual kinship with a layer of the synoptic tradition, which is to be found above all in Q;" and Baasland, "Der Jakobusbrief," 125-26: "This [i.e., the fact that James never actually quotes a synoptic text] may be best explained by positing that James relies not upon the written form of the synoptic tradition, but rather stands very near to the oral Jesus tradition." Baasland may go too far, however, when he suggests that "James might be a student of Jesus" ("Der Jakobusbrief," 127).

28. Dibelius' characterization of James along these lines is well known, and widely accepted; see his *James*, 1-11. For the catholic significance of the "the twelve tribes in the Dispersion" see *James*, 66-67.

29. Dibelius, *James*, 5.

30. Dibelius, *James*, 39-45.

31. More will be said about this qualifying phrase below. One might include 1:9 here as well, but there it is not a poor person, but the "humble" person (ὁ ταπεινὸς) who is exalted. It is interesting also to note that following the destruction of the rich foretold in 5:1-6, when the author turns again to admonish the church (5:7ff.), he or she does not once mention the benefits of their being poor, only the virtue and value of patience and steadfastness.

(5:6), and in the end they shall perish (1:10–11; 5:1,5–6). And yet even these charges do not bring us to the heart of the matter. They are too general and stereotypical and do not square with the intention of at least 2:1–7: if the church's experience of contact with their rich neighbors had been as bad as these charges imply, the author would scarcely have had to convince anyone that to show partiality to the rich is wrong! But perhaps precisely here lies the rub—the rich *are* honored, even in the churches (2:3). And for an older leader, one of the old guard who harps "be steadfast," "be not deceived," "be patient," do not change, hold the line, this could pose a very real problem. A person of means could be an asset to a community generally speaking: he or she could provide a meeting place, the food for banquets, support for the destitute poor, and perhaps provide for defense should the congregation encounter trouble with the authorities. But the person who provides the meeting place also decides when the group can meet; the person providing the food decides what is eaten and by whom; the person providing charity decides who is worthy. Put otherwise, either naturally or by default, the attraction of wealthier persons into local Christian communities would have changed the patterns of leadership within them completely.[32] As local communities began to develop their own local leadership, it was no doubt the wealthier members, with the advantages and services they could render a congregation, who quite naturally began to overshadow the older coterie of wandering radicals and eventually pose a threat to their position of leadership within the communities.[33]

That this is the sort of transition that the author of James was concerned about in the church he or she surveys is shown more clearly when one turns to that part of the letter wherein Dibelius maintains that one has the greatest chance of learning about the particular issues that moved the author to write it, viz. the three "treatises" in 2:1–3:12, "where the structure and lines of thought were apparently shaped by the author himself."[34]

The first of the three consists of 2:1–12 (13).[35] The theme is struck in the

32. The domineering role that might be exercised by a minority of wealthier members within a community is illustrated well by Theissen's discussion of social class within Paul's Corinthian community in "Social Stratification," and "The Strong and the Weak in Corinth." Also of value in this regard is Malherbe's treatment of the subject in his *Social Aspects*, 71–91.

33. I believe that we could speak here of what Theissen has termed "forms of legitimation" for various types of leaders within early Christian groups ("Legitimation and Substance," esp. 42–44, 51–54). The wandering radicals derived legitimation from the witness of their dramatic lifestyle. Theirs was a "charismatic" form of legitimation. Local leaders, on the other hand, had a more "functional legitimation," based upon practical services they might perform for the community. One might debate which form is the most effective or powerful. But it must be admitted that "functional legitimation" is more consistent and reliable over the long haul. A charismatic leader is a rare personality, and such a person comes along only occasionally. The steady basis of leadership within any group is more functional in nature. It would be natural, therefore, as early Christian groups began to settle into a more permanent existence, that there would arise in them leaders whose legitimation within the community was functional in nature.

34. Dibelius, *James*, 5.

35. Dibelius insists that vs 13 is not to be associated with the treatise in vss 1–12 (*James*, 3,

first line: "show no partiality," a general enough theme for the purpose of moral instruction. But why in particular does the author feel compelled to address this subject? The answer lies in the example he or she uses to illustrate this point and his or her subsequent discussion of it:

> [2]For a person with gold rings and in fine clothing also comes into your assembly, and a poor person in shabby clothing also comes in, [3]and you pay attention to the one who wears the fine clothing and say, "Have a seat here, please," while you say to the poor one, "Stand there," or "Sit at my feet," [4]have you not made distinctions among yourselves, and become judges with evil thoughts.

Jas 2:2-4

This is, to be sure, an hypothetical example, and one may not assume that it depicts an historical occurrence within the church.[36] However, the question is not whether 2:2-4 describes a particular historical event, but rather how this example illustrates a type of problem the author sees developing within the churches. The fact that in the subsequent discussion of the example, he or she does not revert back to a general discussion of partiality, but rather delivers some very definite censures having to do specifically with the problem of partiality shown to the rich (2:5-7), shows that there is more to the author's concern than simply the theoretical question of partiality. There is a problem developing in the church involving partiality toward the rich, at the expense of the poor.

Roy B. Ward's analysis of Jas 2:2-4 has helped to clarify more precisely the nature of the problem represented by this example.[37] Ward regards as problematic the usual assumption that the scene presupposed in the example is that of the church gathered for worship and faced with the situation of welcoming strangers, one rich, one poor, into its meeting.[38] Rather, he argues that the rich/poor contrasts of fine clothing/rags and sitting/standing are stereotypical of rabbinic discussions of fairness in the *courtroom*. Two examples from his collection will suffice to illustrate his point:

Deut. Rab. Shofetim 5:6 (to Deut 16:19):

For R. Ishmael said: If before a judge two men appear for judgment, one rich and another poor, the judge should say to the rich man, "Either dress in the same manner as he is dressed, or clothe him as you are clothed."[39]

125-26, 147-48), but others choose to treat vs 13 as an appropriate conclusion to vss 1-12, even though it might have originally been an independent logion (so, e.g., Mussner, *Der Jakobusbrief*, 126; Windisch, *Die Katholischen Briefe*, 13-17). Whether or not vs 13 forms the conclusion to the treatise has no real consequence for the thesis to be offered here, though I would tend to follow Dibelius' analysis.

36. So Dibelius, *James*, 129-30.
37. Ward, "Partiality in the Assembly," 87-97.
38. Ward, "Partiality in the Assembly," 87-88.
39. As cited by Ward ("Partiality in the Assembly," 89) from Cohen, *Midrash Rabbah*.

b. Shebu. 31a:
How do we know that, if two come to court, one clothed in rags and the other in fine raiment worth a hundred manehs, they should say to him, "Either dress like him, or dress him like you"? (followed by reference to Exod 23:7).[40]

Ward summarizes his conclusions thusly:

These texts belong to the rabbinic tradition concerning judicial proceedings—a tradition which is expressly connected with the OT instructions for judging in Lev. 19:15–18; Ex. 23:1–3, 6–9; Deut. 1:16,17 and Deut. 16:18–20. It is an early tradition, reflecting judicial procedure in at least early Tannaitic times. It indicates a concern lest the difference in apparel should lead to partiality and hence unjust judging, and it condemns the practice of having one litigant stand and the other sit as an instance of unjust judging and partiality.[41]

Extrapolating from these rabbinic materials, Ward may go too far in maintaining that the scene presupposed in vss 2–4 is one in which two members of the community have come before the assembled church for judgment.[42] It is, after all, an hypothetical example, and one might question whether there is evidence for Christians holding mock-court exercises such as the language here would suggest. Nonetheless, I would argue that the author of James chooses this juridical example, which has to do with getting a fair hearing, in order to score the general point that within the church it is the wealthy who have been getting the ear of its leaders, while "the poor" are blithely ignored. And to his or her way of thinking this represents a reversal of proper priorities, for "Has not God chosen those who are poor in the world to be rich in faith and heirs of the kingdom which he has promised to those who love him?" (Jas 2:5b).

The first treatise, then, confirms the first part of our hypothesis: the wealthy within the congregations have, in the author's view, too much influence. They have the ear of the community. But what about the second part, that their prominence is being won at the expense of the wandering radicals? Apparently not, at least not in any clear cut way. Here it is not "wandering charismatics" who are losing out, but the poor—or so it would seem. In the example, it is a poor beggar (πτωχός) who is not given a fair hearing. But one should recall that this is an hypothetical situation, not an historical event. And it is interesting that when in vs 5 the author moves now to transfer the lesson of the example to his or her audience ('Ακούσατε, ἀδελφοί μου ἀγαπητοί· [Listen, my beloved brothers]), it is not the "poor" who are in reverse fashion now exalted, but the πτωχοί τῷ κοσμῷ (poor with respect to the world). Even though I cannot acceed to Dibelius' claim that πτωχοί (poor) in this case has

---

40. As cited by Ward ("Partiality in the Assembly," 89–90) from Silverstone, *The Babylonian Talmud.* Ward also cites *Sifra Kedoshim Perek* 4.4 (to Lev 19:15) and *Aboth Rab. Nath.* 1.10.
41. Ward, "Partiality in the Assembly," 90–91.
42. Ward, "Partiality in the Assembly," 94.

become a technical term for the church in general,[43] his sense that that πτωχους τῷ κοσμῷ in 2:5 does not simply mean "poor people" seems quite sound. The antithesis πλουσίους ἐν πίστει (rich with respect to faith) signals that the author has re-signified this term in some particular way, as does the dative qualifier τῷ κοσμῷ (with respect to the world).[44] The question is, how does one interpret τῷ κοσμῷ (and· on the other side, ἐν πίστει)? Dibelius suggests that both are to be read as the *dativus commodi*, or dative of advantage, whereby the contrast would be between their beggarly state *in the worldly sphere* and their wealth *within the sphere of faith*, ἐν πίστει being roughly the equivalent of the similar Pauline formulation ἐν Χριστῷ (in Christ).[45] In other words, these are persons whose poverty is supposed to count for something in the church; their beggarly lifestyle τῷ κοσμῷ is supposed to merit them the higher status of πλούσιοι ἐν πίστει. In the author's view, they are the ones to whom privilege is due and to whom the congregation should turn its ear. In short, the reversal of roles in vs 5 indicates that these πτωχοί are the community's rightful leaders.

One is reminded perhaps of the use of "poor" in Thom 54 as a self-referential term for Thomas Christians, whom I have described as wandering radicals, and it would be tempting now to transfer wholesale everything that has been said about Thomas Christianity's radical life-style to the "poor" in James. But this must be resisted, unless more specific evidence for wandering radicalism is found in James itself.

This brings us to the second treatise, 2:14–26. The general theme for the treatise is, of course, the dilemma posed by the relationship between faith and works. But again one may ask: To what more specific end does the author invoke this theme here? In this regard it is no doubt significant that to illustrate the point he or she uses three examples, each of which has to do with the issue of hospitality.

The point of the first example (2:15–17) is obvious: to give a "brother or sister" a pat on the back and send them on down the road without provisions would be a flagrant violation of the code of hospitality. The second example

---

43. Dibelius, *James*, 39–45; 137–38. To be sure, the author of James seems to identify with the poor, and he or she takes up their cause, but he or she never refers to Christians, or the church in general as "the poor" (πτωχοί). Elsewhere he or she might refer to Christians as "humble" (ταπεινός: 1:9; 4:6), or as "persecuted" (πειράζειν/πειρασμός: 1:2, 12, 13, 14), but πτωχός occurs in James *only* in this hypothetical example (2:2–4) and its discussion (2:5–7). And in neither place can it be taken as a *terminus technicus* in the sense of "Christian." In the example, it refers simply to a poor person, since it is the rich/poor distinction that is the point of this *topos*, as Ward's rabbinic parallels show ("Partiality in the Assembly," 89–90). In the discussion, it also cannot be taken as coterminous with "Christian," for in vs 6 πτωχός is clearly presented as a unique type, distinct from the church at large. This much is shown by the fact that the author speaks here *to* the church using direct address (ὑμεῖς [you]) *about* "the poor," depicted now as a third party. Thus, it cannot be maintained that "poor" and "Christian" in James are to be considered synonymous and interchangeable. If anything, the πτωχοί in James should be seen as a particular type of person within the church.

44. Dibelius, *James*, 137–38.

45. Dibelius, *James*, 137–38.

(2:21–23) is less clear, but fortunately we have once again Ward's clever sleuthing as a guide. Ward argues that the example of Abraham's ἔργα (works) in 21a does not refer to the action of sacrificing Isaac in 21b; if this were the case, the plural ἔργα (as opposed to the singular ἔργον) would not make sense. Instead, Ward guides us again into the world of Jewish lore, where Abraham frequently appears as the "paradigm of the hospitable man":

> Thus in *Aboth de R. Nathan* I, ch. 7, Abraham surpassed even Job in showing hospitality to the poor. The same view of Abraham appears in the *Test. of Abr.* The title "friend" appears to be given Abraham especially because of his hospitality (*Test. Abr.* 1 [long recens.]; 4 [short recens.]), and thus hospitality deters the Angel of Death from touching Abraham (*Test. Abr.* 12 [long recens.]; 13 [short recens.]). In Gen. R. XLIX, 4 the צדקה of Abraham (Gen. 18:19) is interpreted as referring to the hospitality of Abraham (R. Aha in the name of R. Alexandri and R. 'Azariah in the name of R. Judah). So also in Tanḥuma, leka 12 "sowing righteousness" (Prov. 11:18) is applied to Abraham because he fed travelers.
>
> Furthermore, in rabbinic haggada the fact that Abraham is allowed *not* to carry out the action of sacrificing Isaac is understood to be because Abraham had merits, in particular, his hospitality (Gen. R. LVI, 5; cf. LV, 4).[46]

Ward goes on to argue that the example used in 2:15–17 would have been reminiscent of the hospitality tradition associated with Abraham, so that in vs 21a the author would not have had to stop and clarify that to which "works" here refers. Likewise, the offering of Isaac in vs 21b would have been understood in the traditional way, as the trial of Abraham, in which his "works" (i.e., his acts of hospitality) worked for his acquittal.[47] Thus the second example, when viewed critically, serves also to reinforce the theme of hospitality.

In the third example (2:25), the hospitality motif is once again transparent. Even Rahab the harlot was justified by her ἔργα, "when she received the messengers and sent them out another way."

I would suggest that it is not accidental that when the author of James addresses the question of faith and works, he or she chooses to illustrate the point using three examples relating to hospitality. He or she is focused so explicitly here on the hospitality theme that one must surely conclude that the reason the author brings up the subject of faith and works at all is that he or she feels it will be useful in treating what he or she perceives as a problem in the churches: the refusal of hospitality to travelers.

It might prove useful to pause at this point to summarize what has been learned thus far about the particular concerns of James' author in examining

---

46. Ward, "The Works of Abraham," 286–87. The final point is credited to Ginzberg, *Legends of the Jews*, 1.281.

47. Ward provides yet another example to illustrate the point, from *Yashar, wa-yera 42b,* cited after Ginzberg, *The Legends of the Jews,* 1.270–71: "If one was hungry, and he came to Abraham, he would give him what he needed, so that he might eat and drink and be satisfied; and if one was naked, and he came to Abraham, he would clothe him in garments of the poor man's choice, and give him silver and gold, and make known to him the Lord, who had created him and set him on earth."

these first two treatises. In the first treatise he or she protests the treatment of "the poor," whose influence has been supplanted as the churches turn a more sympathetic ear to their more wealthy members. In the second treatise, he or she protests the treatment of itinerants, who have been refused hospitality. Taken together they form a composite sketch of a situation lurking in the shadows behind the paraenetical screen that looks not unlike the situation we have already found in the church as the didachist knew it. It is a church that has grown tired of its itinerant "poor," that has begun to retreat from its inclination to support them and is beginning to find new voices to whom it may turn its ear.

The third treatise (3:1–12) is entirely consistent with this thesis. As has been seen in our treatment of the Didache, it belongs to the role of the wanderers to teach (Did 11:1–2). If the writer of James defends the position of the wandering radicals in the previous two treatises, their right to be heard and give counsel in the first and their right to receive hospitality in the second, in the third he stakes out yet another area of wandering radical turf, the right to teach (which now turns out to be the author's own turf—"we [48] who teach shall be judged"!), attempting to scare away any would-be local rivals. Dibelius is no doubt correct when he argues that we do not have to do here with the replacement of the older charismatic calling to teach with a new institutional office.[49] Indeed, it is precisely the opposite: this amounts to a *defense* of the older charismatic calling against newer teachers who do not share in the older radical life-style. This much is shown by the deliberate way in which the author structures this treatise.

The theme of the treatise is established in vs 1: teaching is a dangerous calling and not meant for just anyone. The rest of the treatise, composed almost entirely of Jewish and hellenistic wisdom sayings, which depend upon some particular thematic context to steer their general applicability onto a specific subject, depends for its interpretation upon vs 1. One must continually refer back to this theme in order to discover the point he or she is trying to make with each maxim.

Verse 2 serves both as a bridge from the theme established in vs 1 to the treatise that follows in vss 3–12,[50] and as an introduction to the treatise itself. It introduces two aspects of the practice of teaching, each of which makes teaching a difficult thing to pursue: 2a points out how easy it is for anyone to make a mistake, and to err (in light of vs 1) is particularly disastrous for the teacher. 2b reminds the aspiring teacher that it is not enough just to teach and not err. The successful teacher, one who does not err, is also a "perfect man ($\tau\acute{\epsilon}\lambda\epsilon\iota os \ \dot{a}v\acute{\eta}\rho$), able to bridle the whole body also."[51] The treatise that follows uses a series of maxims to elaborate on these two aspects.

---

48. The RSV reflects adequately the sense of the third person plural, $\lambda\eta\mu\psi\acute{o}\mu\epsilon\theta a$; it identifies the author with that group who is judged more harshly, viz. the $\delta\iota\delta\acute{a}\sigma\kappa a\lambda o\iota$ (teachers).
49. Dibelius, *James*, 183.
50. Dibelius, *James*, 181–82.
51. The author's failure at this point to present a description of the $\tau\acute{\epsilon}\lambda\iota os$ (perfect) life

Proceeding chiasticly, the author treats the second aspect first in vss 3–5a. Using two familiar figures[52] to present a rationale for the radical expectation that one who teaches must also be a "perfect man," the argument runs as follows: if we expect that a small bit in the mouth of a horse will enable us to control the entire body of the horse (vs 3), and that a small rudder can control the entire huge ship (vs 4), then it is not too much also to expect that the entire body should behave just as the teacher's tongue demands. In this sense the little tongue can boast of great things (vs 5a).

Verse 5b is a transition verse. It picks up the great/small dichotomy with which the author has been playing, but turns it in another direction to score a new point: how such little things can cause so much trouble. This introduces the second half of the treatise, which deals with the subject first broached in vs 2a: how easy it is to make mistakes (and therefore open oneself up to particularly severe judgment if one has chosen to teach.) The second half begins by defining the problem: it is the tongue (vs 6a). The tongue is unrighteous and can thus lead to perdition for the entire body (vs 6). The tongue is unruly and un-tameable (vss 7–8). The tongue is duplicitous and inconsistent (vss 9–12). Referring back to vs 2a, but at the same time now following after vss 3–5a and connected to it via the tongue motif, the point of the second half of the treatise turns out to be two-fold and doubly effective. On the one hand, it underscores how easy it is for people to err by showing how prone to err the human tongue is. On the other hand, if the tongue, the rudder upon which the teacher must rely to steer his or her entire corporeal existence in "perfection" is so prone to err, how utterly difficult it must be to achieve the teacher's status of τέλιος ἀνήρ (perfect man). In the end, the treatise places the ability to teach far beyond the reach of the normal person.

James is a paraenetical document; thus, it will never be possible to describe very concretely who the author is, or what his or her specific concerns were. But what we have found in the three central treatises is a defense of three areas

---

leads me to conclude that his or her intended audience would have known what this meant. It is not unimportant to his argument; thus, had he or she thought that the concept would have been unclear, a fuller account would be expected. This, unfortunately, does not help us, who are consequently left in the dark. The reference to "bridling the body" no doubt suggests some form of ascesis (cf. Kretchmar, "Ein Beitrag," 53–54). Paul perhaps refers to a similar concept of perfection when he appeals in Rom 12:1–2 to the "brethren" (ἀδελφοί) to "present your bodies as a living sacrifice . . . that you may prove what is the will of God, what is good and acceptable and perfect (τέλιον)." But this really does not tell us much more than Jas 3:2. The ascetic motif may perhaps suggest the concept as it was known to Matthew, for whom the life of the τέλιος (perfect) consists in the giving up of possessions, and accepting the life of itinerant disciple (Matt 19:21; cf. Mark 10:21). In adding to Jesus' reply the words εἰ θέλεις τέλιος εἶναι (if you would be perfect), Matthew seems to be acknowledging that there are still τέλιοι in the church who ascribe to this form of discipleship, even though he himself agrees with Mark in thinking this unnecessary for salvation (Matt 19:26; cf. Mark 10:27, where the interpolation first occurs).

52. Dibelius has gathered numerous parallels from hellenistic and Jewish-hellenistic sources (see *James,* 190). I agree with the conclusion he draws from these, viz. that both metaphors are basically optimistic in thrust. However, I do not agree entirely with his reading them in terms of the material that follows in vss 5b-12, as will be clear presently.

in the life of the wandering radical—poverty and the right of the "poor" to be heard; itinerancy and the right of itinerants to receive hospitality; and teaching and the reservation of this right for those who would fulfill some form of ascetic requirement and become "perfect." In addition, the author describes him or herself as one such teacher. We can only offer an hypothesis, but it seems quite likely that the same sort of transition from wandering radical leadership to local authorities that we have already observed in the Didache is part of the part of the picture also in James. The epistle is in part an attempt to defend the position of the wandering radicals within the churches and to recoup some of the ground they have already lost to a newer set of local leaders.

Whether there was an historical connection between the author of James and Thomas Christianity would be impossible to know. But the possibility should not be excluded. Both James and the Gospel of Thomas draw upon the authority of James. The Epistle of James, as has already been pointed out, stands very close to the sayings tradition; aside from the three treatises in 2:1–3:12 and the fictional epistolary introduction, James is simply a collection of wisdom sayings, resembling Thomas even in its extensive use of catchwords.[53] As for its provenance, most commentators are reluctant to locate James very firmly, but as Schenke and Fischer have pointed out, it must derive from an area where James would have been a popular figure, where the synoptic tradition was still alive as oral tradition, and where both Jewish and hellenistic influence had been felt. They therefore suggest Syria. But beyond these rather general observations, it is also noteworthy that James and Thomas correspond in a number of details, some of them interesting, though perhaps insignificant, and others both interesting and quite significant. Of the former one should mention the odd reference to the "Father of Lights" in Jas 1:17 (cf. Thom 83), the reference to peace-making in Jas 3:18 (cf. 106), or the fact that James' hypothetical example in 2:15–26 implies that a typical case of this sort would involve both men and women itinerants (cf. Thom 114). As to the latter, it is of greatest significance that both James and Thomas seem to share a certain attitude of distance or mistrust of the world. In chapter 5 I have already expressed my views on the degree to which this is fundamental to Thomas' outlook. It is to be seen in such sayings as Thom 56, or 111, or in slogans such as "Whoever finds himself is superior to the world." But more importantly, it is to be found at the base of the entire radical ethos that I have attempted to show lies behind Thomas—the wandering life-style, the rejection of wealth and acceptance of the beggarly life, the rejection of family and traditional piety, etc. In James one finds comparable slogans, such as "friendship with the world is enmity with God." (Jas 4:4) But one also finds some of that radical ethos familiar from Thomas strewn throughout James as well. For example, somewhat comparable to Thomas Christianity's critique of popular piety, one reads in 1:27:

53. Cf. Dibelius *James*, 7–11.

Religion that is pure and undefiled before God and the Father is this: to visit orphans and widows in their affliction, and to keep oneself unstained from the world.

Or one might mention the polemic against engaging in commerce in 4:13–14 (cf. Thom 63–65), or what I have argued for as the defense of wandering radicalism in 2:1–3:12. To be sure, James is not out entirely to promote this sort of radical ethos, and there are some issues over which James and Thomas are sharply divided (cf. Jas 5:7–8 and Thom 3, 51, and 113). But there is enough in James to render credible the suggestion that it, like Thomas, comes out of a tradition whose trajectory has been profoundly influenced by the phenomenon of wandering radicalism.

3 and 2 John

The tiny letter of 3 John has generated a flourishing debate throughout the history of modern critical scholarship. Theissen drew attention to it because it seems to allude to a conflict between certain wandering ἀδελφοί (brethren) and a local leader by the name of Diotrephes. Here I wish to look in closer exegetical detail at the social situation behind 3 John, to see what it can add to our understanding of the sorts of conflicts that may have arisen between wandering radicals and local leaders. I will begin by reviewing the main schools of thought regarding the social situation that lay behind 3 John.

Walter Bauer was inclined to read 3 John in terms of the situation he saw reflected in 1 and 2 John. There, he surmised, the conflict had been over a docetic view of Christ held to by certain gnosticizing members of the community. But in view of such passages as 1 John 4:5, Bauer rightly points out that one should not conclude that those who shared the author's orthodox views on this issue were in the majority. Rather, it appears that it is they who have retreated.[54] Bauer projects a similar situation onto 3 John. The orthodox elder, he maintains, has now taken his case on the offensive and sent out missionaries to attempt to influence the views of neighboring communities. The heretical Diotrephes responds in kind, rejecting the authority of the elder and excluding from the community anyone who is sympathetic to him.[55] Thus, for Bauer the conflict behind 3 John was a doctrinal one, and the elder was losing.

Käsemann, too, argued that the conflict reflected in 3 John was basically doctrinal.[56] However, rather than viewing the elder as a proponent of orthodox views attempting to influence the followers of the heretic Diotrephes, Käsemann argued that it was the elder who was suspected of gnostic views and for this reason expelled by the orthodox bishop Diotrephes.[57] Käsemann arrives at

54. W. Bauer, *Orthodoxy and Heresy,* 92.
55. W. Bauer, *Orthodoxy and Heresy,* 93.
56. Käsemann, "Ketzer und Zeuge."
57. Käsemann, "Ketzer und Zeuge," 173–74.

this conclusion via the supporting hypothesis that the elder was none other than the author of the Gospel of John, which, though not to be considered gnostic in the full sense of that term, leans far enough in that direction to lend itself to gnostic interpretation and thus cast a cloud of suspicion over its author.[58] The elder, then, was an elder of Diotrephes' congregation, who has now become a renegade undermining the authority of Diotrephes.

Both Bauer and Käsemann are in agreement in regarding the historical setting of 3 John as dominated by a conflict that is basically *theological* in nature. Yet in 3 John itself there is never any indication that the problem is theological. Diotrephes has refused to accept wandering preachers and rejected the authority of the elder—this is all that the letter tells us. But this is not enough, in the view of both Bauer and Käsemann, to account for the friction between Diotrephes and the elder.[59] This leads each into the dubious procedure of projecting onto the various characters involved that chief incriminator of early Christianity, Gnosticism, under the assumption that this would have been sufficient to produce the level of conflict we see here. Bauer projects the (anti-gnostic?) views of the author of 1 and 2 John onto the elder, even though few would maintain today that these three epistles derive from the same hand. For his part, Käsemann makes the elder responsible for the gnosticizing views of the Gospel of John. Though some would continue to argue that 1 John and the Gospel share common authorship, there is nothing that would suggest the same for 3 John.[60] And both assume alternatively that the elder or Diotrephes would have been so incensed by even the slightest hint of Gnosticism that such a conflict would ensue. One wonders whether at this early date there would have existed the high level of hostility to gnosticizing views among 'orthodox' Christians necessary to support either thesis.

Haenchen's treatment of the question is preferable in that it involves fewer assumptions.[61] For example, he is suspicious of Käsemann's procedure of imputing to the elder what amounts to a summary of the theology of the Gospel of John,[62] and for his own part chooses not to cast the conflict in theological terms at all. Rather, he follows Schnackenburg and Dodd in viewing the problem as having to do foremost with things organizational.[63] This is a battle over 'turf,' not doctrine. Similarly, he rejects Käsemann's thesis that the elder has been expelled from the community by Diotrephes, since in the text itself there is no mention of the elder's expulsion, and his intention to come to Diotrephes to straighten the matter out personally could scarcely be

58. Käsemann, "Ketzer und Zeuge," 177-79.
59. W. Bauer, *Orthodoxy and Heresy*, 93; Käsemann, "Ketzer und Zeuge," 172.
60. For discussions of the problem of authorship of the various Johannine writings see Kümmel, *Introduction*, 442-45; 449-51; Schenke and Fischer, *Einleitung*, 2.209-216; Schnackenburg, *Die Johannesbriefe*, 34-39, 295-301.
61. Haenchen, "Neuere Literatur."
62. Haenchen, "Neuere Literatur," 298.
63. Haenchen, "Neuere Literatur," 303-4. He cites Schnackenburg, *Die Johannesbriefe*, 266; and Dodd, *The Johannine Epistles*, 165.

understood under such circumstances.[64] Instead, Haenchen maintains that the elder in 3 John (and 2 John) is the leader of a church community located nearby to that of Diotrephes, and that it is his attempt to extend his authority beyond his own congregation through the use of missionaries that has led to the conflict with Diotrephes, who sees his actions as an encroachment.[65]

Though I prefer Haenchen's approach insofar as he identifies the conflict as a jurisdictional matter, not chiefly theological, there are questions to be raised regarding his specific reconstruction of the situation. First, there is no indication in the letter that its author is the leader of a community, or that he has personally commissioned and sent out the itinerant "brethren" whom he discusses in vss 5–8, 10. For example, there is no evidence that the "brethren" who have paid the elder a visit in vs 3 are doing anything more than stopping by; they are not necessarily reporting back. The elder does testify to the worth of Demetrius (vs 12), presumably one such itinerant, but in so doing he is merely adding his stamp of approval to that of many others, not giving him a commission. He sends along the greetings of mutual friends (vs 15), but this does not necessarily imply that he is a leader among them. That he may serve as a patron of the "brethren," supplying them with a letter of recommendation to the community of Diotrephes means simply that he, perhaps by virtue of an historical relationship, has (or had!) some standing in that community and thus could be trusted to vouch for the legitimacy of the strangers.[66] It does not necessarily mean that he was a leader among the "brethren." Thus, Haenchen's view of the elder as the leader of a rival community, sending out missionaries to extend his control, seems artificial.

Second, the elder does not seem to be *extending* his influence, but *defending* it. In vs 5 the action of Gaius in aiding the itinerant "brethren" is described as an act of faithfulness (πιστόν), thus implying his adherence to what has been customary up until now. Diotrephes, who refuses to help them, is the one who has been disloyal and taken a new course of action. Likewise, the elder's own authoritative status within the congregation of Diotrephes does not seem new; rather, his confidence that Diotrephes would have to give in if only he should appear in person suggests that he already has some considerable standing there. This view is confirmed by the fact that he already has contacts within the community, including Gaius,[67] and the unnamed "friends" in vs 15. Thus, it does not sound as though the elder is pushing forward into new ecclesiastical frontiers, seeking to expand his influence into previously independent areas, but holding the line on what is already his.

Third, the authority which the elder plans to reclaim is not his alone. It is

---

64. Haenchen, "Neuere Literatur," 304.
65. Haenchen, "Neuere Literatur," 310. Cf. Donfried's similar thesis in "Ecclesiastical Authority."
66. On patronage as a way of coping with strangers in the ancient world, see Malina, "The Received View," 182–83.
67. Note how the elder numbers Gaius among his "children" (τὰ ἐμὰ τέκνα) in vs 5.

said of Diotrephes in vss 9-10 that "he does not acknowledge *us*" (οὐκ ἐπιδέχεται ἡμᾶς), and that he "slanders *us*" (φλυαρῶν ἡμᾶς). Clearly it is not simply the elder's own authority that has been questioned, but that of his group.

We may then describe the situation as follows: the presbyter is part of a group of persons who have in the past enjoyed some amount of respect and authority within the congregation of Diotrephes. Perhaps he had a hand in founding it, or at least in recruiting some of its members (the implication of using the term τὰ ἐμά τέκνα [my children] in vs 4?). But recently a local leader in the community, Diotrephes, has attempted to weaken his relationship to the congregation by not recognizing his authority. Specifically, he has somehow nullified a letter which the presbyter had sent to the church (vs 9),[68] he has slandered the presbyter and his folk (ἡμᾶς; vs 10a), and he has refused to welcome the itinerant "brethren," punishing those who do (vs 10b). This last offense is apparently the most egregious in the elder's view, as the hospitality issue really occupies the focus of the letter from vs 3 to vs 10. This is understandable. The status of the "brethren" in the community of Diotrephes is tied to that of the presbyter, whose patronage by way of a letter of recommendation is all that may assure them of a hospitable reception as insiders, not strangers.[69] Thus, their rebuff, and the rejection of the presbyter's letter constitutes a personal affront to the presbyter. In turning away the "brethren," Diotrephes has shamed the presbyter. He must now attempt to regain his honor in the eyes of this community.[70]

The settling down of the phenomenon of wandering radicalism within synoptic Christianity, and at the same time its continuation in Thomas Christianity help to explain the sort of conflict that we see here. The presbyter, a figure left over from that sub-apostolic period before the rise of the monarchical episcopate,[71] stands for the old guard, intervening on the side of the itinerant "brethren." Whether he was himself an itinerant "brother," thus explaining the mysterious ἡμᾶς (us) in vss 9 and 10, is an open question.[72] At

68. The fate of the letter is not known, perhaps even to the elder. He apparently assumes, however, that Diotrephes had something to do with its being ignored, since it is precisely here that the name of Diotrephes first comes up.

69. That the letter was indeed a letter of recommendation is argued by Dodd, *The Johannine Epistles*, 161–62; Haenchen, "Neuere Literatur," 283; Schackenburg, *Die Johannesbriefe*, 326; Bultmann, *The Johannine Epistles*, 100; Malherbe, *Social Aspects*, 103–4.

70. For a discussion of the issue of honor and shame and how it manifests itself here see Malina, "The Received View," 184. The personal nature of the conflict is acknowledged by Malherbe (*Social Aspects*, 107) as well when he describes the presbyter's view of the matter "as a purely personal issue." Malina and Malherbe are not in substantial conflict on this text, despite Malina's vehement assertions to the contrary.

71. That Diotrephes does not here act with the authority of a "bishop" *per se* is argued by Malherbe, *Social Aspects*, 108–9. What is exercised here is "power" rather than "ecclesiastical authority" (Malherbe, *Social Aspects*, 109). One might perhaps imagine here the sort of figures referred to as "presbyters" by Papias (Eusebius, *Eccles. hist.* 3. 39:4); so Bultmann, *The Johannine Epistles*, 95; and von Campenhausen, *Ecclesiastical Authority*, 122.

72. The fact that he refers to the "brethren" in the third person (vss 3, 5, 6, 7, 8, and 10)

any rate, he takes the rejection of the itinerants personally, and he links it with his own rejection by Diotrephes. Diotrephes, on the other hand, represents the changing of the guard, the new order of indigenous leadership that is home-grown. He is not a heretic, or even a villain. He is simply a local leader chafing at the notion that an itinerant might stop in for a few days at will and attempt to exercise the role of leader of the community, a role that has now been vested in Diotrephes himself.[73] Dodd describes the situation as we might have predicted it on the basis of our study of wandering radicalism in Thomas and the synoptics:

> There must have been a stage at which the authority of local ministers was growing at the expense of the waning authority of the 'apostolic men,' like our Presbyter. It is likely enough that this stage was marked by some tension. Ageing men do not always yield with good grace an authority which under changed conditions they can no longer exercise effectively. Younger men, conscious of the growing needs and opportunities of a fresh generation, are not always considerate in grasping powers which are their due. It may well be that this letter reflects such a stage of transition and perhaps of tension.[74]

As a case study, the conflict reflected in 3 John illustrates the transference of leadership within early Christian communities from wandering radicals to local leaders. Whether there was an actual historical connection between the presbyter who wrote 3 John and Thomas Christianity would be impossible to know. Though if the modern trend to locate the Gospel of John not in Asia Minor, as was traditional, but further east in Syria, serves also to locate the Johannine epistolary corpus further east as well,[75] such a connection would not be out of the question. It is of interest in this regard that the presbyter repeatedly refers to the itinerant preachers as the "brethren," a detail that is somewhat striking when one recalls the Thomas version of the saying preserved in Thom 25: "Love your *brother* like your soul, guard him like the pupil of your eye." Diotrephes, in his attempt to limit the authority and influence of itinerant "brethren," and instead build up the strength of the local community and its leaders, no doubt would have preferred the more domestic, synoptic version of this saying: "Love your neighbor as yourself." For the presbyter, the Thomas version would have functioned quite nicely in his campaign to protect the status of the "brethren."

---

should not trouble. If the term "presbyter" has at least some quasi-titular significance, without implying the full ecclesiastical structure of later times, it might be supposed that he stood as a leader of sorts above the common "brethren" (cf. Bultmann, *The Johannine Epistles*, 97–98), and hence might refer to the "brethren" in such a way. The third person plural in vs 8, which identifies the presbyter as a "fellow worker" along with Gaius may simply be rhetorical. That the presbyter is also a traveler is shown by vs 10.

73. One might say that in terms of ancient codes of hospitality, from the point of view of Diotrephes the wanderers have violated their role as guest by usurping the role of host: taking precedence over the host, making claims or demands on the host, giving orders, etc. (see Malina, "The Received View," 185).

74. *The Johannine Epistles*, 164.

75. Koester, for example, treats them as documents in the battle for Syrian Christianity in his *Introduction*, 2.193–96.

Dodd was inclined to think that in this round, at least, the presbyter ultimately won out, as would be shown by the survival of his correspondence.[76] But one wonders how long the wandering tradition could have held out beyond this. It would have been only a matter of time before the personal influence of leaders like Diotrephes grew to the point of overshadowing that of a leader such as the presbyter. To this end a word should be appended here regarding 2 John.

Whether 2 John is a real letter or a literary fiction based upon 1 and 3 John has long been debated. Many have chosen to treat it as a real letter by the same presbyter responsible for 3 John. Haenchen, for example, regards it so, but stresses that it has its own purpose apart from 3 John and thus should not be interpreted in light of 3 John.[77] In so doing he correctly rejects the thesis that 2 John is the document mentioned in 3 John 9.[78] His own explanation of their differences is quite simple: the two letters were written for different purposes, "the third letter gives support to the mission to the Gentiles, this one [2 John], by contrast, is fighting against Gnosticism."[79] Such differences, in his view, do not justify positing a second author for 2 John.

But one can scarcely say that 3 John is intended to support a mission to the gentiles in light of 3 John 7! Rather, 3 John is written to support the itinerant "brethren," a theme which occupies almost the entire document (vss 3–10). And it is exactly this which makes 2 John most problematic. How could such a staunch supporter of the itinerants in 3 John turn on them so quickly in 2 John? Here one may not appeal to the fight against Gnosticism. Perhaps the charge that they advocated docetism (vs 7), as stereotypical as this charge rings, or the vague charge that they go beyond ($\pi\rho o\acute{\alpha}\gamma\omega\nu$) the doctrine of Christ (vs 9), would have been enough to convince one already predisposed against the itinerants to shut them out. But surely such an avid supporter of the itinerants as the presbyter in 3 John would have extended to them at least the courtesies mandated in Didache 11. As we have already noted, there, if one teaches falsely the community need not listen (11:2), but this provides no grounds for refusing to receive such itinerants (11:4). Not that the specific rules laid out in the Didache would have applied everywhere. They simply illustrate that the level of prestige these itinerants enjoyed could not easily be overridden for doctrinal reasons (cf. Did 11:7!). Only a person who *did not recognize their status to begin with* would have opposed the itinerants on the relatively flimsy grounds offered in 2 John 7 and 10; the presbyter of 3 John is clearly not such a person.

That leaves us with but one inevitable conclusion: 2 and 3 John were not written by the same person. But this would not be new. In his commentary on the Johannine epistles Bultmann argued that 2 John is not a real letter, but an imitation composed by someone wishing to mimic the style and vocabulary of

---

76. Dodd, *The Johannine Epistles*, 165.
77. Haenchen, "Neuere Literatur," 304–307.
78. Haenchen, "Neuere Literatur," 307; *contra* Wendt, *Die Johannesbriefe*, 26.
79. Haenchen, "Neuere Literatur," 307.

1 and 3 John. Bultmann repeatedly points out those places where 2 John parallels very closely 1 and 3 John: In vs 1 πρεσβύτερος (presbyter) could mimic 3 John 1;[80] vs 4 begins the body of the letter in the same manner as 3 John 3, with an expression of joy (ἐχάρην λίαν [I greatly rejoiced]);[81] the characterization of the love commandment in vs 5 as having been received ἀπ' ἀρχῆς (from the beginning) imitates 1 John 2:7;[82] ἵνα ἀγαπῶμεν ἀλλήλους (that we love one another) follows 1 John 3:11, 23; 4:7, 11-12;[83] the ἵνα (that) clause in vs 6a is pedantic and reminiscent of 1 John 2:3-4;[84] vs 6b is super-fluous, and the ἀπ' ἀρχῆς again hearkens to 1 John 2:7; 24; 3:11;[85] the warning in vss 7-9 is identical to that in 1 John 2:18-27, 4:1-6;[86] and the closing in vs 12 is the same as that in 3 John 13-14.[87]

But why would someone compose an imitation Johannine letter? Heise, whose arguments for the inauthenticity of 2 John were published in the same year as Bultmann's commentary, suggests that it was designed "to correct the third letter, as well as Johannine theology in general in the direction of the official Church."[88] Yet, if the problem were really theological, 2 John covers surprisingly little theological ground, and that which it does cover, docetism (vs 7), is surely one area in which Johannine theology would easily have passed the test of the "official Church." And in any event, the charge of docetism likely plays off of the so-called 'test of the spirit' in 1 John 4:2. No, the axe that the author of 2 John is grinding is to be found in vss 10-11, for as Bultmann notes, it is here alone that the pseudo-epistle goes its own way and offers something original:[89]

> [10]If anyone comes to you and does not bring this doctrine, do not receive him into the house or give him any greeting; [11]for anyone who greets him shares in his wicked work.

Here is the rub: to whom shall we extend hospitality? In my view these verses indicate that 2 John was composed not to correct any theological tendencies (which appear nowhere in 3 John), but rather, to counter the presbyter's position in 3 John on the recognition and support of itinerants. This explains both the use of the presbyter as the pseudonymous author and the heretical charges brought against the itinerants. The letter portends to be from the hand of the presbyter in order to give the impression that this most adamant of supporters had changed his position with regard to the itinerants. The vague charges of heresy are included simply to lend credibility to the picture thus

80. Bultmann, *The Johannine Epistles*, 107.
81. Bultmann, *The Johannine Epistles*, 110.
82. Bultmann, *The Johannine Epistles*, 111.
83. Bultmann, *The Johannine Epistles*, 111.
84. Bultmann, *The Johannine Epistles*, 111.
85. Bultmann, *The Johannine Epistles*, 111.
86. Bultmann, *The Johannine Epistles*, 112-14.
87. Bultmann, *The Johannine Epistles*, 115.
88. Heise, *Bleiben*, 170.
89. Bultmann, *The Johannine Epistles*, 114.

created by providing the rationale for the change in his position. Thus, though as Dodd maintains, the presbyter and his itinerant "brethren" may have won the battle that was 3 John, ultimately they appear to have lost the war. After his death (for one can scarcely imagine such an imitation when the presbyter was still alive) the presbyter himself was compromised and his name turned against the itinerants by the pseudonymous composer of 2 John.

Summary

All three of these case studies have helped to confirm two important points: 1) In the latter part of the first century there was a continuing tradition of wandering radicalism especially in the eastern regions of early Christian activity. 2) As predicted, the wandering radicals could not continue to exert influence over local communities without inevitably coming into conflict with a newer set of local leaders. In each case we have found communities in turmoil over the role to be played by wandering radicals still active among the churches. But in addition to this, they have also told us more about the nature of the conflicts that arose. In each case one can see that a transfer of real authority within the communities from wandering radicals to local leaders has either already taken place (as in Didache 11–13), or is under way (as in 3 John and James). And in each case, the resulting conflict has led to dispute over the itinerant's right to receive support from the communities. In two cases (Didache 11–13 and James) part of the controversy has revolved around teaching, disputing either *what* should be taught (Didache 11–13), or *who* is qualified to teach it (James).[90] Finally, in the case of Didache 11–13 and 3 and 2 John it is clear that in the end it was the local authorities who eventually prevailed. In the case of James, we do not know how the letter fared in the churches for which it was intended.

Thus, on the one hand the hypothesis that Thomas Christianity represents a lingering movement of itinerant social radicals, even while synoptic Christianity was progressively settling into communities more conventional in nature, is quite plausible. It is precisely this scenario that we find playing itself out in the second Christian generation. But on the other hand, it has also become evident that the tension created during this period of transition from the older style of wandering charismatic leadership to a newer form of local leadership was considerable. If Thomas Christianity did determine to continue the older, itinerant radical lifestyle of the Jesus movement in the face of a changing church, one should well expect to find in it evidence of this tension and the inevitable conflicts it would have sparked. It is to this problem that we shall now turn.

90. In this respect it is interesting to note that in 2 John, when the pseudonymous author moves to impugn the reputation of the wandering folk, this is done by alleging that their teaching is unacceptable (2 John 7, 9).

8
Itinerant Radicalism and Thomas Theology Kingdom Within and Without

In the preceding chapter I have presented three case histories to illustrate the changing landscape of early Christianity as it moved into the latter part of the first century. In each, one may see the struggle of an older sort of leader, the wandering radical, to maintain his or her status in communities which seem to be turning steadily toward a more local, indigenous leadership. And from these three studies it has been possible to see the sort of problems and conflicts that would have arisen during this awkward transition and the rebuffs one could expect a wandering radical to encounter while attempting to maintain his or her radical life-style in the context of this changing church. Finally, all three cases involve texts from the latter part of the first century in Syria, precisely the period and provenance with which one would associate Thomas.[1] Therefore, if the sketch of Thomas Christianity offered above, wherein the persons who assembled and used the Gospel of Thomas are seen as continuing the tradition of wandering radicalism even while other strands of the Jesus movement were beginning to settle down, has any degree of plausibility, then something of the conflicts we have seen at work in Didache 11–13, James, and 3 and 2 John should be in evidence in the Gospel of Thomas as well. Did our Thomas Christians encounter resistance among the communities they visited, and if so, how did they respond? In this chapter I will argue that they did encounter resistance, and that one may find the fruit of that conflict primarily in the theological reflection of Thomas Christianity that finds its expression in our text.

With this question, however, we must move into an aspect of Thomas Christianity that has not been dealt with in the previous pages. Throughout this study I have attempted to hold the focus on issues of social-historical

---

1. For the date and provenance of Thomas see chapter 4.

interest, desiring first and foremost to supplement the history of scholarship on Thomas, which has until now tended to focus on Thomas' theology and its place within the history of ideas, with a more complete social-historical picture of Thomas Christianity. But now it is necessary to broaden that focus and attempt to integrate what has been learned here about Thomas Christianity's social-historical orientation with what has been gained from previous studies of Thomas' theological tendencies.

This necessity derives from my assumption that these two areas of inquiry cannot truly be regarded as separate spheres. Social history and theology are intricately bound together in the positive construction of a world view. If social history provides the substance of reflection, the experiences, problems, situations which call for interpretation, theological reflection provides the interpretive structure within which life and experience take on meaning and offers the foundation from which a particular self understanding within that structure might develop. Likewise, as persons accept for themselves a particular structure of meaning and develop an understanding of themselves within that structure, they begin also to live out of that self understanding in such a way that their social history is affected. Thus, in a religious community or association social history and theological reflection exist in a kind of mutual relationship, coordinates running together to form a plane of interpreted reality out of which persons attempt to live. Put simply, if there were early Christians who found the Gospel of Thomas useful, they found it so because of its relevance to the situation in which they found themselves. We have already seen how legal sayings in Thomas support the social radicalism of Thomas Christianity in a very concrete way. But this would be but half of the picture, or better, just a small portion of it. For the Gospel of Thomas claims above all to be a document of revelation; its mode of discourse is primarily theological. It remains to be seen, therefore, how Thomas' theological tendencies are related to the social history I have tried to sketch out thus far.

In what follows I would suggest that one may find a mutual interaction of theology and social history in Thomas taking two basic forms, one positive and one negative. Positively, one may observe the coordination of social history and theology in the decisions Thomas makes about what it views as theologically valid. On the other hand, negatively one may observe this complicated interaction also in the decisions Thomas makes against a particular theological standpoint. I will begin with the positive: the relationship between the generally esoteric, or gnosticizing proclivity one finds running through many of Thomas' sayings and the socially radical lifestyle we have described above.

Wandering Radicalism and Thomas' Gnosticizing Proclivity

While it has often been pointed out that Thomas lacks the characteristics of a full-blown Gnosticism, such as an elaborate mythological framework, including metaphysical speculation about aeons, the demiurge and his error, and the redemptive path of the revealer, it cannot be denied that alongside its many legal sayings, wisdom sayings, or parables, Thomas does have a certain amount of gnosticizing content, which lends to Thomas what one might call a distinctly gnosticizing proclivity.[2] Robinson gave articulation to this "between" status of the Gospel of Thomas in locating it as a sayings collection along the LOGOI SOPHON trajectory somewhere between early Christian and Jewish sayings collections standing more firmly within the conceptual framework of the Jewish wisdom tradition, and later manifestations of the genre, such as Thomas the Contender, in which the tendency toward Gnosticism had played itself out more fully.[3] Put otherwise, Thomas is still tied to a traditional Jewish wisdom orientation by its genre, LOGOI SOPHON, yet, in terms of the material content of many of its sayings, it is moving toward a more gnostic orientation. Thus, in the Gospel of Thomas one catches Thomas Christianity in the midst of a basic theological shift or reorientation.

For the purpose at hand—coordinating Thomas' theological affirmations with Thomas Christianity's social history—this on-going reorientation provides a methodological opening. It will be noticed that some Thomas sayings have retained both their wisdom form and content and thus have not been drawn into the shift at all (e.g.,. Thom 25, 26, 31, 32, 34, 35, 41, 45, 47, 54, 86, 94, and 103). Others already show a very gnosticizing tendency (e.g.,. Thom 11, 15,18, 60, 67, 83, 84, and 88) and thus reflect the new orientation, but not necessarily the reorientation process itself, since they do not participate in the earlier wisdom orientation to any great extent. However, there is a small third group of sayings in which the reorientation takes on a very concrete and observable form. These are sayings which have been "gnosticized," or at least "esotericized," in an artificial, plastic way, either 1) through the secondary appending of esoteric, highly symbolic, or otherwise coded language, which serves to obscure the aphoristic meaning of the saying, replacing it with a hidden, or "gnostic" meaning; or 2) through the gathering together of wisdom sayings and combining them with gnosticizing sayings to form primitive gnostic dialogues. Precisely these sayings in which the shift plays itself out most directly are important. For if one may assume that there are issues in the life of Thomas Christianity that correspond to and help bring about this theological reorientation, then these sayings hold out the possibility of identifying those issues: these sayings are given a new interpretation because they deal with the very real issues in the life of Thomas Christianity, which themselves stand in *need* of re-interpretation.

2. While I cannot agree with many of his conclusions regarding individual sayings, Haenchen's work (see esp. *Die Botschaft*) has shown sufficiently the gnostic *Tendenz* operative in many of Thomas' sayings. To maintain that Thomas is simply a wisdom book, as does Davies (*The Gospel of Thomas*) one must simply ignore the work of Haenchen, and others.

3. Robinson, "LOGOI SOPHON." See my summary of Robinson's thesis on pp. 102–4.

The sayings that lend themselves to this sort of analysis fall into two groups: 1) one set of sayings having to do with the radical life and its defense; 2) a second set which speaks of a certain object of seeking or learning.

1. The Radical Life and its Defense

The first saying from this set to come to our attention is Thom 101:

[1]Whoever does not hate [father] and mother as I do cannot be my [disciple], [2]and whoever does [not] love [father and] mother as I do cannot be my [disciple]. [3]For my mother [gave me falsehood][4] but my true [mother] gave me life.

I have already dealt with the place of Thom 101 within the socially radical ethos of Thomas Christianity in chapter 5.[5] The abandoning of family ties that this logion demands seems to have been central to early Christian social radicalism in general.[6] But what is of central interest now is 101:3. Here the simple legal saying is given an esotericizing twist—the mother Jesus hates is the mother of falsehood, the mother he loves, the "true" Mother, is she who gives life. The saying is abstruse enough to defy obvious interpretation, though the importance of "life" and "living" in the Gospel of Thomas as terms of soteriological significance should not pass unnoticed.[7] However, what is more important here than any particular interpretation of this esotericizing conclusion is simply the fact that it is attached to *this* saying, which deals with a particular issue within Thomas Christianity, the rejection of family ties. It says, in effect, to the Thomas radical that he or she has not given up his or her family merely for the sake of an ethos, a movement, an ideology, but rather, as a sign of his or her true identity within the larger cosmic scheme of things.[8] The stakes have been raised, so to speak. The reorientation of one's family ties has taken on life and death importance—"my true Mother gave me life!"

The point here, and with all of the examples to follow, is that Thomas' "gnosticizing" proclivity is not simply an intellectual-theoretical phenomenon. It has its social-historical coordinates as well. For every wandering radical who accepted the call of the Jesus movement, there was a family left behind wondering what had become of their son or daughter, father or mother, husband or wife. The difficulty posed by this requirement is readily imagined, and the temptation to give up one's commitment to the movement and return to one's family must have been great. Why *should* one maintain the socially radical ethos of the Jesus movement? Of what value to ourselves and to the world is that for which we are sacrificing so much? These are the questions that early Christian social radicals must have faced as they attempted to

---

4. This lacuna cannot be filled in with certainty. The text supplied here is the suggestion of Lambdin in Layton, *Nag Hammadi Codex II*, 89.
5. See pp. 134–35.
6. Cf. Theissen, "Wanderradikalismus," 83–84; *Sociology*, 11–12.
7. Cf. Thom 4, 58, 59, 60, 61, 111, 114; also Thom 18, 19, 85.
8. One is reminded of the similar phenomenon in Mark 10:29–30, par.

maintain the itinerant life in the face of a gradually "domesticating" church. They are questions that invite theological reflection. And when one thinks of the fundamental rejection of the (social) world of antiquity embodied in the social radicalism of the Jesus movement, is it any wonder that at least one such group of social radicals found a comfortable theological home in Gnosticism, which looked out upon the world of antiquity in all of its brutality and harshness and called it evil? Gnosticism provided the framework in which the social protest of leaving family and village behind could be re-imagined in theological terms. Within a gnostic framework, social radicalism could become something more than radical *askesis* designed to raise questions about the social world. In Thom 101 it has become a matter of identity and the basis of a claim to life.

Of similar significance is the primitive discourse that has been constructed in Thom 49–50. Once again the opening logion, a beautitude, is familiar from our treatment of its subject matter in chapter 5: "Blessed are the solitary (MONAXOI) and elect, for you will find the kingdom." The MONAXOI (solitary) are those who have taken up the life of the wandering radical—the term has become self-referential for Thomas Christianity.[9] The beatitude is thus entirely comprehensible by itself within the context of Thomas Christianity. Presumably, it is through the insight gained in leading the life of the solitary wanderer that one ultimately finds the kingdom. Nonetheless, beginning with 49:2 the logion starts to work in another direction: "For you have come from it, and you will return there again." The discussion then continues to unfold in Thom 50:

> [1]Jesus said, "If they say to you, 'Where have you come from?' say to them, 'We have come from the light, from the place where the light came into being by itself, established [itself], and appeared in their image.' [2]If they say to you, 'Is it you?' say, 'We are its children, and we are the chosen of the living Father.' [3]If they ask you, 'What is the evidence of your Father in you?' say to them, 'It is motion and rest.'"

Haenchen has correctly drawn attention to the clearly gnostic *Tendenz* in both Thom 49:2 and 50:1–3.[10] By placing them together, Thomas' author/editor has created a primitive gnostic discourse, which takes as its point of departure Thom 49:1. But in terms of the wandering radical ethos, at least ideally, the gnostic additions seem entirely superfluous. The MONAXOI practice a lifestyle that allows them to find the kingdom—there is a social-historical content locked within this term. "Finding" here comes from praxis. There would be no need for further theological elaboration (49:2), no need for instructions and passwords for wending one's way through the cosmic obstacles that stand between the gnostic and the kingdom (50).

But as the above analysis of Didache 11–13, 3 and 2 John, and James has shown, wandering radicalism in the latter part of the first century was not in an ideal situation. The wandering radicals themselves were under fire. Their place in the communities which supported them was no longer secure; they could no longer assume that hospitality and support would be extended to them in compensation for the life they had chosen. In such a situation, wandering radicalism may not have provided its own clear-cut rewards, or its own assurance that the radical existence the wandering charismatics had chosen was in any way necessary. If Didache 13 is a fair indication of the attrition that would have set in, as more and more radicals chose to settle down to a more normal, sedentary life, the radicals' small voice against that of the majority of Christians would have offered little self-generating confidence (cf. Thom 73). Without the moral support of local communities, and with dwindling numbers, what sign was there that they had chosen correctly?

Precisely here the gnosticizing proclivity of the Gospel of Thomas again finds its social-historical coordinates. If assurance was lacking in the social world of the early church, theological reflection within the framework of Gnosticism could result in a deeply felt conviction that the socially radical ethos one had chosen was not in vain. Concepts such as the "children of light," or the "elect of the living Father" clearly raise the stakes for the ⲘⲞⲚⲀⲬⲞⲒ. Their social radicalism has become more than a witness to the communities that had traditionally supported them. It has become a manifestation of their personal worth within the larger cosmic scheme. It is no longer a question of their having chosen correctly. Thom 49:2–50:3 assures them that indeed it is they who have *been* chosen. It matters not what the majority believes (Thom 74, 75) and that their own numbers dwindle. They are the chosen few (Thom 23).

The way in which this kind of siege mentality spirals around and leads to an enhanced self-understanding among Thomas Christians is to be seen finally in the sequence Thom 68–69. Thom 68:1 is a simple wisdom saying, a beatitude which gives positive valuation to the problem of persecution of Thomas Christians. The correlative in 68:2 also has a relatively straightforward meaning: "no place will be found, wherever you have been persecuted." The warning sounds ominous. Thus, the us/them mentality comes clearly to the fore on a rather basic level. But as one moves on to Thom 69, the train of thought spirals back around with the repetition of the first part of the makarism "Blessed are the persecuted . . .", but then reaches up to a new plane of discourse by adding "within themselves" (ϩⲘ̄ ⲠⲞⲨϩⲎⲦ), thus invoking a set of gnosticizing concepts in Thomas centered around the struggle of the Thomas Christian to reach inside of him or herself and grasp an understanding of his or her true nature (cf. Thom 2, 3, 111, and 70).[11] More will be said of this later. For the present, it is enough to notice how the train of thought has spiralled

11. Haenchen ("Spruch 68," 28) rightly sees this as the significance of ϩⲘ̄ ⲠⲞⲨϩⲎⲦ (in their heart) in Thom 69:1; but I cannot agree with his projection of this understanding onto "persecution" in Thom 68 (following Giversen, *Thomasevangeliet*, 248), where the added words of Thom 69's version of the makarism do not occur.

upwards and away from the problems these wandering radicals are experiencing in the world. The movement is completed in the correlative: "They are the ones who have *truly* come to know the Father."

Their special status is confirmed, their experience of hatred and persecution in the world transcended and transformed into the ultimate assurance that it is they "who have truly come to know the Father." Thus, the gnosticizing concepts of correct perception, of having true knowledge that sets one apart from the common herd, has its social-historical coordinates in the difficulties Thomas Christianity is experiencing in the world. They distract one's attention away from the real "persecution" (whether this might refer to something more serious than the refusal of hospitality is impossible to know) and focus upon the special status that comes from the gnostic search for true self.

In each of these examples Thomas Christianity has found in a kind of gnosticizing theology a way to cope with and understand the rejection it seems to have been experiencing. The times were just not right for the radical legacy they sought to carry on. The importance they may have once had has dwindled, and the itinerants naturally had to face the choice of either accepting that reality, giving up the radical life, and melding into the normal fabric of settled community life, or denying the validity of what was happening around them. For those who chose the latter, the very real decline they were experiencing called for explanation; the gnostic notion of the *electi* provided at least the intellectual framework within which they could carry on.

2. The Object of Seeking

The motif of seeking and finding occurs three times in the Gospel of Thomas. In Thom 94 it occurs in the form of a simple wisdom saying, paired with the familiar parallel strain "to [one who knocks] it will be opened." It is a motif which especially lends itself to the tendency to esotericize or gnosticize, for it leaves one with an open-ended suggestion: seek and ye shall find . . . what?! Thom 2 and 92 both take advantage of that open-ended quality of the motif to bend Thomas in a gnosticizing direction. Thom 2 reads:

> [1]Jesus said, "Let one who seeks not stop seeking until he finds. [2]When he finds, he will be disturbed. [3]When he is disturbed, he will marvel, [4]and will reign over all."

In 2:1 one may easily recognize the wisdom logion, complete in itself, and yet, as is endemic to the seeking-finding tradition, begging the question: "Find what?" Thomas seizes the opportunity and shadows in some of the opening with the mysterious contents of 2:2–4. It is interesting, however, to note that here the author/editor does not really answer this question. 2:2–4 describes what happens to the seeker once he or she has found, but it does not say *what* exactly is to be found. Rather than answering the obvious question, 2:2–4 serves only to pique our interest even more! It matters not which of the two versions of this logion represents the original;[12] both versions score essentially

---

12. The Greek version (POxy 654.5–9) is slightly different. It does not mention "the All,"

the same point, though perhaps each in a slightly different history of religions mode: to successfully find, and then master this mysterious object of searching is to attain to salvation. No longer the coaxing of the classroom teacher, the exhortation "seek until you find" has become in Thomas the call to find that thing which is the very key to one's salvation. But what is that all-important thing? Thomas is coyly secretive on this crucial point.

The seeking and finding motif is used similarly in Thom 92. Again the logion begins with the simple wisdom saying: "Seek and you will find." And again the author/editor seizes the opportunity to expand into the vacancy looming at the end of the saying:

[2]In the past, however, I did not tell you the things about which you asked me then. Now I am willing to tell them, but you are not seeking them.

The then/now periodization of history should not lead one to conclude that Jesus speaks here as the risen Lord, "then" referring to his earthly sojourn, "now" referring to a post-resurrection period.[13] Thomas otherwise shows little interest in the death of Jesus and never mentions the resurrection. Rather, Jesus here speaks as the revealer, God's agent of revelation waiting in the wings since the days of old until such time as God deemed it timely to send him forth into the world. Its conceptual framework is therefore similar to the first eleven verses of the prologue to the Gospel of John. And in this sense it has a certain gnosticizing *Tendenz*. It is, however, disappointing. Like the expansion to Thom 2, it has no intention of telling us what it is one should look for, or what one might expect to find. Rather, it moves furtively around this question and instead points an accusing finger. It says essentially: If you do not know what it is you are to seek after, it is your own fault! Your timing is off. You have not asked the appropriate questions at the appropriate time. And it leaves its audience asking: What was it that we were wanting to know? What is it that he wants to tell us? But ultimately, the object of seeking is itself never disclosed.

This saying is not aimed at Thomas Christianity itself. The movement would not likely pummel itself like this. These are, after all, the chosen, the *electi*. Rather, it is part of Thomas Christianity's tantalizing message to outsiders. It scolds those who have refused to listen to them, who have refused to inquire after that which Jesus wishes to disclose through the agency of those who have "become like" him (Thom 108). In this way it participates in the siege mentality that was noticed with respect to Thom 101, 49–50, and 68–69 above. But there is something more here as well. 92:2 is also alluring. It reveals the existence of something secret, something to be communicated, something Jesus wants to say, but stops short of revealing what it is. It attracts the curious,

---

but speaks simply of "ruling" ($\beta\alpha\sigma\iota\lambda\epsilon\acute{\upsilon}\sigma\eta$), then continues with the words (following Attridge's reconstruction in Layton, *Nag Hammadi Codex II*, 113) "and after ruling, he or she shall rest" ($\kappa\alpha[\grave{\iota} \ \beta\alpha\sigma\iota\lambda\epsilon\acute{\upsilon}\sigma\alpha\varsigma \ \grave{\epsilon}\pi\alpha\nu\alpha\pi\alpha]\acute{\eta}\sigma\epsilon\tau\alpha\iota$).

13. So Haenchen, "Literatur," 317; *contra* Grant and Freedman, *Secret Sayings*, 118; Gärtner, *Theology*, 98–101.

the seekers, those who cannot stand to be left out, or who feel they have missed something.

Why should Thomas Christianity draw this furtive, secretive, esotericizing cloak around that which it has to offer? Again we must ask this question not just in terms of the history of religions, but in terms of the social-historical coordinates suggested by these sayings and the attitudes and concerns they betray. For example, if one thinks of the decline in status and prestige within local communities that the wandering radicals were experiencing during the latter years of the first century, it is easy to imagine the functional value of esotericizing the tradition and suggesting that the Thomas Christian has something secret, something desirable, something of tremendous importance. As a strategy for propping up the special status they once enjoyed, one can understand how the esotericizing, or gnosticizing Tendenz within Thomas Christianity would have found its concrete social-historical coordinates.[14] Theological reflection can sometimes be gratuitous.

But if one thinks of esotericism in terms of the day-to-day reality of itinerancy, additional light is shed on the problem of coordinating Thomas' gnosticizing proclivity with a concrete social-historical situation. Itinerants did not stay long in one place; they could not (Did 11:5). They had but a short time to give their pitch, plant their seeds and then move on to other fields. He or she might not return to a given community for some time. In the interim the community would have begun to mull things over, to take what had been given and begin to think as a group in conversation with one another about what the significance of the message had been. By the time the itinerant preacher managed to return to the group, who knows what he or she might find had become of what had been said several months before. And for his or her part, the itinerant probably would not have remained entirely stagnant either, but would have continued to develop his or her thinking. And this would have transpired not in conversation with any particular community, but in the solitude of the itinerant life. By the time itinerant and community were reunited, their views could well have evolved into conflicting positions, which the itinerant must then patch up. Add to this the problem of different itinerants stopping by the same community at different times, and perhaps with different kerygmata, one can easily imagine a situation of extreme chaos.

For the person claiming to bear the very essence of divine revelation itself, this would add up to a situation of real awkwardness. Minds change; revelation does not. Human beings have differing opinions; the voice of the revealer, however, must speak all of one accord. In such a situation the esotericizing of the tradition served the very useful function of providing the itinerant with a way of explaining him or herself and any discrepancies that might arise

---

14. There seems to have been some self-awareness among gnostic groups themselves of the abuse to which such an esotericizing of the tradition could lead. In ApJohn 31.34–37, for example, one finds a curse turned explicitly against those who would exchange gnosis for material support.

between the older message and the new, or between competing wanderers who may have felt differently about the particulars of just what it was that he or she sought after and found. The old position, or the competing voice could be relegated to the status of "public," or "common" (i.e., inferior) knowledge, while that which the itinerant now wishes to reveal—ah!—that is the special, heretofore secret wisdom of the ages, which only now has become available. If what the itinerant brings seems strange, its justification lies close at hand in Thom 17:

> Jesus said, "I will give you what no eye has seen, what no ear has heard, what no hand has touched, what has not arisen in the human heart."

To illustrate the usefulness of this tradition one need go no further than Paul, who makes use of this saying in precisely the sort of situation we have been describing (cf. 1 Cor 2:9). In the opening chapters of 1 Corinthians it is likely that an interpretation of Paul's own baptismal teaching lies at the root of the problem he addresses. Apparently, Paul's own notion of dying and rising with Christ (cf. Romans 6) had lead to the opinion that Christians have already experienced the resurrection in baptism (cf. 1 Corinthians 15) and thence advanced to a superior state of wisdom. In Paul's absence the interpretation of his preaching has lead to consequences which he did not foresee.[15] Complicating the issue, no doubt, was the presence of various other leaders in Corinth besides Paul, whose own esoteric wisdom teaching had led to the situation of competing loyalties to conflicting messages.[16] The resulting factionalism must now be patched up. In this situation, Paul composes a speech (1 Cor 2:6–16) mocking the esoteric wisdom of his opponents,[17] probably even making use of their own material, including the saying in 2:9, which looks remarkably like Thom 17: "What no eye has seen, nor ear heard, nor human heart conceived, what God has prepared for those who love him." His intention, no doubt is to debunk their claims to secret wisdom fit only for advanced ears. But it is most interesting to note that in the end Paul himself invokes the very strategy of his opponents, countering their claims to secret teaching with claims of his own:

> But I, brethren, could not address you as spiritual people, but as people of flesh, as babes in Christ. I fed you with milk, not solid food; for you were not ready for it; and even yet you are not ready, for you are still of the flesh.
>
> (1 Cor 3:1–3a)

15. For this general view of the baptism question in 1 Corinthians, see Robinson, "Kerygma and History," 30–34.

16. On the esoteric wisdom character of the opposition Paul addresses in the opening chapters of 1 Corinthians see Horsley, "PNEUMATIKOS vs. PSYCHIKOS." Horsley takes as his point of departure the earlier work of Dupont, *Gnosis*, 172–80 and Pearson, *PNEU-MATIKOS—PSYCHIKOS Terminology*, 11–12, 17–21.

17. That Paul has composed this speech to mock his opponent's message is argued by Pearson, *PNEUMATIKOS-PSYCHIKOS Terminology*, 27–42. See also Conzelmann, *1 Corinthians*, 57–60.

Thus, to counter those whose claims to secret wisdom has led to an unwelcome re-interpretation of Paul's teaching on baptism, Paul himself lays claim to esoteric tradition of his own, for which the Corinthians are not yet ready.

Similarly, in the letter to the Galatians Paul must work to repair his reputation in Galatia after subsequent visitors had introduced a "different gospel" (Gal 1:6: ἕτερον εὐαγγέλιον). In this situation, however, Paul uses a different tactic, viz., appealing to authority. To enhance his precarious position there he must draw upon both his own personal authority in having received his revelation directly from Christ (1:12) and the recognized authorities in Jerusalem (2:1–10). Turning to the third Thomas saying to be considered in this set, one finds both of these strategies, appealing to authority and falling back on esotericism, working to the Thomas Christian's advantage. Thom 13 begins as a simple scholastic dialogue, which reminds one of the similarly depicted scene at Caesarea Philippi in Mark 8:27–30, par.:

> ¹Jesus said to his disciples, "Compare me to something and tell me what I am like." ²Simon Peter said to him, "You are like a just angel." ³Matthew said to him, "You are like a wise philosopher." ⁴Thomas said to him, "Teacher, my mouth is utterly unable to say what you are like."

But the scene in Thomas begins to take an unusual twist with Jesus' response to Thomas' answer:

> ⁵Jesus said, "I am not your teacher. Because you have drunk, you have become intoxicated from the bubbling spring that I have tended." ⁶And he took him, and withdrew, and spoke three sayings to him. ⁷When Thomas came back to his friends, they asked him, "What did Jesus say to you?" ⁸Thomas said to them, "If I tell you one of the sayings he spoke to me, you will pick up rocks and stone me, and fire will come from the rocks and devour you."

Several things are to be noted about the last half of this dialogue. First, Thomas, remarkably, is elevated by Jesus to a status equal to his own: "I am not your teacher." Thomas has fully understood, he has drunk from the "bubbling spring" that Jesus has "tended." Then, as a consequence of this newly declared status, Jesus withdraws with Thomas, revealing to him the mysterious "sayings," or "words" (ⲛ̅ϣⲁϫⲉ), a secret whose power is most impressive (13:8!). One is reminded again here of Thom 108: Jesus said, "Whoever drinks from my mouth will become like me; I myself shall become that person, and the hidden things will be revealed to him." Thom 13 makes Thomas, in a sense, the prototypical Thomas Christian, who, like Thomas, now enjoys this special authority.

But what are these three words? The Gospel of Thomas does not say. This is a secret, reserved only for those who have attained to the "intoxicated" status. What is more, Thomas makes it very clear that this inner circle did not include the likes of Peter and Matthew. In my view, this may well represent a direct attack upon the gospels that stand in the Petrine (Mark) and Matthean (Matthew) traditions.[18] According to Thom 13, they do not, indeed *cannot* have what the Gospel of Thomas claims to have—the persons to whom they appeal for authority were not there to receive it! Thomas insinuates that they were not worthy of such things. The secret belongs to Thomas and Thomas Christianity alone. When one thinks of the pattern of settling down that we have argued stands behind the synoptic half of the Jesus tradition, one may perhaps think of this polemic in terms that go beyond the rival claims of different communities. It may well reflect the conflict that arose between the older, itinerant radical leadership of the Jesus movement and the newer, settled, local leadership of early Christian communities.

As local communities grew up, we have seen how they developed their own ideas about what constitutes right teaching. 2 John attempts to discredit the itinerants by claiming that their teaching "goes beyond" (vs 9). The Didache places strict limitations on what the wandering teachers could legitimately say in the community and still remain in good standing (11:1–2). In such a situation the claim to have access to secret traditions, words, and mysteries that local authorities could not possibly know about would have served a very useful function. On the one hand it undergirds the authority of the Thomas Christian during a time when the authority of wandering radicals would have been coming more and more under question and doubt. On the other hand, the claim to have such powerful secrets serves to entice the curious, the worried, the ambitious, by suggesting the deficiency of the synoptic message over against the superiority of the Gospel of Thomas. To hear such things, to read such mysteries, one must be special—pearls are not thrown to swine! (Thom 93).

The ultimate outcome of this development leads quite naturally to the Prologue and Thom 1. The tendency to esotericize the tradition would eventually result in cordoning off not just a few well kept secrets, but the entire collection of Jesus' sayings. The Prologue declares the entire collection to be private property—the sayings, all of them, are now secret. The Gospel of Thomas has become a document strictly for insiders. The power of the secret is added in Thom 1: "Whoever discovers the interpretation of these sayings will not taste death." Consequently, those who have these sayings and can mediate their interpretation, hold the key to life and death.

The esotericizing aspect of Thomas' gnosticizing proclivity has its social-historical coordinates in the issue of authority and control. The rise of local leaders, as we have seen, lessened the demand for the role of the wandering radicals. By esotericizing the tradition and claiming sole control over its interpretation, Thomas Christianity had provided itself, whether consciously or unconsciously, with something of value, a lever with which to recoup some

18. So Walls, "References to the Apostles," 269.

of its inevitable losses. It claims to have secrets reserved for the deserving, secrets which hold the key to life beyond death.

Wandering Radicalism and Actualized Eschatology

The wandering radicalism of Thomas Christianity must be coordinated not only with what it accepts theologically, but with what it rejects as well. This too stands to lend insight into the nature of the phenomenon of wandering radicalism in early Christianity. For this, however, it will be necessary to look in Thomas for a different type of saying. Rather than look for sayings that push positively in a gnosticizing direction, in this section the focus will be on more negative, polemical sayings.

Thom 113 reads as follows:

> ¹His disciples said to him, "When will the kingdom come?" ²"It will not come by watching for it. ³It will not be said, "Look, here' or 'Look, there.' ⁴Rather, the Father's kingdom is spread out upon the earth, and people do not see it."

The parallels to Luke 17:20–21 are obvious. Yet, unlike Luke, Thomas does not temper this tradition with anything like Luke 17:22–25; the polemic against a futuristically conceptualized eschatology is allowed to stand without the slightest compromise. Luke is not fundamentally opposed to a futuristic eschatology, only an imminent apocalypse. He is prepared to wait literally 'until kingdom comes.'[19] Thomas, by contrast, appears to be impatient: "It will not come by watching for it!" Rather, it is already here. The problem is simply that people do not see it. It is a theme that surfaces elsewhere in Thomas—the failure to see, to discern. Thom 5:1 enjoins: "Know what is in front of your face, and what is hidden from you will be disclosed to you." And in Thom 91:2, Jesus replies to an anonymous query with the same tone of impatience heard in 113:

> "You examine the face of heaven and earth, but you have not come to know the one who is in your presence, and you do not know how to examine the present moment."

For Thomas the moment is now; this is the time, if only one can be made to perceive it.

Thomas' opposition to any future eschatological schemes is to be found also in Thom 51:

> ¹His disciples said to him, "When will the rest for the dead take place, and when will the new world come?" ²He said to them, "What you are looking forward to has come, but you do not know it."

The notion of the future "rest of the dead" (ⲦⲀⲚⲀⲠⲀⲨⲤⲒⲤ Ⲛ̄ ⲚⲈⲦⲘⲞⲞⲨⲦ), which Thomas here opposes, probably refers to the future repose of the saints

---

19. Conzelmann, *Theology of St. Luke*, 95–136.

in Rev 14:13 and Heb 3:7–4:13. It is not the notion of "rest" itself which attracts the opposition here—elsewhere Thomas offers its own (perhaps) related concept (cf. Thom 2 [Greek version: POxy 654.5–9], 50, and 60). The decisive factor here is the implication that the "rest" is something that one may simply wait for. For Thomas Christianity, there is no rest that is to come, no new world waiting around the corner. The new world is already here. The disciples simply do not recognize it.

This is realized eschatology, but not in the Johannine sense. Thom 3:1–3 polemicizes against any notion of heavenly mansions for which one is qualified by virtue of one's present status:

> [1]Jesus said, "If your leaders say to you, 'Look, the kingdom is in the sky,' then the birds of the sky will precede you. [2]If they say to you, 'It is in the sea,' then the fish will precede you. [3]Rather, the kingdom is within you and it is outside you.

For Thomas, the arrival of the kingdom is no waiting game. Thom 3:4–5 continues with a plan of action:

> When you know yourselves, then you will be known, and you will understand that you are children of the living Father. But if you do not know yourselves, then you live in poverty, and you are the poverty."

Γνῶθι σαυτόν (Know thyself)—the famous maxim of Thales[20] is appropriated here by Thomas Christianity to demonstrate its fundamental conception of the kingdom: it consists, like any other kingdom, of nothing more and nothing less than those who declare themselves to be its subjects. The kingdom is nothing without its constituents, without those who recognize their true identity as its citizens, its loyal "children." The kingdom is *already* spread out upon the earth, its potential resting in every person, waiting for individuals to realize their citizenship in it. Without that realization, the kingdom is nothing, it is invisible (Thom 113, 51, 5, 91), and its constituents are themselves nothing (Thom 3:4–5). The onus for making the kingdom real rests squarely with anyone who desires it to be real. Its power to "save" is nothing if the person desiring salvation does not him or herself empower the soteriological process (Thom 70). Its power to *be* is nothing without the will of its constituents to make it a reality.

In Thom 24 one finds a chreia, the setting of which reminds one very much of John 13:31–14:7, the beginning of John's farewell discourse. There Jesus announces to the disciples his imminent departure, which prompts Peter to inquire: "Lord, where are you going?" (John 13:36). The heart of Jesus' comforting reply comes in 14:1–4:

> [1]"Let not your hearts be troubled; believe in God, believe also in me. [2]In my Father's house are many rooms; if it were not so, would I have told you that I go to prepare a place for you? [3]And when I go and prepare a place for you, I will come

---

20. Diogenes Laertius 1.40.

again and will take you to myself, that where I am you may be also. ⁴And you know the way where I am going."

"Let not your hearts be troubled"—how different this attitude is from that of the Gospel of Thomas (cf. Thom 2!). It is small wonder that in Thomas Jesus responds quite differently to essentially the same question:

¹His disciples said, "Show us the place where you are, for we must seek it." ²He said to them, "Whoever has ears should listen. ³There is light within a person of light, and he²¹ shines on the whole world. If he²² does not shine, he²³ is dark.

Jesus speaks here as the revealer. The saying presupposes a christology similar to that of John 13:31–14:7, but chronologically sets the scene one step further along in the revealer's journey. The revealer has already come and gone, and like John's disciples, the disciples here wish to follow to that "place." But in Thomas, Jesus' response to their query is very different. It begins with the familiar saying "Whoever has ears should listen," as if to say "play close attention." What follows does not seem comforting. Rather, the double-stich saying does not reveal the information the disciples were seeking at all. It refuses to acknowledge that there is a place beyond the present world to which the disciples, or anyone will someday go. Instead, it demythologizes the gnostic myth of salvation, the return of the children of light to the "place where the light came into being," as one finds, for example, in Thom 50, and turns the focus around, back to the world and the present responsibility of the children of light where they are, dwelling in the world. If they have light in themselves, then the entire world becomes the place of light. If it exists in them, it exists also in the world. If they have no light, the light does not exist at all.

Eschatology in Thomas is not future. But nor is it realized eschatology, if one means by this an end that is "already, but not yet." Eschatology in Thomas is "now or never." "The kingdom is within you and it is outside you (Thom 3:3)." But if it is not realized inside of you, it will not exist outside of you. This is not realized eschatology, it is *actualized eschatology*. If the kingdom is to exist at all, it is up to Thomas Christianity to make it exist, to be the leaven (Thom 96), to shine in the world (Thom 24), to enable people to see the kingdom in its full potential: "spread out upon the earth" (Thom 113). In this way the kingdom is present, it is real. It must be tended, lest it slip away (Thom 97); it must be kept in shape, well practiced (Thom 98).

In his treatment of early Syrian Christian asceticism Kretchmar sought to show that Christian ascetic practice there, unlike, for example, in Egypt, was not motivated primarily by metaphysical speculation. Rather, by tracing its roots to the Jesus tradition as it moved east out of Palestine, he attempted to

21. Or: "it".
22. Or: "it".
23. Or: "it".

argue that its primary motivation was eschatological. In this he is aided by Erik Peterson's conclusions reached with regard to eschatology and asceticism in the apocryphal Acts:

> ... in the apocryphal Acts Peter and Thomas are actual apostles, who have been sent to the important centers of the world, and who not only fill the entire world with their teaching, but also with the lived reality of Christ, who intends to become a world power, insofar as *he subverts the world in its present state and duration*. In this sense asceticism has a strong relationship to eschatological faith: it has to do with hastening the coming of the Reign of God.[24] (italics mine)

Peterson here draws into relationship two aspects of Syrian Christianity which were already present in Thomas a generation earlier: asceticism, in the form of wandering radicalism, and eschatology. There are, of course, differences between the apocryphal Acts and the earlier Gospel of Thomas. For example, there is not yet any well developed concept of a world mission in Thomas to proclaim the arrival of the kingdom of God. Nonetheless, what Peterson and Kretchmar have observed about the relationship between asceticism and eschatology is, in my view, crucial for understanding the relationship between actualized eschatology and social radicalism in Thomas. If eschatology is a mythological challenge to the world as it exists, the mythological expression of hope for something better, asceticism offers a real, present challenge to the world. It calls into question the ways of the world, its standards, its goals, its notion of what is meaningful in life. Thomas Christianity's social radicalism, as a form of asceticism, has precisely this effect. It challenges the values of house and home, of financial security. It challenges the convention that "clothes make the person," and that money should be lent, not given away. It challenges conventional piety—prayer and fasting, circumcision, and ritual purity. Through parables it challenges the world's notion of what constitutes sensible business practice, good herding, good fishing. It even calls into question love and devotion to family. Everything that the world of early Christianity has to offer is called into question. This is eschatology demythologized and actualized. Wandering radicalism does not proclaim the (future) *coming* of the kingdom, it brings it directly to the front door. With the knock of the itinerant radical, the old world has already passed away, and the kingdom of God has arrived.[25]

Wandering radicalism provides the social historical coordinates for the theological tendency in Thomas to speak of the kingdom as a present reality whenever the Thomas Christian makes it so. To shine forth, to enable people to see the kingdom in their presence, spread out upon the earth, not to be expected or waited for, but actualized *now*—this is the function of wandering radicalism in Thomas Christianity. It calls the old world into question, thus

24. Peterson, "Einige Beobachtungen," 217–18; as cited by Kretchmar, "Ein Beitrag," 31.
25. Cf. Luke 10:9, 11.

making way for the new world, the presence of the kingdom of God in those who would search within themselves, bring it forth, and find life.

Locating this aspect of Thomas Christianity within the overall development of early Christianity poses problems not encountered with those sayings above, in which Thomas' gnosticizing proclivity could be coordinated with certain problems encountered by wandering radicals in the latter part of the first century. Thomas' actualized eschatology is to be coordinated with the radical lifestyle itself and thus located anywhere along the Thomas trajectory, from its origins in the early Jesus movement, to its outcome in Syrian asceticism. But are there particular moments in the development of early Christianity with which the polemical terms in which this aspect of Thomas' theology might be coordinated?

On one hand, one could argue that such a polemical demythologizing of apocalypticism would represent a way of coping with the failure of apocalyptic expectations—such as one finds, for example, in Mark and Q[2]—to materialize on schedule. It could then be seen as a development parallel to the relativizing of apocalypticism found in in Luke, and thus assigned to the latter part of the first century, when the church began to face this challenge to its apocalyptically dominated conceptuality.

But there is also another option: that this sort of actualized eschatology was part of the Jesus movement from the very beginning. After all, apocalypticism was very common in first-century Palestine and Syria. Early Christianity did not invent apocalypticism, nor was it the first group to hold to such expectations, only to have them disappointed later. John the Baptist's group, for example, had such expectations, if the preaching of John as characterized by the synoptic tradition[26] is any indication of the Baptist's theology. John's followers must have had to come to terms with the failure of his expectations to materialize at least fifty years before Luke was called upon to provide the same service for Christianity near the end of the first century. For surely the failure of something to happen before, or soon after the death of John, would have raised painfully the question whether or not John had been right about the imminence of the cataclysmic day of judgment after all. And if Jesus was in fact baptized by John and thus originally a follower of John, he himself would have had to make a decision on whether or not John had been right. In view of the failure of John's own predictions about the end time, is it possible that Jesus himself could have decided against apocalypticism and opted instead for something like the actualized eschatology one finds in the Gospel of Thomas?

Mark does not portray it so, suggesting that the apocalyptic hopes and expectations that had once been associated with John were rightly transferred to Jesus, for whom John had simply served as precursor (Mark 1:7-8). But this portrayal is not universal in early Christianity. John, for example, also transfers the authority of John the Baptist to Jesus by casting the Baptist in the role of

---

26. Mark 1:4-8; Matt 3:2-12; Luke 3:7-17.

precursor, but he curiously never mentions the apocalyptic aspect of his preaching. There, the Baptist does not foretell the coming day of judgment, but the arrival of the revealer sent from God (John 1:19–34). In this way the fourth evangelist simply dispenses with John's preaching and thus creates a smooth transition from one career to the other (John 1:35–42), without ever having to explain what had been erroneous in John's message.

Perhaps even more important, however, is the voice of Q on this matter. If Kloppenborg is correct in his reconstruction of the redactional history of Q, this branch of the sayings tradition, like Thomas, also did not start from the assumption of an imminent day of apocalyptic judgment. Rather, in its initial phase (Q^1) it presented its logia gathered together into short speeches, which are "controlled . . . by sapiential themes and devices and, notwithstanding several important interpolations, are directed at the Q community in support of its radical mode of existence."[27] Apocalypticism does not make its entry until the later redactional stages of Q (Q^2). The convergence of Thomas and the formative speeches of Q^1 on this point is of critical importance, for it shows that very early on in the Jesus movement, precisely in circles in which a socially radical lifestyle was pursued, there was a break between the apocalyptic preaching of John the Baptist and the socially radical preaching of the Jesus movement.[28] How early did the Jesus movement break with the Baptist on the issue of apocalypticism? Could this break have occurred already in the preaching of Jesus himself? With this question we step beyond the discussion of Thomas Christianity and into another, extremely problematic area of inquiry: the quest of the historical Jesus. To this particular problem we shall turn presently.

Summary

In this chapter I have attempted to show how the social radicalism of Thomas Christianity was related to various strands of Thomas' theology. First, we have seen how the anti-cosmic stance of Gnosticism could have provided the theological framework within which Thomas Christianity strengthened its resolve to continue in its counter-cultural protest. Those whose social radicalism demonstrated their utter rejection of the social world in which they lived might well have found their theological home in the world-condemning strains of Gnosticism. At the same time, Gnosticism's esoteric side could have provided a declining movement of wandering radicals with the leverage they

---

27. Kloppenborg, *Formation*, 171–245; the quote is from 205. The sapiential speeches which Kloppenborg assigns to the formative layer of Q are (cited according to Lukan chapter and verse): 6:20b-49; 9:57–62 + 10:2–16, 21–24; 11:2–4, 9–13; 12: 2–12, 22–34; 13:24–30.

28. In the sapiential speeches of Q's formative layer (Q^1) the subject of John the Baptist's preaching is not broached. Only in Q^2 (Luke 3:7–9//Matt 3:7–10) do we hear anything of John's apocalyptic preaching. In Thomas, John is commented upon only in Thom 46, where he is complimented, but left ultimately in the role of one inferior to the Thomas Christian. The subject of John's preaching is not mentioned.

needed to survive over against an increasingly non-supportive local support network. Finally, I have argued that the rejection of apocalyptic eschatology in favor of the notion that the kingdom might be actualized here and now coordinates well with the social radicalism of this movement. Social radicalism is the attempt to live out of an alternative reality, an alternative dominion. As such, it is the praxis of a theological vision.

The Gospel of Thomas *and the Historical Jesus*

9

Thomas and the Historical Jesus[1] What are the Prospects?

After so much has been said about the place of the Gospel of Thomas in the history of early Christianity, it may seem an awkward move now to shift our focus to a figure whose life predates the Gospel of Thomas by at least forty years: Jesus of Nazareth. Yet it is this person whose sayings the Gospel of Thomas purports to communicate. In fact, much of the initial excitement over the Gospel of Thomas was generated by this claim. Could this new gospel fill in some of the gaps left by the canonical portrayals of Jesus, his life, his preaching? Claims and disclaimers were frequent in the early years of research devoted to Thomas, but as scholars settled down to do the serious work necessary for understanding this text, the focus came to fall ever more on the theology and history of the gospel itself, not the possible revelations it might provide with respect to the historical Jesus. The focus of the present study has for the most part reflected this interest, and rightly so. But the question of the historical Jesus remains, and it is a legitimate question. The fact that many of Thomas' sayings are paralleled independently in the synoptic tradition is enough to show that the traditions Thomas contains are not all the product of the late first century church; many must have a history that extends back into the earliest phase of the Jesus movement. Thus, it is possible that from Thomas we can learn something of the preaching of Jesus himself. The question is how to exploit this possibility effectively. Clearly, a systematic attempt to evaluate all of Thomas' sayings with respect to their plausible attribution to Jesus himself would be a large undertaking, too large for the work at hand. Nonetheless, what follows is a first attempt, however rough, to address this very basic issue. The first part of the chapter will look back over

---

1. A version of this chapter was originally published as "The Gospel of Thomas and the Historical Jesus."

the somewhat meagre role the Gospel of Thomas has played in the Jesus debate since its publication (in translation) in 1958, to the present, in order to summon whatever gains have been made, upon which one might now build. The second part of the chapter will attempt to look ahead to the ways in which adding the Thomas witness to the Jesus debate may help to shape that discussion in the future.

Thomas and the Quest of the Historical Jesus

1. Thomas and the New Quest

When one considers the impact that the Gospel of Thomas might have made on that movement of German and American scholars who took up anew the question of the historical Jesus during the 1950s and 60s, it should be recalled that although the Gospel of Thomas was discovered along with the rest of the Nag Hammadi Library in 1945, due to various (some less than edifying) adventures[2] it was not actually published until 1957, and then only in a rough photographic edition[3] Leipoldt's translation into German in the following year made the text generally available[4] and the Brill critical edition with text and translation appeared only in 1959.[5] These delays, perhaps not serious when compared to the much more vexing problems experienced in the publication of another great manuscript find of the same year, the Qumran scrolls, were nonetheless costly. For it was in 1953, at a now famous meeting of the "Old Marburgers" at Jugenheim, West Germany, that Ernst Käsemann delivered his lecture "Das Problem des historischen Jesus,"[6] thus launching what would soon become known as the "New Quest of the Historical Jesus."[7] The New Quest began where the last quest left off, viz., with the assumption that the gospels as we have them are not historical accounts, but products of the early Christian preaching about Jesus. If there is anything in them upon which to base a discussion of the historical Jesus, it would only be individual sayings or perhaps isolated historical reminiscences that could be separated from the later settings into which they had been cast in the service of the early Christian kerygma. This meant that in the New Quest, the *sayings* of Jesus would be of the utmost importance as the new discussion took shape.

---

2. For an account of the discovery and the subsequent fate of the Nag Hammadi Library see Robinson, "Discovery of the Nag Hammadi Codices," and "Getting the Nag Hammadi Library into English."

3. Labib, *Coptic Gnostic Papyri.*

4. Leipoldt, "Ein neues Evangelium."

5. Guillaumont, et al., *The Gospel According to Thomas,* published simultaneously in Dutch, German, and French.

6. The lecture was published in 1954 as an essay by the same title in *Zeitschrift für Theologie und Kirche* and made available to American audiences in Käsemann's translated essays, *Essays on New Testament Themes,* 15–47.

7. The standard account of this movement is that of Robinson, *New Quest.*

How exciting it would have been for a new source of sayings—without the encumbrance of a secondary biographical framework—to have been placed on the table just as the new discussion was getting started. But by 1959 it was too late. Most of the "New Questers" had by this time made their definitive contributions to the discussion.[8] But even the relative late-comers, such as Gerhard Ebeling (1962)[9] and Herbert Braun (1969),[10] apparently did not consider the Gospel of Thomas relevant to their views.

There were perhaps several reasons for this. One is no doubt the fact that much of the early work on Thomas tended to have a rather conservative ring to it. When one looks at those who argued early on for Thomas as an independent tradition, not a one was part of the post-Bultmannian movement. By 1961 the only Bultmannian to have entered into the discussion was Ernst Haenchen, and he argued that Thomas was a later gnostic interpretation of the gospel tradition, whose more original kerygmatic cast had already been set in the canonical gospels.[11]

A second reason may also be related to Haenchen's work. Haenchen recognized that in Thomas one finds a quite different kerygma, a different proclamation from that which we have in the canonical gospels. When one recalls that the New Quest was pursued not simply by an analysis of the sayings tradition, but rather by asking whether the claims of the early Christian kerygma were somehow anticipated in Jesus' own teaching as reflected in the sayings tradition, the problem comes clearly into view. The realization that Thomas, with its own kerygmatic claims, represents a tradition that is both independent of, and roughly contemporaneous with the canonical gospels would have meant the recognition that early Christian claims about Jesus were quite multiple and diverse. If this were true, then the entire question posed by the New Quest would have to be rephrased: how might Jesus himself have anticipated the claims of *various early Christian kerygmata*. Eventually such a program emerged from out of the Bultmannian camp with Helmut Koester's influential article of 1965, "GNOMAI DIAPHOROI." But by the time Koester had figured out how the Gospel of Thomas might properly impact the New Quest, the New Quest was all but over.

2. Thomas and the "Third Quest"

After a long hiatus, during which a number of advances have served to reopen the exploration of the gospels as theological literature, including redac-

---

8. Among the better known "New Questers" one should recall that Günther Bornkamm's book *Jesus von Nazareth* was published in 1956; Hans Conzelmann's famous article "Jesus Christus," was published in the 3rd edition of *RGG*, which appeared in 1959; Ernst Fuchs' studies, which were published together in 1960 in his *Zur Frage nach dem historischen Jesus*, were all originally published or conceived in 1959, really too late to take much cognizance of the newly discovered gospel.

9. Ebeling, *Theologie und Verkündigung*.

10. Braun, *Jesus—Der Man aus Nazareth*.

11. Haenchen, *Die Botschaft*.

tion criticism and the newer literary criticism, recent years have once again brought about a resurgence of interest in the question of who Jesus was in history.[12] The 1980's saw the publication of several new monographs on the subject, such that some have begun now to speak of yet another distinct phase in the quest for the historical Jesus, a so-called "Third Quest."[13] But even though the Gospel of Thomas has been readily available now for over twenty years, a fast perusal of these latest contributions to the Jesus discussion yields scarcely a word on how it may (or may not) be relevant to the question as it is now being posed.

Given the very high quality of many of these newest contributions, it is unlikely that their silence on the matter of Thomas is simply the result of oversight. And while some of these "Third Questers" will no doubt have excluded the Thomas material as a result of lingering doubts over the question of whether Thomas does indeed represent a tradition independent from that which comes down to us via the synoptic gospels, the reason for its omission may ultimately lie once again in the manner in which the question has been posed. Unlike the "New Questers," who tended to concentrate on the *sayings* of Jesus to the exclusion any events alleged to have effected the course of Jesus' life, the "Third Questers" have tended to reverse this trend. E. P. Sanders is typical of this new breed—broadly skeptical of the results of the New Quest in its attempt to arrive at a core of authentic sayings of Jesus, upon which a plausible reconstruction might be based, and eager to ground their studies in certain "almost indisputable facts" about Jesus' life, such as his association with John the Baptist, or his crucifixion at the hands of the Roman authorities.[14] Without passing judgment on the relative worth of either approach, it need only be pointed out that this new emphasis on significant events in Jesus' life will leave the Gospel of Thomas, which contains almost nothing of biographical significance, languishing on the side-lines.

3. Taking Thomas Seriously

Yet even though the Gospel of Thomas, for one reason or another, has not played a significant role in either the New Quest or the so-called Third Quest, it has not been left out of the discussion altogether. Over the years a number of studies have carefully been laying the methodological and substantive ground work for incorporating Thomas into the mainstream of the debate. Not long after the discovery of the new gospel, several studies appeared which attempted to take seriously the proposition that Thomas, if indeed represen-

12. See Borg, "Renaissance."
13. Among these "Third Questers" may be named Ben Meyer (*The Aims of Jesus*), A. E. Harvey (*Jesus and the Constraints of History*), Marcus Borg (*Conflict, Holiness and Politics in the Teachings of Jesus* and more recently *Jesus: A New Vision*), E. P. Sanders (*Jesus and Judaism*), Richard Horsley (*Jesus and the Spiral of Violence*), and Sean Freyne (*Galilee, Jesus, and the Gospels*) among others.
14. Sanders' "facts" are to be found in *Jesus and Judaism*, 11.

tative of an autonomous tradition of Jesus' sayings, might actually provide historians with worthwhile primary data for discussing who Jesus was.

Gilles Quispel, of course, must be mentioned as the first to do this. Already in his 1957 article in *Vigiliae Christianae* Quispel argued that Thomas drew its synoptic-like sayings not from the canonical Gospels, but from the now lost Gospel of the Hebrews, "nothing else than the Gospel used by the descendents of the primitive Christian community of Jerusalem."[15] And if this is the case, argued Quispel, then the close similarity of these sayings to their synoptic counterparts allows us to

> . . . see clearly that the almost nihilistic skepticism of certain "Histories of the Synoptic Tradition" about the authenticity of the words attributed to Jesus in our Scripture has not such solid foundations as it claims to have. In this sense the Gospel of Thomas confirms the trustworthiness of the Bible.[16]

While few today would accept Quispel's thesis regarding Thomas' relationship to the lost Gospel of the Hebrews,[17] his assertion that Thomas represents an autonomous tradition has received wide assent.[18] However, his assessment of that datum relative to the quest of the historical Jesus is, of course, highly dubious. To be sure, viewing Thomas as an independent tradition does mean that many sayings found in both Thomas and the synoptic gospels may now be seen to enjoy independent multiple attestation within the tradition. But while independent multiple attestation may serve to locate a saying relatively early in the history of the tradition, it in no way guarantees that the saying comes from Jesus. Moreover, it is difficult to see how such parallels could be so construed as to guarantee the reliability of the entire tradition. Such claims fail to consider the broader significance of form and redaction criticism for our understanding of the nature of the tradition.

In any event, Quispel's proposal is important for two reasons. First, the highly polemical nature of his tone over against the Bultmannians may help to explain why the "New Questers" were reluctant to do much with Thomas. Scholarship too has its political dimension, and Thomas was claimed early on for the conservative backlash against the form-critical school. Secondly, the remarks quoted above suggest a motive for Quispel's work that became typical for the early attempts to work Thomas into the Jesus debate. Thomas was not incorporated into the debate with the expectation that its evidence would alter or adjust the view of Jesus already provided by the canonical gospels; rather, early interest was sparked by the way in which Thomas might serve to confirm that view.

This was true, for example, of the work of Johannes Bauer.[19] Bauer, who

15. Quispel, "The Gospel of Thomas and the New Testament," 5.
16. Quispel, "The Gospel of Thomas and the New Testament," 16.
17. See the thorough refutation by Haenchen, "Literatur," 3–4.
18. An account of the scholarly debate on this issue is to be found in Fallon and Cameron, "The Gospel of Thomas," 4213–24. For my own position, see Part I of this study.
19. J.-B. Bauer, "Echte Jesusworte."

accepted Quispel's thesis regarding the sources for Thomas' sayings, carried out a more extensive evaluation of the Thomas tradition, asking which of its sayings might be considered "authentic" sayings of Jesus. While Bauer includes in his study a number of sayings which have no synoptic parallels, the basis of his evaluation is consistently whether or not a given saying may be seen to agree in its thrust or intention with material found in the synoptic tradition. For each saying he regards as authentic, Bauer proposes an interpretive context, that is, a plausible setting in the (synoptic) life of Jesus, in which one might imagine Jesus saying such a thing. In this way he argues that many of these sayings could well have come from the preaching of Jesus.[20] In the end, however, his method rather foreordains that the Gospel of Thomas will not substantively change the view we already had of Jesus based upon the synoptic tradition alone.

R. McL. Wilson's highly regarded study,[21] while more comprehensive in scope than that of Bauer, proceeds on precisely the same terms laid down by Bauer. Wilson writes:

> Of the possibility that some of these sayings may be authentic words of Jesus, not much may yet be said. It depends upon our ability to trace back a regular line of connection. If we have here no more than Gnostic composition based upon our Gospels, authenticity for any of these sayings is practically out of the question; if, on the other hand, it becomes possible to isolate with confidence an element of genuine early tradition, then the sayings within this section must have a claim to consideration. One important criterion here has already been used by Bauer, namely, that it should be possible to fit such sayings into the context of the life of Jesus.[22]

As may be expected, Wilson's study did not produce any revolutionary disclosures. In the end only a handful of sayings from Thomas manage to survive the *Sitz im Leben Jesu* criterion in Wilson's work, and these tend to have synoptic parallels.[23]

A turning point in the discussion, in my view, is marked by the sixth edition of Joachim Jeremias' classic, *Die Gleichnisse Jesu*, published in 1962, which included into its revised framework all of the parables found in Thomas. Jeremias' work is distinguished by the fact that here for the first time a major form-critical study of the Jesus tradition makes extensive use of the Gospel of Thomas as a tool for piecing together the history of the transmission of this material, and ultimately for assembling what Jeremias takes to be the original proclamation of Jesus. Often Jeremias judges the Thomas version of a parable

20. In Bauer's analysis Thom 82, 81, 58, 51, 52 are allowed the possibility of authenticity; 53 and 102 are ruled out. The parables of the kingdom in Thomas (Thom 20, 57, 76, 96, 97, 98, 107) are held to be gnostic or gnostic adaptations of their more authentic synoptic parallels.
21. Wilson, *Studies.*
22. Wilson, *Studies,* 151.
23. Cf. Wilson's remarks on Thom 31 (*Studies,* 60), 32 (p. 61), 39 (p. 75–76), 102 (p. 76–77), 45 (p. 77), and 47 (p. 77–79).

to be more original than its synoptic counterpart. He frequently contrasts the simpler Thomas parable to the synoptic version to illustrate the tendency of the synoptic tradition to embellish, allegorize, to incorporate allusions to the Septuagint and other popular lore, and other secondary features. Of course, Thomas' parables themselves also frequently exhibit their own secondary features of like manner, thus confirming the notion that such secondary features characterized the development of the oral tradition generally speaking, not just the synoptic tradition alone.[24] When in the end Jeremias summarily draws together the proclamation of Jesus as expressed in the parables, the parables from Thomas play no small role. Thomas' version of the Great Supper (Thom 64) and the Parable of the Tenants (Thom 65), for example, illustrate God's mercy for sinners.[25] Thomas' version of the Parable of the Leaven (Thom 96) and the Parable of the Mustard Seed (Thom 20) illustrate Jesus' assurance and unwavering trust in God.[26] Material from Thomas is used generously throughout this section of Jeremias' book, thus leaving the impression that the Thomas material had played a major role in shaping the outcome of this study. In reality, however, although Jeremias was pioneering in his readiness to make use of Thomas, especially to re-write the tradition history of the parables, in the final analysis the incorporation of the Thomas evidence did not really have much of an effect on his reading of the Jesus tradition. There is very little difference between the Fifth Edition of his book, without the Thomas evidence, and the Sixth Edition, which includes it. The Thomas material was simply analyzed and slipped into the various categories at which Jeremias had already arrived from a study of the synoptic evidence alone.

What Jeremias accomplished with the parables tradition was attempted by his student, Norman Perrin, with respect to the tradition of Jesus' sayings as a whole. The resulting study, *Rediscovering the Teaching of Jesus*, has become standard in the field. Like his *Doktorvater* before him, Perrin also takes care to note the relevance of the Gospel of Thomas to the discussion of Jesus' teaching. Upon laying down the arguments for viewing Thomas as an independent tradition, Perrin concludes:

> This may not justify the absolute claim that Thomas is independent of the canonical synoptic tradition, but it certainly justifies the acceptance of this as a working hypothesis, and hence the use of Thomas material, where relevant, in addition to the canonical material in an attempt to reconstruct the history of the tradition and to arrive at the earliest form of the saying or parable.[27]

Perrin here seems to be fully prepared to give Thomas due consideration in his

---

24. Cf. Montefiore, "A Comparison."
25. Jeremias, *Gleichnisse Jesu*, 128.
26. Jeremias, *Gleichnisse Jesu*, 145–49, 152.
27. Perrin, *Rediscovering*, 37.

work. And indeed, on at least two occasions Perrin draws upon the Thomas version of a parable to help underscore a point.[28]

But as with Jeremias, one wonders how much the material incorporated from the Gospel of Thomas has really been allowed to help shape Perrin's conclusions about the teaching of Jesus. This may be illustrated from pp. 68–74 of *Rediscovering the Teaching of Jesus*, where Perrin makes extensive use of Thom 3 and 113 alongside Luke 17:20–21 in building a case for viewing Jesus' preaching as fundamentally prophetic rather than apocalyptic. However, the conclusions he draws in this section of the book are precisely those at which he had arrived already in his Göttingen dissertation several years earlier, there relying solely on an analysis of Luke 17:20–21 with little regard for the Thomas parallels.[29] At another crucial juncture Perrin fails to notice the significance of Thomas' evidence for his thesis altogether. In chapter 4 on "Jesus and the Future," Perrin argues that none of the apocalyptic Son of Man sayings may be attributed correctly to Jesus; all derive from the later preaching of the early church.[30] On this score it would have been of greatest significance to his thesis had Perrin noticed that in Thomas, an autonomous witness to the Jesus' sayings tradition, the apocalyptic image of the Son of Man does not occur at all.[31] If this indicates, as Koester would suggest in an article published just one year later,[32] that there existed an early stage in the development of the tradition in which such speculation had not yet occurred, Thomas as a whole confirms Perrin's position that the appropriation of this apocalyptic image was relatively late.

However tentative these two early attempts to bring Thomas into the discussion may have been, they are nonetheless very important for having laid the ground work for those who would come later. They make it clear that so long as one proposes to focus upon Jesus' sayings as the route by which one might approach the quest for the historical Jesus, Thomas' independent witness to the sayings tradition cannot be ignored. Their efforts have born fruit, for example, in more recent treatments of the parables tradition. John Dominic Crossan has been particularly diligent in insisting on the value of Thomas parallels to synoptic texts for reconstructing the tradition-historical process; Crossan makes extensive use of Thomas both in his book on parables,[33] and in his later work on the aphorisms attributed to Jesus.[34] However, it is still

---

28. In his section entitled "Recognition and Response" Perrin notes the originality of Thom 64 (*Rediscovering*, 111–113), and uses it to build his case. So also Thom 98 (pp. 126–27). Thom 9 figures well in his section on "Confidence in God's Future" (pp. 155–56).

29. Perrin, *The Kingdom of God*, 174–78. POxy 654.3 is mentioned here, but dismissed as "foreign to the teaching of Jesus" (176).

30. Perrin, *Kingdom of God*, 197–98.

31. The use of Son of Man in Thom 86 is not titular, but generic; so Koester, "One Jesus," 170–71 (esp. n. 34).

32. Koester, "One Jesus," 170–72. This essay was originally published in 1968 in the *Harvard Theological Review*.

33. Crossan, *In Parables*.

34. Crossan, *In Fragments*.

unclear how in the end Thomas' material will affect Crossan's answer to the question "Who was Jesus?" These two books are actually preliminary tradition-historical work; his statement on Jesus has only just appeared.[35] James Breech may also be mentioned as one who has made use of the Thomas material,[36] as well as the very recent work by Bernard Brandon Scott.[37] Both use Thomas' parables in particular for doing the work of tradition-historical analysis. Without passing judgment on the results of either of these significant pieces of work, suffice it to say that their honest attempts to work through these issues contribute further to the legacy upon which we can now build.

Sifting the Tradition

One will have noticed that among the chief methodological concerns raised throughout the review offered above is that the Gospel of Thomas not be viewed simply as an ancillary source to be mined for material that tends only to confirm various positions on the question of who Jesus was already arrived at using the synoptic tradition. The tendency to do this is understandable. For even though most modern scholars have come to realize (through the work of Wrede, Schmidt, Bultmann and others) that the synoptic gospels are in no way to be seen as biographies of Jesus, there has nonetheless grown up around them a kind of normative status for the historian. While John "spiritualized" the gospel, and Paul recast it in the form of the "syncretistic" Christ cult, the synoptics alone were seen to have retained at least some contact with the historical person of Jesus, perhaps because they place so much emphasis upon his sayings and parables, long considered the bedrock of the tradition, and thus the most promising material for the purposes of the historian. However flawed the synoptics may be as pure history, their view of Jesus as an apocalyptic preacher with a mission to Israel, who thought of himself as a Messiah and reflected upon the significance of his inevitable death, has held a rather firm grip on scholarship at least since the days of Schweitzer. But the Gospel of Thomas, building upon that same bedrock of tradition, presents us with a view of Jesus that is quite different. And while it would be equally erroneous now to elevate Thomas' Jesus to the position once reserved for the Jesus of the synoptic gospels, having another view at our disposal does give us a way of placing the synoptic Jesus in critical relief. Thomas and the synoptic gospels, in a sense, represent two diverging trajectories moving out and away from a common beginning in an early Jesus movement grounded in the legacy of Jesus' sayings, or words (λόγοι). By using Thomas and the synoptic gospels to play these two trajectories off one against the other, it may be possible to catch at least a glimpse of that common beginning, extremely important for understanding who Jesus was, even while at the same time arriving at a greater

35. Crossan, *The Historical Jesus*. Regretably, Crossan's results are not incorporated here.
36. Breech, *The Silence of Jesus*.
37. Scott, *Hear Then the Parable*.

appreciation of the theological effort to understand the significance of Jesus that was underway in each of these trajectories. In the following rough sketch of the prospects for how Thomas may ultimately come to re-shape our view of who Jesus was in history, this sort of tradition-historical work forms a basic point of departure.

1. Jesus According to Thomas

Beginning with the Thomas trajectory, a good deal may already be said about its tendencies. Chief among them is Thomas' gnosticizing proclivity, or at the very least its tendency to esotericize the sayings tradition. This, of course, was one of the results of Robinson's seminal article on the early Christian sayings tradition, "LOGOI SOPHON." Using the self-designation "sayings" (λόγοι) as a means of tracing the development of the literary genre to which the early Christian sayings collections Q and the Gospel of Thomas belong, Robinson demonstrated how over time the genre itself became the preferred vehicle for interpreting the sayings of Jesus as the words of a gnostic redeemer, a process whose end point is marked by such early Christian gnostic works as Thomas the Contender and Pistis Sophia.

Thomas, to be sure, is not a full blown gnostic gospel entirely comparable to a work like Thomas the Contender, but one may see in many of Thomas' sayings the tendency to cast Jesus in the role of the descending/ascending redeemer mythos, so important to the gnostic interpretation of Jesus. In Thom 28, for example, Jesus speaks as the redeemer who has come from God, only to find the objects of his efforts unable to respond, a theme typical of the redeemer myth:

> Jesus said, "I took my stand in the midst of the world, and in the flesh I appeared to them. I found them all drunk, and I did not find any of them thirsty. My soul ached for the children of humanity, because they are blind in their hearts and do not see, for they came into the world empty, and they also seek to depart from the world empty. But now they are drunk. When they shake off their wine, then they will repent."

The task of the redeemer in gnostic lore is to descend to earth and tell the "children of humanity" of their true origin in a world, an aeon, far beyond the present evil world, wherein dwells the one true God, an alien in distant remove from the world. Their plight is their loss of memory, their stupification which prevents them from re-ascending to the realm of their origin.[38] In chapter 8 we have already had recourse to look once at Thom 49–50, also crucial for understanding Thomas' brand of gnostic theology. Here Jesus speaks the message of the redeemer, reminding the lost souls of their identity as the chosen, and providing them with the passwords that will enable them to re-ascend to their place or origin:[39]

---

38. The classic account, still unsurpassed, is that of Jonas, *The Gnostic Religion.*
39. So Haenchen, *Die Botschaft,* 39–41, 44.

49 ¹Jesus said, "Blessed are those who are alone and chosen, for you will find the kingdom. ²For you have come from it, and you will return there again." 50 ¹Jesus said, "If they say to you, 'Where have you come from?' say to them, 'We have come from the light, from the place where the light came into being by itself, established [itself], and appeared in their image.' ²If they say to you, 'Is it you?' say, 'We are its children, and we are the chosen of the living Father.' ³If they ask you, 'What is the evidence of your Father in you?' say to them, 'It is motion and rest.'"

Davies has objected to the characterization of the Gospel of Thomas as "gnostic," arguing instead that it be seen as falling within the tradition of Jewish wisdom speculation, such as one finds, for example, in Philo of Alexandria.[40] Thomas' Jesus is not a gnostic redeemer, according to Davies, but an incarnation of Sophia. Davies, of course, is partially correct. He is justified, for example, in locating Thomas within the tradition of Jewish wisdom. As Robinson has shown, the early Christian practice of collecting Jesus' sayings continues the Jewish tradition of collecting words of wisdom, such as one finds in Proverbs 1–8, Wisdom of Solomon, etc.[41] He is also correct in pointing out that Thomas is not a full-blown gnostic gospel, complete with their typically intricate descriptions of the cosmos, the origin of the world, and other features common to later gnostic tractates. But neither is Thomas simply a book of Jewish wisdom speculation. Coptic words which might render the Greek words σόφος/σοφία (wise/wisdom) occur only four times in Thomas,[42] and only once with reference to Jesus (and this in error!).[43] Its words are not wise words so much as they are "secret words."[44] Rather, what we have in Thomas is a book which stands between the wisdom collection on the one hand, and the gnostic revelation dialogue, in which the redeemer reveals to his followers secret words of knowledge (γνῶσις)[45] on the other. It therefore helps to document that very important, though murky point of modulation between Jewish wisdom (and other Near Eastern traditions which make use of the descending/ascending redeemer mythos) and Gnosticism.

In any event, Gnosticism seems to provide the most likely theological framework within which to understand the esotericizing trend one finds throughout Thomas. It may be seen in a number of sayings unique to Thomas, whose meaning has become almost entirely opaque.[46] But more importantly, it can be seen in the manner in which Thomas treats a number of sayings known also from the synoptic tradition.[47] Thus, if one uses the synoptic tradition to

---

40. Davies, *The Gospel of Thomas,* 18–61.
41. Robinson, "LOGOI SOPHON," esp. 103–111.
42. ⲡⲙⲛ̄ϩⲏⲧ: Thom 8:1, 2; 13:3; ⲥⲁⲃⲉ: Thom 76:2.
43. ⲣⲙⲛ̄ϩⲏⲧ: Thom 13:3.
44. Recall that the *incipit* to the Gospel of Thomas reads: "These are the secret sayings (ⲛ̄ϣⲁϫⲉ ⲉⲑⲏⲡ) that the living Jesus spoke and Didymos Judas Thomas recorded."
45. Note that this word too is relatively rare in Thomas. It occurs only in Thom 39:1.
46. E.g., Thom 7, 11, 15, 18, 37, 60, 67, 83, 84, and 88.
47. E.g., Thom 2 and 92 (cf. Matt 7:8); Thom 3 (cf. Luke 17:20–21, Q [?]); Thom 11 (cf. Mark 13:31, par.); Thom 22 (cf. Mark 10:13–16); Thom 68–69a (cf. Matt 5:10–12//Luke 6:22–

throw the Thomas trajectory into critical relief, one discovers that its own tendency is to esotericize the traditions about Jesus.[48] This is unique to Thomas,[49] and thus may be isolated to the interpretive effort going on within the Thomas trajectory. Jesus himself probably did not preach in such terms.

2. Jesus According to the Synoptics

We may now reverse this procedure, using Thomas as a means of throwing the synoptic trajectory into critical relief. In this part of the work the parables provide a particularly fruitful point of departure for two reasons. First, since the work of Jülicher, it has long been generally recognized that there is a tendency within the tradition for parables to be transformed secondarily into allegories in the interpretive work of the early church. Most of the parables were not originally intended as allegories. Second, while the tendency to allegorize appears to have been prominent in the synoptic trajectory, in the Thomas trajectory, for whatever reason, this was not the case.[50] Therefore, one relatively easy way to begin to isolate the interpretive effort underway in the synoptic trajectory is simply to hold its allegorized versions of the parables up against their non-allegorized Thomas counterparts.

The Parable of the Tenants (Matt 21:33-46; Mark 12:1-12; Luke 20:9-19; Thom 65) is a good place to begin, since there are versions of it in all three of the synoptic gospels (Matthew and Luke presumably having taken the parable from their common source Mark) as well as in the Gospel of Thomas. I will presuppose here what I have argued for already in treating this parable in Chapter 2 of this study: 1) that Thomas represents an attestation to the parable that is essentially independent from that found in the synoptic gospels; 2) that Thomas' version is not an allegory, but a parable properly speaking; and 3) that the allegorization of this parable in Mark, and its further development in Matthew and Luke, are all secondary features.[51] The important thing to notice for the present study is the theological direction in which the allegorization of the parable has taken it. Mark 12:1-12 is no longer a parable about absentee landlords and rebellious tenants, but an allegory about the death of Jesus. It ends on a note of foreboding, anticipating the avenging judgment of God that is to come. Matthew and Luke, while customizing the parable to the nuances of their own social, political, and theological situations, do not stray from this basic understanding of the story as an allegory for Jesus' death and the impending divine judgment. None of this, of course, is present in the Thomas

---

23, Q); Thom 101 (cf. Matt 10:37-39//Luke 14:26-27, Q). Many of these sayings have been addressed already in chapter 8.

48. One should perhaps exercise caution against overstating this point. One does well to heed the warning of Grobel ("How Gnostic is the Gospel of Thomas?"), and more recently Davies (*The Gospel of Thomas, passim*) not to read too much into these sayings when a gnostic interpretation is not altogether obvious.

49. That is, over against the synoptic tradition. Thomas, of course, shares this tendency to some degree with John.

50. So Montefiore, "A Comparison," 335-38.

51. See chapter 2, pp. 48-51.

version of the parable; it is limited to the allegorical interpretation found only in the synoptic trajectory, and thus to be isolated there.

The interpretive problem posed by Jesus' death and the question of the coming judgment assert themselves through allegorization of the tradition in the case of another parable as well, the Parable of the Great Supper, attested in both Matthew and Luke (Matt 22:1-14//Luke 14:15-24; Q), and independently in Thomas (Thom 64).[52] Of these, the most thoroughly allegorized version is that found in Matthew. Added here are the references to killing the king's servants (vs 6), and the king's subsequent vengeance for that killing (vs 7). Both of these hearken back to the Parable of the Tenants, which in Matthew occurs not long before the Great Supper. The resulting scheme no doubt insinuates allegorically that the destruction of Jerusalem is to be viewed as God's judgment against Israel, whom Matthew sees as responsible for the death of Jesus. Finally, the consummation of judgment is intimated in Matthew's final addition to the parable (vss 11-14), in which the king arrives at the banquet, only to punish those spur-of-the-moment guests caught without a wedding garment. Their fate is that of all who fall under God's final judgment in Matthew: they are cast "into the outer darkness; there they will weep and gnash their teeth" (vs 13b).

None of these elements are present in Luke. Luke does see the parable as an allegory, viz., for the Messianic banquet to be enjoyed in the kingdom of God. But he effects an allegorical reading not by altering the internal structure of the parable, but rather by introducing the parable with his vs 15. The parable itself probably remains much as Luke found it in his source, Q.[53] Neither are these features to be found in Thomas. The interpretation of the parable found in Thomas' version is no doubt also secondary, but it is asserted without serious distortion of the parabolic structure by simply adding a line to the end: "Buyers and merchants [will] not enter the places of my Father." (Thom 64:12)[54] The parable itself shows no particular signs of allegorization. Thus, if one assumes that Thomas (without 64:12) and Q (roughly Luke 14:16-24) represent the gist of the parable in its original form, again one may clearly observe a distinct synoptic tendency to introduce into the tradition reflection upon the death of Jesus and the impending judgment of God.

That this is particularly characteristic of Matthew may be seen again in yet a third parable, the Parable of the Fisher, of which both Matthew (13:47-50) and Thomas (Thom 8) preserve an exemplar. The original *topos* is no doubt very old, as the similar story from Aesop clearly suggests.[55] But that both Matthew and Thomas stem from a common early Christian parable based

---

52. See chapter 2, pp. 77-78.

53. For Luke's version and its close relationship to Q see the summary discussion in Schulz, *Q*, 391-98.

54. Whether a Thomas redactor has added this comment or whether it has been attached to the parable in the process of oral transmission is difficult to say. Cameron ("parable and Interpretation," 16-19) argues for the latter. For our purposes this is of little consequence; it is at any rate to be isolated to the Thomas trajectory.

55. Aesop, Fable 4 (Perry, *Babrius and Phaedrus*, 9-10).

upon it, is shown by the similar way in which both of our examples twist the focus of the story. In Aesop the focus is on the fish in the catch—the big ones are caught while the little ones escape through the holes in the net. The moral of the story is clear: with greatness comes risk. In Matthew and Thomas, however, the focus is not on the fish, but on the fisher, and what the fisher does once the catch is in hand. Yet within the early Christian sample our two exemplars are themselves quite different. In Thom 8 we encounter a fisher who makes a most unusual choice: he throws all (ⲧⲏⲣⲟⲩ) the small fish back, only to keep a single large fish. While this may be good advice when fishing the local farm pond, a professional fisher would not last long using this technique. It is puzzling, a parable, and the final phrase invites one to reflect upon its depth: "Whoever has ears to hear should hear" (8:4). In Matthew, however, the story is no puzzle. Instead Matthew has created from it an allegory for the final judgment. Just as the fisher sorts out the good fish from the bad,

> So will it be at the close of the age. The angels will come out and separate the evil from the righteous, and throw them into the furnace of fire; there people will weep and gnash their teeth.
>
> Matt 13:49–50

That this sort of reflection on the death of Jesus and the impending judgment that is to come can be isolated consistently to the synoptic trajectory should not be surprising. A cursory comparison of Thomas and the synoptics might have indicated as much. It is not at all insignificant that the synoptic gospels have preserved the sayings tradition only by embedding it in a biographical framework that presents Jesus as the suffering martyr marching slowly and deliberately to his death on a cross. Martin Kähler's dictum that the Gospel of Mark is nothing other than "a passion narrative with an extended introduction" has not yet outlived its usefulness.[56] And just before the climactic events unfold, Jesus delivers his final discourse, a prophetic speech of foreboding doom for the world that has not accepted his words (Mark 13:3–37, par.; cf. Matt 24:23–28, 37–42//Luke 17:22–37, Q).

Thomas, of course has none of this. There is no apocalyptic scenario,[57] and Thomas seems scarcely aware of the tradition in which Jesus' death had become the focal point of theological reflection.[58] Moreover, the highly nu-

---

56. Kähler, *The So-Called Historical Jesus*, 80, n. 11.

57. One must be careful not to read into Thomas a note of apocalypticism based upon sayings whose synoptic parallels are given an apocalyptic interpretation in the canonical tradition. For example Thom 103 (cf. Matt 24:43–44//Luke 12:39–40, Q) simply advocates vigilance, not necessarily watchfulness in anticipation of the coming Son of Man. Thom 57 is a parable about the good winning out in the end, not an allegory for the last judgment (cf. Matt 13:24–30). Similar caution should be exercised in reading Thom 21:9; 10; 40; and 91.

58. There are three possible references to the death of Jesus in Thomas: Thom 66, 104:3, and 55. The first two are probably secondary additions to the original text of Thomas (see chapter 2, pp. 48–51 [for Thom 66], and 80–81 [for Thom 104:3]). If the reference to the cross

anced understanding of the early stages of the synoptic tradition that has begun to emerge in more recent years suggests that these elements did not always dominate the synoptic trajectory either. Of particular importance in this regard is Kloppenborg's influential study of the redaction of Q.[59] Just as we have already seen that Thomas and Q[1] agree in opting for a non-apocalyptic interpretation of Jesus preaching,[60] so also now it is to be noticed that neither Thomas nor Q[1] seem to be much interested in Jesus' death. It is, at any rate, not a primary point of departure in their respective theological orientations. The convergence of Thomas and Q[1] on these points is very important, for it helps us clearly to locate reflection upon the death of Jesus and the use of apocalyptic scenarios in the sayings tradition to the synoptic trajectory alone, and to its later stages at that. It is becoming ever more difficult to imagine a Jesus who reflected upon his own death, and preached an imminent apocalyptic judgment to be visited upon the world.

3. Common Ground

Having peeled away those elements which may be isolated to the interpretive effort underway in the Thomas trajectory on the one hand, and the synoptic trajectory on the other, what is left in the sayings tradition that does not stand out in critical relief when the two trajectories are compared? What is left that forms a kind of common ground out of which both trajectories would likely have proceeded? To isolate this common ground of material is an essential step toward understanding the preaching of Jesus, for it is this common ground which stands the best chance of holding a more or less direct connection to the preaching of Jesus himself. The prospects depend upon the degree to which elements within this core can be freed from the early Christian urge to reformulate traditional material to kerygmatic ends. This will require an effort far beyond the scope or capacity of the present study; nonetheless, something may be learned already from a cursory overview of the material at hand. Within this mass of remaining material, three prominent corpora stand out: a) a large number of wisdom sayings; and b) a large number of sayings of various forms which seem to advocate an attitude of social radicalism; and c) the parables.

a) Wisdom Sayings

The sayings themselves do not require extensive comment. Much is indicated by a simple listing of the wisdom sayings which occur in both trajectories.

---

in Thom 55 is original, then this may be the sole reference to the death of Jesus in the entire document. Yet even here it may be possible to understand the cross simply as a metaphor for discipleship.

59. Kloppenborg, *Formation.*

60. See pp. 212–13.

Wisdom Sayings in the Common Tradition

Thom	Matt	Mark	Luke
2:1	7:7		11:9 (Q)
4:2	19:30; 20:16	10:31	13:30
5:2	10:26	4:22	8:17; 12:2 (Q/Mark)
6:5–6	10:26	4:22	8:17; 12:2 (Q/Mark)
26	7:3–5		6:41–42 (Q)
31	13:57	6:4	4:24
32	5:14b		
33:2–3	5:15	4:21	11:33; 8:16 (Q/MK)
34	15:14		6:39 (Q)
35	12:29	3:27	11:21f. (Q/Mark)
39:3	10:16b		
41	13:12; 25:29	4:25	8:18b; 19:26 (Q/Mark)
45:1	7:16b		6:44b (Q)
45:2–3	12:35		6:45a (Q)
45:4	12:34b		6:45b (Q)
47:2	6:24		16:13 (Q)
47:5	9:16–17	2:21–22	5:36–39
62:2	6:3		
89	23:25–26		11:39–41 (Q)
92:1	7:7		11:9 (Q)
93	7:6		
94	7:7		11:9 (Q)

This list could perhaps be expanded (for example, I have not included beat-itudes, woes, or parables) or adjusted in other ways,[61] but the point to be made here will not suffer from minor changes. Jesus scholars, especially those influenced by the New Quest, have been reluctant in the past to attribute such sayings to Jesus or ascribe to them much historical value. The criterion of dissimilarity all but guarantees that sayings of such an ordinary sort will fall by the wayside in the quest for what is distinctive about Jesus. But when one notices just how many wisdom sayings are paralleled in Thomas and either Q or Mark—that is, in the earliest common sayings tradition which we can with certainty identify—it becomes ever more difficult to deny the historical implications of this datum. While we will never be able to say with certainty that Jesus in fact uttered this or that particular wisdom saying, the fact that the earliest Christian voice we hear recollects a Jesus who made ample use of common wisdom warrants serious consideration of the hypothesis that Jesus was a wisdom teacher, and that the early Jesus movement thought of itself as a kind of wisdom school.

Such beginnings could account for much within the diversity of earliest Christianity. The emergence of a document like that which Kloppenborg has

---

61. Cf. Koester's list in "One Jesus," 179–80.

proposed for the first edition of Q (Q¹), a collection of wisdom speeches, would be readily explicable. The modulation of this into the more apocalyptic orientation of later synoptic Christianity could then be followed forward via the second redaction of Q (Q²), as proposed by Kloppenborg,[62] and on into Matthew, which successfully combines wisdom mythology with apocalypticism.[63] The martyrological themes surrounding the death of Jesus tradition such as one finds in the Gospel of Mark could be grounded in reflection upon the wisdom motif of the death of the righteous sage, using the "genre" of the persecuted righteous one traced by George Nickelsburg through Genesis 37–50, Wisdom 2–5, and ultimately through Mark's passion narrative.[64] By moving the wisdom mode of discourse in a more speculative direction, one could account, on the one hand, for the wisdom-oriented opponents of Paul reprimanded in 1 Corinthians,[65] and on the other, for the emergence of the descending/ascending revealer Christology that comes to predominate later in the Gospel of Thomas and in John. Such developments need not be thought of as particularly late, but could well have begun to take shape quite early on. Something of this wisdom oriented reflection upon the person of Jesus is to be seen already in Thom 17, a saying whose antiquity is assured by its independent multiple attestation in Q (Matt 13:16–17//Luke 10:23–24), 1 Cor 2:9, DialSav 140.1–4, as well as in many other sources of later date.[66]

b) Social Radicalism

But while much of the wisdom tradition tends toward the conservative and conventional, on the whole this could not be said to characterize this early layer of the sayings tradition. For alongside all of this wisdom material is a large amount of commonly held material that is extremely *unconventional.* Among these sayings we find the many legal sayings and community rules used in chapter 5 to reconstruct the social history of Thomas Christianity. Such sayings are widely paralleled throughout the Jesus tradition and they form perhaps the most distinctive group of sayings in this common ground of material from which both the Thomas and synoptic trajectories emerge.

Among these one finds the well known lament about homelessness:

"[Foxes have] their dens and birds have their nests, but the child of humanity[67] has no place to lay his head and rest."

---

62. Kloppenborg, *Formation,* 102–170.
63. For wisdom in Matthew see Suggs, *Wisdom, Christology, and Law.*
64. Nickelsburg, "Genre and Function."
65. For this interpretation of the Corinthian opponents see Dupont, *Gnosis,* 172–80; Pearson, *PNEUMATIKOS-PSYCHIKOS Terminology,* 11–12, 17–21; and Horsley, "PNEU-MATIKOS vs. PSYCHIKOS."
66. Helmut Koester posits an early Christian sayings collection from which all four of these early versions of the saying might ultimately derive (*Ancient Christian Gospels,* 55–62). If Koester is correct, this is one of the earliest kerygmatic claims associated with Jesus' person. For a complete list of the later manifestations of this saying see Stone and Strugnell, *The Books of Elijah,* 42–73.
67. This is Meyer's (in Kloppenborg, et al., *Q-Thomas Reader,* 149) rendering of ⲡϣⲏⲣⲉ

Cited here in its Thomas version (Thom 86), there is, of course, a close parallel in Q (Matt 8:20//Luke 9:58). As I have argued in Chapter 5, this is closely related to the injunction to leave house and home, and abandon family ties and responsibilities in order to become part of the Jesus movement (Thom 55 and 101:1–2, par. Matt 10:37–39//Luke 14:26–27, Q).[68] The saying decrying the rejection of local prophets (Thom 31, par. Matt 13:57//Mark 6:4// Luke 4:24) is probably also be related to this radical ethos. One who rejects home and family could certainly have expected equally harsh treatment from the local community which he or she had abandoned.[69]

Thomas and Q share in their advocacy of the lifestyle of the wandering beggar. The tradition preserved in Thom 14:4 (par. Luke 10:8–9, Q) perhaps best reflects its practical dimensions:

Thom 14:4
When you go into any country and walk from place to place, when the people receive you, eat what they serve you and care for[70] the sick among them.

Luke 10:8–9
Whenever you enter a town and they receive you, eat what is set before you; heal the sick in it, and say to them, 'The kingdom of God has come near to you.'

Utterly destitute, the wise sage is called upon to dispose of his or her money (Thom 95, par. Matt 5:42//Luke 6:34–35a, Q), and to take no care for such necessities as clothing (Thom 36 [Coptic], par. Matt 6:25–33//Luke 12:22–30, Q) or food (Thom 69:2, par. Matt 5:6//Luke 6:21a, Q). Their poverty is to be a sign of blessing (Thom 54, par. Matt 5:3//Luke 6:20b, Q).

Another aspect of the social radicalism encountered at the base of the sayings tradition has to do with traditional standards of purity. This, too, has already been discussed with respect to the Thomas tradition in Chapter 5. Two of these sayings are related to dietary practices. In Thom 89 (par. Matt 23:25–26//Luke 11:39–41, Q) the notion of washing to maintain ritual purity is ridiculed using the figure of washing a cup: is it not more important to have a cup that is clean on the inside than one which is clean only on the outside? In Thom 14, cited above, the injunction to eat whatever is placed before you is followed by another saying from the common tradition:

ⲙ̄ⲡⲣⲱⲙⲉ ("Son of Man"). The term here is not titular, but refers to the plight of homelessness common in Jesus' day (cf. n. 31; also ch. 5, pp. 133–34).

68. Cf. also Thom 99, par. Matt 12:46–50//Mark 3:31–35//Luke 8:19–21; and Thom 16, par. Matt 10:34–36//Luke 12:51–53, Q.

69. So Theissen, Sociology, 12.

70. The Coptic here simply transliterates θεραπεύειν from the Greek original. It is usually translated "to heal," but in the broader sense the term may mean simply to give care to the sick (LSJ, s.v. θεραπεύω). The point is that these instructions are real; they do not presuppose a nostalgic look back to an idealized past when apostles could perform such miracles as healing the sick.

For what goes into your mouth will not defile you; rather, it is what comes out of your mouth that will defile you.

Thom 14:5

Mark 7:15 (par. Matt 5:11) provides a close parallel:

There is nothing outside a person which by going in can defile; but the things which come out of a person are what defile.

Thus dietary laws regulating purity are abrogated. Finally, it is arguable that the general indictment of the Pharisees and scribes found in Thom 39:1-2 (par. Matt 23:13//Luke 11:52, Q) is also related in some way to this radical position over against purity:

Thom 39:1-2

Jesus said, "The Pharisees and the scribes have taken the keys of knowledge and have hidden them. They have not entered, nor have they allowed those who want to enter to do so."

Matt 23:13

"But woe to you,, scribes and Pharisees, hypocrites! for you lock the kingdom of Heaven away from people; for you neither enter yourselves, nor allow those who are trying to enter to go in."

Luke 11:52

"Woe to you lawyers! for you have taken away the key of knowledge; you yourselves did not enter, and you prevented those who were trying to enter."

One can only guess about the actual content of the criticism here, but if one associates these groups with the law and its interpretation, one could plausibly argue that it has something to do with the sayings tradition's radical position on purity laws.

Finally, there is a group of sayings which seem generally to promote an attitude of social, possibly even political subversion. One of these is Thom 10 (par. Luke 12:49, Q[71]):

Thom 10

Jesus said, "I have set a[72] fire upon the world, and behold, I am guarding it until it blazes."

Luke 12:49

I have come to bring fire upon the earth; and how I wish that it were already kindled.

Outside of the context of the apocalyptically oriented synoptic trajectory this

---

71. For Luke 12:49 as deriving from Q see Arens, ΗΛΘΟΝ-*Sayings*, 68–69; Ernst, *Das Evangelium nach Lukas*, 412; März, "Feuer auf die Erde," 481–485.

72. Meyer (in Kloppenborg, et al., *Q-Thomas Reader*, 10) translates "cast." The Coptic is ΝΟΥϪΕ, which translates the Greek βάλλειν; but the latter may mean simply "place" or "put," not necessarily "throw" (*LSJ*, *s.v.* Βάλλω*). The latter seems more appropriate here.

need not be seen as an apocalyptic image.[73] But it is a threatening image. Fire was a threat in the ancient world, whether in an urban environment, where large disastrous fires were notorious, or in the countryside, where an enemy or pillaging army could destroy the year's crop without warning. Jesus as arsonist—a subversive image indeed!

More overtly political is the saying preserved in Thom 100 (par. Matt 22:15–22//Mark 12:13–17//Luke 20:20–26):

Thom 100
They showed Jesus a gold coin and said to him, "Caesar's people demand taxes from us." He said to them, "Give Caesar the things that are Caesar's, give God the things that are God's, *and give me what is mine.*"

Mark 12:13–17
And they came and said to him, . . . "Is it lawful to pay taxes to Caesar, or not?" . . . And he said to them, "Whose likeness and inscription is this?" And they said to him, "Caesar's." Jesus said to them, "Render to Caesar the things that are Caesar's, and to God the things that are God's."

It is generally recognized that the final phrase in Thom 100 (italics) represents the editorial work of Thomas,[74] but exactly to what end, remains a question. Since the present focus is on the common tradition, not on Thomas alone, no attempt will be made to settle that matter here. With respect to the rest of the saying, paralleled closely in the Markan version and its derivatives, it is enough to point out how much recent studies have exposed as erroneous a reading of this chreia which bows to the modern notion of the separate but compatible realms of politics and religion. In a first century Palestinian context, God and Caesar were not viewed as compatible options, but strongly competing loyalties; there is little question that the claim of God is absolute, and the more compelling of the two claims presented.[75] The surreptitious message here is subversive indeed: Caesar receives nothing.

A somewhat more enigmatic saying is to be found in Thom 71:

Jesus said, "I shall destroy [this] house, and no one will be able to build it [. . .]."

If the saying intends, as do its parallels (Matt 26:61; 27:40//Mark 14:58; 15:29; Matt 24:2//Mark 13:2//Luke 21:6), to refer to the Temple, then the common tradition could be said to take on the Temple system, with all of the social, political, and religious ramifications of such a stance.[76] If it does not, there may be other possibilities, depending on how one wishes to understand "house" here. There were various "houses" in first century Palestine. The king's house, for example, the house of David, now occupied by an illegitimate Herodian "house," seems, in my view, not to be out of the question.

73. Only in Q may the saying be understood apocalyptically; see Patterson, "Fire and Dissension," 134–35.
74. See the treatment of this saying and its parallels in chapter 2, pp. 68–69.
75. For such a reading see, e.g., Horsley, *Jesus and the Spiral of Violence,* 306–17.
76. For a detailed exposition see Theissen, "Die Templeweissagung Jesu."

Such an enigmatic saying could well have had profoundly threatening political overtones.[77] Such a reading is complimented by Thom 78 (par. Matt 11:7-9//Luke 7:24-26, Q), with its biting critique of kingship. The saying is essentially, of course, the opposite of the popular adage "clothes make the person." But it is significant that the saying chooses "rulers" or "kings" as the rule-breaking example: "They are dressed in soft clothing, and cannot understand truth." The politically subversive qualities of the saying are readily transparent.[78] It reminds one of the sort of witty criticism of kingship heard among Cynics of the period, which tended to earn them the ire of the emperor and periodic expulsion from Rome.[79]

To these sayings perhaps others can be added, including those which occur only in Thomas or Q or Mark, but which cohere well with this group. However, those collected above serve adequately to make the point: the earliest sayings tradition common to both Thomas and the synoptics is neither conservative nor conventional. Its attitudes toward family life, toward money and property, toward piety, and toward political life are all quite radical. Its ethos may be described as social radicalism.

Such an ethos at the base of the common tradition could also account for much of what one finds spread throughout early Christianity in all of its diverse forms. Whether one speaks of Paul, for whom the present evil age is coming to a rapid end, or Mark and Kloppenborg's second edition of Q, both of which view the world as an evil place, worthy only of apocalyptic destruction, or John, whose community has come to know the "hatred" of the world (John 15:18-16:4), a place hostile to it and its claims about Jesus, or Thomas, for whom the world is but a corpse to be overcome and left behind (Thom 56)—all of these various early Christian interpretations of the gospel hold in common the basic conviction that the kerygma brings them fundamentally into conflict with the world. While their preaching becomes ever more charged with the mythic language of apocalypticism or Gnosticism, all of these early Christian groups maintain a basic existential hostility to their social world, whose first manifestation may well have been the social radicalism sketched out above. In any event, with such a strong element of social radicalism at the very core of the sayings tradition, alongside the notion of Jesus as wisdom teacher one must also be ready to entertain the hypothesis that Jesus offered in his preaching a strong dose of radical social criticism.

c) Parables

The third grouping consists of the several parables shared in common by both trajectories of the sayings tradition.

77. Cf. the discussion in chapter 5, pp. 149-50.
78. Again, cf. the discussion in chapter 5, p. 150.
79. Cf. Diogenes Laertius 2.25; Lucian, *Dem.* 41; Epictetus, *Disc.* 1.24.7; Ps.-Crates 23; Lucian, *Perig.* 17-19. That emperors regarded such critique as a serious threat is indicated by the fact that Nero, Vespaian, and Domitian all expelled the philosophers from Rome when their criticism became too censorious; see Dudley, *History of Cynicism*, 125-42, and Toynbee, "Dictators and Philosophers," 43-58.

Parables of the Common Tradition

	Thom	Matt	Mark	Luke
The Fisher	8	13:47-50		
The Sower	9	13:3-9	4:2-9	8:4-8
The Mustard Seed	20	13:31-32	4:30-32	13:18-19
The Weeds	57	13:24-30		
The Rich Farmer	63			12:16-21
The Great Supper	64	22:1-14		14:15-24 (Q)
The Tenants	65	21:33-41	12:1-9	20:9-16
The Pearl	76	13:45-46		
The Leaven	96	13:33		13:20-21 (Q)
The Shepherd	107	18:12-14		15:3-7 (Q)
The Treasure	109	13:44		

Owing to the very important role parables have traditionally played in research on the preaching of Jesus, it is here among this list that the most work needs to be done. The task is threefold: 1) to reconstruct the gist of each parable's earliest narrative form using the tools of tradition-historical analysis; 2) to arrive at a reading of each as a parable apart from the secondary narrative and allegorical features attaching to many; and 3) to offer an interpretation of them that coheres not with the secondary (synoptic or Thomas) context in which they are presently found, but with the basic core of common material we have been able to identify thus far. This, of course, is a large undertaking. For the present, I will simply offer a few suggestions about where such analysis might lead.

First, it is to be noted that not all of these parables are parables of the kingdom. In particular, the Rich Farmer, the Great Supper, and the Tenants were probably not so designed.[80] They are, rather, parables of social criticism—parables of the world. The Rich Farmer (Thom 57; Matt 13:24-30) is transparently so: it is a parable about the foolishness of a life based on the acquisition of wealth. The Great Supper (Thom 64; Matt 22:1-14//Luke 14:15-24, Q) is also rather obvious in its social critique. It is a parable designed to undermine and overturn the normal worldly assumptions about privilege and class. When the host is stood up, and suffers shame at the hands of his peers, he refuses to bear this humiliation, but turns instead to those who had previously been to him "outsiders." By this reversal he demonstrates how possible it is to live without regard for the social reinforcement of class and protocol. The Tenants (Thom 65; Matt 21:33-41//Mark 12:1-9//Luke 20:9-16), though perhaps more complex in its criticism, may also be understood in terms of its radical social critique. If the original narrative ended, as it does in Thomas, with the murder of the owner's son, then the parable can be seen as a

---

80. Of the three, only the Great Supper was ever treated as such, and this only in Matthew, where the parable has become an allegory for the coming apocalyptic kingdom.

radical criticism of the economically exploitive system of absentee land ownership. In the end the owner receives for his reward only the loss of his investment, and the death of his son. For their part, the tenants are given but two equally poor choices: either to suffer under the exploitive arrangement of tenancy or to use violence and suffer the risks and shame that would inevitably come with such drastic measures. In neither case do they truly emerge as winners. There are no winners in this parable; all ultimately fall victim to a poor and unjust economic arrangement. The social critique of property and its acquisition is very thorough.

As for the remainder of this list, most are parables of the kingdom.[81] Yet four of these may also be read in terms of their socially radical stance over against the world insofar as their parabolic depiction of the kingdom tends to focus on characters who are themselves counter-cultural. The Parable of the Shepherd Thom 107; Matt 18:12–14//Luke 15:3–7, Q) has as its focus a foolish herder who leaves ninety-nine sheep unattended in the wilderness while he searches for a single stray.[82] His love for the lost makes him careless with the flock—the kingdom is like that. In the Parable of the Pearl (Thom 76; Matt 13:45–46) a merchant has a going-out-of-business sale in order to buy a single pearl, a bauble, for himself. His infatuation with the beauty of what he has discovered leads him to cash in his livelihood—the kingdom is like that. The Fisher is a fool (Thom 8; Matt 13:47–50). He throws back the entire catch for the sake of the single prize fish.[83] His infatuation with the largest allows him to abandon the day's work back into the sea—the kingdom is like that. The Parable of the Treasure (Thom 109; Matt 13:44) also may be grouped with these parables of foolishness.[84] According to Jewish law (*b. B. Mes.* 118a) the prevailing rule here is "finders keepers." So long as the laborer was hired simply to work the field, and so long as the treasure does not have an owner (if the land owner was willing to sell the field we may presume that he was ignorant of the treasure, and therefore not its rightful owner) the laborer in this story is allowed to keep the treasure as his own.[85] The laborer could have claimed the treasure simply by virtue of his having found it; he did not have to go so far as to buy the entire field. Yet that is what he does. In his excitement he rushes out, sells everything, and buys the land. He "overdoes it." The kingdom is like that.

In the workaday world of shrewd economics, of scraping by, of making ends

---

81. The only exception is the Parable of the Sower.

82. Most commentators have noted the irresponsibility of the shepherd; see Scott, *Hear Then the Parable*, 415, for a representative discussion.

83. Presuming that these two parables in fact derive from a common origin (a point often disputed; see, e.g., Hunzinger, "Unbekannte Gleichnisse," 217) Thom 8 gives us the closest approximation of the original narrative. It is, at any rate, preferable to Matthew's allegory for the final judgment (see chapter 2, pp. 72–73).

84. I would follow Jeremias (*Gleichnisse Jesu*, 28–29) in supposing that the Thomas version has been reshaped along the lines of the Rabbinic story from *Midr. Cant. Rab.* 4.12.1. The Matthean version likely comes closer to the original parabolic narrative.

85. See Crossan, *Finding is the First Act*, 91; also Scott, *Hear Then the Parable*, 398–400.

meet, these characters are fools. Their enthusiasm for a surprising discovery, their exuberance for the find, quickly overrides any common sense response that the world has to recommend. By the world's standards, the kingdom is pure foolishness. Yet by the same measure, if one accepts the odd wisdom of this parabolic world, is not the real world with its enthusiasms of buying and selling, herding and fishing, finding, saving, and investing now exposed as foolishness in truth? In this sense these parables may all be grounded in social critique.

Two of the kingdom parables may be seen as counter-cultural in another sense: the Parable of the Mustard Seed (Thom 20; Matt 13:31–32//Mark 4:30–32//Luke 13:18–19) and the Parable of the Leaven (Thom 96; Matt 13:33//Luke 13:20–21, Q). Both liken the kingdom to objects of loathing and nuisance. So prolific[86] was mustard that it was forbidden even to plant it in one's garden, lest it threaten to take over the entire area.[87] One should call this the Parable of the Mustard *Weed*, rather than the Mustard Seed.[88] And yet that is what the kingdom is like: it grows from the smallest of seeds to become the most loathsome of weeds. Leaven is similarly tinged. Within the context of Jewish and hellenistic culture alike it is a element of corruption.[89] "In the view of all antiquity, Semitic and non-Semitic, panary fermentation represented a process of corruption and putrefaction in the mass of dough."[90] Even within the New Testament it is used metaphorically to connote base desire and evil intent.[91] This parable's use of it is particularly insidious: in each version the leaven is "hidden"(!) in the flour. Pity the baker who suddenly discovers the "process of corruption and putrefaction" ruining the dough so carefully mixed. A small thing can be a very large nuisance. Such is the kingdom.

These are provocative images. They suggest a kingdom that is threatening, impure in the world of things clean and unclean. It is small, yet insidious, and impossible to control once it has been implanted. It stands to take over, to invade, to change the way things are. The kingdom that is mustard, the kingdom that is leaven: this is a subversive kingdom. Yet it is a kingdom which seems assured of success. This seems to me to be the gist of the Wheat and the Weeds and the Parable of the Sower. Though hampered by weedy beginnings, in the end the harvest of the kingdom will win out—so says the parable of the Wheat and the Weeds (Thom 57; Matt 13:24–30).[92] In the Parable of the

---

86. See Pliny, *Nat. Hist.*, 19.170.

87. See Jeremias, *Gleichnisse Jesu*, 22, n. 3.

88. For this reading of the parable see Oakman, *Jesus and the Economic Questions of His Day*, 123–28, esp. 127: "It is hard to escape the conclusion that Jesus deliberately likens the rule of God to a weed."

89. Windisch, "Ζυμή, ζυμόω, ἄζυμος," 903–6; see also the summary discussion in Scott, *"Hear Then the Parable,"* 374–75.

90. Kennedy, "Leaven," 2754, as cited by Scott, *Hear Then the Parable*, 324.

91. Cf. Matt 16:6//Mark 8:15//Luke 12:1; 1 Cor 5:6–8.

92. As pointed out above, outside of the apocalyptic context of the synoptic gospels the image here employed need not necessarily be seen as apocalyptic.

Sower (Thom 9; Matt 13:3–9//Mark 4:2–9//Luke 8:4–8) it matters not that the sower throws the seed willy nilly on the paths, the rocks, the bad soil as well as the good. In the end, the yield is still a "hundredfold."[93] This preaching of the kingdom is brash and bold; it proclaims its own destiny of triumph.

Whether this rough and ready reading of the parables will stand up to more rigorous analysis remains to be seen. But I have tried, at least in a preliminary way, to provide a reading that finds its cogency within the social radicalism of the early sayings tradition common to both the synoptic and Thomas trajectories. If it is this common tradition which has the best chance of holding a direct connection to the preaching of Jesus, the parables will also have to be drawn into this web in some coherent way.

Summary

In this chapter I have tried to sketch out in rough lines the way in which the Gospel of Thomas has made an impact on the study of the historical Jesus, and how we can expect its evidence to contribute to the discussion in the future. While work to date has tended to make use of Thomas only when it could be seen to confirm what is already suspected about Jesus on the basis of canonical materials, such a limited approach does not tap the full potential of the Gospel of Thomas for the question of the historical Jesus. Thus, I have tried to lay out what I think is a more reasonable way of proceeding, together with the results of my own initial plumbs into the sayings tradition. By playing Thomas and the synoptic tradition off one against the other, I have argued that it is possible to arrive at a very early stratum in the sayings tradition, which stands the best chance of preserving some continuity with the preaching of Jesus. Within that common tradition are a number of wisdom sayings, and a large corpus of sayings whose ethos may be described roughly as social radicalism. Several parables comprise a third corpus within that early common tradition. They too may be read in terms of the cultural criticism offered by the socially radical aphoristic tradition. Whether my own hunches presented here will ultimately bear fruit remains to be seen. Much more work lies ahead. But at least for this much I would stake a rather firm claim: no new quest of the historical Jesus can proceed now without giving due attention to the Thomas tradition. As an independent reading of the Jesus tradition, it provides us with a crucial and indispensable tool for gaining critical distance on the synoptic tradition, which has so long dominated the Jesus discussion.

---

93. Or even one hundred and twenty-fold(!), if the Thomas version is not pure embellishment.

Works Cited

A. Adam. "Erwägungen zur Herkunft der Didache." *ZKG* 68 (1957) 1–47.

E. Arens. *The* ΗΛΘΟΝ *Sayings in the Synoptic Tradition.* Orbis Biblicus et Orientalis 10. Freiburg: Universitätsverlag/Göttingen: Vandenhoeck & Ruprecht, 1976.

H. Attridge. *"The Greek Fragments."* Pp. 95–128 in B. Layton, ed. *Nag Hammadi Codex II.*

———. "The Original Text of Gos. Thom., Saying 30." *BASP* 16 (1979) 153–57.

J.-P. Audet. *La Didachè. Instructions des apôtres.* Paris: Libraire Lecoffre, 1958.

T. Baarda. "Jesus said, Be Passers-by. On the meaning and origin of Logion 42 of the Gospel of Thomas." Pp. 179–205 in idem. *Early Transmission of Words of Jesus: Thomas, Tatian, and the Text of the New Testament.* Amsterdam: VU Boek-handel/Uitgeverij, 1983.

———. "Luke 12, 13–14: Text and Transmission from Marcion to Augustine." Pp. 105–62 in J. Neusner, ed. *Christianity, Judaism and Other Greco-Roman Cults: Studies for Morton Smith at Sixty; Part One: New Testament.* Leiden: Brill, 1975.

E. Baasland. "Der Jakobusbrief als Neutestamentliche Weisheitsschrift." *StTh* 36 (1982) 119–139.

A. Baker. "Early Syriac Asceticism." *DR* 88 (1970) 393–409.

———. "'Fasting to the World.'" *JBL* 84 (1965) 291–94.

———. "Syriac and the Origins of Monasticism." *DR* 86 (1968) 342–53.

G. Barth. "Matthew's Interpretation of the Law." Pp. 58–164 in G. Bornkamm, G. Barth, and H. J. Held. *Tradition and Interpretation in Matthew.* New Testament Library. London: SCM, 1963.

J.-B. Bauer. "Das milde Joch und die Ruhe, Matth. 11, 20–30." *TZ* 17 (1961) 99–106.

———. "Echte Jesusworte." Pp. 108–50 in W. C. van Unnik. *Evangelien aus dem Nilsand.* Frankfurt: Verlag Heinrich Scheffer, 1960.

W. Bauer. *Rechtgläubigkeit und Ketzerei im ältesten Christentum.* BHT 10. Tübingen: Mohr (Siebeck), 1934. ET: *Orthodoxy and Heresy in Earliest Christianity.* Trans. by a team from the Philadelphia Seminar on Christian Origins; Robert Kraft and Gerhard Krodel, eds. Philadelphia: Fortress, 1971.

F. W. Beare. *The Gospel According to Matthew.* San Francisco: Harper and Row, 1981.

K. Berger. "Zur Diskussion über die Herkunft von I Kor. 11.9." *NTS* 24 (1977/78) 271–83.

H. D. Betz. "The Logion of the Easy Yoke and of Rest (Mt 11:28–30)." *JBL* 86 (1967) 10–24.

————. *Essays on the Sermon on the Mount.* Philadelphia: Fortress, 1985.

J. N. Birdsall. "Luke XII.16ff. and the Gospel of Thomas." *JTS* 13 (1962) 332–36.

C. L. Blomberg. "Tradition and Redaction in the Parables of the Gospel of Thomas." Pp. 177–205 in D. Wenham, ed. *Gospel Perspectives 5: The Jesus Tradition Outside the Gospels.* Sheffield: JSOT Press, 1984.

M. Borg. *Conflict, Holiness and Politics in the Teachings of Jesus.* New York: E. Mellon Press, 1984.

————. *Jesus: A New Vision.* San Francisco: Harper and Row, 1988.

————. "A Renaissance in Jesus Studies." *Theology Today* (October, 1988) 280–92.

G. Bornkamm. *Jesus von Nazareth.* Stuttgart: Kohlhammer, 1956.

H. Braun. *Jesus—Der Man aus Nazareth und seine Zeit.* Stuttgart: Kreuz, 1969.

J. Breech. *The Silence of Jesus.* Philadelphia: Fortress, 1983.

J. P. Brown. "An Early Revision of the Gospel of Mark." *JBL* 78 (1959) 215–27.

R. Bultmann. *Die Geschichte der synoptischen Tradition.* 9th Edition. Göttingen: Vandenhoek & Ruprecht, 1979.

————. *Die Geschichte der synoptischen Tradition: Ergänzungsheft.* 5th Edition. Gerd Theissen and Philipp Vielhauer, eds. Göttingen: Vandenhoeck & Ruprecht, 1979.

————. *The Gospel of John: A Commentary.* Trans. by G. R. Beasley-Murray, et al. Philadelphia: Fortress, 1971.

————. *The Johannine Epistles.* Trans. by Philip O'Hara, et al.; Robert Funk, ed. Philadelphia: Fortress, 1973.

W. Bussmann. *Synoptische Studien.* Vol. 2: *Zur Redenquelle.* Halle (Saale): Buchhandlung des Waisenhauses, 1929.

A. T. Cadoux. *The Parables of Jesus.* London: James Clark, 1931.

R. Cameron. *The Other Gospels: Non-Canonical Gospel Texts.* Philadelphia: Westminster, 1982.

————. "Parable and Interpretation in the Gospel of Thomas." *Foundations and Facets Forum* 2,2 (1986) 3–34.

————. *Sayings Traditions in the Apocryphon of James.* HTS 34. Philadelphia: Fortress, 1984.

————. "'What Have You Come Out to See?' Characterization of John and Jesus in the Gospels." Pp. 35–69 in idem. *Semeia 49: The Apocryphal Gospels and Christian Origins.* Atlanta: Scholars Press, 1990.

H. von Campenhausen. *Ecclesiastical Authority and Spiritual Power in the Church of the First Three Centuries.* Trans. by J. A. Baker. London: Adam and Charles Black, 1969.

E. Castelli. "Virginity and its Meaning for Women's Sexuality in Early Christianity." *Journal of Feminist Studies in Religion* 2 (1986) 61–88.

L. Cerfaux and G. Garitte. "Les paraboles du Royaume dans L'Évangile de Thomas." *Muséon* 70 (1957) 307–27.

H. Chadwick. *The Sentences of Sextus: A Contribution to the History of Christian Ethics.* Cambridge: Cambridge University Press, 1959.

B. Chilton. "The Gospel According to Thomas as a Source of Jesus' Teaching." Pp. 155-75 in D. Wenham, ed. *Gospel Perspectives 5: The Jesus Tradition Outside the Gospels*. Sheffield: JSOT Press, 1984.

A. Cohen. *Midrash Rabbah*. London: Soncino, 1938.

H. Conzelmann. *1 Corinthians: A Commentary on the First Epistle to the Corinthians*. Trans. by James W. Leitch; George MacRae, ed. Philadelphia: Fortress, 1975.

_____. *The Theology of St. Luke*. Trans. by Geoffrey Buswell. Philadelphia: Fortress, 1982.

J. D. Crossan. *Finding is the First Act*. Semeia Supplements. Philadelphia: Fortress/Missoula: Scholars Press, 1979.

_____. *Four Other Gospels: Shadows on the Contours of Canon*. Sonoma, CA: Polebridge Press, 1992.

_____. *In Fragments: The Aphorisms of Jesus*. San Francisco: Harper and Row, 1983.

_____. *The Historical Jesus: The Life of a Mediterranean Jewish Peasant*. San Francisco: HarperCollins, 1991.

_____. *In Parables: The Challenge of the Historical Jesus*. Sonoma, CA: Polebridge Press, 1992.

_____. "The Parable of the Wicked Husbandmen." *JBL* 90 (1971) 251-65.

_____. "The Seed Parables of Jesus." *JBL* 92 (1973) 244-66.

W. E. Crum. *A Coptic Dictionary*. Oxford: at the Clarendon Press, 1939.

O. Cullmann. "Das Thomasevangelium und die Frage nach dem Alter in ihm enthaltenen Tradition." *TLZ* 85 (1960) 321-34.

S. Davies. *The Gospel of Thomas and Christian Wisdom*. New York: Seabury, 1983.

B. Dehandschutter. "L'Évangile de Thomas comme collection de paroles de Jésus." Pp. 507-15 in J. Delobel, ed. *Logia: Les Paroles de Jésus—The Sayings of Jesus* (Mémorial Joseph Coppens). BETL 59. Leuven: Uitgeverij Peeters/Leuven University Press, 1982.

_____. "The Gospel of Thomas and the Synoptics: The Status Quaestionis." Pp. 157-60 in E. A. Livingstone, ed. *StEv* 7. TU 126. Berlin: Akademie-Verlag, 1982.

_____. "La parabole de vignerons homicides (Mc XII, 1-12)" Pp. 203-219 in M. Sabbe, ed. *L'évangile selon Marc, Tradition et rédaction*. BETL 34. Leuven: Leuven University Press, 1974.

_____. "Les paraboles de l'Évangile selon Thomas: La Parabole du Trèsor caché (log. 109)." *EThL* 47 (1971) 199-219.

M. Devisch. "La relation entre l'évangile de Marc et le document Q." Pp. 59-91 in M. Sabbe, ed. *L'évangile selon Marc, Tradition et rédaction*. BETL 34. Leuven: Leuven University Press, 1974.

M. Dibelius. *Die Formgeschichte des Evangeliums*. 6th Edition. Günter Bornkamm, ed. Tübingen: Mohr (Siebeck) 1971.

_____. *James: A Commentary on the Epistle of James*. 11th ed., revised by Heinrich Greeven. Trans. by Michael A. Williams; Helmut Koester, ed. Philadelphia: Fortress, 1975.

C. H. Dodd. *The Johannine Epistles*. 2nd ed. London/New York: Harper & Brothers, 1947.

_____. *The Parables of the Kingdom*. London: Nisbet, 1936.

P. Donfried. "Ecclesiastical Authority in 2-3 John." Pp. 325-33 in M. de Jonge, ed. *L'Évangile de Jean. Sources, rédaction, théologie*. BETL 44. Leuven: University Press, 1977.

J. Doresse. *Les livres secrets des gnostiques d'Egypt.* Vol. II: *L'Évangile selon Thomas ou les paroles secrètes Jésus.* Paris: Libraire Plon, 1965.

D. R. Dudley. *A History of Cynicism.* London: Methuen, 1937.

J. Dupont. *Gnosis: La connaissance religieuse dans les épitres de Saint Paul.* Paris: Gabalda, 1949.

G. Ebeling. *Theologie und Verkündigung.* Tübingen: Mohr (Siebeck), 1962.

B. Ehlers (Aland). "Kann das Thomasevangelium aus Edessa stammen." *NovT* 12 (1970) 284–317.

J. Ernst. *Das Evangelium nach Lukas.* Regensburger Neuestestament 3. Regensburg: Pustet, 1977.

F. T. Fallon and R. Cameron. "The Gospel of Thomas: A Forschungsbericht and Analysis." Pp. 4213–24 in W. Haase and W. Temporini. *ANRW* II 25.6. Berlin/ New York: De Gruyter, 1988.

J. A. Fitzmyer. "The Oxyphynchus LOGOI of Jesus and the Coptic Gospel According to Thomas." Pp. 355–433 in idem, *Essays on the Semitic Background of the New Testament.* SBLSBS 5. Missoula: Scholars Press, 1974.

R. Fortna. *The Fourth Gospel and Its Predecessor: From Narrative Source to Present Gospel.* Philadelphia: Fortress, 1988.

H. Freedman and M. Simon, eds. *Midrash Rabbah: Song of Songs.* London: Soncino Press, 1939.

S. Freyne. *Galilee, Jesus, and the Gospels: Literary Approaches and Historical Investigations.* Philadelphia: Fortress, 1988.

E. Fuchs. *Zur Frage nach dem historischen Jesus. Gesammelte Aufsätze* (vol. 2). Tübingen: Mohr (Siebeck), 1960.

R. Funk. *New Gospel Parallels.* Philadelphia: Fortress, 1985.

B. Gärtner. *The Theology of the Gospel of Thomas.* Trans. by E. J. Sharpe. London: Collins/New York: Harper, 1961.

G. Garitte. "Le premier volume de l'edition photographique des manuscrits gnostiques Coptes et l' Évangile de Thomas." *Muséon* 70 (1957) 60–73.

L. Ginzberg. *The Legends of the Jews.* Philadelphia: The Jewish Publication Society of America, 1909.

S. Giversen. *Thomasevangeliet. Indledung, ag Kommentarer.* København: G.E.C. Gad, 1959.

T. F. Glasson. "The Gospel of Thomas 3, and Deuteronomy xxx, 11–14." *ExpT* 78 (1976–77) 151–52.

J. Gnilka. *Das Evangelium nach Markus* (2 vols.). EKK 2. Zürich: Benzinger Verlag/Neukirchen-Vluyn: Neukirchener Verlag, 1978.

J. Goldin. *The Fathers According to Rabbi Nathan.* New Haven: Yale University Press, 1955.

L. Goldmann. "Die Soziologie der Literatur." In J. Bark, ed. *Literatur-soziologie.* Stuttgart: Kohlhammer, 1974.

R. M. Grant. "Notes on the Gospel of Thomas." *VC* 13 (1959) 170–80.

R. M. Grant and D. N. Freedman. *The Secret Sayings of Jesus.* (With an English Translation of the Gospel of Thomas by William R. Schoedel.) Garden City: Doubleday/London: Collins, 1960.

B. P. Grenfell and A. S. Hunt. ΛΟΓΙΑ ΙΗΣΟΥ: *Sayings of Our Lord.* London: Henry Frowde, 1897.

———. *The Oxyphynchus Papyri, Part 1.* London: Egypt Exploration Fund, 1898.

K. Grobel. "How Gnostic is the Gospel of Thomas?" *NTS* 8 (1961/62) 367-73.

A. Guillaumont. "Semitismes dans les logia de Jésus retrouvés Nag-Hammadi." *Journal Asiatique* 246 (1958) 113-23.

A. Guillaumont, H.-Ch. Puech, G. Quispel, W. C. Till, Y. 'Abd al Masih. *The Gospel According to Thomas: Coptic Text Established and Translated.* Leiden: Brill/London: Collins/New York: Harper, 1959; published simultaneously in Dutch (Leiden: Brill); German (Leiden: Brill); and French (Paris: Presses Universitaires de France/Leiden: Brill).

J. Guey. "Comment le 'denier de César' de l' Évangile a-t-il pu devenir une pièce d' or." *Bulletin de la Societé française de Numismatique* 15 (1960) 478-79.

F. Hahn. *Christologische Hoheitstitel.* 4th Edition. FRLANT 83. Göttingen: Vandenhoeck & Ruprecht, 1974.

E. Haenchen. "Die Anthropologie des Thomas-Evangeliums." Pp. 207-27 in Hans Dieter Betz and Luise Schottroff, eds. *Neues Testament und christliche Existenz: Festschrift für Herbert Braun zum 70. Geburtstag am 4. Mai 1973.* Tübingen: Mohr (Siebeck), 1973.

_____. *Die Botschaft des Thomas-Evangeliums.* Theologische Bibliotek Töpelmann 6. Berlin: Töpelmann, 1961.

_____. "Johanneische Probleme." *ZThK* 56 (1959) 19-22.

_____. "Literatur zum Thomasevangelium." *ThR* n. F. 27 (1961/62) 147-78, 306-38.

_____. "Neuere Literatur zu den Johannesbriefen." *ThR* n. F. 26 (1960) 1-43, 267-91. Reprinted: pp. 235-311 in idem. *Die Bibel und Wir: Gesammelte Aufsätze.* Tübingen: Mohr (Siebeck), 1968.

_____. "Spruch 68 des Thomasevangeliums." *Muséon* 75 (1962) 19-29.

_____. *Der Weg Jesu: Eine Erklärung des Markus-evangeliums und der kanonischen Parallelen.* Berlin: Töpelmann, 1966.

A. von Harnack. *Lehre der zwölf Apostle. Untersuchungen zur ältesten Geschichte der Kirchenverfassung und des Kirchenrechts* (2 fascicles). TU 2. Leipzig: Hinrichs, 1884.

_____. *Sprüche und Reden Jesu.* Beiträge zur Einleitung in das Neue Testament, Vol. 2. Leipzig: Hinrichs, 1907. ET: *The Sayings of Jesus: The Second Source of St. Matthew and St. Luke.* Trans. by J. R. Wilkenson. New York: Putnam's, 1908.

A. E. Harvey. *Jesus and the Constraints of History.* Philadelphia: Westminster, 1979.

F. Hauck. "μαργαρίτης." TDNT 4:472-73.

M. Hengel. "Das Gleichnis von den Weingärtnern. Mc 12,1-12 im Lichte der Zenonpapyri und der rabbinischen Gleichnisse." *ZNW* 59 (1968) 1-39.

E. Hennecke. *Neutestamentliche Apokryphen.* 4th Edition. W. Schneemelcher, ed. Tübingen: Mohr (Siebeck) 1958. ET: *New Testament Apocrypha.* Trans. by A. J. B. Higgins, G. Ogg, R. E. Taylor and R. McL. Wilson; R. McL. Wilson, ed. Philadelphia: Westminster, 1963 and 1965.

J. Heise. *Bleiben. Menein in den Johanneischen Schriften.* Tübingen: Mohr (Siebeck), 1967.

A. J. B. Higgins. "Non-Gnostic Sayings in the Gospel of Thomas." *NovT* 4 (1960) 292-306.

P. Hoffmann. *Studien zur Theologie der Logienquelle.* NTAbh, n.f. 8. Münster: Aschendorf, 1975.

J. Horman. "The Parable of the Sower in the Gospel of Thomas." *NovT* 21 (1979) 326-43.

G. Horner. *The Coptic Version of the New Testament: Sahidic and Thebaic.* Oxford: at the Clarendon Press, 1911.

R. Horsley. *Jesus and the Spiral of Violence: Popular Jewish Resistence in Roman Palestine.* San Francisco: Harper and Row: 1987.

———. "PNEUMATIKOS vs. PSYCHIKOS: Distinctions of Spiritual Status among the Corinthians." *HTR* 69 (1976) 269–88.

———. *Sociology and the Jesus Movement.* New York: Crossroad, 1989.

R. Horsley and J. Hanson. *Bandits, Prophets, and Messiahs: Popular Movements at the Time of Jesus.* San Francisco: Harper and Row, 1985.

C.-H. Hunzinger. "Außersynoptisches Traditionsgut im Thomas-Evangelium." *TLZ* 85 (1960) 843–46.

———. "Unbekannte Gleichnisse Jesu aus dem Thomas-Evangelium." Pp. 209–20 in W. Eltester, ed. *Judentum, Urchristentum, Kirche: Festschrift für Joachim Jeremias.* BZNS 26. Berlin: Töpelmann, 1964.

J. C. Hurd. *The Origin of I Corinthians.* London: SPCK/New York: Seabury, 1965.

A. Jacobson. "Wisdom Christology in Q." PhD Dissertation, Claremont, 1978.

H. Jackson. *The Lion Becomes a Man: The Gnostic Leontomorphic Creator and the Platonic Tradition.* SBLDS 81. Atlanta: Scholars Press, 1985.

J. Jeremias. *Die Gleichnisse Jesu.* 10th Edition. Göttingen: Vandenhoeck & Ruprecht, 1984.

———. *Unbekannte Jesuworte.* 2nd Paperback Edition. Gütersloh: Gütersloher Verlagshaus Mohn, 1983.

H. Jonas. *The Gnostic Religion.* Boston: Beacon, 1958.

A. Jülicher. *Die Gleichnisreden Jesu.* Tübingen: Mohr (Siebeck), 1898.

M. Kähler. *The So-Called Historical Jesus and the Historic Biblical Christ.* Philadelphia: Fortress, 1964.

E. Käsemann. "Ketzer und Zeuge—Zum Johanneischen Verfasserproblem." *ZThK* 48 (1951) 292–311. Reprinted: pp. 168–87 in idem. *Exegetische Versuche und Besinnungen.* Göttingen: Vandenhoeck & Ruprecht, 1960.

———. "Das Problem des historischen Jesus." *ZThK* 51 (1954) 125–53. ET: "The Problem of the Historical Jesus." Pp. 15–47 in idem. *Essays on New Testament Themes.* Studies in Biblical Theology 41. Naperville, IL: Allenson, 1964.

R. Kasser. *L'Évangile selon Thomas: Présentation et commentaire theologique.* Bibliotèque théologique. Neuchâtel: Delachaux et Niestlé 1961.

A. R. S. Kennedy. "Leaven." Cols. 2752–54 in T. K. Cheyne and J. S. Black, eds. *Encylopaedia Biblica* (vol. 3). New York/London: MacMillan, 1902.

K. King. "Kingdom in the Gospel of Thomas." *Foundations and Facets Forum* 3,1 (1987) 48–97.

A. F. J. Klijn. "Christianity in Edessa and the Gospel of Thomas: On Barbara Ehlers,' Kann das Thomasevangelium aus Edessa stammen?" *NovT* 14 (1972) 70–77.

———. "John XIV 22 and the Name Judas Thomas." Pp. 88–96 in *Studies in John Presented to Prof. J. N. Sevenster On the Occasion of his Seventieth Birthday.* Supplements to NovT 24. Leiden: Brill, 1970.

———. "The 'Single One' in the Gospel of Thomas." *JBL* 81 (1962) 271–78.

J. Kloppenborg. *The Formation of Q: Trajectories in Ancient Wisdom Collections.* Studies in Antiquity and Christianity. Philadelphia: Fortress, 1987.

———. "Wisdom Christology in Q." *Laval théologique et philosophique* 34 (1978) 129–48.

J. Kloppenborg, M. Meyer, S. Patterson and M. Steinhauser. *Q—Thomas Reader*. Sonoma, CA: Polebridge, 1990.

E. Klostermann, *Das Matthäusevangelium*. HNT 4. 4th Edition. Tübingen: Mohr (Siebeck), 1971.

D.-A. Koch. *Die Bedeutung der Wundererzählungen für die Christologie des Markusevangeliums*. BZNW 42. Berlin: Töpelmann, 1975.

H. Koester. *Ancient Christian Gospels: Their History and Development*. Philadelphia: Trinity/London: SCM: 1990.

_____. "Apocryphal and Canonical Gospels." *HTR* 73 (1980) 105–30.

_____. "Dialog und Spruchüberlieferung in den gnostischen Texten von Nag Hammadi." *EvTh* 34 (1979) 532–556.

_____. "GNOMAI DIAPHOROI: The Origin and Nature of Diversification in the History of Early Christianity." *HTR* 58 (1965) 279–318. Reprinted: pp. 114–57 in idem and James M. Robinson. *Trajectories*.

_____. "Gnostic Writings as Witnesses for the Development of the Sayings Tradition." Pp. 238–56 in B. Layton, ed. *The Rediscovery of Gnosticism;* Vol. I: *The School of Valentinus*. Studies in the History of Religions 16. Leiden: Brill, 1980.

_____. "History and Development of Mark's Gospel (From Mark to Secret Mark and 'Canonical' Mark)." Pp. 35–57 in Bruce Corley, ed. *Colloquy on New Testament Studies: A Time for Reappraisal and Fresh Approaches*. Macon, GA: Mercer University Press, 1983.

_____. "Introduction [to the Gospel of Thomas]." Pp. 38–49 in B. Layton, ed. *Nag Hammadi Codex II*.

_____. *Introduction to the New Testament*. Philadelphia: Fortress, 1982.

_____. "One Jesus and Four Primitive Gospels." *HTR* 61 (1968) 203–47. Reprinted in idem and James M. Robinson. *Trajectories*, 158–204.

_____. *Synoptische Überlieferung bei den apostolischen Vätern*. TU 65. Berlin: Akademie-Verlag, 1957.

_____. "Three Thomas Parables." Pp. 195–203 in A.H.B. Logan and J. M. Wedderburn, eds. *The New Testament and Gnosis: Essays in Honor or Robert McL. Wilson*. Edinburgh: T. & T. Clark, 1983.

G. Kretschmar. "Ein Beitrag zur Frage nach dem Ursprung frühchristlicher Askese." *ZThK* 61 (1964) 27–67.

W. G. Kümmel. *Introduction to the New Testament*. Revised edition. Translated by H. C. Kee. Nashville: Abingdon, 1975.

H.-W. Kuhn. *Ältere Sammlungen im Markusevangelium*. SUNT 8. Göttingen: Vandenhoeck & Ruprecht, 1971.

K. H. Kuhn. "Some Observations on the Coptic Gospel According to Thomas." *Muséon* 73 (1960) 317–23.

P. Labib. *Coptic Gnostic Papyri in the Coptic Museum at Old Cairo* (vol. 1). Cairo: Government Press (Antiquities Department), 1956.

R. Laufen. *Die Doppelüberlieferung der Logienquelle und des Markus-evangeliums*. BBB 54. Bonn: Peter Hanstein Verlag, 1980.

B. Layton. *The Gnostic Scriptures*. New York: Doubleday, 1987.

_____. "The Hypostasis of the Archons." *HTR* 67 (1974) 351–425.

B. Layton, ed., *Nag Hammadi Codex II,2–7 together with XII,2 Brit. Lib. Or. 4926 (1), and P. Oxy 1, 654, 655;* Vol. 1: *Gospel According to Thomas, Gospel According to Philip, Hypostasis of the Archons, and Indexes*. Nag Hammadi Studies 20. Leiden: Brill, 1989.

L.-Th. Lefort. *Les Pères apostoliques en copte.* CSCO 135; Scriptores Coptici 17. Louvain: L. Durbecq, 1952.

J. Leipoldt. *Das Evangelium nach Thomas: Koptisch und Deutsch.* TU 101. Berlin: Akademie-Verlag, 1967.

———. "Ein neues Evangelium: Das Koptisch Thomasevangelium übersetzt und besprochen." *TLZ* 83 (1958) cols. 481–96.

M. Lelyfeld. *Les Logia de la vie dans l' Évangile selon Thomas: a la recherche d' une tradition et d' une rédaction.* NHS 34. Leiden: Brill, 1987.

B. Lincoln. "Thomas-Gospel and Thomas-Community: A New Approach to a Familiar Text." *NovT* 19 (1977) 65–76.

A. Lindemann. "Zur Gleichnisinterpretation im Thomas-Evangelium." *ZNW* 71 (1980) 214–43.

O. Linton. "Evidence for a Second-Century Revised Edition of St. Mark's Gospel." *NTS* 14 (1967–68) 321–35.

D. Lührmann. *Die Redaktion der Logienquelle.* WMANT 33. Neukirchen-Vluyn: Neukirchener Verlag, 1969.

B. Mack. "The Kingdom that Didn't Come: A Social History of the Q Tradents." Pp. 606–635 in D. J. Lull, ed. *Society of Biblical Literature 1988 Seminar Papers.* Atlanta: Scholars Press, 1988.

G. W. MacRae. "The Gospel of Thomas—LOGIA IESOU?" *CBQ* 22 (1960) 56–71.

Cl.-P. März. "Feuer auf die Erde." Pp. 479–511 in *À cause de l' évangile. Études sur les Synoptiques et les Actes offertes au P. Jacques Dupont, O. S. B. l' occasion de son 70e anniversaire.* Paris: Cerf, 1985.

A. Malherbe. *Social Aspects of Early Christianity.* 2nd Enlarged Edition. Philadelphia: Fortress, 1983.

B. Malina. "The Received View and What It Cannot Do: III John and Hospitality." Pp. 171–89 in J. H. Elliott, ed. *Semeia 35: Social-Scientific Criticism of the New Testament and Its Social World.* Atlanta: Scholars Press, 1986.

T. W. Manson. *The Sayings of Jesus.* London: SCM, 1949.

M. Marchovich. "Textual Criticism on the Gospel of Thomas." *JTS* 20 (1969) 229–42.

H. K. McArthur. "The Dependence of the Gospel of Thomas on the Synoptics." *ET* 71 (1959/60) 286–87.

———. "The Gospel According to Thomas." Pp. 43–77 in idem, ed. *New Testament Sidelights: Essays in Honor of Alexander Converse Purdy.* Hartford: The Hartford Seminary Foundation Press, 1960.

W. A. Meeks. *The First Urban Christians: The Social World of the Apostle Paul.* New Haven: Yale University Press, 1983.

———. "The Image of the Androgyne: Some Uses of a Symbol in Earliest Christianity." *HR* 13 (1974) 165–208.

J.-E. Ménard. "La datation des manuscrits." *Histoire et archéologie* 70 (1983) 12–13.

———. *L'Évangile selon Thomas.* NHS 5. Leiden: Brill, 1975.

———. "La tradition synoptique et l'Évangile selon Thomas." Pp. 411–26 in F. Paschke, ed. *Überlieferungsgeschichtliche Untersuchungen.* TU 125. Berlin: Akademie-Verlag, 1981.

B. Meyer. *The Aims of Jesus.* London: SCM, 1979.

M. W. Meyer. "Making Mary Male: The Categories 'Male' and 'Female' in the Gospel of Thomas." *NTS* 31 (1985) 554–570.

———. "The Youth in the Secret Gospel of Mark." Pp. 129–53 in R. Cameron, ed.

Semeia 49: *The Apocryphal Jesus and Christian Origins.* Atlanta: Scholars Press, 1990.

R. Miller, ed. *The Complete Gospels.* Sonoma, CA: Polebridge Press, 1992.

C. G. Montefiore and H. Loewe. *A Rabbinic Anthology.* New York: Macmillan, 1938.

H. Montefiore. "A Comparison of the Parables of the Gospel According to Thomas and the Synoptic Gospels." *NTS* 7 (1960/61) 220-48.

H. Montefiore and H. E. W. Turner. *Thomas and the Evangelists.* Studies in Biblical Theology 35. Naperville: Allenson, 1962.

J. Munck. "Bemerkungen zum koptischen Thomasevangelium." *StTh* 14 (1960) 130-47.

F. Mussner. *Der Jakobusbrief.* HTKNT 13,1. Freiburg: Herder, 1964.

F. Neirynck. "The Study of Q." Pp. 29-75 in J. Delobel, ed. *Logia: Les Paroles de Jésus—The Sayings of Jesus (Mémorial Joseph Coppens).* BETL 59. Leuven: Uitgeverij Peeters/Leuven University Press, 1982.

_____. "John and the Synoptics." Pp. 73-106 in M. de Jonge, ed. *L'Évangile de Jean. Sources, rédaction, théologie.* BETL 44. Gembloux: Duculot/Louvain: University Press, 1977.

K. V. Neller. "Diversity in the Gospel of Thomas: Clues for a New Direction." *The Second Century* 7 (1989-90) 1-18.

G. E. Nickelsburg. "The Genre and Function of the Markan Passion Narrative." *HTR* 73 (1980) 153-84.

K. Niederwimmer. "Zur Entwicklungsgeschichte des Wanderradikalismus im Traditionsbereich der Didache." *Wiener Studien* n. F. 11 (1977) 145-67.

D. Oakman. *Jesus and the Economic Questions of His Day.* Studies in the Bible and Early Christianity 8. Lewiston/Queenston: Edwin Mellen Press, 1986.

S.J. Patterson. "Fire and Dissesion: Ipsissima Vox Jesu in Q 12:49, 51-52?" *Foundations and Facets Forum* 5,2 (1989) 121-39.

_____. "Outside the Bible: Can It Be Jesus?" *The Fourth R* 3,3 (1990) 3-5.

_____. "The Gospel of Thomas and the Historical Jesus: *Prospectus* and *Retrospectus*." Pp. 614-36 in D. J. Lull, ed. *Society of Biblical Literature 1990 Seminar Papers.* Atlanta: Scholars Press, 1990.

_____. "Paul and the Jesus Tradition: It is Time for Another Look." *HTR* 84 (1991) 23-41.

S.J. Patterson and C. Jefford. "A Note on *Didache* 12.2a (Coptic)." *The Second Century* 7 (1989-90) 65-75.

B. Pearson. *The PNEUMATIKOS-PSYCHIKOS Terminology in 1 Corinthians.* SBLDS 12. Missoula: Scholars Press, 1973.

N. Perrin. *The Kingdom of God in the Teaching of Jesus.* Philadelphia: Westminster, 1963.

_____. *Rediscovering the Teaching of Jesus.* New York: Harper and Row, 1967.

B. Perry. *Babrius and Phaedrus.* LCL. Cambridge: Harvard University Press, 1965.

E. Peterson. "Einige Beobachtungen zu den Anfängen der christlichen Askese." Pp. 209-220 in idem. *Frühkirche, Judentum, und Gnosis. Studien und Untersuchungen.* Freiburg: Herder, 1959.

W. L. Petersen. "The Parable of the Lost Sheep in the Gospel of Thomas and the Synoptics." *NovT* 23 (1981) 128-47.

O. Piper. "The Gospel of Thomas." *The Princeton Seminary Bulletin* 53:2 (1959) 18-24.

W. Pratscher. *Der Herrenbruder Jakobus und die Jakobustradition.* FRLANT 139. Göttingen: Vandenhoeck & Ruprecht, 1987.

H.-Ch. Puech. "Das Thomasevangelium." Pp. 199–223 in E. Hennecke. *Neutestamentliche Apokryphen* (vol. 1). ET: Trans. and ed. by R. McL. Wilson. "The Gospel of Thomas." Pp. 278–307 in E. Henneke, *New Testament Apocrypha* (vol. 1).

G. Quispel. "L'Évangile selon Thomas et le Diatessaron." *VC* 13 (1959) 87–117. Reprinted: pp. 31–55 in idem. *Gnostic Studies* (vol. 2).

––––––. "L'Évangile selon Thomas et les origines de l'ascèse chrétienne." Pp. 35–51 in *Aspects du judéo-christianisme: Colloque de Strasbourg 23–25 avril 1964.* Bibliotèque des Centres d'Études supérieures spécialisés. Paris: Presses Universitaires de France, 1965. Reprinted: pp. 98–112 in idem. *Gnostic Studies* (vol. 2).

––––––. "L'Évangile selon Thomas et le 'texte occidental' du Nouveau Testament." *VC* 14 (1960) 204–15. Reprinted: pp. 59–69 in idem. *Gnostic Studies* (vol. 2).

––––––. *Gnostic Studies* (2 vols). Istanbul: Nederlands Historisch-Archaeologisch Instituut te Istanbul, 1975.

––––––. "The Gospel of Thomas and the New Testament." *VC* 11 (1957) 189–207. Reprinted: pp. 3–16 in idem. *Gnostic Studies* (vol. 2).

––––––. "The Gospel of Thomas Revisited." Pp. 218–66 in B. Barc, ed. *Colloque international sur les textes de Nag Hammadi (Québec, 22–25 aot 1978).* Bibliothèque copte de Nag Hammadi, Section "Études." Québec: Laval University Press/Louvain: Peeters, 1981.

––––––. *Makarius. Das Thomasevangelium und das Lied von der Perle.* NovT Supplements 15. Leiden: Brill, 1967.

––––––. "Some Remarks on the Gospel of Thomas." *NTS* 5 (1958/59) 276–90.

––––––. *Tatian and the Gospel of Thomas: Studies in the History of the Western Diatessaron.* Leiden: Brill, 1975.

––––––. *Das Thomasevangelium und das Lied von der Perle.* NovT Supplements 15. Leiden: Brill, 1967.

G. Quispel and D. Gerschensen. "Meristae." *VC* 12 (1958) 19–26.

J. M. Robinson. "The Discovery of the Nag Hammadi Codices." *BA* 42,4 (1979) 206–24.

––––––. "Getting the Nag Hammadi Library into English." *BA* 42,4 (1979) 239–48.

––––––. "The Johannine Trajectory." Pp. 232–68 in idem and H. Koester. *Trajectories.*

––––––. "Kerygma and History in the New Testament." Pp. 114–50 in J. P. Hyatt, ed. *The Bible in Modern Scholarship.* Nashville: Abingdon/London: Lutterworth, 1965. Reprinted: pp. 20–70 in idem and H. Koester. *Trajectories.*

––––––. "*LOGOI SOPHON:* Zur Gattung der Spruchquelle." Pp. 77–96 in E. Dinkler, ed. *Zeit und Geschichte. Dankesgabe an Rudolf Bultmann.* Tübingen: Mohr (Siebeck), 1964. Revised ET: "*LOGOI SOPHON:* On the Gattung of Q." Pp. 71–113 in idem and H. Koester. *Trajectories.*

––––––. *A New Quest of the Historical Jesus (and Other Essays).* Philadelphia: Fortress, 1983.

––––––. "On Bridging the Gulf from Q to the Gospel of Thomas (or *vice versa*)." Pp. 127–55 in C. W. Hedrick and R. Hodgson, Jr. eds. *Nag Hammadi, Gnosticism, and Early Christianity.* Peabody, MA: Hendrickson Publishers, 1986.

J. M. Robinson, General Editor. *The Nag Hammadi Library in English.* Revised Edition. San Francisco: Harper & Row, 1988.

J. M. Robinson and H. Koester. *Trajectories Through Early Christianity.* Philadelphia: Fortress, 1971.

W. Rordorf and A. Tuilier. *La doctrine des douze apôtres (Didachè).* Sources chrétiennes 248. Paris: Les éditions du Cerf, 1978.

K. Rudolph. *Gnosis: The Nature and History of Gnosticism.* Trans. by R. McL. Wilson. San Francisco: Harper and Row, 1983.

T. Säve-Söderbergh. "Gnostic and Canonical Gospel Traditions, with special reference to the Gospel of Thomas." Pp. 552–59 in H. Bianchi, ed. *Le Origini dello Gnosticismo, Colloquio di Messina, 13–18 Aprile, 1966.* Leiden: Brill, 1967.

S. Safrai and M. Stern. *The Jewish People in the First Century* (2 vols.). Compendium Rerum Judaicarum ad Novum Testamentum 1. Philadelphia: Fortress, 1976.

E. P. Sanders. *Jesus and Judaism.* Philadelphia: Fortress, 1985.

H.-M. Schenke. Review of Ménard: "L'Évangile de Thomas. Son importance pour l'étude des paroles de Jésus et ue gnosticisme chrétien." *ETR* 54 (1979) 375–396.

––––––. "The Mystery of the Gospel of Mark." *The Second Century* 4 (1984) 65–82.

––––––. Review of Schrage, *Das Verhältnis. TLZ* 93 (1968) 36–38.

––––––. "Die Tendenz der Weisheit zur Gnosis." Pp. 351–72 in B. Aland, ed. *Gnosis. Festschrift Hans Jonas.* Göttingen: Vandenhoek & Ruprecht, 1978.

H.-M. Schenke and K. M. Fischer. *Einleitung in die Schriften des Neuen Testaments.* Berlin: Evangelische Verlagsanhalt, 1979.

G. Schille. "Das Recht der Propheten und Apostle. Gemeinderechtliche Beobachtungen zu Didache Kapitel 11–13." Pp. 84–103 in idem and P. Wätzel, eds. *Theologische Versuche* (vol. 1). Berlin: Töppelmann, 1966.

J. Schmid. *Matthäus und Lukas. Eine Untersuchung des Verhältnisses ihrer Evangelien.* BibS (F) 23. Freiburg: Herder, 1930.

C. Schmidt. "Das koptische Didache-Fragment des British Museum." *ZNW* 24 (1925) 81–99.

K. Schmidt. *Der Rahmen der Geschicte Jesu.* Berlin: Trowitzsch & Son, 1919.

W. Schmithals. "Kritik der Formkritik." *ZThK* 77 (1980) 149–85.

R. Schnackenburg. *Die Johannesbriefe.* HTKNT 13, 3. Freiburg: Herder, 1963.

F. Schnider. "Das Gleichnis vom verlorenen Schaf und seine Redaktion: Ein intertextuellen Vergleich." *Kairos* 19 (1977) 146–54.

W. R. Schoedel. "Parables in the Gospel of Thomas." *Concordia Theological Monthly* 43 (1972) 548–60.

W. Schrage. "Evengelienzitate in den Oxyrhynchus-Logien und im koptischen Thomas-Evangelium." Pp. 251–68 in W. Eltester, ed. *Apophoreta: Festschrift für Ernst Haenchen zu seinem siebzigsten Geburtstag.* BZNW 30. Berlin: Töppelmann, 1964.

––––––. *Das Verhältnis des Thomas-Evangeliums zur synoptischen Tradition und zu den koptischen Evangelienübersetzungen. Zugleich ein Beitrag zur gnostischen Synoptikerdeutung.* BZNW 29. Berlin: Töppelmann, 1964.

T. Schramm. *Der Markus-Stoff bei Lukas. Eine literarkritische und redaktionsgeschichtliche Untersuchung.* SNTSMS 14. Cambridge: Cambridge University Press, 1971.

H. Schürmann. *Das Lukasevangelium.* HTKNT 3,1. Freiburg: Herder, 1969.

––––––. "Das Thomas Evangelium and das lukanische Sondergut." *BZ* 7 (1963) 236–60.

S. Schulz. *Q. Die Spruchquelle der Evangelisten.* Zürich: Theologischer Verlag, 1972.

E. Schweizer. *The Good News According to Matthew.* Trans. by David E. Green. Atlanta: John Knox Press, 1975.

B. Scott. *Hear Then the Parable*. Minneapolis: Fortress, 1983.

P. Sellew. "Reconstruction of Q 12:33–59." Pp. 617–68 in K. H. Richards, ed. *Society of Biblical Literature 1987 Seminar Papers*. Atlanta: Scholars Press, 1987.

J. Sheppard. "A Study of the Parables Common to the Synoptic Gospels and the Coptic Gospel of Thomas." PhD Dissertation, Emory, 1965.

A. E. Silverstone. *The Babylonian Talmud*. London: Soncino, 1935.

J. Sieber. "A Redactional Analysis of the Synoptic Gospels with regard to the Question of the Sources of the Gospel According to Thomas." PhD Dissertation, Claremont, 1965.

J. Z. Smith. "The Garments of Shame." *HR* 5 (1965/66) 217–38.

K. L. Snodgrass. "The Gospel of Thomas: A Secondary Gospel." *The Second Century* 7 (1989–90) 19–38.

―――. "The Parable of the Wicked Husbandmen: Is the Gospel of Thomas Version the Original?" *NTS* 21 (1974) 142–44.

W. Stegemann. "Wanderradikalismus im Urchristentum? Historische und theologische Auseinandersetzung mit einer interessanten These." Pp. 94–120 in idem and Willy Schottroff. *Der Gott der kleinen Leute. Sozial-geschichtliche Bibelauslegungen;* Vol. 2: *Neues Testament*. München: Chr. Kaiser Verlag, 1979. ET: "Vagabond Radicalism in Early Christianity? A Historical and Theological Discussion of a Thesis Proposed by Gerd Theissen. Pp. 148–68 in idem and Willy Schottroff. *God of the Lowly: Socio-Historical Interpretation of the Bible*. Maryknoll, N.Y. : Orbis, 1984.

M. E. Stone and J. Strugnell. *The Books of Elijah, Parts 1 and 2*. Society of Biblical Literature Texts and Translations 18, Pseudepigrapha Series 8. Missoula: Scholars Press, 1979.

H. L. Strack and P. Billerbeck. *Kommentar zum Neuen Testament aus Talmud und Midrasch* (3 vols.). München: C. H. Beck, 1922–28.

G. Strecker. "Die Antithesen der Bergpredigt (Mt. 5:21–48, Par.)." *ZNW* 69 (1978) 36–72.

―――. *Das Judenchristentum in den Pseudoklementinen*. TU 15. Berlin: Akademie-Verlag, 1958.

―――. "Die Makarismen der Bergpredigt." *NTS* 17 (1971) 255–75.

―――. *Der Weg der Gerechtigkeit*. 2nd Edition. FRLANT 82. Göttingen: Vandenhoeck & Ruprecht, 1966.

A. Strobel. "Textgeschichtliches zum Thomas' Logion 86 (Mt 8, 20/Luk 9, 58)." *VC* 17 (1963) 211–44.

M. J. Suggs. *Wisdom, Christology, and Law in Matthew's Gospel*. Cambridge: Harvard University Press, 1970.

A. Suhl. *Die Funktion der alttestamentlichen Zitate und Anspielungen im Markusevangelium*. Gütersloh: Mohn, 1965.

V. Taylor. "The Order of Q." *JTS* NS 4 (1953) 27–31. Reprinted: pp. 90–94 in idem. *New Testament Essays*. London: Epworth, 1970/Grand Rapids: Eerdmann's, 1972.

―――. "The Original Order of Q." Pp. 246–49 in A. J. B. Higgins, ed. *New Testament Essays: Studies in Honor of T. W. Manson*. Manchester: Manchester University, 1959. Reprinted: pp. 95–118 in V. Taylor. *New Testament Essays*. London: Epworth, 1970/Grand Rapids: Eerdmanns, 1972.

G. Theissen. "Legitimation und Lebensunterhalt: Ein Beitrag zur Soziologie des hellenistischen Urchristentums." *NTS* 21 (1975) 192–221. Reprinted: pp. 201–

30 in idem. *Studien*. ET: "Legitimation and Substance: An Essay on the Sociology of Early Christian Missionaries." Pp. 27–67 in idem. *Social Setting*.

———. *The Social Setting of Pauline Christianity*. Trans. by John Schütz. Philadelphia: Fortress, 1982.

———. "Soziale Schichtung in der korinthischen Gemeinde: Ein Beitrag zur Soziologie des hellenistischen Urchristentums." *ZNW* 65 (1974) 232–72. Reprinted: pp. 231–71 in idem. *Studien*. ET: "Social Stratification in the Corinthian Community: A Contribution to the Sociology of Early Hellenistic Christianity." Pp. 69–119 in idem. *Social Setting*.

———. *Soziologie der Jesusbewegung*. München: Chr. Kaiser Verlag, 1977. ET: *The Sociology of Early Palestinian Christianity*. Trans. by John Bowden. Philadelphia: Fortress, 1978.

———. "Die soziologische Auswertung religiöser Überlieferungen. Ihre methodologischen Probleme am Biespiel des Urchristentums." *Kairos* 17 (1975) 284–299. Reprinted: pp. 35–54 in idem. *Studien*. ET: "The Sociological Interpretation of Religious Traditions: Its Methodological Problems as Exemplified in Early Christianity." Pp. 175–200 in idem. *Social Setting*.

———. "Die Starken und Schwachen in Korinth. Soziologische Analyse eines theologischen Streites." *ET* 35 (1975) 155–72. Reprinted: pp. 272–89 in *Studien*. ET: "The Strong and the Weak in Corinth: A Sociological Analysis of a Theological Quarrel." Pp. 121–43 in idem. *Social Setting*.

———. *Studien zur Soziologie des Urchristentums*. 2nd Edition. WUNT 19. Tübingen: Mohr (Siebeck), 1983.

———. "Die Templewissagung Jesu. Prophetie im Spannungsfeld von Stadt und Land," *TZ* 32 (1976) 144–58. Reprinted: pp. 142–59 in idem. *Studien*.

———. "Theoretische Probleme religionssoziologischer Forschung und die Analyse des Urchristentums." *Neue Zeitschrift für Systematische Theologie und Religionsphilosophie* 16 (1974) 35–56. Reprinted: pp. 55–76 in *Studien*.

———. "Wanderradikalismus. Literatursoziologische Aspekte der Überlieferung von Worten Jesu im Urchristentum." *ZThK* 70 (1973) 245–71. Reprinted: 79–105 in idem. *Studien*. ET: "Itinerant Radicalism: The Tradition of Jesus Sayings from the Perspective of the Sociology of Literature." Trans. by A. Wire. *Radical Religion* 2 (1976) 84–93.

———. "Zur Forschungsgeschichtlichen Einordnung der soziologischen Fragestellung." Pp. 3–34 in idem. *Studien*.

W. Till. *Koptische Grammatik*. Leipzig: VEB Verlag Enzyklopädie, 1986.

———. "New Sayings of Jesus in the Recently Discovered Coptic Gospel of Thomas." *BJRL* 41,2 (1959) 446–458.

J. M. C. Toynbee. "Dictators and Philosophers in the First Century AD." *GR* 13 (1944) 43–58.

K. Toyoshima. "Neue Vorschläge zur Lesung und Übersetzung von Thomasevangelium Log. 21, 103 und 68b." *AJBI* 9 (1983) 230–41.

W. Trillig. *Das wahre Israel*. 3rd Edition. SANT 10. München: Kösel, 1964.

J. B. Tyson. "Sequential Parallelism in the Synoptic Gospels." *NTS* 22 (1976) 276–308.

L. Vaage. "Q: The Ethos and Ethics of an Itinerant Intelligence." PhD Dissertation, Claremont, 1987.

P. Vassiliadis. "The Original Order of Q. Some Residual Cases." Pp. 379–87 in J. Delobel, ed. *Logia: Les Paroles de Jésus—The Sayings of Jesus (Mémorial Joseph Coppens)*. BETL 59. Leuven: Uitgeverij Peeters/Leuven University Press, 1982.

P. Vielhauer. "ΑΝΑΠΑΥΣΙΣ. Zum gnostischen Hintergrund des Thomasevangeliums." Pp. 281–99 in W. Eltester, ed. *Apophoreta. Festschrift für Ernst Haenchen.* BZNW 30. Berlin: Töpelmann, 1964.

———. "Gottesreich and Menschensohn in der Verkündigung Jesu." Pp. 51–79 in W. Schneemelcher, ed. *Festschrift für Günther Dehn.* Neukirken: Kreis Moers, 1957. Reprinted: pp. 55–91 in idem. *Aufsäzte zum Neuen Testament.* München: Kaiser, 1965.

———. "Jesus und der Menschensohn." *ZThK* 60 (1963) 133–77. Reprinted: pp. 92–140 in idem. *Aufsätze zum Neuen Testament.* München: Kaiser, 1965.

———. *Geschichte der urchristlichen Literatur.* Berlin: De Gruyter, 1975.

A. Vööbus. *History of Asceticism in the Syrian Orient: A Contribution to the History of Culture in the Near East.* Vol. 1: *The Origin of Asceticism. Early Monasticism in Persia.* Scriptorum Christianorum Orientalium 184. Louvain: Secrétariat du Corpus SCO, 1958.

A. F. Walls. "The Reference to the Apostles in the Gospel of Thomas." *NTS* 7 (1960/61) 266–70.

J. Wanke. "Kommentarworte. Älteste Kommentierung von Herrenworten." *BZ* n.f. 24 (1980) 208–33.

R. B. Ward. "Partiality in the Assembly: James 2:2–4." *HTR* 62 (1969) 87–97.

———. "The Works of Abraham: James 2:14–26." *HTR* 61 (1968) 283–90.

E. Wendling. *Die Entstehung des Markus-Evangeliums.* Tübingen: Mohr (Siebeck), 1908.

H. H. Wendt. *Die Johannesbriefe und das johanneische Christentum.* Halle/Salle: Buchhandlung des Waisenhauses, 1925.

P. Wernle. *Die synoptische Frage.* Freiburg: Mohr, 1899.

R. L. Wilken, ed. *Aspects of Wisdom in Judaism and early Christianity.* Notre Dame: University of Notre Dame Press, 1975.

U. Wilckens. *Weisheit und Torheit.* BHTh 26. Tübingen: Mohr (Siebeck) 1959.

B. R. Wilson. *Magic and Millenium.* New York: Harper & Row, 1973.

R. McL. Wilson. *Studies in the Gospel of Thomas.* London: A.R. Mowbray, 1960.

———. "Thomas and the Growth of the Gospels." *HTR* 53 (1960) 231–50.

V. L. Wimbush. *Renunciation Towards Social Engeneering.* The Institute for Antiquity and Christianity Occasional Papers 9. Claremont: The Institute for Antiquity and Christianity, 1986.

H. Windisch. "Ζυμή, ζυμόω, ἄζυμος." *TDNT* 2:902–6.

———. *Die Katholischen Briefe.* HNT 15. Tübingen: Mohr (Siebeck) 1951.

H.-T. Wrege. *Die Überlieferungsgeschichte der Bergpredigt.* WUNT 9. Tübingen: Mohr (Siebeck), 1968.

Index of Authors

Index of Passages

Jewish Scriptures

Jewish Apocrypha

Christian Apocrypha

Apostolic and Early Christian Authors

Rabbinic Texts

Greek and Roman Authors

CPSIA information can be obtained at www.ICGtesting.com
Printed in the USA
BVOW020516160412

287676BV00001B/2/P